140°

20°

Acapulco

MARQUESAS
IS

SOCIETY IS

TUAMOTU
ARCH.

AUSTRAL IS

Pitcairn I

· Easter I

0   1000   2000
kilometres

140°   120°   100°

D1294255

WHERE THE WAVES FALL

Pacific Islands Monograph Series, No. 2

WHERE THE WAVES FALL

*A new South Sea Islands history
from first settlement to colonial rule*

K R HOWE

Center for Pacific Islands Studies
University of Hawaii
UNIVERSITY OF HAWAII PRESS
Honolulu

© K R Howe 1984

First published in paperback 1988

This book is copyright under the Berne Convention. All rights reserved. No reproduction without permission

Library of Congress Cataloguing in Publication Data:

Howe, K R
Where the waves fall,
(Pacific islands monograph series; no. 2)
Bibliography; p.
Includes index,
1. Islands of the Pacific—History,   2. New Zealand—
History—to 1843.   I. Title, II. Series.
DU$_{28.3}$.H68 1984 990 83 18295
ISBN 0-8248-0921-1
ISBN 0-8248-1186-0

Set in Monophoto Garamond
by Asco Trade Typesetting Ltd, Hong Kong
Printed by Kim Hup Lee Printing Co Pte Ltd, Singapore

an ocean ... where the waves fall on
innumerable reefs, and a great wind blows
from the south-east with the revolving world

J C Beaglehole, *The Life of Captain James Cook*

As waves break upon the coral ringed shores of
the South Seas, each one overtaken by the next
before its energy is quite spent, so has the history of the Pacific been marked by successive
and merging phases.

J W Davidson, European penetration of the South
Pacific

for Nicholas
and my mother and father

Contents

Epilogue

16   Considering the new historiography   347

Maps

Illustrations

The past has no independent existence. It exists only in the present. Even the ten thousand year old artefact exists now; it has no previous context other than that given by our intellect and imagination. Historians thus essentially create the past in the light of current perceptions, priorities, and assumptions. Those who gaze into the past are in essence facing a mirror. It is their own and their society's reflections that they see. Historians who might challenge these notions might consider that quantum physicists— surely the most 'scientific' of researchers—accepted these views about the nature of knowledge well over fifty years ago.

European historians writing about Europe are perhaps less conscious of this autobiographical role of history than are European historians examining the non-European world, for it is in trying to cross culture as well as time that we become so aware of our own. European historians must of necessity tell as much about themselves and their times as about the non-Europeans they might claim to study.

The last major reorientation of European historical perception of non-Europeans occurred about the time of the Second World War and its immediate aftermath. By then the days of Anglo-Saxon global dominance were well on the wane. Empires in India, Africa, China and Indochina, and Latin America were gradually abandoned by or wrested from former white masters. The Third World began to stir. What would have been heresies to former European overlords became the new gospel, proclaimed in institutions like the United Nations—the equality and dignity of all people, and their right to self-rule and self-determination.

Historians reflected these changing intellectual assumptions. As colonies became decolonised, so historians began to decolonise history. Attention became focused on the oppressed rather than the oppressors. Africa, south Asia, Latin America were studied not as the playthings of empire but for their own sakes. Where the written history of these places had been a history of white men as agents of empire, now the indigenous peoples themselves were deemed fit subjects for academic research.

The decolonisation of Pacific islands history owed much to Professor J W Davidson, foundation professor of the Department of Pacific History at the Australian National University, Canberra, in the early 1950s. As with other colonised regions of the globe, the history of the Pacific islands had consisted of a history of imperial agents—explorers, missionaries, administrators—in the islands. And their activities were viewed from mission, commercial, and government headquarters in England, the United States, Germany, or France. The Pacific Islanders themselves seldom featured in the books, and when they did they were usually portrayed as helpless, passive, inferior, the objects of European initiatives not subjects in themselves. The 'new' Pacific islands history under Davidson, paralleling historiographic developments for other countries, rejected this imperial overview. The islands became the focus. Events there were to be interpreted not as they reflected imperial concerns, but as they affected the lives of the inhabitants.[1] This change to an island-oriented perspective had two main consequences for the historian. First, imperial history had, in Davidson's words, to 'give way to the history of European expansion'[2] in the Pacific and that meant looking at many influences other than the predominant concerns of the imperial historian. It was not sufficient to concentrate on explorers, missionaries, and government agents. A lowly beachcomber, an impoverished sandalwood trader, a ragged whaling crew in search of rest and recreation might perform activities or make observations as significant as those of any top-hatted evangelist or ostrich-plumed governor. Davidson likened European penetration to a series of waves, each one breaking, as he put it 'upon the coral ringed shores of the South Seas, each one overtaken by the next before its energy is quite spent.'[3]

The second main consequence of his new perspective has meant appreciating that Europeans in the Pacific were influenced by local conditions and especially by the indigenous societies. Pacific islands history had to be seen in terms of cultural interaction, which necessarily meant studying both sides. The Islanders were brought into the picture. Their communities were now credited with having histories of their own that were worthy of serious academic study. Modern historians of the Pacific islands have concentrated on the social, economic, political, and intellectual changes experienced by island societies as a result of their ever increasing interaction with Europeans and Western influences generally.

In order to achieve this, the new generation of Pacific islands historians had to supplement the usual archival research with fieldwork in island communities, and to familiarise themselves with the relevant findings of prehistorians, linguists, demographers, and anthropologists. Pacific islands history became a somewhat interdisciplinary subject. Staff and students in Davidson's department have been responsible for a significant amount of this new history, especially since the mid-1960s. Over the past decade other universities in Australia, New Zealand, the Pacific, and the United States, often employing graduates from Canberra, have also contributed to the now large stockpile of detailed historical information.

However, as I have argued elsewhere,[4] for all its excellence this detailed research has been rather unsystematic. Pacific islands history, partly because the islands are so 'splendidly splittable into Ph.D. topics',[5] has become a breeding ground for highly specialised and self-contained articles, monographs, and symposia. More and more is being discovered about less and less. Consequently the audience is very small. Pacific historians are in danger of writing merely to be read by each other. It is timely that an attempt should be made to remould their material and present it to a wider reading public. After all, the only substantive general history, Douglas Oliver's *The Pacific Islands*, was first published in 1951. In spite of revisions, it still necessarily reproduces the perceptions and information which predate modern Pacific history.

This book is an attempt to survey the detailed findings of modern Pacific historians and present them to the layman in a less obscure and inaccessible form than they now exist. But it is more than just a compilation of this research. I have endeavoured to provide a synoptic overview, to take the detailed and self-contained studies and place them into a wider thematic framework. Events on selected islands are compared and contrasted to give a broader regional perspective. In this book I have also attempted to assess the implications of modern Pacific islands history in a historiographic context.

I make no claim to comprehensiveness. This is not a historical encyclopaedia or a reference book. For example, not all major islands or island groups are examined. In part this reflects the absence of historical knowledge for certain localities—the islands of much of Micronesia are a glaring example. But in part too it results from a decision to avoid unnecessary repetition, the piling of example on example, which, if taken too far, replicates the fragmented nature of research findings themselves. I have chosen to illustrate certain key themes of culture contact, rather than endlessly narrate its events. Furthermore some islands which have been left out, such as the Marquesas, the Cooks, and the Gilbert and Ellice Islands have had modern histories appear after this book was all but written.[6]

For its geographical framework, this book looks at the insular as opposed to the Oceanic Pacific which takes account of continental hinterlands.[7] This division is itself not very logical and can be justified only since two separate historical genres are involved. Even the notion of an insular Pacific has its own inconsistencies. For example, New Zealand is usually left to those whose 'territory' is New Zealand history rather than Pacific islands history. I have placed New Zealand in what, for my purposes anyway, is its appropriate place. Australia since 1788 is not covered because the history of Aboriginal-European relations is difficult to fit readily into a

Pacific islands context, not necessarily because these relations might be different but more because Australia's historiographic traditions are, to date, so dissimilar. The tale of culture contact in New Guinea, but not its prehistory, is also omitted because it falls mainly outside my time scale. In essence this book is about regions commonly called Polynesia and Island Melanesia.

The period covered is from 50 000 years ago, when humans first came to the Ocean's western fringes until the imposition of colonial rule in the nineteenth century. Within this vast time scale, emphasis is placed on the period of culture contact from the sixteenth century onward as Islanders and Europeans began to interact with each other. Although the beginning of this study is fairly obvious, its ending is less so in a chronological sense, since the formal establishment of colonial control occurred at different times for different islands throughout the nineteenth century. The logic for this thematic as opposed to chronological cut-off point is threefold. First, there is very little historical analysis of colonial systems on Pacific islands. Modern Pacific history has been far more concerned with precolonial culture contact than with issues of colonisation and decolonisation. Second, where such colonial studies have been undertaken they represent rather different historical approaches and techniques and are often models or experiences from Africa and elsewhere applied to Pacific islands situations. A Pacific or indigenous development of colonial and postcolonial studies is still in its infancy. Third, the changes that occur in historiographic perceptions as they now exist when passing from precolonial to colonial times can result in certain opinions about colonial experiences being projected backward to earlier years, so distorting interpretations of what took place. While Cook and other explorers or early missionaries might indeed have been the forerunners of colonial rule, it would be misleading to interpret early culture contact simply as a prelude to annexation. Not only is this an anachronism but it denies the role played by Islanders in precolonial times and therefore is in essence a replay of older imperial views of Pacific history which see Europeans as the initiating and predominant force. By contrast, a basic theme of this study, and one that reflects the new Pacific historiography, is how processes and developments in many precolonial culture contact situations were greatly influenced not by European decree but by the initiatives of various Islanders and by their respective social and political arrangements. As Davidson argued, in spite of the growing European presence in island communities 'the indigenous cultures . . . were like islands whose coastal regions outsiders might penetrate but whose heartlands they could never conquer.'[8] The relevance of this view is becoming more and more apparent, especially on those islands now in postcolonial situations.

Research for this book has been confined to printed sources, both primary and modern. To have attempted a study of this scope by going back to the myriad unpublished sources would not only have taken many decades but would have produced tomes which, like so much recent research, would have been so detailed, fragmented, and highly specialised as to defeat my purpose. This book is one interpretation of the state of the art of modern Pacific history. It is therefore fixed in time and place. It is in the main the product of European, specifically English, and even more specifically Australasian scholarship. There will be people, especially in the islands, who might disapprove of this bias. But the modern Pacific history exists in the absence of as yet established alternative perceptions, not by the suppression of them. And I am just as aware of likely criticisms from the other side. In 'playing the generalist game'[9] it is all too easy to upset the specialist in some narrow aspect of some island's history. But it is time such a game was played. There are more than enough discrete parts waiting to be placed into a synoptic framework. My hope is that the result does justice to all those authors whose findings appear in the following pages.

Massey University
November, 1982

Acknowledgments

I owe a very great debt to all those prehistorians and historians whose work I have so liberally borrowed for this study. Unfortunately there are far too many to list here. I would like them to accept their names in the references and bibliography as recognition (unfortunately all too token) of my grateful reliance upon them.

In addition some of these people, and others, have helped me more directly in both personal and academic ways, for which I am very thankful. Many of them are associated with the Australian National University where I spent three years in the early 1970s and where in 1980 I was a Visiting Fellow in the Department of Pacific and Southeast Asian History: the late J W Davidson, Gavan Daws, Niel Gunson, Hank Nelson, Deryck Scarr, Oskar Spate, Dorothy Shineberg, Robert Langdon, Norma McArthur. I am also very grateful to Robin Fisher of Simon Fraser University (British Columbia), and Mary Boyd of Victoria University (New Zealand). At Massey University I owe a particular debt to W H Oliver, John Owens, Barrie Macdonald, and Judy Bennett.

I also wish to acknowledge assistance of a more technical nature: much of the illustrative material was provided by the Alexander Turnbull Library, Wellington, New Zealand, and Massey University's photographic unit, the latter reproducing all those illustrations not otherwise acknowledged: Keith Mitchell very kindly drew the maps; Heather Read and Glenis Foster typed the manuscript; and Chris Bloore lent me drawing equipment for the sketches.

Finally I must thank my family for their constant support and patience.

Explanatory notes

Place names

Some of the islands dealt with in this book have had name changes this century. I have retained the older and more usual names for the sake of convenience and for a measure of historical accuracy. To have sandalwood traders in the 1840s going to Vanuatu would be as misleading as having Columbus sailing to the United States in 1492. Hence I use, for example,

New Hebrides instead of Vanuatu
Gilbert Islands instead of Kiribati
Ellice Islands instead of Tuvalu
New Guinea instead of Papua New Guinea and/or Irian Jaya
Samoa instead of Western Samoa and/or American Samoa

Even so, it should be noted that this practice is not always historically correct. Some islands were known to Europeans by names which sooner or later went out of fashion. For example, the Hawaiian Islands, Samoa, and Tonga (terms I use) were once called, respectively, the Sandwich Islands, the Navigators' Islands, and the Friendly Islands.

More general terms like the South Sea or the Pacific similarly have had complex patterns of usage; see Spate, 'South Sea to Pacific Ocean'.

Even where nomenclature has remained unchanged, spelling sometimes has not, especially of late with attempts to 'de-Europeanise' the rendition of certain indigenous names. Where standardisation is not yet well established, or is debated, I have used spellings which at least are in common use.

Fijian orthography

In Fijian usage, the following letters are pronounced:

b	as	*mb*	in	*number*
c	as	*th*	in	*that*
d	as	*nd*	in	*end*

g   as   *ng*   in   *singer*
q   as   *ng*   in   *finger*

Measurements

All measurements are metric.

Dating

For dates before about 2000 years ago BP (before the present), rather than BC, is used, for example 50 000 BP (instead of 48 000 BC). For more recent dates the more usual form is used, for example 1284 AD.

In the sea's eye

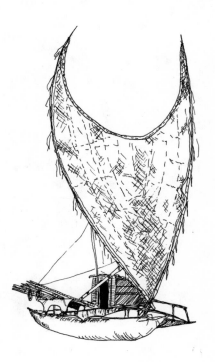

Ocean-going canoe, Santa Cruz

Whence and how

The story of the first human settlement of the Pacific islands is now known at least in broad outline. Modern scholarship in such fields as archaeology, linguistics, and ethno-botany has removed much of the fanciful myth and romance that enshroud so many popular views of Pacific prehistory. Yet the tale as scholars now tell it is no less dramatic and has lost none of the epic qualities in its accounts of ancient seafarers exploring, discovering, exploiting, settling some of the most remote specks of habitable land on earth. Human ventures into an oceanic world are significant not only for Pacific prehistory, but also for world prehistory. In the Southeast Asian archipelago and western Pacific fringes—Australia and New Guinea— physical anthropologists and archaeologists are dealing with some of the world's earliest civilisations and tracing the evolution of such fundamental steps in human prehistory as horticulture and animal domestication. These developments seem to be quite independent from, and in some aspects may even predate, similar events in the Old World. In eastern Pacific islands we can witness perhaps the very last stages in the long process of exploration and initial settlement of the habitable parts of the globe. Humans first evolved in Africa several million years ago; just over one thousand years ago some individuals finally reached the most isolated islands in the midst of the world's largest ocean—Hawaii, Easter Island, and New Zealand.

Southeast Asia

The ancient homeland of Pacific island populations was in Southeast Asia. Early people, *Homo erectus*, reached there two million years ago. Throughout much of the Pleistocene period sea levels were much lower than they are today and the Southeast Asian landmass encompassed the western half of the present-day archipelago (Map 1). This now partly submerged continent is known as the Sunda Shelf and the remains of *Homo erectus* have been found on its southern shoreline, present-day Java. Very little is known of their paleolithic culture. Modern people, *Homo sapiens*, arrived in the region perhaps sixty thousand years ago and their traces,

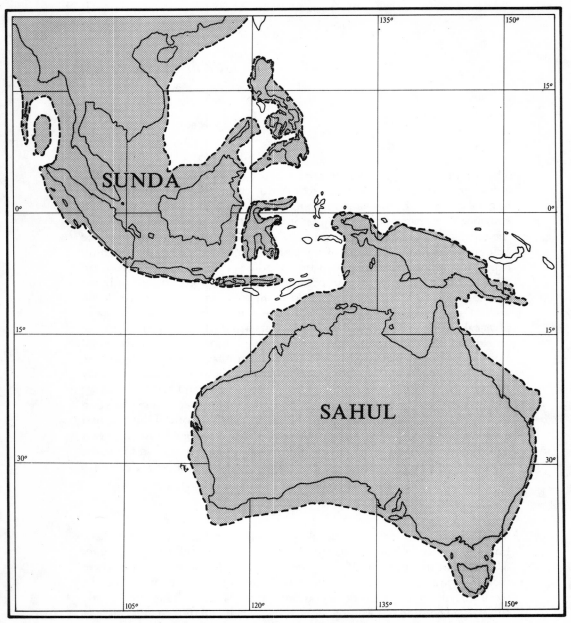

1   Sunda and Sahul. Extended land areas during Pleistocene glaciation.

mainly flaked tools, are found with increasing frequency throughout Sunda. Like their predecessors, these people were hunters and gatherers, but they were more venturesome, and determined to find what lay beyond Sunda's shores.[1]

Australia

Because of their proximity to Southeast Asia, both New Guinea and Australia, which as recently as 8000 years ago were still physically joined, are of vital importance. On these large land masses one can follow the fortunes of those hunter-gatherers who left their Southeast Asian homelands to cross the seas to the south and east. Even at the ocean's lowest point at the height of the Pleistocene Ice Age, a sea crossing of some considerable distance was required to reach the Australia–New Guinea continent from the Sunda Shelf. Human settlement was widespread over what is now the Australian continent by at least 30 000 years ago, which means that the initial human entry was much earlier. It is still not known whether Australia was populated by a single migration or a series of them. Nor can it yet be determined to what extent Aboriginal culture was a product of local evolution, subsequent diffusion, or the later introduction of techniques from elsewhere. This particular problem is highlighted by the contemporaneous existence, at least to some 8000 years ago, of two apparently different skull types—a robust and seemingly archaic form and a more modern gracile variety. There is some debate as to whether these skulls have different origins or whether they are extreme variations of a basic stock. The unravelling of such mysteries will open a window not only on Australia's past but possibly on the whole question of human physical evolution. Skulls of *Homo sapiens* found in both Southeast Asia and Australia date back some 30 000 to 40 000 years, to a time when 'Neanderthal man had not yet departed the European scene', and suggest that there was 'a separate and parallel evolution of *Homo sapiens* in different regions of the world from already regionally diversified *Homo erectus* ancestors'.[2]

One of the most notable characteristics of Aboriginal culture is its stability and longevity. This does not mean that it was static. The continent was subject to considerable climatic changes over tens of thousands of years. Some areas now arid were once lakes teeming with marine and other life. Vegetation patterns were radically affected by such changes, as well as by fires of natural or human origin. Further, as the last Ice Age ended, the rising of the seas flooded about one third of the land that was dry when humans first arrived. By 8000 years ago New Guinea had finally become an island, and so had Tasmania. Although such changes may appear extremely dramatic, they took place gradually over thousands of years, and many generations might have noticed little or no change. Nevertheless the basic hunter-gatherer existence clearly did adapt to local conditions and environments over a period of time, to an extent which has perhaps not been fully appreciated. The textbook view of Aborigines as kangaroo catching desert dwellers needs to be substantially qualified, for they occupied 'every ecological niche that hunter-gatherers anywhere in the world have entered, except the snowbound: upland, lowland, swamp and lake, maritime, riverine, tropical and temperate, rain forest, open forest, grassland and desert'.[3] Local or regional cultural adaptation was thus encouraged to some extent.

There is some evidence too of possibly imported innovations. About 6000 to 7000 years ago there was a detectable modification in tools throughout the continent, but not in Tasmania for by this time that land was isolated from the mainland by a wide and dangerous strait. The dingo, too, seems to have been a late arrival on the mainland for it also failed to reach Tasmania. The extent to which mainland Aborigines had contact with or even knowledge of the outside world is yet unclear, though it is now thought to have been quite substantial at least in the far north. In the most recent prehistoric times—the last two centuries before 1770—Aborigines in the far north may have had some dealings with the Portuguese who were trading as far south as Timor. At the same time they certainly did have contact with Indonesian fishermen from the port of Macassar in the Celebes, hundreds of whom ranged from the Kimberleys to the Gulf of Carpentaria each summer in search of the edible sea-slug or bêche-de-mer.[4] There were also longstanding links between the Aborigines of the Cape York region, the Islanders of Torres Strait, and neighbouring New Guineans. This latter contact in particular highlights one of the more puzzling aspects of Australian prehistory. For some 5000 years, New Guineans along with most peoples of the Southeast Asian archipelago have been horticulturalists and domesticators of animals. Aborigines, however, remained hunter-gatherers, and obviously not because of ignorance of a planting economy—at least not in the far north.[5]

One explanation is that Aborigines were too mentally inferior to cope with the imagined 'sophistication' of a gardening economy, a belief based on the fallacious assumption that the lifestyle of a nomadic hunter-gatherer is less 'evolved' than that of a more 'civilised' agricultural settlement. Another and more common view is that Australia was too arid and in other ways ecologically unsuited for the development of Aboriginal agricultural pursuits. Modern scholarship has advanced a rather different explanation. Many areas of Australia were perfectly capable of supporting a gardening economy and Aborigines, it is suggested, were quite capable of changing their economic habits but simply chose not to because there was no good reason why they should. It is now thought that their hunter-gatherer existence was so well attuned to supplying their needs, physical as well as emotional, that any changes were quite unnecessary. This view was most persuasively argued in Blainey's *Triumph of the Nomads*, which suggested that Aborigines, far from belonging to the most primitive, degraded human cultures as popular folklore has it, were in fact members of one of the world's first affluent societies.[6] That Aborigines preferred to continue their age-old lifestyles was a matter of choice.

The hunter-gatherers who entered the Australian continent sustained a way of life that was relatively unchanging for some 40 000 years. Such longevity and stability have not been found elsewhere in the story of the settlement of Oceania.

New Guinea

Earliest evidence of human settlement in New Guinea is in the highland areas and dates back at least 25 000 years. Such a date roughly correlates with early settlement of Australia, which is only to be expected in view of the physical union of the two land masses at that time. We may speculate that there may have been some movement of population between the two regions until about 8000 years ago, when rising sea levels finally severed the land bridge. The linguistic origins of Australian Aborigines and most New Guineans (except those in some coastal regions) point to a common ancestry. Early cultural divergence between the New Guinea highlanders and those groups occupying what is now Australia was probably more subtle than it later became, and was probably initially stimulated by the marked climatic differences between the two regions—the forested New Guinea highlands were particularly wet at this stage. As early as 10 000 years ago there were detectable differences in some of the tools used in the highlands and those used in what was becoming (because sea levels were rising) continental Australia. Such developments indicate a degree of economic specialisation as the various communities adapted to their respective environments. However, the common hunter-gatherer economies were maintained.

But just as a wide sea finally separated New Guinea and Australia, so too did basic cultural patterns come to differ markedly, not only by internal adaptation but also because of the 'Austronesian' advance through New Guinea coastal regions and ultimately beyond, about 6000 years ago. The Austronesians appear to represent a 'second wave' of migrants from the Southeast Asian region, and they were in many respects very different from the neolithic hunter-gatherers who preceded them to New Guinea–Australia by at least 30 000 years.[7] The newcomers and their culture were the products of later developments in Southeast Asia and in what had by then become its archipelago. Two such developments in particular seem to have stimulated Austronesian expansion. First, the adoption of the sail and outrigger canoes made journeys across the broad waterways separating the archipelago islands much safer and more certain. Second, the use of root

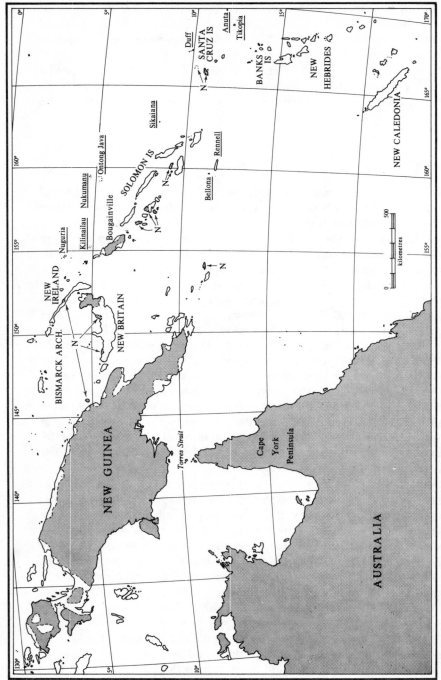

2 *Southwest Pacific. Non-Austronesian language areas are shaded, or marked N. The remaining areas are Austronesian. Polynesian outliers are underlined. (Based on Chowning An Introduction to the Peoples and Cultures of Melanesia)*

crops and pig farming, which had recently evolved and rapidly became widespread, encouraged settlement of other lands, some of which would have been unable to support a hunter-gatherer existence.[8] Ultimately, such a means of travel and mode of sustenance made possible the discovery and settlement of the islands of the Pacific Ocean.

Approximately 5000 to 7000 years ago a number of related events— having to do with such an unlikely combination as pigs, pottery, post-holes and polished adzes—all point to Austronesian settlement in coastal and riverine New Guinea and subsequent influences on existing New Guinea societies. Pig bones definitely appear in the highland's archaeological record some 6000 years ago, and were probably present much earlier. Since pigs were not indigenous to New Guinea they must have been introduced by humans, and these people were probably agriculturalists, for the domestication of the pig requires feeding and a relatively settled existence. Whether horticultural techniques were entirely introduced to New Guinea from further west or whether introduced techniques merely stimulated a simple horticulture that might already have been evolving independently in New Guinea is not yet clear, especially as fragments of polished adze heads, usually associated with cutting trees, appeared some 10 000 years ago in the highlands. Furthermore, at Kuk, what appear to be pig wallowing-holes occurred at these early times. Certainly a main, but not necessarily only impetus for agriculture came with the Austronesians who also probably introduced the dog and the chicken along with the pig, as well as intensive exploitation of root crops like yam and taro. Root cropping and pig domestication seem to have been speedily adopted and adapted right through the country, including the highland regions that most Austronesians seem not to have settled. Pollen analysis and related studies suggest that by 5000 years ago large areas of the highlands had been cleared of forest, indicative of a slash and burn horticulture that still exists in areas of Melanesia. By 2000 years ago the presence of a sophisticated agriculture throughout both highland and lowland regions is evidenced by wooden implements, widespread drainage of swamps, irrigation ditches for intensive taro planting, and permanent village settlements typical of an agricultural existence. Along with the first signs of agriculture are other cultural remnants generally associated with Austronesian presence, such as quadrangular adzes, and pottery. Such artefacts do not predate Austronesian settlement in the New Guinea region, and are subsequently found consistently not only there but throughout the rest of Oceania.[9] Finally, linguistic analysis provides very strong evidence of the advance of this new culture out of Southeast Asia and eastward into the Pacific islands from about 6000 years ago. The very numerous languages of Australian Aborigines and most New Guineans are generally classified as Non-Austronesian. Such languages are based on those of the first settler populations of tens of thousands of years ago and are not to be found elsewhere (except in some pockets in Indonesia and northern Island Melanesia). A second and much more recent family of languages, referred to as Austronesian, encompasses all the surrounding regions—most of island Southeast Asia, the Philippines, and all the remaining islands of the Pacific. The exact relationship between Non-Austronesian and Austronesian languages is difficult to ascertain, but there seems little doubt that the latter represent a much more recent movement of population out from Southeast Asia, a movement intimately associated with the sail and outrigger canoe complex, agriculture, and pottery making.[10] A linguistic map of the Australian–New Guinea region is very suggestive of such a wave of newcomers.[11] All the languages of Australia are Non-Austronesian. So too are the languages of New Guinea except for pockets of Austronesian languages in the 'bird's head' in the far west and in narrow enclaves along the northern coast and the 'tail' in the eastern end. In the Melanesian island chain the situation is reversed: Austronesian languages predominate, with Non-Austronesian languages confined to small areas of New Britain, a tiny enclave on New Ireland, interior regions of Bougainville, tiny pockets on and near New Georgia, and on the Santa Cruz islands—the southeasterly limit. The rest of island Melanesia and the remaining Pacific islands are Austronesian (Map 2).

Island Melanesia

The early hunter-gatherers of New Guinea probably did not penetrate much beyond New Britain, New Ireland, and Bougainville, at least not for any great length of time. First, they did not have the marine technology for a ready means of exploration. Second, and perhaps more important, these mainly pre-agricultural people would have been unable to survive for very long in southern Melanesia, which is very poor in edible flora and fauna compared with New Guinea and Australia. The first permanent inhabitants of most of island Melanesia were the Austronesians whose root crop and pig agriculture enabled them to survive where hunter-gatherers could not. By 4000 years ago they had settled as far south as New Caledonia and its dependencies and some 500 years later had reached Fiji. Settlement of most of island Melanesia was thus relatively recent and probably took place rapidly, perhaps well within 1000 years.[12]

It would be misleading to imagine that there was necessarily a sequential progression down the island chain. Rather there were probably very complex patterns of settlement—some travellers moving quickly, bypassing islands, others moving slowly, perhaps settling in inland regions and quickly becoming isolated. Other migrants perhaps moved northward again, while new waves of people bringing with them different genes and ideas entered the region. Such cultural infusion combined with an ongoing local adaptation and innovation helps to explain why 'Melanesian' culture by the time of European contact seemed so diverse. This complex pre-history resulted in an amazing proliferation of languages and a remarkable diversity of customs and sociopolitical arrangements. It is impossible to speak of 'Melanesian' culture as in any way homogeneous. Yet the region did have elements of a cultural coherence of a different kind, as illustrated by the widespread use of Lapita pottery between 4000 and 2000 years ago. Lapita pottery—so called because of an excavated site at Lapita in New Caledonia—is characterised by particular stamped and incised surface designs.[13] One of the significant aspects of such a ceramic tradition is its wide distribution, from Watom Island off New Britain, through many parts of island Melanesia and Fiji, to Samoa and Tonga. Roger Green has suggested that Lapita pottery was a 'new specialisation within a more generalised horticultural, maritime-based Austronesian adaptation, a de-velopment dependent on the evolution of an efficient internal-exchange network maintained by effective two-way voyaging over distances of up to 600 km.'[14] He claimed that the Lapita makers had a relatively coherent cultural complex, which possibly originated in the Bismarck Archipelago and made its way across to the central Pacific islands. Green distinguished a basic Western Lapita adaptation, which maintained itself by internal ex-change as far as Santa Cruz, and an Eastern Lapita which was eventually isolated from continued contact with the west and evolved into its own, proto-Polynesian forms. Meanwhile the Lapita tradition in the west had, by about the first centuries AD, either been abandoned or absorbed (perhaps by conquest), or evolved into quite new forms. It seems likely that these ancient Lapita makers were not the direct ancestors of today's 'Melanesians'. So-called Melanesian culture most probably evolved more recently and from subsequent migrations into that region of the Pacific. There is still a good deal of speculation as to the implications of Lapita ware, and much work to do relating it to other contemporaneous and later ceramic traditions throughout Melanesia and the central Pacific.[15] One conclusion seems fairly clear: some 3000 to 4000 years ago a people with an identifiable cultural tradition extended human settlement from northeastern Melanesia to New Caledonia, Fiji, and as far afield as Samoa and Tonga. While they were in some way eclipsed in Melanesia by succeeding cultural traditions, these gardening, Lapita-making, ocean-going specialists were in the van-guard of human discovery and settlement of the western and central Pacific islands and were the ancestors of the people whom we now call Polynesians.

Micronesia

Settlement sequences of Micronesia are still quite tentative, mainly because very little archaeological work has been undertaken there.[16] Radiocarbon dates for human presence on the high volcanic Marianas go back some 4000 years, and though there has been no similar dating for the Carolines, other archaeological evidence suggests that settlement of at least Yap and Palau probably occurred about the same time. The Marianas and Yap were probably settled from the Philippines, and Palau from the Celebes region. These dates perhaps tie in with the general movement of the Austronesian-speaking communities beyond the Southeast Asian archipelago. Linguistic evidence suggests, however, that the inhabitants of Saipan, Yap, Palau, and surrounding islands penetrated no further eastward and that the tiny coral atolls that comprise the remaining Caroline, Marshall, and Gilbert Islands were subsequently settled from somewhere in eastern Melanesia; some linguists suggest the Santa Cruz–northern New Hebrides as a possible point of origin. Such a movement to the north and west reached as far as a small group of islands southwest of Palau (Sonsorol, Pulo Anna, and others). Though two basic linguistic types are present in Micronesia, possibly attesting to two different points of entry by the earliest settlers, internal migrations and local adaptations to environments have tended to blur any formerly clear-cut cultural divisions. Nor in suggesting that the first settlement of most of Micronesia was from the southeast is it implied that cultural diffusion necessarily followed this general route. There is ample evidence, for example in evolving fishing technology, that later influences from as far afield as Japan were not uncommon. And doubtless because of their relative proximity to the Asian mainland, the northern and western regions of Micronesia received various Asiatic influences, more so than, say, the Gilbert Islands far to the east.

Central and eastern Pacific islands

Fiji, which the Lapita makers had reached about 3500 years ago,[17] is generally regarded as the more immediate place of ancestry for those travellers who moved further eastward into the wide expanses of Polynesia. Much has been made of Fiji as some sort of border territory between the cultural regions commonly defined as Melanesia and Polynesia. There has been some debate as to whether the first settlers in Fiji came via the Melanesian island chain or through Micronesia. Some physical anthropologists, like William Howells, argued for a Micronesian route on the grounds that certain physical characteristics of Polynesians imply that their more immediate ancestors came through the Caroline Islands. Such characteristics, as they emerged in Fiji (it is claimed), would have been rather different or hybridised if they had been transmitted through Melanesia.[18] At present there is considerable evidence to the contrary.[19] As already mentioned, linguistic studies indicate that most Micronesian languages (except for those in the far west) derive from those of eastern Melanesia, which suggests that much of Micronesia was settled from the south and east. Archaeologists also point out that Lapita pottery has not yet been found in Micronesia, though pots of a different sort were made there. This suggests that the people of eastern Melanesia who migrated to Micronesian islands either did not come from a Lapita-making tradition when it was current or moved off after Lapita potting had become a vanished art. In the latter case, Fiji was already long settled. Whatever the explanation, the lack of Lapita pottery in Micronesia is a major problem for those who claim that the first settlers in Fiji, who were Lapita potters, did not come from the Melanesian islands. Furthermore, some root crops and animals, in particular the pig, that arrived in Fiji clearly came via Melanesia and with the Austronesians. Such plants and animals would have been unlikely to have survived for long on small atolls, and not surprisingly are absent from the archaeological record in the eastern regions of Micronesia. Finally, the case advanced by Howells, some would argue, seems based on the assumption that Polynesians or at least proto-Polynesians moved into the Pacific as a physically identifiable group from somewhere in the Southeast Asian region, bypassing Melanesia, and that if this group had moved through Melanesia the inhabitants already there would have left an unmistakable genetic imprint on the migrants. Such a conclusion, however, seems to rest on the questionable view that the early settlers in the Melanesian island chain could be identified as culturally 'Melanesian' in the same way as they are today. But, as will be described in the following chapter, by the time Fiji was settled there was no 'Melanesian' culture in this sense. Such a development came later, probably from 'hybridisation within Melanesia, resulting in gene flow from New Guinea (already long occupied)'.[20] By then some of the Austronesian settlers of Fiji had moved into the remoter Polynesian islands where they were unaffected by such developments within Melanesia. This is not to suggest that no one ever reached Fiji directly out of Southeast Asia via Micronesia, but it seems likely, on current evidence, that Fiji's first settlers and the predominant culture of that region (which was quickly transmitted further eastward) emerged out of the Melanesian island chain.

From Fiji, the Lapita seafarers ranged ever onward and had settled Tonga by about 3200 BP and Samoa by 3000 BP (possibly earlier).[21] The Tongan-Samoan region is often referred to as the cradle of Polynesia for it was here, over a period of perhaps 1000 years and in apparent relative isolation that the inhabitants developed those linguistic and cultural characteristics that are commonly known as 'Polynesian', or more accurately west Polynesian.[22] Within that regional complex there also evolved more specific, local traits which resulted in the development of the respective Tongan and Samoan cultures. This Tongan-Samoan differentiation was subsequently reflected across the rest of Polynesia. The proto-Polynesian languages that evolved in this region have been divided into Tongic, which includes Tonga and Niue, and Nuclear Polynesian, which includes Samoa and all eastern Polynesian islands. Early cultural assemblages in eastern

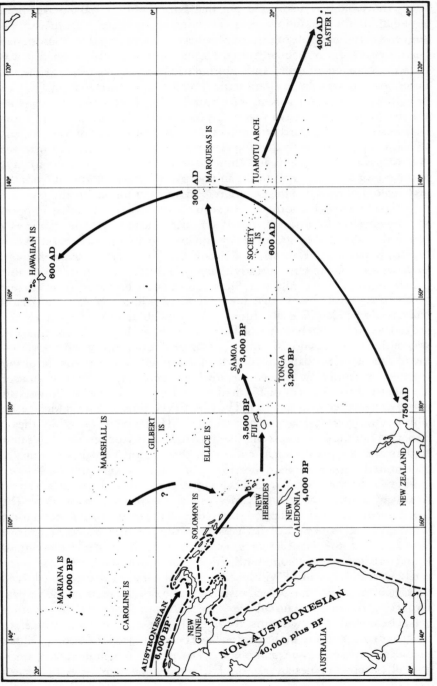

3   *Pacific settlement*

Polynesia also suggest that Samoa, rather than Tonga, was the more likely
principal point of departure for the first travellers to eastern Polynesian
outposts, though some artefacts and influences on these islands can also be
traced back directly to Fiji and to western Polynesian complexes generally.[23]

The next reliable date for human settlement further to the east appears,
somewhat surprisingly, as late as about AD 300 and as far away from Samoa-
Tonga as the Marquesas.[24] The Marquesas, or possibly some other nearby
islands, appear to have been a dispersal point for subsequent discovery and
settlement of most of the rest of Polynesia. It would appear that exploratory
voyages ranged out from this area like the rays of the sun. There is evidence
of human habitation on Easter Island by AD 400, the Society Islands, Cook
Islands, and Hawaii by AD 600, and New Zealand by AD 750.[25] The earliest
material remnants of these islands clearly derive from a 'common ancestral
East Polynesian type ... [which] had evolved by AD 600–800 out of an
earlier type which is exemplified by the earliest Marquesan materials of AD
300 to 600. The latter can be regarded as a continuation of the ancestral
Polynesian tradition, now best represented by Samoan materials from 200
BC to AD 200, with certain important modifications.'[26]

Polynesian or 'Samoan' outliers

The story of the settlement of the Pacific islands does not end with the
discovery and habitation of the islands at the far ends of the Polynesian
triangle—Hawaii, Easter Island, New Zealand. Samoa, which seems to
have been an important homeland for the explorers who moved further
east, was also a major point of departure for voyagers to the north and west
at later dates. The Tokelaus were settled about AD 1000 and the Ellice
perhaps as late as AD 1400. Other groups of people from the Samoan region,
either by accident or design, found themselves off the eastern flank of island
Melanesia at various times in the last 1500 years. Many of these travellers
were either killed or culturally absorbed by local inhabitants. However, a
surprising number established their own little communities, usually on
small offshore islands (Map 2). On these Polynesian outliers—like
Nukumanu, Ontong Java, Sikaiana, Bellona, Rennell, Anuta, Tikopia—
are tiny pockets of (west) Polynesian culture, modified to a greater or lesser
extent by new environments and neighbouring cultures. For a long time
they excited the imaginations of scholars seeking to find the supposed
homeland of the Polynesians. Until quite recently it was assumed that Polynesians, as Polynesians, entered the Pacific from somewhere in Southeast
Asia and migrated around cultures already in the western Pacific until they
eventually came to these uninhabited islands where they finally settled. The
problem was to find traces of this migration, and the outliers fitted the bill
perfectly. They were, it was claimed, the cultural footprints left by the

Polynesian migrants as they skirted around the northeastern fringes of island Melanesia. Modern scholarship has found that these outliers were not the first traces of Polynesian culture in the Pacific. On the contrary, they represent some of the last stages of Polynesian expansion, long after the development of Polynesian cultures in the central and eastern Pacific islands. Polynesians had almost returned to those western gateways where their Austronesian ancestors had first entered the Pacific Ocean thousands of years earlier.

Polynesian origins

The grandiose quest for the mythical Polynesian homeland outside the Pacific—like some Antipodean Holy Grail—has haunted scholars since Cook's voyages.[27] The question 'Where did the Polynesians come from?' now has a nicely deflating answer, in the words of one prehistorian: 'Polynesians did not strictly come from anywhere'.[28] The *ancestors* of these people came from Southeast Asia, and after a long process of adaptation, developed, in the central Pacific region, cultural forms which we call (western) Polynesian and which were further evolved as these people settled more easterly islands and finally Hawaii and New Zealand.

The evidence for Southeast Asian origins of all Pacific islands cultures, as they existed by the time of first European contact, is overwhelming. Radiocarbon dating shows that settlement progressed in roughly an easterly direction. Earliest dates for human occupation are in the western Pacific, the most recent in the east. Linguists have performed the remarkable task of ultimately relating all Pacific islands languages back to Southeast Asia.[29] Physical anthropologists and geneticists can similarly point to Southeast Asia as the Islanders' ancient homeland.[30] Archaeologists can trace the development of various artefacts and their use along the routes of migration into the Pacific from the west.[31] Botanists can show that most plants (with the notable exception of one or two) and animals likewise originated in Southeast Asia and must have been carried by humans into the far extremes of Oceania.[32]

In spite of such evidence, the Asian origin of some Pacific cultures—especially Polynesian—still does not command popular as opposed to academic support. Opinions that Polynesians came from spaceships or Mesopotamia can excite a good deal of interest, as does the seemingly more plausible view advanced by Thor Heyerdahl that the first settlers of Polynesia came from South America.[33] This particular theory, though thoroughly demolished by modern scholarship, will probably always find a cosy niche in Pacific historiography, if only because of Heyerdahl's epic raft voyage from Peru to the wave-lashed reefs of the Tuamotus. Contrary to Heyerdahl's claim, this adventure proved nothing beyond the fact that

Thor Heyerdahl could, with some initial mechanical assistance, sail a raft from Peru to eastern Polynesia. Not only is the view that Polynesian culture derived from the Americas completely untenable, but there is not yet any evidence that there was even any significant contact in prehistoric times between Polynesian islands and such distant continental coasts. Easter Island, the closest part of Polynesia to South America, though separated by well over 3000 kilometres of empty ocean, has long been thought of as a place where South American influences prevailed. Careful scrutiny of supposedly South American features such as the famous stone statues has left no doubt that they are typically Polynesian. Similar constructions can be found elsewhere in eastern Polynesia, and Austronesian communities throughout Melanesia and Polynesia built stone megaliths of one sort or another. On the other hand, definite South American traces that one *should* be able to find if there had been significant contact are notably absent. Where, for example, are South American linguistic influences? It is quite possible that some South Americans might have made their way to eastern Polynesia, but there is no evidence that such travellers had any impact on existing cultures, let alone formed the basis of Polynesian society.[34]

As proponents of the South American connection are quick to point out, the sweet potato poses a particular problem, for there seems little doubt that this plant originated on that continent. It is also believed to have been present in eastern Polynesia at the time of first human settlement there. Indeed, the sweet potato may well have enabled some communities to survive, particularly in New Zealand where the climate is too cold for most of the tropical foodplants that the first settlers tried to bring with them. How the sweet potato reached Polynesia from South America is unknown, though the strong inference is that it must have been by human hand. The further spread of the sweet potato across the Pacific is also something of a mystery. It was doubtless disseminated widely throughout eastern Polynesia by roving seafarers, and probably into island Melanesia as well. However, its arrival farther west seems to have been very much later. Possibly not until the sixteenth century did it reach the highlands of New Guinea, perhaps from the Philippines (via Indonesia) where it could have been introduced by Spanish galleons travelling to Manila from South American ports.[35]

The spread of the coconut across the tropical Pacific Ocean is also suggestive of early long-distance voyaging by humans. The coconut probably originated in the Southeast Asian–Melanesian region. It was also established on the Pacific coast of the Panama-Colombia area by at least AD 1500. If, as seems likely, this plant crossed the Pacific from west to east, the question is did it drift or was it carried? Tests of the nuts' viability floating in water for long periods, and computer simulations of likely drift directions, together with chances of natural reestablishment in new lands have indicated that it was 'highly unlikely that the coconut could have crossed the central Pacific in either direction as an unaided voyager'.[36] Thus both the coconut and the sweet potato provide some, albeit highly circumstantial, evidence for trans-Pacific journeys by people long before Magellan.

Navigation

In recent years another debate has been rather more fruitful than that over the question of South American origins for Polynesian cultures. If one accepts that Pacific Islanders ultimately emerged from Southeast Asia, the problem is no longer *where* they came from but *how* they came. How were they able to reach virtually every speck of land dotted right across the vast ocean surface? Scholars of earlier generations assumed that most Islanders were skilled sailors with efficient craft and expertise in the arts of direction finding. Peter Buck called them the 'Vikings of the Sunrise'. In the late 1950s and early 1960s Andrew Sharp sparked off a lively debate by suggesting that Islanders had neither suitable canoes nor navigating techniques to permit deliberate voyages of settlement, or even to allow them to navigate successfully to and fro over open oceans. These controversial views were advanced in *Ancient Voyagers in the Pacific* and *Ancient Voyagers in Polynesia*. Sharp began by noting, obviously enough, that every island was first discovered by accident. But he then went on to deny that once travellers had chanced upon land, they could sail back to their point of departure and subsequently return to their new discovery. Sharp thus challenged the orthodox views about the 'triple voyage'—one to discover an island, one to return home, one to return to the new island—at least for any appreciable distance. He maintained that Islanders were incapable of navigating to a known destination more than 480 kilometres away, where navigation is defined as an ability to hold a course to a given destination. According to Sharp, the settlement of the Pacific islands resulted from a series of accidental drift voyages, or even planned voyages of exploration, mostly in an easterly direction. And they were, he claimed, essentially voyages of no return. The first discoverers of an island were thus its first settlers.[37]

Sharp believed that sailors were unable to navigate (though they could journey randomly) over empty seas to a known destination because of his conviction that they had no means of detecting their lateral (sideways) drift caused by winds and currents. The magnitude of lateral error would, he claimed, increase according to the distance the canoe travelled. He also questioned the skills the Islanders were supposed to have in navigating by the stars. His view was that since rays of starlight were parallel by the time they reached earth, a particular star at any given time appeared to all observers on the same latitude to be in the same place. Stars might help indicate distance north or south of a target, but could not indicate whether one was east or west of it—again the problem of lateral displacement. And then there was the problem of not being able to see stars at all on cloudy nights. Further, Sharp questioned the effectiveness of other directional aids commonly attributed to these early sailors. The use of migrating or homing birds was limited, in his view, because they were unaffected by ocean currents, and also they could not be seen at night. Birds might indicate the general direction of land, but they could not show the extent of lateral drift.[38] Finally, Sharp suggested that the Islanders' seagoing canoes were not reliable, seaworthy craft as many people assumed. He argued that most were cumbersome, could not be pointed into the wind, and were generally unsafe and incapable of holding a given course. The vagaries of wind and wave were, in Sharp's view, the basic determinants of direction.[39] Such arguments provoked considerable controversy[40] and while most of Sharp's suggestions are now given relatively little credence, his studies did inspire the first really detailed investigations into the Islanders' navigating techniques. Ironically, thanks to Sharp, the sailing and direction-finding skills of some Pacific communities have been proven to be far more sophisticated than even earlier scholars like Buck imagined. David Lewis has been amongst those researchers most responsible for unearthing these maritime skills. Lewis has successfully combined detailed historical documentary analysis with practical small boat seamanship in the islands. One of this century's more remarkable navigators himself, Lewis sailed with and learnt much from the few surviving Micronesian and Polynesian navigators who still practise some of the traditional skills—the last exponents of a vanishing art. As Lewis claimed, this has enabled him to put theoretical knowledge to the 'hard test of landfall'. His findings appear in numerous publications, perhaps most authoritatively in *We the Navigators*.

Contrary to Sharp's view, Lewis believed that the three-way or triple voyage was possible even over many hundreds of kilometres of seemingly empty ocean. He argued that having once discovered an island (obviously by chance) the early navigators were able to reverse their course to their point of departure, and, using the signs learnt on these two trips, deliberately make their way back to their discovery again. Lewis began by examining the very complex and sophisticated methods of astral navigation whereby various horizon stars in particular were of great benefit in establishing direction. His findings make Sharp's comments about such things as parallel starlight seem singularly simplistic and ill informed. Lewis's research indicated that the ancient navigators had, and some still have, a vast mental storehouse of knowledge about the direction and movements of the various heavenly bodies. This was a highly respected and prestigious knowledge handed down through countless generations, often in various navigators' 'schools' where pupils spent years learning about such things as star 'compasses' and putting them to the test at sea. Courses set either by horizon or zenith stars were often confirmed or corrected by other directional aids, particularly certain wind and wave patterns. Star 'compasses' were often incorporated with seasonal wind directions. According to Lewis, the problem of lateral drift was not the great impediment to accurate direction finding that Sharp suggested. Furthermore, in Lewis's view a long voyage did not necessarily increase the lateral error, for sideways drifting was seldom consistent. Rather, a complex and random series of cross-currents and winds was more likely to cancel than to multiply errors. And if there was a persistent sideways drift, said Lewis, the skilled mariner would be aware of it and would correct his course accordingly.[41] In this respect the navigators' knowledge of seasonal and local winds and currents was of crucial importance, and, said Lewis, their expertise in such matters would often surpass 'in detail and accuracy that in European hydrographic publications'.[42]

In addition to such knowledge and experience, there were quite different techniques for spatial orientation than those normally used by Westerners.[43] Whereas the latter tend to interpret movement as progress from point A to point B, some Pacific Islanders see it rather differently. For example, Lewis carefully demonstrated what is often called the concept of *etak* whereby (to take the simplest case) a passage from A to B is seen in relation to a third and usually equidistant point, or island, off to the right or left—point C. As the voyage from A to B progresses, point C appears under different and known horizon and other stars. The skilled navigator knows when he is nearing target B, for reference point C will have moved under the appropriate rising or setting star. In practice, the mental visualizations are often rather more complex than this simple example. The concept of *etak* is particularly useful when tacking into the wind (knowing how far to keep on each tack before turning on to the other) and when reorienting after being driven off course by storms, once the skies clear again. What, in brief, the navigator visualizes is a pattern of islands moving and changing their directional relationships with each other. The canoe, to all intents and purposes, remains still. The islands move past. Some of the old navigators interviewed by Lewis had as much difficulty understanding our birdseye concept of static islands placed immovably on a map as we have in grasping their 'wholly dynamic' mental image of 'moving islands'.[44]

Combined with such arts of direction finding is the concept of the 'expanded target' which the lay European may find much easier to understand (though certainly not practise!) To most Europeans, Pacific islands represent little more than dots on a map, all seemingly separated by large featureless areas of blue ocean. That a navigator can make deliberate landfall, even if his craft can maintain a reasonably steady course, seems a remarkable feat. But the difficulty is really more in Western-oriented conceptualising (for example the preoccupation with latitude and longitude), and ignorance. The navigators had a somewhat different attitude. For them, island targets were not pinpoints of land, nor was the ocean devoid of tell-tale signs for the traveller. The island targets could be 'expanded' and could loom almost like the proverbial barn door.[45]

Even the smallest atoll creates certain phenomena that effectively make it a bigger target than it might appear on a map. It can be 'expanded' to a target 'block' some 100 kilometres wide. In other words such an island can have a target zone of about 50 kilometres radius. And since many Pacific islands are found in clusters or archipelagos they can collectively form a vast target area since their individual blocks will overlap to form a 'screen' of islands. For example, the Hawaiian island chain has a screen of at least 1600 kilometres. The distant navigator aims for a screen rather than any individual island in the group, and having made landfall navigates 'internally' to reach the desired island. Further, Lewis argued, it must be remembered that even without so expanding island targets 'it is possible to sail from Southeast Asia to all the inhabited islands of Oceania, save only Hawaii, New Zealand and Easter Island, without ever making a sea crossing longer than 310 miles [496 kilometres].'[46]

Islands are expanded in several ways. The higher islands can be seen from up to 128 kilometres away. Tahiti rises to over 2000 metres, Hawaii to almost 4000 metres. Certain tell-tale cloud formations above such landmasses can extend this range even further. Other cloud formations are often just as effective in indicating the presence of even the lowest islands, especially atolls whose lagoon surfaces are reflected on the cloud's undersides.

Homing birds flying to islands in the evening and away from them at dawn can be useful indicators. For example, boobies range from 50 to 80 kilometres offshore during the day, terns and noddies 30 to 40 kilometres. Thus a flock of terns seen flying along at dusk not only gives the direction of their nightly home but indicates that it is less than 40 kilometres away.

Swell patterns formed by waves bouncing off or being deflected by islands are another sign of land. The experienced navigator can sense (rather than often actually see) three or four differing cross swells at a time. At night, deep phosphorescence sometimes flashes seemingly from the direction of land up to 130 to 160 kilometres away, and disappears as the land gets closer. All sorts of drift objects—coconuts, seaweed, twigs— indicate the presence of land. The trained eye can also detect changes in sea colour which tell of deep reefs.

Broad expanses of sea, which to most Europeans are featureless (and generally full of menace), were something quite different to the trained island mariner. To him the sea was a friendly place and as full of signs as a road map is to a European.

Finally, Lewis challenged Sharp's opinion that the Islanders' canoes were not suitable for deliberate voyaging to distant destinations, and showed how many Pacific canoe designs ultimately derive from the rich maritime technology of the Southeast Asian region. Constant modification in design to suit particular island conditions produced a range of vessels that were eminently suitable for long distance navigation and displayed

XVIII

*1   Ocean-going outrigger, Caroline Islands. Note asymmetrical hull in front view.
(Choris Voyage Pittoresque Autour du Monde. Alexander Turnbull Library)*

very considerable sophistication in their many varieties of hull and sail shape and construction.[47] Again, the problem of interpretation lies mostly in Western preconceptions. Anything 'different' and not of Western manufacture and design is frequently considered 'primitive' and less effective: a canoe is popularly seen as a hollowed-out log. The voyaging canoes of Oceania were anything but hollowed-out logs. They ranged from the giant ribbed and planked double-hulled vessels of some 24 metres length found in parts of tropical Polynesia to the similarly constructed but smaller mainhull plus single outrigger canoes of Micronesia. Many oceangoing craft featured such 'modern' designs as deep vee hulls, some of which were asymmetrically shaped to reduce drag and lateral drift when sailing to windward, and carefully rigged and shaped sails which 'spilled' just enough wind to reduce pressure on the sail's leeward surface and again improve speed and direction into the wind. Apart from other 'modern' features such as planking, ribbing, and caulking, techniques quite atypical of anything in European marine technology were developed. In particular, cunning use was made of double-ended outrigger canoes. The foot of the mast was shifted from one end to the other (as was the steering oar) to enable the vessel to tack into the wind using the 'stern' as the 'bow' and vice versa on the other tack, permitting the outrigger to be kept always to windward.

So many of the navigating techniques that Lewis and others have painstakingly recorded[48] and often actually tested at sea, were evolved and refined over hundreds of years. As local knowledge and practical experience built up, it was handed on through the generations. Once the equatorial

2   *Double-hull travelling canoes, Tonga.*
(*Cook* A Voyage towards the South Pole.... *Alexander Turnbull Library*)

regions of the Pacific Ocean were settled, a great deal of evidence indicates constant and deliberate voyaging to and fro over many hundreds of kilometres. The ancient navigators had both the skills and the capabilities to ensure that, contrary to Sharp's view, a journey to distant islands was not just another voyage of no return.

Yet there remains the question of whether such deliberate journeys were possible over the extreme distances to the outermost regions, notably Hawaii, New Zealand, and Easter Island. A recent computer study has advanced some interesting conclusions which may or may not be confirmed by future research. The authors of *The Settlement of Polynesia: A Computer Simulation* posed two questions: was a purely drift settlement of Polynesia possible, or was a navigated one necessary?[49] The computer was programmed to simulate many thousands of voyages from various islands. Built into its programme were such variables as starting times (seasons), wind shifts, current movements, probabilities of storms, life expectancies of crews, and other similar factors. The general findings indicated that drift voyages were unlikely to have reached Fiji from southern Melanesia but were possible from southern Micronesia. Nor was it likely that drift voyages from Fiji could have reached the Polynesian dispersal point in the vicinity of the Marquesas. To reach here from Fiji–Samoa–Tonga, the computer findings suggested that a deliberate course, even if one way, was necessary. Perhaps the explorer opted for a particular direction—following the rising sun, or a star course? Once in the Marquesas–Society Islands region the computer found that it was highly possible to drift to most of the rest of Polynesia, with the notable exception of Hawaii, Easter Island, and

New Zealand. The chances of drifting to the latter were given as very remote, and impossible for the first two. The suggestion is that to reach the extremities of Polynesia it was necessary to be able to hold a deliberate course.[50]

Such a computer exercise is of course little more than an academic experiment and can offer only the most circumstantial evidence. Yet when placed in the context of other research it perhaps adds weight to the views of scholars like Lewis and detracts from Sharp's hypotheses. The case for some navigated voyages of exploration to the outermost islands at least looks promising. One might speculate that just over a thousand years ago communities in eastern Polynesia sent forth a series of exploratory probes. Perhaps they were given certain courses to follow for so long and then return if they found no new lands. Such voyages might have radiated out from eastern Polynesia like the rays of the sun. Some undoubtedly sailed on into oblivion, some might have returned from landless seas, and some made new discoveries, such as New Zealand and Hawaii. Whether these travellers were able to make their way back home over such vast distances is unknown and the weight of evidence at present indicates that they did not. Perhaps in these remote regions the successful exploratory voyage was likely to be one of no return.

2

Civilisations in the making

A popular misconception is the belief that once people established themselves on an island their subsequent culture was somehow fixed and self perpetuating until 'disturbed' by European contact. The logical conclusion of such an opinion is that there was a unilinear cultural development as settlement advanced: that, for example, the people who entered Melanesia became 'Melanesians' and that some of them travelled across to the central Pacific where they evolved into 'Polynesians' who subsequently settled the eastern and fringe areas of Polynesia. Such an interpretation is without foundation, and it distorts the rather more complex and subtle developments that took place in any one area after it was initially populated. The Pacific cultures described by the first European explorers do not necessarily bear any detectable relationship with the earliest cultures established on any particular island. Early European accounts are seldom a clear window back into the Pacific islands' more distant prehistory. Further, 'Melanesians' did not become 'Polynesians' in the central Pacific. In fact many of the communities we call 'Melanesian' in places like the Solomon Islands, New Hebrides, and New Caledonia developed there due to highly complex and localised ethnolinguistic developments after the initial Austronesian communities had already sent off those daughter communities who moved eastwards and evolved what we now call 'Polynesian cultures'.

To gain a greater appreciation of the progress of settlement, which so far has been expressed largely in spatial or geographic terms, one must now add the dimension of time. With few exceptions, no initial settlement led to an unchanging culture. The cultural baggage brought by the first settlers to any one island was constantly modified by adaptation to new (and sometimes changing) environments and by further cultural innovations from new arrivals or new ideas and techniques. In order to describe such developments prehistorians study culture sequences or histories. An area or region is selected and the changes that human settlement patterns and cultures undergo are outlined. This approach highlights the fallacy of assuming that any given culture was static from the time of its establishment, and shows that the complexity of culture sequences in particular areas sometimes makes it very difficult to justify using the three main cultural categories for Pacific Islanders. This is not to suggest that there were no elements of continuity or even uniformity in prehistoric times—after all most Pacific Islanders share a distant cultural heritage—but it is to suggest that each community was also subject to changes in sociopolitical organisation, economic activities, settlement patterns, and lifestyles generally which could give it its own particular identity. There is a danger in unthinkingly placing Pacific peoples in categories that have been artificially and arbitrarily imposed to suit European administrative and racial convenience. The terms Melanesian, Micronesian, and Polynesian should perhaps be used to designate geographic rather than culture areas. It might be convenient to call people from Tana Melanesian or New Hebridean but neither term says anything about their Tanese culture. Pacific peoples have specific culture histories and identities—they are Tongans or Tokelauans—as well as sharing characteristics of a more general and perhaps less easily defined regional culture history.

It is tempting to suggest that the longer an area has been settled the more likelihood there is of culture change and evolution. Yet the notable exception of Australia makes such a generalisation misleading. Both New Guinea and Australia have been settled for tens of thousands of years, and both are relatively close to the Asian mainland and therefore likely to be recipients of new settlers and ideas. Whereas Australian Aboriginal culture remained relatively unchanging, the culture history of New Guinea was dramatically different. Neither is the reverse of the generalisation necessarily true—that the last islands settled show the least amount of culture change. New Zealand, settled only 1000 years before European contact, and in one of the most isolated parts of the ocean, witnessed very considerable culture change. The extent and degree of culture modification is not necessarily related to the age of human settlement. Changes result from all manner of quite arbitrary factors such as the environment, the preferences of the inhabitants, the ability of or necessity for people to adapt to a variety of exotic and indigenous pressures, and stimuli for change, whether technological, military, demographic, economic, political, or spiritual.

The study of such culture histories is still in its infancy. A few islands, such as Western Samoa, and one or two small areas in the New Guinea highlands have been subject to considerable though still far from complete archaeological investigation. On some other islands such work is only just beginning, and numerous others, especially in Micronesia, have still to be scratched by the modern archaeologist's trowel. The findings so far, incomplete as they may be, nevertheless add greatly to our understanding of life in early Pacific communities and certainly indicate that the Islanders' prehistories were far more complex and more subject to change than is commonly imagined.

New Guinea

Early New Guinea prehistory[1] must be set against a background of geological time. Sea levels have altered markedly since humans first arrived in New Guinea, reaching the lowest level (some 120 metres below today's shorelines) 18 000 to 20 000 years ago. By 8000 years ago the earth had warmed sufficiently to begin to melt edges of the polar ice, thus raising sea levels and cutting off New Guinea from the Australian continent. Climatic changes have also been considerable over the last 25 000 years. The Pleistocene glaciation lasted till about 14 000 years ago, bringing snow in New Guinea down to much lower levels than today, and perhaps giving a much wetter climate. From 14 000 to 8000 years ago, the climate warmed, melting glaciers and allowing vegetation to grow at higher levels. There was possibly less rain. From 8000 to 5000 years ago the weather was warmer and more humid than today and since then there has been a 'modern' climate.

The earliest archaeological sites so far known are in the highlands of Papua New Guinea. Some 25 000 years ago, and perhaps much earlier, 'unspecialised' hunter-gatherers roamed the forests and grasslands. Their tools were waisted blades (presumably shaped so they could be lashed onto a haft) and flaked axe-adzes. It is suggested that this stone technology has more affinity with that in Japan at that time than with the tool kits of either Australia or Southeast Asia—although it is not dissimilar from the kits in the latter region. Similar tools have been found in New Britain and Bougainville (at sites as yet undated), which could mean that these early settlers were established there.

From 11 000 to 6000 years ago there is evidence of a new stone technology, which might indicate the arrival of other people. Ground and polished stone tools now appeared, and coincided with forest clearing, perhaps indicating rudimentary and localised attempts to cultivate crops. Even so, economic life continued to be based on hunting and gathering such foodstuffs as pandanus. At this time too, the highlanders began to trade with the people occupying lowland sites, as some pig bones and many seashells (both presumably from coastal regions) are to be found in the highlands. From 6000 to 3000 years ago cultivation of root crops became widespread in the highlands, possibly following similar developments in the lowlands where the Austronesian-speaking horticulturalists were now well established. The hunter-gatherer existence was not abandoned in favour of a horticultural economy, but economic life was substantially modified in this period. Widespread clearing of forests was undertaken, presumably for agricultural purposes. The pig became domesticated on a large scale. Over the last 3000 years the highlands have been further influenced by developments in lowland regions. Certain axe or adze shapes

unmistakably reflect Southeast Asian influences. These tools were introduced by the Austronesians and subsequently traded into the interior
ranges. Horticulture also became more intensive, with the draining of
swamps and construction of sophisticated irrigation ditches.[2] Wooden
tools appeared. Such developments probably reflect both the introduction
of new technologies and a growing population—the one stimulating the
other. Agricultural life seems to have become more sedentary. In addition
to the age-old shelter sites, huts and villages were noticeable. Some 400
years ago the sweet potato had a major impact on economic life in the
highlands. Originating in South America, this plant was possibly transported across the Pacific in the sixteenth century by the Spanish to Manila,
and thence into Southeast Asia by Spanish, Portuguese, and other travellers. East Indonesia was possibly the immediate source of the highland
sweet potato, whose relatively easy cultivation and ability to grow above
the limits of taro permitted the growth and sustenance of some of the
largest groups of people to be found in the Pacific islands.

Archaeological investigation of lowland sites is less advanced. There are
yet no published findings of early settlements but it is assumed that some
hunter-gatherers were in river and coastal regions at the same time they
were in the highlands some 25 000 years ago. Dated lowland sites go back
2500 to 4000 years and show, as expected, evidence of an agricultural lifestyle, presumably belonging to Austronesian settlers. Pig bones abound.
There was also widespread trade to the highlands and the Solomon Islands
in obsidian, pottery, tool stones, and shells. Local adaptation and/or
possibly new arrivals resulted in a complex range of economic activity and
lowland settlement patterns. Some communities specialised in maritime
economy and trading. Others concentrated more on agriculture. Full or
part-time hunting and gathering also continued, resulting in a 'discon-
tinuity and complexity of settlement history on any given site'. Overall, it
has been suggested, the 'peoples of Papua New Guinea did not proceed
through a series of economic phases, but rather retained their existing
repertoire, while adding new techniques and filling economic niches with
the aid of new technology. Trade had been crucial in supplying certain
essential raw materials to areas lacking in them, and in permitting areas to
be settled that were formerly inadequate to support relatively self-sufficient
settlement. It has also undoubtedly been a great stimulus to prehistoric
culture change.'[3]

Solomon Islands

A brief outline by Roger Green of aspects of Solomon Islands culture
history provides an excellent example of various and sometimes contemporaneous culture sequences. As he said, 'Three separate bodies of

material point to the settlement of the Solomon Islands more than 3000 years ago by groups of people already culturally different from each other. None of these groups can be positively identified with a specific tribal society now living in the Solomon Islands.'[4]

Evidence of very early settlement on Guadalcanal comes from excavations in a large cave (Fotoruma) which revealed strata dating from 3000 years ago to Japanese presence in World War II. The cultural remnants found in most of the occupation layers—shell and stone adzes, money beads, shell arm rings, chert flakes—are, Green suggested, 'artifact types typical of traditional Guadalcanal societies.' Unexpectedly, no pottery was found on this site, although it is present elsewhere in the Solomons. Green concluded that these findings illustrated that 'parts of Guadalcanal have been occupied for at least 3000 years by groups of culturally related people who are ancestors of some traditional societies now resident on Guadalcanal. . . . The materials from the cave sequence . . . belong to one cultural tradition.'[5]

A second Solomon Islands tradition is associated with the Lapita makers. Lapita sites in the Santa Cruz region similarly date back at least 3000 years and continue to about 2600 BP. The people appear to have been coastal dwellers and, like Lapita-making communities elsewhere in island Melanesia, Fiji, and western Polynesia, expert seamen. Obsidian originating from New Britain and even the Admiralty Islands is often found at these Lapita sites indicating some system of long-range exchange. The Solomon Islands Lapita makers seem to have lived in permanent villages, planted crops, and domesticated pigs. Green believed that one of the cultural traits handed on to later Solomon Islanders was the 'sea-based exchange of goods which characterise many of the later specialist trade systems'[6] found throughout Melanesia, for example the well-known Kula ring complex.

A third early cultural tradition is evidenced by the remains of the first settlers on Anuta dating from 3000 to 2600 BP. In more recent times this island was settled by people from Polynesia, and is now classified as a Polynesian outlier. The first inhabitants, though, were makers of plain pots and appear to have made more use of shell than stone tools. Green suggests that in these respects their culture differed from the contemporaneous Lapita makers, yet at the same time illustrated sufficient similarity to suggest a common origin at some much earlier stage.[7] The islands Santa Ana and Bellona also have evidence of plain pottery makers sometime during the period 3000–2000 BP.

These three cultural traditions indicate that from 4000 to 2000 years ago Austronesian-speaking horticulturalists with various specialist skills, especially pot making, were establishing communities throughout the Solomon Islands. Later cultural sequences have also been detected, and are often more directly related to contact populations. Some sequences in parts of the western Solomons are based on aceramic traditions, such as those on Shortland Island which lasted from AD 800 to the nineteenth century. Also in western regions, irrigation terraces for taro growing were developed. Those on New Georgia date back to as recently as the sixteenth and seventeenth centuries. Similar terraces were constructed several thousand years earlier in parts of highland New Guinea and New Caledonia.

While archaeological investigation of the Solomons is just getting under way, there is already sufficient evidence to illustrate the complexity of Solomon Islands culture history, and the early development, consolidation, and further evolution of local cultural traditions. This helps to explain the cultural diversity found amongst many communities at the time of European contact.

New Hebrides

Most archaeological work in the New Hebrides has been concerned with unravelling a very complex series of pottery sequences found mainly in the central islands of the group.[8] In addition to the ubiquitous Lapita ware (which dates back to about 3000 years ago and has close affinity with the Lapita pots of Watom far to the north) there is a quite separate ceramic tradition known as Mangaasi. This incised and appliqué ware dates from 600 BC to AD 1300 and can be divided (at AD 800) into early and late phases. The same style also appears in Fiji and New Caledonia. Likewise, in the central New Hebrides is a paddle-impressed pottery similar to that found in Fiji. On Tongoa is yet another style—incorporating internal incised designs—which appeared about AD 1000 and disappeared by the time of the island's eruption in AD 1400. All pottery making disappeared from the central New Hebrides about AD 1300 to 1400. José Garanger, who has done so much to unearth all these pottery traditions, suggests that subsequent aceramic cultures might be due to the arrival of new people from the south—as tradition has it—where pottery was never made. Alternatively, the ending of the pottery tradition might have been related to what appears to have been substantial volcanic activity about that time.[9] In the north of the group were several pottery traditions, including a red-slipped design which is still made on Espiritu Santo. In the far south, however, no pottery industry has been found, which is all the more surprising since settlement was well established during the time of pottery making elsewhere in the New Hebrides, and other artefacts show common cultural links within the group as a whole.

Garanger's overall conclusion is that the incised and appliqué ware is 'truly characteristic only of the central New Hebridean archipelago' where it lasted some 2000 years.[10] It never reached the south of the group, yet it appears in New Caledonia about AD 300 and in Fiji about AD 1100. The Lapita ware also indicates links with Bougainville and Watom. It is not yet clear exactly what can be deduced about culture change in this central New

Hebridean area on the basis of pottery making. Obviously communities living here had, at various times, relations with other peoples over almost the whole of the southwest Pacific—from Watom to Fiji. Further research may indicate the main directions of these various ceramic traditions and shed light on the nature of local cultural innovations and exotic influences.

New Caledonia

New Caledonia poses one of the more interesting problems in Oceanic archaeology. The Melanesian island chain was settled 3000 to 4000 years ago by ceramic-making, Austronesian-speaking horticulturalists.

Yet on mainland New Caledonia and the Isle of Pines there are several hundred conical tumuli, about 2.5 metres high and 9 metres in diameter. They are made of iron-oxide gravel and have an inner cylinder composed of hard lime mortar. They are clearly of human making, though for what purpose no one knows, and are sometimes associated with post-holes and ring ditches. No other artefacts have been found with them, as yet. Three radiocarbon dates put their age at about 7000, 9500, and 13 000 years. These amazing dates may simply result from the testing of material that was long dead before being used to build the tumuli. On the other hand it is possible that the dates are correct. The tumuli might conceivably have been constructed by a prehorticultural, preceramic people such as those who lived in New Guinea at this time. It might well be that thousands of years before Austronesian settlement of New Caledonia, the first settlers were hunter-gatherers who had made their way from the north.[11] Such people perhaps could not sustain themselves for very long in this region of Melanesia because of the paucity of edible flora and fauna, which were abundant in New Guinea.

The later Austronesian settlement of New Caledonia is much more definite in the archaeological record, with Lapita pottery dating to 4000 BP, the earliest date (so far) for Lapita pottery anywhere in Oceania—another paradox of New Caledonian prehistory.[12] The Lapita traditions disappeared here, as elsewhere, about the beginning of the Christian era. Another pottery style—paddle-impressed—coexisted with Lapita ware and lasted longer, to about AD 300–400. A third tradition—incised ware—began about AD 300 and was apparently related to New Hebridean and Fijian ceramic styles. This particular tradition has lasted through to late prehistoric times on New Caledonia.[13]

As with the New Hebrides, the unravelling of such pottery sequences for New Caledonia raises as many questions about prehistoric cultures as it answers. Settlement of New Caledonia, at least by 4000 BP, was, it seems, contemporaneous with the Austronesians both adapting to local conditions and having some contact with other southwest Pacific peoples. The agricultural techniques of these settlers reached a peak of sophistication in New

Caledonia, with the extensive irrigation systems in the mountains of the mainland.[14] This may account for the somewhat larger population on New Caledonia than was usual throughout the rest of island Melanesia.

In more recent prehistoric times, and continuing into the historic period, New Caledonia and its neighbouring Isle of Pines and Loyalty Islands, were the landfall for numerous Polynesians who had drifted mainly from the Samoan-Tongan areas. As will be described later, these newcomers had considerable influence on New Caledonian lifestyles.

Fiji

Fiji is commonly considered the borderland between Polynesia and Melanesia—the people of the western main islands of the group being more 'Melanesian' in appearance, and those in the eastern approaches (the Lau group) more 'Polynesian'. Such a view is oversimplistic and gives a misleading interpretation of Fijian prehistory. Evidence now gathered by archaeologists illustrates the fallacy of assuming that the current or early contact communities of Fiji were similar to Fiji's first settlers, some of whom moved further east to Samoa and Tonga and there became 'Polynesians'. There was no such unilinear cultural development. As will be explained shortly, the so-called Melanesian and Polynesian cultural boundaries did not exist when people first moved into Fiji. They are, if one accepts their validity at all, a much more recent development.

Fijian prehistory has been divided into several phases, again based mainly on various ceramic traditions.[15] First was the Sigatoka phase, characterised by Lapita pottery, which dated from first settlement, about 3500 BP, to the disappearance of Lapita ware about 1400 years later. This pottery was closely related to the Lapita styles in island Melanesia, and predated several of them. Fijian Lapita ware was also associated with such characteristic adzes as the quadrangular sectional adze kits familiar in early tool assemblages in Southeast Asia and New Guinea, and with various shell and stone artefacts common in early island Melanesian settlements. The second, or Navatu phase had a very different ceramic style, that of paddle-impressed relief ware, and dated from just before the end of the Lapita sequence through to about AD 1100. A third phase, known as the Vuda, was typified by plain pottery, some of it incised, and dated from about AD 1250 to the eighteenth century.

These three traditions, as already described, were also widely distributed in various locations in the New Hebrides and New Caledonia, suggesting some close associations through trade and/or migration.[16] For example, the Fijian incised ware (from the Vuda phase) was 'exactly the same' as that found at Mangaasi on Efaté in the central New Hebrides, and its disappearance there coincided with its appearance and development in Fiji.[17] Both the Vuda and the preceding Navatu ceramic traditions may be evidence of two new waves of migrants into Fiji after the earlier Lapita makers. But it is not yet clear whether it was so much a question of considerable numbers of new arrivals bearing new techniques as the introduction of new cultural traditions themselves, perhaps by only a handful of travellers. It is thought, for example, that the people who brought the impressed ware did not alter the existing adze kit which had persisted largely unchanged since Lapita times, and nor was the earlier Fijian language much affected by them.[18] It would be misleading to credit all culture change in early Fijian societies to external influences. Linguists have tended to stress local adaptations and evolutions within Fiji itself leading to a 'variety of sub-cultures', which also contributed to the apparent diversity of Fijian society by the early nineteenth century.[19]

To emphasise internal adaptations does not imply a cultural isolation. There is ample evidence of fairly regular contacts amongst Samoa, Tonga, and Fiji, over at least several centuries before European contact. Links with New Caledonia and the New Hebrides, though perhaps less frequent, had clearly been of some consequence in earlier times.

Archaeological remains other than pottery also offer clues to phases in Fijian prehistory, in particular the large ring-ditch fortifications. On Viti Levu these are to be found mainly along the wet, eastern region especially in the fertile deltas of the Rewa and Waimara rivers.[20] The suggestion is that the rich alluvial soils enabled intensive and specialised horticulture, especially of taro. This in turn sustained a larger resident population than was normally associated with a slash and burn horticulture. Considerable pressure was placed on resources and defensive positions evolved. The idea of constructing a circular ditch around gardens and settlements was a logical approach, though the ditches could have easily been any other shape. In higher areas, away from the alluvial flats, some ring ditches were built, but these appear to have been later constructions and were probably modelled on those of the lowlands. However, because of the rather different topography, and rather smaller populations in the areas where a slash and burn gardening technique was employed, there are many more ditches which vary from the original lowland prototype. They are more linear and are often called ridge forts. The dating of these forts presents, as yet, something of a problem, but on Wakaya Island some of them contain Navatu phase pottery. It is possible that some of the techniques of Fijian fort building could have been exported to Samoa.

Tonga

Both Tonga and Samoa have claims to be the homeland of the Polynesians. Tonga has generally been accepted by scholars, though the recent discovery of Lapita ware on Samoa has once again brought Samoa close to the forefront. Yet there is also the possibility that any such homeland might

lie elsewhere. As Roger Green and Janet Davidson suggest: 'It seems unlikely, if most islands of the Tongan and Samoan groups were reached and
settled by people using Lapita pottery, that other islands of West Polynesia
(Futuna, Uvea, Niue, Nuiafo'ou) had not also been discovered and settled
at the same time.'[21]

Both Tonga and Samoa were first settled by the voyaging Lapita makers,
and both Tongan and Samoan cultures derive from a single basic source.
Unlike many areas of Melanesia, both groups show a high degree of
cultural continuity. Yet in language and cultural assemblages each group
also developed its own particular identity within an evolving and more
general western Polynesian cultural complex. There is evidence of later
external contact, with Fiji for example, and as far away as the New
Hebrides, but this does not seem to have made a major impact on either
Tongan or Samoan lifestyles. In Tonga, the Lapita sequence was modified
to a plain ware which in turn was abandoned in the first few centuries AD.[22]
Relatively little more has been found out about Tongan culture history to
about AD 1000. From about that time, and again paralleling developments
in Samoa, various earthwork mounds appear. One inference is that they
indicate the emergence of a more stratified society, with a larger population
and an increasingly centralised system of authority. This ties in with oral
traditions which claim that the Tu'i Tonga dynasty appeared on Tongatapu
in the tenth century AD and began a gradual process of centralisation which
finally culminated in the establishment of the Tongan monarchy in the
nineteenth century. The earliest earthwork fortification is found on
Tongatapu and, it is suggested, may be connected 'with the special requirements of a capital and royal residence'.[23] Most other fortifications on
Tonga are much more recent, many belonging to the eighteenth and early
nineteenth centuries—a time when civil strife associated with the Tu'i
Tonga's attempts to reestablish hegemony over local and regional leaders
reached its height. From about AD 1200, then, Tongan society was probably
becoming more organised and complex, so acquiring some of the characteristics witnessed by the earliest Europeans to land there.[24] Contacts with
Fiji and Samoa may have played some part in such developments, as oral
tradition claims. Perhaps the forts of later prehistoric times were inspired
by the Fijian and Samoan example, but there is no hard evidence for this as
yet. Certainly Tongans extended their influence far beyond their immediate
group to Uvea, Rotuma, Futuna, Samoa, Niue, and the Lau islands of Fiji
where, tradition has it, the Tongans were sometimes able to establish a
form of sovereignty and exact tribute.

Western Samoa

Western Samoa has received as much detailed archaeological scrutiny as
anywhere else in Polynesia, and justifiably so since this central Pacific

region is crucial in the culture history of Polynesia. Like Tonga's, Samoan culture sequences display a high level of continuity. As its excavators have commented, 'Change there was .... Still, it can be documented without recourse to a period or stage model. Without such a model, the principal feature of the Samoan sequence is its continuity ... [and] the Samoan sequence ... provides the one good case in Western Polynesia for continuity between the ancestral Lapita horizon and the Polynesian cultural complex which developed from it in the course of the next 2000 years.'[25]

As in Tonga, the Lapita pottery style merged into a plain ware which lasted from about 300 BC to AD 300. This was a time when settlement extended along the coastal regions and also began to move inland. That expansion developed apace after AD 300 is evidenced by widespread clearing of forests and continuity of residence in the vicinity.[26] The abandonment of pottery in Samoa was probably for 'functional and sociological reasons'. It is suggested that certain social roles closely associated with Lapita ware may have been changed or abandoned. This may explain why wooden vessels (which ultimately replaced ceramics and were used for many of the same purposes) were readily accepted.[27] By inference, the same sorts of explanation may also be applicable to Tonga.

After the tenth century AD certain shaped mounds were constructed. Some were house platforms, others seem to have had various specialised functions, such as huge stone walls and large ceremonial roads. Again as for Tonga, it is tempting to see such constructions indicating the evolution of a 'social stratification and supra-local authority',[28] features of Samoan society so prevalent by the time of European contact. Warfare, another such characteristic, seems to have been widespread according to the number and size of earthwork fortifications, some of which date back some 1500 years. Numerous oral traditions record Tongan raids and even invasions of Samoa, and it has been suggested that some of the Samoan forts were actually built by Tongans. However this seems unlikely since most of the fortifications on Tonga, and especially Tongatapu, were built in historic times whereas those in Samoa are prehistoric. Green and Davidson claimed that it was unlikely that 'Tongans would have been able to teach the Samoans anything about fortification, particularly on the Samoans' home ground.' Fiji is a more likely source of origin, they said, 'if Samoan forts require a source.' In the few centuries before European arrival, Tongan raids on Samoa appear to have been fairly frequent, but the older view that Tongans sometimes ruled Samoa seems unlikely. More probably, a number of Tongan raiding parties got themselves involved 'with one or other party in Samoan internal wars.'[29]

Archaeologists have also pointed out that certain other characteristics of Samoan society, noted in the early historic period, were probably more the result of European contact than any prehistoric developments. Contrary to the popular view, Samoans were not primarily shore dwellers, as they became from the 1830s. Rather settlements were widespread over both coastal and inland areas.[30] It was the arrival of European shipping, and missionary activity that tended to attract Samoans out of the hills.

Another commonly accepted view, about not only Samoa but most Pacific islands, is that populations at the time of European contact were the largest they had ever been. The assumption is that initial settler groups continued to grow by natural increase and sometimes immigration. In Samoa there is some evidence that the estimated 38 000 inhabitants in the 1840s may have been considerably less than in previous centuries. As Green and Davidson pointed out: 'It seems that only a population twice the size of that in the 1840s, or one with a radically different subsistence-settlement pattern basis, would require the amount of arable land which archaeology indicates was once in use.'[31]

West Polynesia as a culture area

Respective culture histories of Samoa and Tonga have many common elements, yet at the same time there are differences which take on a particular significance for the evolution of 'Polynesian' culture traits. Andrew Pawley and Roger Green maintained that 'one of the most important discoveries in recent work in Fiji, Tonga, and Samoa is that the innovations in artefact forms which led to what are generally called characteristic "Polynesian types", appear in the Samoan record but not in the Tongan. These distinctive types appear in East Polynesia which thus groups with Samoa. Tonga falls outside of this Polynesian area, archaeologically speaking.'[32] For example, where the 'basic Lapita adze kit' was used with little change in Fiji and Tonga, from the second century AD the Samoan kit was modified by the addition of the 'Polynesian' triangular cross-sectioned adze. This was transported eastward and was present in early settlement times in eastern Polynesia. It seems the modification in Samoa resulted from 'the crossing of the Andesite Line, which runs between Fiji-Tonga and Samoa. Being restricted in Samoa largely to olivine basalt rocks typical of volcanic islands, flaking techniques developed at the expense of pecking and grinding techniques more suited to the denser, harder rocks of Melanesian (including Tongan) islands.'[33]

Nevertheless, culturally speaking Tonga and Samoa evolved as the key centres of what is often called a west Polynesian tradition. The cultural boundary between this region and eastern Polynesia soon became more marked. Roger Green believed an important reason was that, 'continuous two-way voyaging . . . took place within West Polynesia, probably throughout its prehistory, in contrast to a lack of similar continuity in contact between West and East Polynesia after the settlement of the latter.' He also noted that just as 'later West Polynesian traits such as mounds or wooden *kava* bowls do not penetrate into East Polynesia, neither do later East

Polynesian traits, such as a wide variety of simple fishhooks, gripped adzes, and pounders, ever establish themselves in West Polynesia. It would seem that this boundary ... was not often crossed in either direction once East Polynesia was settled.'[34]

Furthermore, these differences were accentuated by later contact 'between West Polynesia and the neighbouring islands of Melanesia, in particular, Fiji, the Lau group, and Rotuma. For by the 1st century AD various non-Polynesian cultures with new types of pottery, new forms of adzes, and many other traits thought of as typically Melanesian had established themselves in New Caledonia and Fiji and some traits associated with them found their way into West Polynesia but not into East Polynesia.'[35] Thus, argued Green, it was only with these later Melanesian cultural traditions, dating from just before this time, that there emerged any cultural boundary between 'Melanesia' and 'Polynesia'. The notable ethnographic differences between the people of the southern Melanesian islands and those of west Polynesia are thus relatively recent. As Green said, 'At an earlier period this boundary simply did not exist, and Polynesia, as a cultural area, had yet to come into being.'[36]

Cultural evolution and change was not a unilinear process that followed the first settlers across the Pacific islands. To begin to understand the culture histories of individual islands and regions it is necessary to consider a much more dynamic framework, and one which incorporates the dimension of time as well as space. Although the Melanesian islands were settled first, many so-called 'Melanesian' cultural traits are very recent, and even post-date some of those characteristics usually associated with Polynesian traditions.

Marquesas

Culture histories of eastern Polynesian islands are generally much more continuous than in the west, mainly because of the recency of human occupation. Even so, such continuity does not imply a lack of change. On the contrary, cultural innovation could be just as marked here as elsewhere in the Pacific. What is different is that changes were invariably stimulated by internal factors. Eastern Polynesia was far too isolated to receive periodic influxes of new people and ideas as happened in Melanesia.

The earliest recorded settlement east of Samoa-Tonga was in the Marquesas and it is generally thought that these islands, or at least islands in this vicinity, were a dispersal point for subsequent settlement of the rest of Polynesia. Archaeologists have suggested four phases of cultural development.[37] The first or initial settlement period lasted from AD 300 to 600. The first inhabitants appear to have concentrated on hook and line fishing and catching turtles and seabirds. Horticulture seems not to have been very prominent, for stone pounders and vegetable scrapers have not been found. These people also initially possessed some plain pottery. A few sherds have been recovered and have proved by petrographic analysis to have come from the Rewa River delta of Fiji's Viti Levu (possibly via Tonga).[38] However, as has already been mentioned, various artefacts like adzes, as well as linguistic evidence, point to Samoa as the more dominant cultural homeland of those who settled far to the east. These travellers also brought dogs with them, but as yet there is no hard evidence of their bringing pigs and chickens. Phase two lasted from AD 600 to 1300, and was characterised by an increase in population and extension of settlement along the coasts and into the hinterlands. The material culture remained largely unchanged though there was possibly an increased reliance on horticulture to supplement sea foods. Pigs now appear in the archaeological record. Phase three, from 1300 to 1600, saw settlement extend to most habitable areas on most islands of the archipelago. Various artefacts disappeared, such as whale-tooth pendants and shell discs, or changed noticeably, like house-building techniques. New items appeared, in particular conical stone pounders. The classic phase, from 1600 to the eighteenth century, was marked less by changes in artefacts than by structural developments associated with religious or ceremonial constructions, notably the *marae* complexes. As in other parts of the central and eastern Pacific, the inference is that social organisations were becoming larger and more complex, with social stratification and more powerful leadership emerging.

Society Islands

The Society Islands were probably settled from the Marquesas by about AD 600. Relatively little archaeological work has been carried out to date, though it is already apparent that the earliest cultural remnants bear a close relationship to those belonging to the first phase of Marquesan settlement. Equally noteworthy, some bear an even closer resemblance to the earliest artefacts found in New Zealand, dated around AD 900–1100.[39]

Like most island groups in eastern Polynesia, the Society Islands culture history emphasises internal adaptations rather than exotic influences. As expected, archaeological findings indicate the further evolution of an 'eastern Polynesian' technological complex with regard to such items as adze forms, food pounders, and fishing gear. One of the most conspicuous features that changed over the years was the design of the *marae*. Kenneth Emory has described a series of forms beginning with relatively simple arrangements and ending with elaborate structures dominated by altar-like constructions. The largest of these are found in coastal regions and were probably built after 1600.[40] Again the suggestion is that various ceremonies were becoming more elaborate and reflecting the growing complexity of sociopolitical organisation. It is believed they reflect the increased geographic and economic power of certain chiefships which were able to dominate smaller political entities. Irving Goldman expressed it nicely when he commented that 'the size of marae was the constant Polynesian index of political standing'.[41] Douglas Oliver's massive, three-volumed *Ancient Tahitian Society* supported this interpretation. In discussing the evolution of Tahitian social relations against a background of Society Islands prehistory, he wrote:

> *The picture I perceive . . . is of numerous landings on the Society Islands throughout a millennium or more, from other archipelagos near and far, and ranging in size from a lone and near-dead survivor in a drifting canoe to a modest-sized fleet. Most newcomers would have added some new ideas and objects to the local cultural inventory, and during the earlier centuries some of the larger-scale immigrations were probably near revolutionary in their influence. But as time passed and the local population made settlements on all islands of the archipelago, subsequent new arrivals, (say after about A.D. 1200), even large-scale ones, could not have been large enough, or culturally 'superior' enough, to have effected radical changes in the technological and social patterns that had by then become fairly well consolidated.[42]*

The technological and social patterns of about AD 1200, he suggested, would have been: a technology not very different from that of 1767 when Europeans first saw Tahiti; tribal units would have been smaller and less complex than those in 1767 (having more of a kin basis than the later more overtly 'political' arrangements) and marked by less social and economic specialisation and less complex forms of social stratification than those that so impressed early European visitors. Oliver believed that the underlying factor for such changes was a steady and substantial increase in population.[43]

Hawaiian Islands

In spite of a good deal of detailed archaeological investigation of the Hawaiian Islands, there have been few attempts to synthesise results into an overall sequence. One of those proposed three periods.[44] The first was that of Initial Settlement from about AD 600 when small communities with 'simple ranking' systems established themselves permanently in the wet windward areas and in the few fertile valleys of the much drier leeward regions. Their cultural remains are typically early east Polynesian and seem to have close affinity with the first phase of Marquesan settlement. A preponderance of fishing artefacts and fish and shell remains points to a basically maritime economy. Yet it is difficult to pinpoint the precise origin of the first Hawaiian settlers—at least simply on archaeological grounds— because the dispersal to such distant lands as Hawaii and New Zealand may have occurred over a very short space of time, and when there was an initial widespread cultural uniformity throughout much of the Marquesas–Society Islands region.[45]

The second or New Adaptation Period dated from about AD 1100 onward, when settlement was extended inland and to dry leeward areas. Such a movement was made possible by the evolution of various agricultural techniques, such as terracing to capture and channel water for root-crop gardening. The third or Complex Chiefdom Period began about the sixteenth century and was marked by the creation of larger areas of political control and an associated ranking of the population. The rapidly increasing communities were becoming harnessed to the exploitation of agricultural and other resources by the more aggressive leaders struggling for paramountcy in their various regions. As in Samoa, Tonga, and the Society Islands the various physical trappings of such power—in Hawaii's case large residences, temples, ornate burial grounds—appear in the archaeological record. By 1778 when Cook arrived, Hawaiian society was rigidly stratified with perhaps the most complex sociopolitical bureaucracy in all Polynesia.[46]

As in Tahiti, population increases probably helped to account for the highly structured and elitist nature of political control and for the patterns of tribal warfare that existed by the late eighteenth century. Indeed, such are the apparent similarities between the cultures of Tahiti and Hawaii that scholars have long argued for significant and sometimes regular contact between the two island groups.[47] This argument is reinforced, some would claim, by a recent return canoe voyage using 'ancient directions'.[48] Modern research does not support this view. Because Hawaii is so far from eastern Polynesia, few if any subsequent contacts seem likely. Even if there was the odd voyage from the Society Islands there is no evidence of any significant cultural contributions from outside. Hawaiian culture as described by the first European visitors was one which had originated far to the southeast and had been adapting for over a thousand years to the landscape and resources of the Hawaiian Islands.

New Zealand

The ancient discoverers of all the Pacific islands from New Guinea to Easter Island to Hawaii were within the tropical zone. Though there were obvious ecological differences between an atoll in the Gilberts and a fertile valley on Tahiti, all habitable islands offered various familiar if not always common resources as well as some obvious new ones. In many cases these were supplemented by the introduced root crops, pigs, chickens, dogs, and rats, some or all of which could readily be established throughout most of the tropical Pacific islands where there was adequate water and soil. There was considerable regional variation of staples according to conditions. For example the yam became less important to the east of Tonga where taro and breadfruit came to the fore. Pandanus, which can withstand rigorous conditions including soaking in sea-water during cyclones, was a staple in the more marginal atolls of southeastern Micronesia. On the whole the tropical Pacific islands were not inhospitable places. Having a warm climate and sharing a combination of exotic and indigenous plant and animal life, most could, and did, support permanent populations. Once the founder communities were well established there is little to indicate that island life in the tropics was just one long struggle for survival.

The earliest settlers in New Zealand, however, found themselves in a rather different situation.[49] Their new home was very much colder, and winter conditions especially must have made life thoroughly miserable. Of the tropical plants the settlers brought with them, the taro, yam, gourd, cabbage tree (*ti pore*), and paper mulberry survived. Of these, the potentially useful taro and yam tended to remain poor specimens and never became staples. Fortunately for generations to come, the imported sweet potato grew well, though only in the far north could the tubers be kept alive during the winter. Pigs and chickens were either not brought, or did not survive, though the dog and rat did. There were some familiar indigenous resources, such as seafoods, and there were new sources of food in the very rich bird life, including the large flightless *moa*, lizards, insects, seals, roots, and berries. In spite of such an apparent variety of foodstuffs, the early diet was probably based mostly on shellfish, fish, and wild fern root. Contrary to popular opinion, the first people in New Zealand did not live exclusively on the *moa*, until its extinction which resulted from ruthless hunting and the burning of its forest home.

The initial or Archaic settlement phase in New Zealand was marked by the settlers' efforts to come to terms with a temperate and strange environment. They could exploit their traditional maritime skills, and found plenty of new materials like greenstone and obsidian to maintain and further evolve many aspects of eastern Polynesian material culture. But at the same time they had to lead rather different lifestyles. They were less sedentary and forced to adopt more of a hunter-gatherer existence. Horticulture was not, at this stage, a major economic activity. Settlement or rather camp sites appear to have been widespread throughout coastal regions, but few were permanent. Mobility was high, mainly because of the marked seasonal nature of the climate and consequent availability of edible resources.

The so-called Classic Maori culture that Cook described in 1769 was in many respects rather different from the Archaic. Several major developments help to explain such significant cultural evolution. Changes were not uniform, however, and tended to vary according to regional ecologies. In general, changes tended to occur first in northern regions and were sometimes transferred southward. But even by the final Classic phase Maori culture was still far from homogeneous. As Janet Davidson has remarked, 'contemporary communities in the northern North Island and southern South Island were probably less alike than were communities living in one area 500 years apart'.[50]

Changes in vegetation appear to have been a major factor. The reduction of the original podocarp forest was probably an ongoing natural process which began long before humans arrived in New Zealand. But it was certainly stimulated by their firing, which laid bare large areas of bush. Thus did many birds, including the *moa*, gradually disappear. In the South Island, forest clearance led to a reemphasis on coastal and maritime economic activity. In the North Island areas cleared by fire often sprouted a bracken fern that provided a valuable edible root. In addition there is evidence that by the twelfth and thirteenth centuries, especially in the northern North Island where conditions were more suitable, agriculture became more important and particularly sweet potato cultivation. This provided an additional reason for firing the bush. The sweet potato, which had survived in the far north since its arrival with the first settlers, was initially of relatively little importance because of the difficulty of keeping it alive during the winter. Cultivation on a large scale was not possible until the twelfth and thirteenth centuries, when underground winter storage techniques had been developed. Substantial quantities of the vegetable were then grown in the far north and further south. The sweet potato enabled more Maoris to settle, in larger numbers and more permanently, throughout most of the North Island and halfway down the South Island (where the sweet potato reached its climatic limits).

Forest clearance, sweet potato cultivation, and the subsequent extension of more permanent settlements helped to form those cultural characteristics typical of Classic Maori society. Population increases led to pressure on existing resources and on land which had the potential for agricultural development. From about the fifteenth century, fortified *pa* sites appear in the archaeological record. These were most numerous in areas like the Auckland isthmus where plentiful seafoods and other resources became threatened by increasing local populations, migrants, and invaders. Tribal kin and political affiliations probably became more marked as communities tried to lay claim to new or defend existing territories, and strengthen their own identities.

Such changes in lifestyles from about the thirteenth to the sixteenth centuries have generally been attributed to the arrival from 'Hawaiki', somewhere in eastern Polynesia, of the legendary Great Migration. This was supposed to comprise a fleet of canoes that made landfall in the Bay of Plenty. The travellers, it is claimed, brought with them the sweet potato and other cultural baggage which led to the formation of the Classic phase. They are also credited with forming various tribal groups which many Maoris today look back to as their line of descent.[51] Over the last ten to fifteen years, modern scholarship has effectively demolished the legend, though it still remains widely accepted (and taught) outside academic circles. David Simmons has been most responsible for dissecting the various elements of the legend.[52] He has demonstrated how it was in large part the creation of several later nineteenth century 'ethnographers' like

Percy Smith, who freely reinterpreted a number of Maori traditions to come up with a coherent though mainly fictional story. Simmons has examined numerous (and often conflicting) tribal legends about a past 'migration' and suggested that these may well refer to a considerable exodus of people from Northland and their settlement further south, especially in the Bay of Plenty region. Such an internal migration was possibly stimulated by the newly perfected means of sweet potato cultivation. Simmons convincingly argued that the mythical 'Hawaiki', fabled homeland of many central North Island tribes, may be none other than the northland coast. There is also a good deal of negative archaeological evidence to refute the notion of a new wave of migrants from Polynesia. In general, various artefacts and other developments, such as the *marae* complex, which evolved in eastern Polynesia after the initial settlement of New Zealand were not subsequently introduced. This is not to suggest that no one else ever reached New Zealand after the initial settlement, but that no detectable cultural innovations were imported after this time.

Modern scholarship maintains that the changes from Archaic to Classic came about by internal developments. It is both unwarranted and unnecessary to put them down to external influences. It seems New Zealand was isolated from eastern Polynesia for about a thousand years, until Cook's *Endeavour* bore Tupaia from Tahiti to Poverty Bay in 1769.

The last few centuries before this time saw the further evolution and extension of Classic Maori culture to most parts of the country. There was an emphasis on planting and harvesting of the sweet potato, the gathering of fern root and seafood, many settlements were permanent or semipermanent, and warfare was constant as tribal groups vied with each other for women, land, and other possessions. Overall the temperate climate seems to have ensured that life was harder in New Zealand than, say, Tahiti. Perhaps not without good reason did the early European travellers contrast the 'hard primitives' of New Zealand with the 'soft primitives' of Tahiti.

3

Ethnographic moments

In the late eighteenth and early nineteenth centuries many Pacific islands societies were caught in the act by itinerant newcomers who recorded what they saw and collected artefacts. Thus began the study of Pacific ethnography—the depicting of island lifestyles. So immense is the ethnographic record today, amounting to tens of thousands of books and articles, that it is all too easy to lose sight of the fact that descriptions of societies at that particular time have frozen but a particular moment in hundreds or even thousands of years of cultural evolution in the Pacific. Because the sheer bulk of material can easily give the impression that Pacific communities were static and stable, the problem in describing that moment is to convey a sense of its essential transience, even though many features of the pre-European cultures are still observable in various island societies. Furthermore, the writer who attempts to sketch broad generalisations about the nature of Pacific islands communities immediately runs into the problem of all the exceptions and variations. So much published ethnography consists of highly specialised case studies. The challenge is to rise above the microcosmic view and try to see patterns, themes, and variations for the islands as a whole.

Populations

Estimates of island populations at the time of first Western contact must obviously be tentative. Many of the first Europeans who set foot on islands in the late eighteenth and nineteenth centuries did little more than guess at the number of people who lived there, often adopting highly questionable assumptions, such as a large island must support a large population and vice versa.[1] It was often decades before missionaries and administrators settled amongst island communities and could give a more accurate picture. But by then population numbers could have been altered dramatically by epidemic disease introduced by earlier European travellers. For example, the first reasonable estimates for the Solomon Islands were made in

3   Cultural eavesdropping—Cook witnesses a human sacrifice on Tahiti.
(*Cook* A Voyage to the Pacific Ocean. *Alexander Turnbull Library*)

the 1930s, whereas sporadic European contact dates back to the 1830s and much more intensive contact in the form of the labour trade began in the 1870s. An even more extreme case is the New Guinea highlands. Only forty years ago did the Western world realize that there were a million people living there.

Fortunately demographers have served us well.[2] They have analyzed the original estimates for many island groups and have traced the paths and consequences of epidemics for the nineteenth and twentieth centuries. On the basis of recent censuses they have been able to make numerous cross-checks and tentative projections backward. The dubious habit of guessing about earlier guesses has been refined at least to the extent of being able to discard the more extreme figures. It is now believed that the total population of Polynesia in the late eighteenth century was at least half a million. A total figure for Melanesia is more difficult to give since the first estimates for its southern regions were made in the 1850s and 1860s, but for New Guinea not until the 1940s and 1950s. By adding all the estimates from the early contact periods, wherever and whenever they were, the total comes to some 3.5 million, of which 3 million belong to New Guinea and 500 000 to the rest of Melanesia including Fiji. For Micronesia, the estimated total was about 120 000, and for Australia between 250 000 and 300 000. These figures can tentatively be broken down as shown in Table 1.

It is even more difficult to know what was happening, in a demographic

Table 1   Estimates of Pacific populations at early contact

	Time of estimate	Estimated population
Australia	1790s	250 000–300 000
Melanesia		
New Guinea	post 1940s	3 000 000
Solomons	1930s	94 000
New Hebrides	mid-late 1800s	70 000–100 000
New Caledonia	mid 1800s	45 000
Fiji	mid 1800s	200 000
Micronesia		
Marianas	1600s	50 000
Carolines	mid-late 1800s	25 000
Marshalls	mid-late 1800s	10 000
Gilberts	mid-late 1800s	32 000
Polynesia		
Samoa	1830s	40 000–60 000
Tonga	mid 1800s	20 000–30 000 +
Cooks	mid 1800s	10 000
French Polynesia (Marquesas, Society, Tuamotu)	late 1700s, early 1800s	50 000–100 000 +
Hawaii	late 1700s	200 000–250 000
New Zealand	late 1700s	100 000–120 000

Sources: Principal sources are Alkire *An Introduction to the Peoples and Cultures of Micronesia*; Brookfield with Hart *Melanesia* pp. 65–8; Green *Adaptation and Change in Maori Culture* pp. 32–3; Howells *The Pacific Islanders* pp. 14–19; McArthur *Island Populations of the Pacific* and *Condominium of the New Hebrides*; Oliver *Ancient Tahitian Society* 1: 26–39; Schmitt 'New estimates of the pre-censal population of Hawaii' pp. 237–43.

sense, to these communities. Samoa, as mentioned above, might have supported a larger population at a much earlier time than it did by the 1840s, though this does not mean that the Samoan population by the time of early European contact was in any state of numerical decline. On the other hand it seems unlikely, at least from the archaeological record, that the larger islands like Fiji and New Zealand were experiencing or had experienced any decrease in population, but rather the reverse. Some writers early in this century who were deeply influenced by neo-Darwinian views commonly held that Pacific communities were dying out before Europeans arrived.[3] Modern demographers now rule this out. It seems that prehistoric population growth, at least amongst those communities which survived, had been steady, though not without fluctuations caused by wars, famines, natural disasters, and migrations. In remoter regions, where the first settlers were more likely to be the only ones, very small founder populations were in theory required. A group of three pairs had, according to computer simulations, almost a 50 : 50 chance of establishing a viable community.[4] Furthermore, if a group of twenty were to increase at the rate of 1 per cent per year, within 850 years they could number 100 000.[5] Of course, many islands, especially atolls, could not sustain such potentially high natural increases. Unacceptable population growth was controlled by contraception, abortion, infanticide, and emigration. As Pirie has commented, 'We should expect to find in the Pacific islands evidence of long phase ecological cycles in which population densities mount, are relieved and mount again. The inherent power of these populations is far in excess of the capacity that most island environments have to provide them ...'[6]

Health and ill-health

Early European explorers generally considered Islanders robust and healthy. The first Islanders ever described in any detail were from the Solomons. The Spaniard Alvaro de Mendaña on his first Pacific voyage spent several months in their region in 1568. The people were, he said, 'well-grown and good-looking' and lived on 'healthy' islands. There were no signs of 'any conspicuous malady, or contagious disease'.[7] First descriptions of Polynesians came from Pedro Fernandez de Quiros, chief pilot on Mendaña's second Pacific crossing in 1595, when they touched at the Marquesas. Instantly they were surrounded by

> *more than four hundred natives, white, and of very agreeable appearance, tall and strong, large limbed, and so well made that they had greatly the advantage over us; with handsome teeth, eyes and mouth, hands and feet, and most beautiful flowing hair, and many of them very fair.... and indeed, for savage people, naked and of so little reason, at sight of them there was much cause to praise God who created them. Let this not be taken for exaggeration.*[8]

Some of the Marquesan women, with their 'small waists, and graceful forms' were considered 'prettier than the ladies of Lima, who are famed for their beauty'.[9] Such enraptured accounts came more than 150 years before the late eighteenth century explorers like Frenchman Louis Antoine de Bougainville waxed lyrical about Tahitians being living examples of Rousseau's recently popularized Noble Savage. Said Bougainville, 'I never saw men better made, and whose limbs were more proportionate: in order to paint Hercules or a Mars, one could no where find such beautiful models'.[10] Tahitian women, for their part, were the epitome of Venus. Somewhat less literary descriptions were given by more workmanlike explorers. William Wales, on Cook's second expedition, thought that the New Hebrideans were 'well shaped & Clean made enough'.[11] Cook's opinion of the New Zealanders was that they were 'a strong raw boned well made Active people rather above than under the common size ... [who seemed] to injoy a good state of hilth'.[12] Similar comments about most other Islanders abound in the early records.

To some extent the apparent healthiness of island communities resulted from the survival of the physically fittest. The seriously ill either recovered or died. Those unfortunate people who were seriously mentally or physically handicapped at birth, or who later became so by accident or injury, also usually died by design or fate. There were exceptions. Cook's sailors at Hawaii saw 'more deform'd people than in all the other Islands put together, some had prominences before & behind, or were what we call humpd backd; one young man, had neither feet or hands; We saw two dwarfs ... & many of their lower class of people were ill made.'[13] Dwarfism was also known on Tahiti.

Initial appearances could be deceiving, and overall standards of health were probably not as high as is commonly imagined. Most Islanders were free from epidemic diseases mainly because their geographic isolation protected them from viruses which periodically swept across continental land masses. However the price Islanders were to pay later for this was a total lack of immunity to a range of epidemic diseases introduced by Europeans. Influenza, measles, and whooping cough were fatal. There were, though, many other debilitating and even fatal diseases which survived indefinitely in small, isolated communities during (and well after) prehistoric times. Malaria was prevalent in most of Melanesia as far south as the New Hebrides. Throughout the Pacific there were lung infections, types of pneumonias, which caused considerable mortality, especially amongst the young. There were a wide variety of sores and swellings variously attributed to filarial infections, along with tropical ulcers and yaws.[14] Cook recorded on New Caledonia: 'Swelled and ulcerated legs and feet are very common amongst the Men; swelled Testicles are likewise very Common ...'[15] At Ha'apai in the Tongan group he found more people affected with 'the Leprous or some other Scrofulous disease' than anywhere else. One of his officers added that

> More than half of them are affect'd with the tetter or ringworm, which leaves behind a whitish mark; boils & blotches are often met with, & inflam'd sore Eyes are frequent. ... other disorders which affect their appearance, but not common, are large broad ulcers which appear in every part of the body. ... We also saw several people with their Arms & legs swelld the whole length to a prodigious size. Not withstanding these disorders, they may be considerd as uncommonly healthy, for I never heard of any one being seen confin'd sick in his house, & all their actions shew that they are not debilitated by diseases ...[16]

Tahitians, too, were not all moulded in the images of Greek gods. There is evidence of ruptures, rheumatism, elephantiasis (of limbs and testicles), and body sores.[17] William Bligh, admittedly deliberately looking for evidence of this kind (and recording events twenty years after first European contact there) expressed an extreme though probably not totally inaccurate view:

> *I do not believe that they have superior blessing with respect to health; we already see them with dreadful Cancers, Consumptions, Fevers, Fits and the Scropula in a Shocking degree, and we may infer many incidental diseases besides. The fertile Country and delightfull Climate of the Society Islands does not therefore exempt its Inhabitants from the attendant miseries of ill health.*[18]

Some of the Islanders' health problems were self-induced. Excessive kava drinking was widespread, and particularly noticeable amongst the chiefly ranks in Hawaii:

> *The Excess with which the Chief[s] drink the Kava, destroys their Strength & makes them sad objects of Debauchery; they far outdo in the use of this pernicious root all the other Indians we have visit'd; the more Scaly their bodies are, the more honourable it is with them . . . . Many before they are forty are the most miserable Objects, their whole frame trembles, their Eyes are so sore, & redned, that they seem in Constant pain.*[19]

Modern studies of skeletal remains from around the Pacific indicate a high incidence of degenerative disease, especially forms of arthritis, generally attributed to hard physical labour.[20] It was noticeable that some of the lower class citizens of Polynesia fared far worse than their rulers. For example, on the island of Kauai in the Hawaiian group, it was remarked that

> *the lower Class ... are very tawny, thin & small mean looking people, which doubtless arises from their constant exposure to the heat of the Sun, their being mostly employd in fishing or other hard labour on shore, & to their spare diet. But the figure of the better sort of people is very different ...*[21]

Dental wear and decay was potentially a very serious problem. Life became marginal for those who lost their teeth early, especially where diets were rough and gritty. Maoris in late prehistoric New Zealand seemed to have a particular problem with their teeth.[22] Elsewhere, presumably because of softer foodstuffs, teeth might suffer a little less wear and decay.[23] At the other extreme, teeth remains from Hawaii indicate, in the words of one recent researcher that, 'dental conditions ... [were] generally better than our own American population'.[24]

Overall, studies of skeletal remains suggest that life expectancy was short, by present-day standards. Infant mortality was high, and those who survived to adulthood usually died at about 30 years of age, often physically worn out by this time. Women, on average, died a little earlier, probably because of the rigours of childbirth. Old age meant reaching about 40.

Some European explorers mentioned meeting Islanders who were very old, sometimes 100 years of age. If there were such old people they were probably exceptions. Moreover such (by our standards) was the usual rapid rate of physical degeneration that a 40-year-old could well look like one of today's octogenarians. Such short lives should cause us no surprise. As one writer said, they are 'comparable to that of ancient Greeks and Romans and of many people in the world today, such as the living Egyptians, American Indians, and Chinese.'[25] Only in quite recent times, and in modern Western societies, has the adage three score and ten had any general relevance.

Ironically, such relatively short life expectancy in the Pacific helped to make the prehistoric populations appear healthier than they might have been. Diseases which plague our society, such as cancer and coronary troubles, were rare simply because most Islanders did not live long enough to develop them.

Short lives also had important social as well as medical implications. Parents normally died while their offspring were still young, since a woman's reproductive years (if she survived) ranged from about fifteen to her early to mid-twenties. Extended families were essential simply to look after bereaved children.[26]

Medical knowledge and health care in the pre-European Pacific was less rudimentary than Westerners commonly assumed. Most societies had people who carried out the most delicate operations to repair wounds, set broken bones, and treated sores and minor ailments with herbal remedies. But their most potent weapons against disease were supernatural ones. Ill fortune, including sickness, was attributed to angry spirit-beings whose malice could be destroyed or placated only by stronger spiritual forces. Hence medical 'treatment' was as much concerned to influence the appropriate spirits, and the mental state of the patient, as with tending the body. The incantations, curses, and death wishes which Europeans dismissed as 'superstitious' were as real and potent to Islanders as antibiotics are to us.

Settlement patterns

Late prehistoric settlement patterns are difficult to analyse because of their inherent flexibility owing to wars, migrations, and the fortunes of agriculture. In addition, some of the first European arrivals, particularly missionaries and traders, caused local populations to congregate in hitherto lightly populated areas, for example near harbours and landing places where Islanders could be nearer to Westerners and their goods. By the time ethnographers came along, the settlement patterns which they described could well have been radically different from what they were in earlier days.

By far the largest concentration of Oceanic people was in the New Guinea highlands where some million of them lived. One explanation is that the introduction of the sweet potato about the sixteenth or seventeenth century precipitated a marked increase in population since the tuber not only thrived, but could be cultivated well above levels where taro was not so bountiful and (perhaps more important) malarial mosquitoes were absent.[27] This view is challenged to some extent by the discovery of widespread horticultural systems dating back some 6000 years, which suggests that a large population might well have been present before the sweet potato was introduced. Many coastal and lowland regions of New Guinea, such as the mighty Fly River delta, though to a European eye potentially very fertile, were sparsely populated, sometimes even completely uninhabited. In some of these areas almost perpetual torrential rainfall doubtless made settlement far too unpleasant a prospect. Likewise, regions where malarial mosquitoes were abundant were usually avoided.[28] Malaria also probably influenced settlement patterns in the Solomon Islands and the New Hebrides. It may possibly explain why some of the smaller and apparently less fertile islands of these groups had relatively higher population densities, and may even account for the construction of small artificial islets just offshore. Such islands may also have been built as defensive positions and perhaps even to escape from supernatural villains.[29] Elsewhere throughout the New Hebrides and Solomon Islands settlements were sparsely scattered both inland and along the shores.

Overall, communities in New Guinea (with the exception of some highland regions), the Solomon Islands, and the New Hebrides were very small, averaging from about 70 to 300 people in small villages or clusters of hamlets.[30] Such communities were likely to be autonomous. Partly because of the sparse and isolated nature of settlement, due in turn to mountainous and generally difficult terrain, they tended to be inward looking and, apart from trading links with the outside, relatively self-sufficient. Travel into regions where one did not have kin ties (unless for purposes of trade) was fraught with danger. Strangers were often killed, which was a further inducement to stay home, so encouraging physical isolation and more specific local cultural evolution. While many writers have exaggerated the hostility of many of these Melanesian communities to outsiders, such antipathy was an important—perhaps major—consideration for those early Europeans who dared venture there.

In New Caledonia and (western) Fiji, still ethnographically part of Melanesia, there was no malaria, nor such extreme rainfall as in parts of New Guinea. Settlement patterns seem to have conformed more obviously to supplies of fresh water and soil fertility. Populations were likely to be concentrated along the coasts and in river valleys, the most notable example being the fertile Rewa delta on Fiji's Viti Levu. In both these groups of islands sociopolitical units tended to be larger and more stratified than elsewhere in Melanesia, perhaps because of the nature of their ecological basis—though this issue will be discussed more fully later.

In the aptly named region of Micronesia, the greatest influence on settlement patterns was simply the shortage of land. Micronesia's 2000 islands comprise less than 2600 square kilometres of dry land, and half of this amount is made up of three islands—Guam (58 000 hectares), Babeldaob in the Palaus (40 000 hectares), and Ponape (33 000 hectares). Most of the remaining islands, whether volcanic as in the Marianas and parts of the Carolines, or raised or low atolls as elsewhere in Micronesia, are mere fragments of land. Some inhabited atolls are as small as several hundred square metres. Communities were usually quite small, not only because of shortage of land, but because of limited water supplies especially in the scattered eastern atolls. Nevertheless density of settlement was often quite high in comparison to, for example, the vast lowland regions of New Guinea. Communities in the Marianas ranged from 50 to 600 people grouped in coastal villages, with some inland settlement on the larger islands. Settlement throughout the Carolines showed the greatest amount of diversity. In the Palau islands, ancient hillside terracing suggests interior as well as coastal settlement. Yap was at the centre of what is sometimes referred to as its 'Empire', which reached some 1100 kilometres into the central Carolines. Leaders on Yap controlled and extracted tribute from their tiny far-flung colonial outposts. On Yap itself settlement patterns were influenced by rigid sociopolitical rules that forced the lower-class people to live inland and provide food and labour for the upper class, who owned all the land and lived around the coast. Throughout the rest of the Carolines (except for 'large' Ponape), as well as the Marshalls and the Gilberts, extreme shortage of land left people no choice as to where they might live.[31]

In Polynesia the interplay of both ecological and political considerations helps to explain the diversity of settlement patterns. For example, communities in Samoa formed separate villages inland and on the coast, whereas the coastal ribbon settlements of Tahiti made separate village units less easily apparent. Oliver refers to them as scattered 'households' or neighbourhoods.[32] Such non-nucleated settlements are more often found in Polynesia than in Melanesia. Cook described settlement on Tahiti rather more poetically:

> *Between the foot of the ridges and the sea is a border of low land surrounding the whole Island, except in a few places where ridges rise directly from the Sea, this low land is of various breadths but no where exceeds a mile and a half; the soil is rich and fertile being for the most part well stocked with fruit trees and small plantations and well water'd by a number of small rivulets of excellent water which comes from adjacent hills. It is upon this low land that the greatest part of the inhabitants live, not in towns or Villages but dispersed everywhere round the whole Island.*[33]

Cook was even more enraptured by parts of Tonga,

> *wholy laid out in Plantations in which are some of the richest Productions of Nature, in these plantations are the greatest part of the Houses of the Inhabitants built with no other order than conveniency requires, paths leading from one to a nother and publick lanes which open free communications to every part of the Island.*[34]

Why settlement patterns in Samoa were rather different probably had to do with the relative suitability of the interior for settlement (as opposed to Tahiti's razor-backed mountains), and with the localisation of political authority which made village identities and village life so important. It is probably no coincidence that both Tahiti and Tonga had much larger units of political authority superimposed on them. In New Zealand and Hawaii, on the other hand, ecological factors seem to have been paramount in influencing settlement patterns. Most Maoris lived in the warmer northern half of the North Island and near harbours and rivers that were rich in resources. As in Fiji's Rewa delta, the richest areas, like the Auckland isthmus, were quite densely settled and offered numerous defensive positions. Parts of the Hawaiian islands were far more rugged or dry and the presence or absence of fresh water was of fundamental importance. Settlements were concentrated in wetter coastal regions, river valleys, and other areas where water might be collected and conduited. Since no more than about 16 per cent of the land area is cultivable, settlement was probably quite dense. Much of it was non-nucleated or of the 'neighbourhood' type, though there were separate villages in some localities.

Subsistence agriculture

At the time of first Western contact, most island societies seem to have achieved a balance between population and essential resources. A few communities lived miserably in abject poverty, but most appeared to have sufficient food and other resources for their physical and cultural needs, and some had more than enough. By this time then, and indeed long before it seems, most Pacific Islanders could be considered successful colonists. They had discovered, explored, and settled almost every island in the ocean. They had adapted to and modified aspects of their environments. Long gone were the days when they might have grubbed out a tenuous existence in new and perhaps strange lands. They made the islands their own. What the first European travellers saw were communities evolving and developing their own cultural identities and civilisations generally. The economic basis was often a complex and subtle subsistence agriculture. Basic foods fell into three broad categories: seafoods, domestic animals (dogs, pigs, poultry), and root and tree crops.

Fish, shellfish, sea mammals like dolphins, seals, (stranded) whales, and turtles were all variously exploited throughout the islands. In some places at some times such marine foods were a major item in diets, in other places and at other times they were less significant. Fishing technology consisted of nets, spears, hooks, lures, and poisons. These were widely distributed, though there does seem to have been some regional variation in fishhooks, which were much more prominent and sophisticated (and included trolling lures) in parts of Micronesia and in eastern Polynesia. One possible explanation is that atoll or small island dwellers were simply more marine oriented than, say, villagers in inland Fiji or Malekula. Another is that these hooks and lures derived from Japan, passing through Micronesia and across to the eastern Pacific.[35]

Pigs, dogs, chickens, and rats were brought to most islands by the early settlers, though their distribution by the time of early European contact was fairly uneven. For example, there is no evidence that pigs and dogs reached New Caledonia, though they were very common elsewhere in Melanesia and even reached Hawaii; dogs became extinct in the Marquesas though they survived in New Zealand, whereas pigs and chickens which survived in the Marquesas never reached New Zealand.[36]

The principal root crops were various species of yams, taro, and the sweet potato, the former two originating in Southeast Asia, the latter in America. To have made their way right across the Pacific obviously required human transport and cultivation. For mainly ecological reasons, yams were more important in Melanesia, with taro more prominent in Micronesia and Polynesia. The sweet potato seems to have entered Polynesia long before it reached parts of Melanesia, where even by the nineteenth century its presence, with the notable exception of the New Guinea highlands, was minimal. Main tree crops were coconuts (which were not as widespread as they have become in historic times), breadfruit, especially in Polynesia and Micronesia, and varieties of both wild and cultivated bananas. Pandanus was also widespread and was most useful on the remoter atolls such as those in the eastern reaches of Micronesia and the Tuamotus because of its hardiness and its ability to stand flooding by seawater during storms. Sugar cane was another useful crop in New Guinea and surrounding regions. The Islanders' equivalents of tobacco and alcohol also came from trees and shrubs. The betel-nut palm reached to about midway down the Melanesian island chain, and the shrub used for making kava was found throughout Fiji and central Polynesia. Another tree worth mentioning was the widespread paper mulberry used for making tapa cloth.[37]

Food plants were cultivated virtually everywhere in the Pacific, with the major exception of Australia, where Aborigines remained nomadic hunters and gatherers. Subsistence horticulture throughout the islands ranged from the simple to the complex, depending on such variables as climate, topography, soil fertility, population pressures, and cultural preferences.[38]

In Melanesia, the non-swampy coastal regions did not normally support extensive horticulture, partly because of poor soil fertility and salt winds, and partly because of the availability of marine foods, which were not only consumed but traded for vegetables grown by inland communities. There was even less gardening in swamp lowlands, which were very extensive in many coastal regions of New Guinea. Sago thrives naturally in these conditions and was the main crop, sometimes cultivated, sometimes foraged. Other crops were limited because of the necessity to build ridges and drainage ditches, and, again, vegetable foods could be traded for. In the drier regions of New Guinea and the leeward areas of the southern New Hebrides, New Caledonia, and Fiji, vegetation is mainly grassland, scrub, and savannah. Here shifting agriculture, or slash and burn farming, has been practised for generations. An area of bush would be felled, left to dry, and then burnt off. Yam and taro tubers were then planted in the exposed soil. This locality might be used as a garden for up to five or six years and then left fallow. Depending on the amount of reuse of the area, the original vegetation cover might never be reestablished, hence the gradual spread of grass and scrub lands. Both yams and taro need considerable moisture, and once an area was extensively cleared of forest some form of fixed gardening became necessary, as it always had been in even drier regions. Here yams were planted in long ridges on hillsides or in terraced, crescent shaped formations on valley floors, all cunningly designed to trap surface water. Taro requires even more moisture and that meant proper irrigation in the drier areas. By far the most complex system was that of the terraced hillsides and valley floor taro gardens on New Caledonia. Similar techniques were adopted in parts of New Guinea, the New Hebrides, and Fiji. Cook's description of New Caledonian gardens has yet to be bettered:

> *The Tarro Plantations were prettily Watered by little rills, continually supplyed from the main Channel where the Water was conducted by art from a River at the foot of the mountains. They have two methods in Planting and raising these Roots, some are planted in square or oblong Plantations which lay perfectly horizontal and sunk below the common level of the adjacent lands, so that they can let in as much water upon them as is necessary. I have generally seen them wholy covered 2 or 3 inches deep, But I do not know if this is always necessary; others are planted in ridges about 4 feet Broad and $2\frac{1}{2}$ in in height, on the middle or top of the ridge is a narrow gutter along which is conveyed a small stream of Water which Waters the roots planted on each side, the plantations are so judiciously laid out that the same stream will Water several. These ridges are sometimes the divisions to the horizontal plantations where this method is used not an Inch of ground is lost.*[39]

Most of the remaining areas of Melanesia consist of rain forest foothills and mountain ranges. Here taro was the staple crop, and cultivated on a shifting basis where possible. The highland regions of New Guinea form the last separate horticultural region in Melanesia. Since yams, taro, bananas, and some other plants common to the rest of Melanesia become marginal over about 1500 metres, here the sweet potato came into its own. It was cultivated by complex systems of drainage ditches, sometimes covering several acres of valley floors. However, as has been mentioned, such methods of cultivation were used some thousands of years before the sweet potato was introduced. Even with the sweet potato some other vegetables were grown intensively, with the garden requiring much composting and covering of soil to keep it warm enough.

The low coral islands and atolls of Polynesia and Micronesia are not usually suitable for any extensive horticulture, though pockets of soil can sometimes be cultivated intensively. Taro was the most likely crop, grown in damp pits with compost. Semi-foraging of coconuts, pandanus, and sometimes breadfruit was usually more important, and of course dwellers on such islands supplemented diets with pigs, chickens, or fish. The high volcanic and continental islands of Polynesia and Micronesia could usually support more plant cultivation though the variety of crops decreased across the Pacific from west to east. Cultivation was mostly fixed and intensive, rather than shifting, with regional variations quite marked. For example, yams were very important only on the western fringes of Polynesia—Fiji, Samoa, Tonga—and in Micronesia only on Yap and Ponape. Staple plants for the remainder of Polynesia and Micronesia were taro, banana, and breadfruit, which in turn had regional variations: breadfruit predominated in the Marquesas, the Society Islands, and Truk, versus taro in the southern Cooks and the Australs. Other plants seem to have been almost the preserve of some islands. The *fe'i* banana was eaten more frequently in Tahiti than elsewhere, and New Zealanders specialised in fern root.

For the most part, European explorers were impressed with the Islanders' gardens and appreciated the technical skills and hard work put into them. The general picture of food supplies that emerges from Cook's journals is at worst one of adequate sufficiency, at best bounteous abundance. The lower to middling points in this range are adequately represented in New Zealand. In Queen Charlotte Sound in the South Island, one community of 300–400 people lived 'disperse'd along the Shores in search of their daly bread which is fish and firn roots for they cultivate no part of the lands.'[40] In other parts of the country there were cultivations:

> *The ground is compleatly cleared of all weeds—the mold broke with as much care as that of our best gardens. The Sweet potatoes are set in distinct little molehills which are ranged in some in straight lines, in others in quincunx … The Arum [taro] is planted in little circular concaves, exactly in the manner our Gard'ners plant Melons …. The yams are planted in like manner with the sweet potatoes: these Cultivated spots are enclosed with a perfectly close pailing of reeds about twenty inches high …. It is agreed that there are a hundred acres of ground cultivated in this [Tolaga] Bay.*[41]

Maori food, thought Cook, was of 'no great variety', consisting of 'Firn roots, Dogs, Fish and wild fowl', supplemented in some regions by yams and sweet potatoes. Fern root was perhaps the single most important vegetable. The roots were heated over a fire then beaten out 'over a stone with a wooden Mallet, after this they are fit for eating in the doing of which they suck out the moist and glutinous part and spit out the fibrous parts.'[42]

The larger tropical islands were likely to be more bountiful, especially Tahiti and Tonga. Cook positively drooled when he listed Tahitian food: breadfruit, bananas, sweet potatoes, yams, sugar cane, chestnuts, pandanus . . .

> *All these articles the Earth almost spontaniously produces or at least they are rais'd with very little labour, in the article of food these people may almost be said to be exempt from the curse of our fore fathers; scarcely can it be said that they earn their bread with the sweet of their brow, benevolent nature hath not only supply'd them with necessarys but with abundance of superfluities.*

And then there were seafoods, pigs, fowls, and dogs, the latter tasting like 'English Lamb'.[43]

Tongans, in Cook's opinion, were equally well off:

> *I thought I was transported into one of the most fertile plains in Europe, here was not an inch of waste ground, the roads occupied no more space than was absolutely necessary .... Nature, assisted by a little art, no where appears in a more flourishing state than at this isle.*

But, he thought, Tongans, unlike Tahitians,

> *cannot be said to be wholy exempt from the curs[e] of our forefathers, part of their Bread must be earned with the sweat of their brows, the high state of cultivation these isles are in must have cost them immense labour and this is now amply rewarded by their vast produce of which everyone seems to partake.*[44]

Trade

Economic activity involved far more than raising, growing, catching, or finding food. Most island communities were involved in various trading arrangements, among the most extensive being the several regional networks of Melanesia. The most well-known is the Kula ring, which encompassed the Trobriand and D'Entrecasteaux islands, southern Papua, and beyond. It was a very complex, formalised network of trade and exchange in both basic commodities (like sago, yams, stone axes, and pottery) and decorative or ceremonial items (like shells and armbands). These various goods went right around the trading circle, though the people trading them did not. Such an institutionalised exchange of goods was more than just a simple matter of economic supply and demand, having a wide range of social and political (as well as economic) features. The trading was usually associated with some form of sociopolitical obligation or expression, and was as much a means in itself as a way to some narrow economic goal.[45] While the Kula might be the most well known it was just one of many such networks, though perhaps the most formalised. Others seem to have been based more on market forces of supply and demand, such as one in Vitiaz Strait, encompassing New Britain and the Huon Peninsula of northeast New Guinea. Other networks linked various parts of the New Guinea highlands with coastal areas.[46] The Solomon Islands, New Hebrides and New Caledonia had similar regional trading networks, based on mutual needs, and usually with sociopolitical links as an essential feature.[47]

Along with all these and other regional trading systems in Melanesia, were some interregional ones that were probably rather more tenuous and therefore much harder to substantiate. Nevertheless the fact that Lapita ware can be found from Watom to Samoa and Tonga suggests at least some transfer of goods over vast distances, though it was probably more common in the Melanesian island chain than across the watery expanses to the east.

The regional networks show a fairly high degree of economic specialisation, and to this extent there was an element of mutual economic interdependence, which in itself stimulated further specialisation. Such trading networks are a good illustration of the oft-claimed 'Melanesian' propensity for wheeling and dealing in commodities, their 'capitalist' attitudes, their 'entrepreneurial' skills. Certainly a high level of commercial interchange was apparent in many regions of Melanesia, and material possessions lay at the basis of many of its sociopolitical organisations, as will be described shortly. It is worth noting too that in Melanesian communities so notorious for their geographic fragmentation and mutual distrust or overt hostility to each other, there should be such cooperation in matters of trade and exchange. While these networks did not usually involve large-scale geographic mobility for the majority of the participants, they did ensure that communities were not isolated either from news about or material goods from the wider world. The West 'discovered' the New Guinea highland populations only some thirty to forty years ago. But in Melanesia, where news can travel at the speed of sound, these hidden people had a good hundred years forewarning of what to expect.

Trade in Polynesia was different in some respects, reflecting both geography and the often larger sociopolitical groups found there. The more isolated Islanders clearly had no chance to develop Kula-type operations. Those islands or island groups within reasonable sailing distance of each other did have some forms of exchange. For example, Tongans received mats from Samoa and canoes from Fiji, and gave women in return.[48] Even so, it was perhaps more a case of social interaction underpinned by economic reciprocity than a strictly commercial enterprise. Throughout most of Polynesia, self-sufficiency rather than specialisation was a dominant characteristic. Furthermore, the large, more stratified societies that were common in Polynesia meant that economic exchange was more likely to be internal, with the commodities more often being monopolised by those of chiefly rank than distributed amongst geographically separated peoples and/or islands. There were of course exceptions. In New Zealand, obsidian, or volcanic glass, from Mayor Island in the Bay of Plenty and greenstone from the Southern Alps were taken along trade routes all over the country.[49]

Micronesian islands, like many of those of Polynesia, engaged in relatively little overseas trade as opposed to internal redistribution, the notable exception being the tribute and exchange system of the Yap 'Empire'.

Sociopolitical organisations

Once early Pacific economies had developed beyond the point where life was just an endless struggle to find food to keep alive, there was some time to dream, to think, and to create. There evolved all the visible trappings and paraphernalia of a settled existence—fortifications, stone megaliths, buildings, canoes, weapons, gardens, decorations—as well as the invisible features such as personal identities and perceptions of the world around.

All these physical and human resources were ultimately managed through a wide variety of sociopolitical arrangements. In the two hundred years since Europeans began the study of island societies, writers have been preoccupied with analysing and classifying social structures and have produced numerous highly detailed case studies of individual communities. Considerable agreement exists amongst anthropologists about such basic issues as the nature of kin relationships and whether societies were matrilineal or patrilineal, avunculocal or uxorilocal, and so on. In this sense there are reasonably reliable 'social' maps of the islands. But there is far less agreement about how communities operated in practice as opposed to static theory. Of particular interest has been the nature of leadership— what constitutes it, how does it work, why has it assumed the forms it has? One of the more common generalisations outlines two basic models of sociopolitical structure. First was a 'Melanesian' one characterised by small communities lacking much social stratification. Economic competition was a paramount concern whereby virtually anyone with sufficient skill and cunning could manipulate material wealth (usually pigs), get others into debt and hence become a leader or Big-Man. The jargon description is that these societies displayed achieved status with little or no institutionalised stratification or hierarchy. Second was the 'Polynesian' model comprised of large, stratified societies where people were born into their rank (ascribed status) and where chiefs of royal blood held sway over the majority from the top of a well controlled social pyramid.[50]

Such rigid stereotyping is open to several objections. First, it is misleading to classify any particular organisation as 'Polynesian' or 'Melanesian' for there was no typical Polynesian or Melanesian model. Within these two broad geographic regions was a wide range of sociopolitical organisations, some so diverse that it becomes necessary to explain how so-called Polynesian models were to be found in Melanesia and vice versa. Further, by juxtaposing the supposedly small, competitive, Big-Man societies of Melanesia with the large, stratified, chiefly societies of Polynesia, it is all too easy to conclude that Polynesians were politically more sophisticated, more 'evolved' than their simple Melanesian cousins. Perhaps the most acceptable generalisation—and it is so general as to be not very helpful—is to say that small, achieved societies were more prevalent in Melanesia and larger, ascribed, chiefly societies were more prevalent in Polynesia. Any attempt to be more specific requires studies of particular communities, and then local complexities immediately become apparent and bedevil the formulation of neat rules of thumb and meaningful generalisations. Within any one region, even within neighbouring communities, there could be great diversity. Furthermore, Islanders' did not organise themselves by reference to static models in anthropological textbooks. The dynamics of island politics, characterised by the constant interplay of precedent and pragmatism according to changing local circumstances, make it extremely difficult to generalise from the particular.

There is no point here in examining in detail the sociopolitical structures of each major island or island group. Where relevant this will be done in later sections that deal with early culture contact between Islanders and Europeans. However, a brief survey of the kinds of arrangements that existed in the main geographic (but not necessarily cultural) regions will help to highlight some of the issues.[51]

Nowhere is the complexity and diversity of sociopolitical structures more apparent than in Melanesia where a self-governing entity could range from twenty to thirty people high in an isolated mountain valley in Espiritu Santo, to the several thousand members of a stratified, chiefly society as in New Caledonia and Fiji. None of the organisations within these extremes can be classified as 'Melanesian', nor is it implied that there is any ranking in an evolutionary sense from the simple to the complex, or from the primitive to the sophisticated.

While there was no typical sociopolitical organisation in Melanesia, many communities did have some common characteristics (though again these must not be termed 'Melanesian'). With the exception of New Caledonia and Fiji, and a few other scattered localities, there were few numerically or geographically large areas of political control. European visitors used to comment that there were no kings and kingdoms, such as were thought to exist in Tonga, Tahiti, and Hawaii. Both settlement patterns and political jurisdictions were more often than not highly fragmented. Mendaña, in the Solomons in 1568, wrote:

> *The people of this island are very brave, and there is no friendship between them. This is easily seen, because we had been two months and a half in the island of Santa Ysabel, and all the island was not acquainted with our coming except here and there; for at every league, six little canoes, or two or three, ventured out and discharged two dozen arrows at us: whereas, if they had been a people under the power of a principal chief whom they were bound to obey, seeing a brigantine with so few men in it, they could with great facility have done us considerable injury by persevering in the fight, if three or four hundred canoes had assembled.*[52]

Self-governing communities were commonly made up of 70 to 300 individuals living in scattered hamlets or small villages. Their leaders are most commonly referred to by anthropologists as Big-Men rather than chiefs.[53] Most male members of the community, so anthropological theories maintain, were capable of achieving Big-Man status if they had certain qualities. The aspiring leader had to be shrewd, hard working, and charismatic. He might have some specialist skill, such as in oratory or dancing or carving. Most important, he had to try to amass material wealth, which usually consisted of pigs and other items such as garden produce, shells, stones, or sharks' teeth. These he would distribute in such a way that other people would become indebted to him, for example, by putting on a feast, or paying a young man's bride-price. In turn, the recipients would present gifts or be obligated to work for the Big-Man when required. Wealth so accumulated could later be redistributed, to the Big-Man's further advantage. The theoretical equality of opportunity for intelligent men to rise to Big-Man status should not be taken too far. Certain individuals, for example a son of an existing Big-Man, clearly stood a better chance, though they still had to prove themselves capable of leadership. Fools and inefficiency were not tolerated and to this extent there was an element of leadership by the fittest. The authority of the Big-Men was very far from absolute, since they were not leaders by any established rights of ancestry nor did they have divine backing. Their influence was based on a reciprocal network of personal and economic ties that they themselves had forged. Their positions were inherently unstable, with authority maintained by consultation and consensus. A high-handed autocrat would not last long, since Big-Men were generally answerable to their followers.

Examples of communities which fit this theoretical prescription (or rather those from which such descriptions were derived) were the Siuai of Bougainville and the Kaoka of Guadalcanal.[54] But there were endless variations. The smallest interior bush communities might not even have a titular leader, decisions being made by consensus, or by the strongest or oldest male. Other societies had much more elaborate organisations. Some

Big-Men societies had elements of social stratification, as did the Nduindui of Aoba in the New Hebrides, where a Big-Man who had achieved his position by economic competition then had his status expressed and confirmed by social ritual and henceforth occupied an office that was based on more than just his ability to manipulate wealth and people.[55] Other societies, such as the Big Namba of Malekula, had even stronger elements of ascription and stratification. Boys and youths spent much of their day in secret ritual, gradually rising up through a ranking system, and leaders were frequently of high birth.[56] In recent years more and more societies throughout Melanesia have been found not to conform to the ideal model of the Big-Man community, but to have various degrees of stratification, ascription, and hereditary succession to leadership.[57] In some cases leaders were treated with the utmost deference, a number even being spoken to in special languages. Few, if any, seem to have had despotic powers.

Likewise, 'Polynesian' outliers in Melanesia are not, as was once assumed, simply replicas of supposedly 'Polynesian' cultures. Local adaptation is most marked in sociopolitical organisation. In the more northerly outliers (Sikaiana, Ontong Java, Nukumanu, Nuguria) the social structure was based on a system of rank which in turn was based upon wealth rather than birth. Those to the south (Tikopia, Anuta, Rennell, Bellona) had more pronounced stratification, with rather more influential chiefs whose status was based on lineage. There was also a system of primogeniture, succession going from father to son.[58]

Finally, and still within the geographic area of Melanesia, there were the larger, stratified, chiefly societies of New Caledonia and its dependencies (Loyalty Islands and Isle of Pines) and Fiji. In New Caledonia, leaders of local kin groups were, in theory, the eldest males directly descended from the extended family's founding couple. Several such groups joined to form clans, each with a chief who was theoretically the eldest male of the oldest kin group and was the symbolic father of the clan. Clans were further grouped into territorial alliances, or tribes, with the most powerful clan chief becoming the tribal chief. Succession normally though not invariably went to clan and tribal chiefs' eldest sons. Both clans and tribes were hierarchical. Social stratification was marked, especially at the upper levels with chiefs being paid the most extreme deference and often having their own 'court' language. Under the tribal chiefs were a range of ministers, advisers, and councils of various kinds all forming a complex bureaucracy. Arbitrary chiefly power was rare. Chiefs were seen as symbols of tribal unity and the repository of tribal knowledge, and were expected to assume responsibility for the well-being of the tribe as a whole.[59]

Similar chiefly societies, though sometimes numerically and geographically larger, were to be found throughout Polynesia. On the surface such sociopolitical organisations might appear relatively homogeneous, yet while there was not quite the same diversity as can be found in Melanesia, there were major differences nonetheless. A number of writers have tried to classify 'Polynesian' structures into groups according to their degree of stratification, but there is yet no general agreement since not all researchers accept the same criteria for measuring hierarchy and the relative importance of ability and heredity in determining leadership. Goldman, for example, has proposed three basic categories. First, was the Traditional Class where rank was based mainly on ascribed genealogical status (that is, primogeniture in the male line), although effective political power also owed something to achievement—a high birth was not in itself a blank cheque to authority. Society was stratified but there were no rigid classes as such. Goldman cited New Zealand, Tikopia, Tongareva, Manihiki-Rakahanga, Uvea, Futuna, Tokelau, Pukapuka, and Ontong Java as examples. Second according to Goldman, were the Open Societies (like Mangaia, Easter Island, Marquesas, Samoa, Niue) where achievement, especially by warriors in battle, was a way to political power, though hereditary chiefs could still retain high status alongside warrior-chiefs. Stability was maintained more by secular powers than was necessary in the traditional class. Third, Goldman proposed a category of Stratified Societies (such as Tahiti, Tonga, Hawaii) which were like large social pyramids with clear-cut classes and barriers against marriage between classes. Strong, centralised authority was monopolised by a small élite, and sometimes extended over whole groups of islands. Leadership was largely dependent upon high rank by birth, and succession was usually by primogeniture.[60] These were the places where early Europeans believed they could distinguish parallels with society in the Old World—slaves, peasants, landed aristocracies, princes, attendant lords, kings, and empires.

In Micronesia, ranked chiefdoms were found on most islands, with society usually divided into the nobility (the land owners), high-ranked commoners, and low-ranked commoners. The small islands and populations of much of Micronesia often made sociopolitical stratification less apparent to Europeans. Yet it must be appreciated that a society's own perception of its social rankings should not be confused with the presence or absence of the visible trappings of status and power such as were obvious in places like Tahiti or Tonga. Yap was unique in that its lower classes were isolated inland where they provided labour and produce for the higher class which owned the land and lived around the coast. Also the rulers of Yap, as has been mentioned, maintained a form of sovereignty over, and extracted tribute from a widely scattered 'empire' in the western Carolines.[61]

No simple models are adequate to encompass all the sociopolitical organisations across the Pacific. Once the notion of a 'Melanesian' or 'Polynesian' system is abandoned, there remains a much more complex and dynamic picture where for each system the relative importance of ascription and achievement and the varying degrees of social stratification must be studied against each local, and possibly changing, background. It becomes necessary to consider the effects of someone's rank as distinct from influence; the relationship between divinely sanctioned and secular power; and the importance of precedents as opposed to the opportunism of the moment.

Why any one sociopolitical system should have taken the form it did raises another host of questions. Sahlins some years ago suggested that the evolution of the highly stratified societies of Polynesia was intimately related to island ecologies. He argued that very small islands and especially atolls simply did not have the human or natural resources to enable or even require distribution through a complex sociopolitical hierarchy, hence the lack of powerful chiefs in such places. One the other hand, went his argument, on larger and more bountiful islands such as Tahiti the capacity for surplus production enabled ambitious and capable leaders to evolve methods of redistribution which in turn encouraged the growth of bureaucracy and social stratification.[62] This view has not been widely accepted, mainly because exceptions to the general outline can be found— small, poor islands where there is considerable stratification, and richer ones where there is not. Goldman suggested that status rivalry might account for the development of stratification, and tentatively concluded that Polynesian aristocracies probably evolved along the direction of his three categories—from Traditional to Open to Stratified, with the last state being a synthesis of the former two.[63] Whether this opinion will stand up to further review will depend on future studies.

Whatever the particular nature of the sociopolitical organisations that were found throughout the islands, the practices of those in authority probably differed more in degree than in kind. To a greater or lesser extent they adopted universal methods for achieving their particular goals in public life—the use and abuse of spiritual and secular sanctions, deceit, diplomacy, tact, cunning, force, and leverage over resources and production. Early Europeans in the Pacific almost inevitably found themselves having to cope not just with strange new environments and people, but with the often daunting vicissitudes of indigenous political life.

Most daunting of all for newcomers was the level of violence both within and between communities. In most island societies what we would now regard as personal insecurity and tension was an everyday feature of life. People feared evil spirits, their priests, often their leaders, and certainly their enemies. Fighting was universally endemic. By Western standards a life was held in scant regard. Violence was institutionalised in the prescribed punishments (usually some form of mutilation) for wrongdoing, or was of a more ritual nature such as the strangling of widows. In battle there were varying degrees of torture and sadism. While it may be unfashionable to say so, the Hobbesian view of island life—'continuous fear and danger of violent death; and the life of men solitary, poor, nasty, brutish and short'—is closer to the mark than the romantic views of the philosophers who saw in island living echoes of arcadian golden ages.

Beliefs

The intangible aspects of island cultures are obviously the most difficult for outsiders to appreciate, particularly Islanders' beliefs and self-perceptions. Yet it is precisely these features that might hold the key to any understanding of what a community can be seen to do. All societies are shaped by a host of invisible influences, of which buildings, decorations, and material cultures generally are tangible expressions. Describing an artefact is not necessarily the same as understanding its full significance for those who made and used it. A study of the architecture of a thirteenth-century French cathedral will not necessarily give insights into the potent spiritual and political forces that caused it to be built.

For most Islanders, what Westerners call supernatural forces or beings were ever present. The modern Western dichotomy between the sacred and the secular had no real equivalent, though some societies shared a minor element of it; for example, Maoris distinguished between *tapu* (sacred) and *noa* (non-sacred). All cause and effect was usually attributed to invisible deities and spirit-beings of numerous kinds who were capable of wielding supernatural powers and forces. Most societies had major deities or culture heroes who had been responsible for the creation of the visible world, including humans and the cosmos generally. Other deities, or the same ones, regulated such phenomena as the cycles of day and night, the phases of the moon, the changing seasons, the rise and fall of tides. There might also be a whole range of lesser, independent deities or spirit-beings. Some were responsible for the fertility of crops and women, success in battle, or survival at sea. Such potentially benevolent patrons were opposed by an equally wide range of malevolent demons, evil spirits, and ghosts who brought sickness, trouble, doom, and disaster upon those who offended them. Most Islanders also believed in the continuation of a spiritual life after physical death with one's soul or spirit either remaining nearby or going to some gathering place. The spirits of the dead were commonly divided into the long ago dead and the more recent dead, who were sometimes represented by their bones, teeth, hair, and fingernails.

Most Islanders felt that their everyday lives were influenced or capable of being affected by some or all of these supernatural beings, and there was a good deal of both private and public activity to placate potentially evil forces and to try to get assistance or protection from the beneficent beings. In some communities ritual was highly elaborate with mediums, sorcerers, priests, sometimes even priestly societies, practising their solemn arts in special places of worship or invocation. At the other end of the scale, rituals in a small community may have been private and quite informal, though nonetheless purposeful. Whether there was a formalised cosmology or hierarchy of deities and spirits, and whether they were represented by specially constructed or natural objects (or not physically represented at all) depended on the individual community. In general, the more elaborately stratified the society, the more likelihood there was of an institutionalised belief system, partly because of the potential social and economic controls powerful leaders could exert by exploiting spiritual sanctions and claiming legitimacy from the gods.

Such generalisations do not imply a relative homogeneity of beliefs throughout the islands. Any apparent homogeneity is more likely the result of outsiders' ignorance and presumptions. An eighteenth-century Samoan anthropologist studying European religions might equally validly come up with almost identical generalisations. Humans everywhere have usually lived with the terrors and comforts offered by the supernatural. To say this is to say little.

But there were other dimensions to beliefs, and these, being more esoteric perceptions, are even less easy to comprehend. In a great many communities there existed a binary world view whereby dual categories were set in opposition to each other. The most common and potent was the male-female dichotomy where 'male' qualities represented goodness, strength, light, and 'female' phenomena were nasty, weak, dangerous, dark (but paradoxically also essential as the givers of life). In parts of Melanesia this division was given physical expression with villages divided into male and female sectors. Such perceptions were but part of the wider world of symbol and metaphor, seldom glimpsed by outsiders, that justified and gave purpose to the inner and outer workings of a community. Yet, since all human societies have their own symbols and metaphors, how were island ways *in essence* different from those of Europe? Greg Dening offers one provocative suggestion. Speaking of the Marquesans he said,

> *They were savage because of their sense of time.*
>
> *Civilizing them in its essence was giving them a different sense of time.... It removed the cyclical time of rituals in which a legendary past was re-enacted to legitimate and prolong the present.... Their present was not without change, but the fundamental mode of their existence was continually to re-establish their land in its metaphors. To become civilized, they needed an emptiness in their souls that left room for the future.*[64]

From cold lands

Harrison's chronometer

4

Suspected continents

No European saw the Pacific Ocean until 1513 when Vasco Nuñez de Balboa, gazing out from Darien, claimed it for Spain. It took another three hundred years for European explorers to master the same winds and currents, the same great expanses of sea that had challenged the first Pacific sailors millennia beforehand. Just as the Austronesian voyagers eventually sighted almost every island in such vastness, so did their European counterparts gradually do the same—with the difference that the new-comers were emissaries of powerful nation-states from the other side of the world. On their maps they filled in what had been, to them, a totally unknown third of the globe. The marks that represented their three hundred years of basic explorations meant nothing to the islands' inhab-itants who had no global aspirations. Yet the cartographers' markings on parchment oceans meant that all the islands and their communities were eventually drawn into the wider world. They became part of global strategies, never again to be isolated and left to chart their own destinies. Gods may have caused fiery mountains to rise from beneath the seas, and mythical fishermen may have hauled up still more land, but Spanish, Dutch, English, and French seafarers 'with long barbed lines across a map hauled it to Europe'.[1]

Europe looks outward

As early as 4000–6000 years ago, Austronesians had a maritime technology that enabled them to cross extreme distances of ocean, setting the first courses through unknown Pacific seas. Egyptians and Arabs were probing along the coastlines of Africa and India in such early times. In the first millennium AD Irishmen and Vikings sailed to North America. But the Atlantic countries that dominated the so-called great age of European discovery—Portugal, Spain, the Netherlands, France, and Britain—entered the scene comparatively late.[2] Their rise to prominence in ship-building, navigation, and oceanic exploration was intimately tied to expanding commerce, growing political centralisation, and the surge in technological development that characterised Renaissance Europe. By the fifteenth century there were emerging several nation-states that generated both psychological and economic pressures for expansion beyond continental Europe. At the same time, rapid development of maritime technology, which borrowed heavily from Arabic experience, provided the means for exploratory forays across the seas. Vessels were much larger, up to 1000 tonnes or more, were flat keeled, steered by stern rudder, multi-masted, and square rigged. Navigational skills were advancing rapidly too, and of necessity. The simple box compass and dead reckoning might have been adequate for the land-locked Mediterranean, but were hardly sufficient for the Atlantic. The Portuguese were probably among the first in Europe to experiment with astronomical navigation, 'measuring' the altitude of the Pole Star and the sun. Before the end of the fifteenth century the astrolabe and the quadrant, developed for this purpose, were quite widely used and the first crude latitude tables had been produced. These devices were the forerunners of the more accurate quadrants and tables of the seventeenth century. But the real difficulty was not so much finding one's latitude, the distance north or south of the equator, but one's longitude, the distance east or west of any given point. Not until the chronometer was invented in the late eighteenth century could longitudes be calculated accurately. Until then various makeshift methods were employed such as attempts at using lunar distances (which were usually unsatisfactory), measuring compass declination, and trying to measure the distance made by timing the movement past a hull of pieces of wood thrown overboard. Yet even two hundred years after Magellan first crossed the Pacific, most vessels in these waters had only the roughest idea of where they were in relation to the coasts of Asia and the Americas.

The Portuguese took an early lead in oceanic voyaging, largely through the inspiration of Prince Henry 'the Navigator'. By 1488 they had sailed along Africa's west coast as far as the Cape of Good Hope. Shortly afterward Vasco da Gama sailed up Africa's east coast so opening sea routes to India, the Spice Islands of Southeast Asia, and beyond. During the first two decades of the sixteenth century, the Portuguese established a trading empire in the Southeast Asian archipelago. The westward limits of the Atlantic were probed by Christopher Columbus (an Italian who sailed for Spain), who reached the Bahamas in 1492. Several further decades of exploration revealed that Columbus's initial landfall was not, as was first thought, the Southeast Asian Spice Islands but a long continental mass barring a direct approach to these sought-after islands from the east. That this continent did not stretch as far west as Asia was suggested by Balboa's sighting of a sea. The area we know now as the Pacific Ocean was thus initially defined in broad outline by default. Europeans had travelled eastward round the world as far as Southeast Asia, and westward as far as the Americas. But what lay in between?

Cartographers and geographers did not leave the space between the Spice Islands and Darien blank on their globes. Even by the twelfth century it was commonly accepted that the European–North African–Asian land-masses must have an antipodean equivalent to keep the world balanced and spinning evenly. And, as the fable grew, this land mass, named Terra Australis Incognita (by Oronce Finé in 1531), was assumed to be rich beyond compare in minerals and spices. By the early sixteenth century, when the outlines of Africa, Southeast Asia, and the central east coast of America were roughly determined, Terra Australis had shrunken a little from those earliest speculations and now occupied the still huge space we call the Pacific Ocean.

The Spanish 'lake'

The search for suspected continents was far more than a matter of hardy souls setting brave new courses for new hemispheres. The two early leaders in the race for discovery—Spain and Portugal—were rivals in a bitter geopolitical contest of the most grandiose proportions. With what now seems monstrous arrogance, a Papal Bull of 1493 divided the world into two, with an imaginary line running from the North Pole to the South, passing just to the west of the Azores. All lands to the east belonged to Portugal, to the west Spain. The 1494 Treaty of Tordesillas confirmed this general division and sorted out a few minor details. The great unknown, however, was just where did these two spheres of exploitation meet on the other side of the world: what would happen when they did, and in whose sphere did the Spice Islands lie?

The Portuguese thrust eastward, around Africa, and the Spanish west-ward, to the Americas. To confuse matters slightly, the man who led the Spanish furthest, and indeed right around the world, was originally from Portugal—Ferdinand Magellan. Piqued in various ways over his treatment by Portuguese authorities, Magellan offered his services to Spain and was accepted. After an arduous and mutinous time sailing down the east coast of South America, Magellan navigated the wild straits that now bear his name and, twelve months after leaving Spain, sailed into Balboa's ocean. Pigafetta, Magellan's Captain-General wrote:

Wednesday, the twenty-eighth of November, 1520, we came forth out of the said strait, and entered into the Pacific sea, where we remained three months and twenty days without taking in provisions or other refreshments, and we only ate old biscuit reduced to powder, and full of grubs, and stinking from the dirt which the rats had made on it when eating the good biscuit, and we drank water that was yellow and stinking. We also ate the ox hides which were under the main-yard, so that the yard should not break the rigging: they were very hard on account of the sun, rain, and wind, and we left them for four or five days in the sea, and then we put them a little on the embers, and so ate them; also the sawdust of wood, and rats which cost half-a-

crown each, moreover enough of them were not to be got. Besides the above-named evils, this misfortune which I will mention was the worst, it was that the upper and lower gums of most of our men grew so much that they could not eat, and in this way so many suffered, that nineteen died, and the other giant, and an Indian from the county of Verzin. Besides those who died, twenty-five or thirty fell ill of divers sicknesses, both in the arms and legs, and other places, in such manner that very few remained healthy. However, thanks be to the Lord, I had no sickness. During those three months and twenty days we went in an open sea, while we ran fully four thousand leagues in the Pacific sea. This was well named Pacific, for during this same time we met with no storm, and saw no land except two small uninhabited islands, in which we found only birds and trees. We named them the Unfortunate Islands . . . .[3]

These were Pukapuka, Fakahina, or Fangatau of the Tuamotus, and Caroline, Vostock, or Flint of the Line Islands. Magellan's route was one generally followed by those who came after: pushed by currents and prevailing winds, as well as by a desire to head for warmer climes, vessels swept northwestward after rounding South America and passed through equatorial waters, so missing the multitude of islands in south Pacific latitudes.

Magellan finally made landfall at Guam in the southern Marianas. The Islanders swarmed on board taking everything they could, including one of the boat's skiffs. Forty armed Spaniards were landed immediately and 'burned forty or fifty houses, with several small boats, and killed seven men'.[4] In spite of this violence, there was some hesitant trading for fresh fruit. Three days later Magellan's vessels departed and within a week had reached the Philippines, marking the end of the first European crossing of the Pacific. It took another eighteen months to complete the journey to Seville.

Ironically, though Magellan had given up his Portuguese citizenship in some disgust and sailed in the name of the Spanish King, his voyage showed that the Moluccas—the Spice Islands—lay on the Portuguese side of the Papal line. But it was not until 1529, after several disastrous attempts (by Loaysa and del Cano, and Alvaro de Saavedra) to reach the Moluccas following Magellan's trans-Pacific route, that Charles V of Spain officially recognised Portuguese rights to these islands—in return for 350 000 ducats.

While the Portuguese strengthened their presence in the Moluccas, the Spanish empire was gradually extended in the Americas by the conquistadores. By the 1530s the Aztec empire had been destroyed and from its ruins arose New Spain. Within a few more years, the conquistadores had similarly dealt with the Incas in Peru and Chile. Spanish attention could again be turned to the far east via the Pacific. In Oskar Spate's words: 'The Pacific littorals of Neuva España and Peru were the bases by which, in the half century succeeding the half century of the Conquista, the Ocean was turned into virtually a Spanish lake'.[5]

But it was not a placid lake. Early Pacific expeditions from these bases, such as those led by Grijalva (1537) and Villalobos (1542) were hazardous in the extreme and generally ended in disaster for the crews. Even if captains could overcome the perils of an ocean crossing with its attendant problems of mutinous crews, thirst, starvation, and disease, there was the seemingly impossible task of returning head on into the prevailing winds from the east. Nevertheless in 1565 the Spanish finally established a firm foothold in the Far East when Miguel Lopez de Legaspi crossed the Pacific and founded a colony in the Philippines, Spain's answer to the Moluccan empire of the Portuguese. Almost at the same time, pilot Andres de Urdaneta fortuitously solved the problem of the return voyage to the Americas by sailing high into the north Pacific, so catching the prevailing westerlies. Thus began the famous Spanish galleon trade which lasted until the early nineteenth century. Vessels left Acapulco between November and April, driven by the northeast trade winds then blowing reliably in latitudes ranging from 11–14 degrees north. The return trip from Manila was completed between May and September, when southwest monsoons sped the vessels northeast to the Japan current where they caught the prevailing westerlies which swept them into latitudes as high as 40 degrees for a landfall somewhere in the Californias or further north.[6] These routes out and back took the Spanish through some of the emptiest regions in the ocean. Sometimes islands were sighted on the way to Manila, usually those belonging to the widely scattered equatorial groups—the Gilberts, Marshalls, Carolines, and Marianas.[7] Most had nothing to offer the sailors; indeed they were hazardous to navigation. Only Guam, which lay conveniently on the approaches to the Philippines, was a regular landing place. Returning home, vessels usually passed north or south of the Hawaiian group. In spite of longstanding theories that Spaniards landed there, no conclusive proof has yet been found for pre-Cook contact.

Another island whose presence was noted early was New Guinea. The Portuguese Jorge de Meneses visited its northern coastline in 1527, and it was seen by Saavedra in 1529. Some survivors of Grijalva's ill-fated expedition of 1537 ended up on some of its northerly off-shore islands. Ironically, New Guinea and neighbouring islands to the east and southeast (the Solomons and the New Hebrides) were among the first Pacific islands ever visited by Europeans, but among the last to be explored. For it was to the southwest Pacific that the Spanish next turned their attention, in search of the fabled Islands of Solomon.

The Islands of Solomon

King Solomon's mines had been a goal of explorers since Biblical times. The idea of a place of great wealth had for long blended well with notions of Terra Australis Incognita.[8] In the mid-sixteenth century added impetus to find this land came from some rather hopeful Spanish interpolations of a Peruvian myth, which claimed that the Inca Tupac Yupanqui had brought back great riches from islands to the west. The fertile imagination and boundless energy of Pedro Sarmiento de Gamboa led to three Spanish voyages from Peru in search of these islands.

The first was led by Alvaro de Mendaña in 1567. He made landfall amongst the group now known as the Solomon Islands and spent some six months charting coastlines and skirmishing with the inhabitants. Mendaña sailed again in 1595 with Pedro Fernandez de Quiros, this time not only looking for Solomon's treasure but intending to found a godly colony. They came first upon islands which still retain the name the Spanish gave them—the Marquesas. They spent two weeks there and killed some 200 Islanders. Travelling on, they sighted several small islands in the central Pacific and came at last to a much larger island they named Santa Cruz. It was Ndeni, among the group still known as Santa Cruz. Relations with the Islanders ranged from mutual distrust to open conflict, and the planned settlement proved unworkable, not least because of demoralisation and bitterness amongst the colonists themselves. After two miserable months of complaint, rancour, and violence the disillusioned settlers sailed for the comforts of Manila. The final Spanish probe of the era was made by Quiros (with Luis Vaez de Torres) in 1605. Undaunted by the experiences of his voyage with Mendaña, he set off with high hopes of founding another colony—the New Jerusalem on Terra Australis, which was still thought to be in that same southwestern region of the ocean. As with the previous two voyages, several islands were sighted, and brief landings were made on Hao in the Tuamotus and Rakahanga in the northern Cooks. Coming finally to the Santa Cruz group, Quiros journeyed further south to the New Hebrides where he landed on the large island he named Espiritu Santo. There he would found his Kingdom of God on Earth.

But the interminable conflicts with the Islanders, together with the predictable jealousies, deceits, and insubordinations amongst the godly settlers, saw the Spanish depart within a month. A defeated Quiros made it back to Spain via Mexico, while de Torres, whose vessel had become separated from Quiros's, sailed to Manila on a route taking him between Australia and New Guinea. Said Beaglehole, 'With Quiros died the heroic age of Spain.'[9] The Manila-Acapulco trade continued, but Spanish explorations into other regions of the ocean were not revived until the 1770s. In the meantime, the Dutch and the English entered the Spanish lake.

Spain's Pacific legacy

That the Spanish legacy to those Islanders whom they met had not been a happy one, was not by design. For their part, Mendaña and Quiros were motivated by the highest ideals of their times—strict conformity to then accepted standards of Christian living, a spirit of humanity toward all people and zeal to convert the 'heathen'. Philip II's instructions for the conduct of expeditions forbade stealing, or harassing other peoples, and encouraged the friendly exchange of trinkets and tools for fresh provisions.[10] Yet the great gulf between Spanish imperial idealism in practice and the Islanders' own perceptions inevitably led to misunderstandings and frequent violence.

First moments of contact were usually, though not invariably, friendly. In 1568 Mendaña was welcomed ashore on Santa Ysabel. He exchanged names with Bilebanara, a local leader, and Spanish sailors and villagers spontaneously danced to Spanish guitars and Melanesian pipes. Bilebanara supplied food while he could, but he hardly had the resources to keep 100 hungry Spaniards content for too long. He thus took to the bush and the Spanish were forced to find food for themselves. Lofty instructions were given to food-gathering parties about not stealing or damaging property, but out of sight of their commanders soldiers and sailors cared little for such niceties. Indeed, their conquistador mentality was aggravated by both their hunger and increasing harassment by Islanders in the bush. Attack provoked counter attack. From the villagers' point of view, even the presence of so many strangers was a great threat to their economy and well-being generally. Other Solomon Island communities were openly hostile to strangers per se, whether Solomon Islanders or not. Guerrilla skirmishing soon became a constant feature of relations with the Spanish during their travels about the Solomons. Typical was an incident on Guadalcanal when a Spanish watering party of ten went ashore in a small boat. The Islanders

came out from an ambuscade with weapons, and set upon them, and they did not leave any alive but a negro . . . who had escaped; and the greater part of them they cut into pieces; cutting off their heads and arms and legs, taking out their tongues, and sucking out their brains with great ferocity.[11]

Sarmiento was ordered ashore 'with as many people as he could muster, to chastise them. He burned several villages, and killed more than twenty Indians.'[12]

When the Marquesas were reached in 1595, some 400 Islanders came out to Mendaña's vessels in canoes. In a manner typical of the way many societies in Polynesia welcomed strangers, food was offered and speeches were made.[13] According to custom, all the strangers' goods then belonged to their hosts. The Islanders swarmed aboard grabbing everything they could. 'Some cut slices from our bacon and meat with knives made of cane, and wanted to take other things.'[14] The Spanish were uneasy. A shot was fired and the Islanders leapt overboard. One who insisted on hanging on had his hand chopped with a sword. Some Islanders tied a rope to the bowsprit and tried to tow their claimed prize ashore. The Spanish aimed their arquebuses 'but, as it had been raining, the powder would not ignite.'[15]

The vessels sailed to a neighbouring island, where violence broke out again. Soldiers began to shoot Islanders as 'examples'. Wrote Quiros:

> *The cruelty of the Spaniards was such that there were not wanting those who said that the bullet wounds, so fierce and ugly, would frighten the other natives, and that the swords, making wide wounds, would have the same effect. In order that the natives might see, it was ordered that the bodies should be taken on shore, that the Camp Master might hang them up where they would be seen by the natives. It was said that this was done in order that the natives, if they came with false intent in their canoes, might know what the Spaniards could do. But it seemed to me that four armed ships had little to fear from unarmed natives in canoes. The Camp Master hung up the three natives in a place best adapted for the intended object. A certain person came to see them, who gave one of the bodies a lance-thrust, and praised what had been done. At night the natives took the bodies away.*[16]

Quiros calculated that 200 Marquesans were killed during the short visit.[17] The story of hesitant meetings, misunderstandings, anger, attacks, and counter attacks was repeated time after time when this expedition went on to the Santa Cruz group, and during Quiros's later voyage to the New Hebrides.

But it would be wrong to assume that sixteenth-century Spaniards with their swords and arquebuses were always able to impose their will on Pacific Islanders. On the contrary, as Dorothy Shineberg has argued,[18] Spanish arms and fighting tactics sometimes proved of limited use. The arquebus itself was neither reliable nor very accurate, nor did it have much of a range. Powder dampness was a major problem in humid coastal areas and there were numerous occasions similar to that already mentioned when the powder would simply not ignite. The difficulty of quickly reloading these cumbersome weapons also made them unsuitable for guerrilla skirmishing, which was the usual method of attack adopted by, for example, Solomon Islanders. Once they realised that they were too vulnerable in an open frontal advance, Solomon Islanders quickly adopted other effective tactics in order to counter the potential killing power of firearms. They soon learnt that arquebuses would not fire when wet, and doused them at every opportunity or attacked when it was raining. They realised too the significance of matches and would refuse to come close until they had been extinguished. Shineberg also gives examples of how some Islanders were quick enough to take advantage of the momentary delay between the flash in the arquebus pan and the ignition of the powder in the barrel. They would draw fire then duck underwater or behind a tree only to emerge when the marksman was helplessly reloading. In Guadalcanal some Islanders constructed sand ramparts to protect them from arquebus fire. The longer the Spanish were in any one locality, the more adept the Islanders became at countering Spanish firepower.

It is possible only to guess at what impact the sixteenth-century Spaniards had on the people they encountered on the islands of the Marquesas, Solomons, Santa Cruz, and New Hebrides. It was to be another two hundred years at least before other Europeans visited these places, and by then there were no obvious signs of early Spanish presence or even memories of these long ago visitors.[19] The exception was the island of Guam, which became a Spanish colony (at least in name) some three centuries before the rest of the islands in the Pacific were taken over by the imperial powers.[20]

In 1565 Lopez de Legaspi, on his way to claim the Philippines for Spain, announced Spanish sovereignty over Guam, though this meant little to the Islanders since no resident Spanish administration was established until more than a century later, in 1676. Theoretically Guam was ruled by the viceroy of Mexico. Meanwhile since Guam lay on the direct route to Manila it was an ideal place for replenishing galleons and other Spanish vessels. English and Dutch adventurers also made surreptitious landings for provisions and fresh water in the late sixteenth and early seventeenth centuries. Trading with the Islanders, or Chamorro as they were called, was usually peaceful, especially after the Islanders gained experience in dealing with sailors and vice versa, though there were occasional instances of violence. Spanish grip tightened with the arrival in 1668 of Jesuit missionaries and a small garrison force. Initial relations proved easy enough, though social divisions within the Chamorro contributed to increasing tensions. Chiefs and leading landowners tried to monopolise what benefits the Spanish church had to offer, and objected vigorously to the lower classes being offered possibility for social mobility and status through baptism and participation in church affairs. More general opposition to Jesuit proselytising arose when the more zealous of them used soldiers to prohibit and generally interfere with various Chamorro customs. Fighting between certain sections of the Chamorro and Spanish soldiers (the Spanish-Chamorro wars) dragged on intermittently until the 1670s and 1680s.

In 1676 the first resident governor arrived, with more soldiers, and a long and often brutal campaign of 'pacifying' the Chamorro began, not only on Guam but also on other islands of the Marianas. Forced resettlement of island communities was a common strategy. By 1695 this campaign was completed. It has been estimated that the population was reduced during this time from some 50 000 to 5000. Such massive depopulation has been attributed both to Spanish killings and to a smallpox epidemic of 1688. By the end of the seventeenth century, Spanish colonial rule was firmly entrenched on Guam and throughout the Marianas. Characteristically, most of the surviving Islanders, especially those on Guam, had been brought 'under the bells'—communities had been resettled in groups of households surrounding a church and under the spiritual jurisdiction of the priests. Some of the leading Chamorro families profited handsomely by this arrangement, managing to keep or even increase their former social, economic, and political influence over their followers by institutionalising themselves in the church hierarchy. Superimposed over all was the Spanish administration consisting of a governor, a military commander with police and soldiers aplenty, and a complex bureaucracy which managed the various municipalities into which Guam had been carefully divided.

Spain's great century of Pacific exploration, from Balboa in 1513 to Quiros in 1606, revealed much of a hitherto unknown third of the globe. Spanish navigators delineated much of the ocean's surrounding shore-line—from Tierra del Fuego to Queen Charlotte Islands in the east, and from New Guinea to Japan in the west. Although most of the islands that they came across in between were 'cartographically floating',[21] the Spanish nevertheless saw most of the islands of Micronesia. In Polynesia they noted some of the Tuamotus, Marquesas, Line Islands, northern Cooks, and Ellice Islands. And in Melanesia they visited the Solomons, Santa Cruz, northern New Hebrides, and parts of New Guinea.[22] Yet much of the ocean, especially south of the equator, was still blank on the map, or rather was still represented by imaginative cartographers as the admittedly shrinking but still magnificent Terra Australis. It took another two hundred years before the myth was finally dispelled.

Dutch entry

In 1581 the Netherlands declared their independence from Philip II, monarch of Spain and Portugal. And as the political and economic fortunes of the Dutch rose, whilst those of Spain (and Portugal) now began to ebb, Dutchmen embarked upon a global search for trading commodities and soon became the leading Pacific explorers of the seventeenth century. Defying Philip's now futile prohibitions, the Dutch eyed the East Indies, hitherto the preserve of the Portuguese. In 1602 the Dutch East India Company was formed to exploit the riches of these lands. Initial attempts to reach them via the Straits of Magellan proved too risky and unreliable, and the Dutch concentrated instead on the much safer route around Africa. By the 1640s they had safeguarded their route eastward by establishing settlements at the Cape of Good Hope, Mauritius, Madagascar, Ceylon, and India, and they had conquered much of the Southeast Asian archipelago and held a powerful commercial and military hegemony in the region: 'The possession of the East Indies, as once the possession of the Americas, was now the key to the ocean'.[23]

Where early Spanish explorers were motivated by grandiose schemes to enhance the glory of the Spanish empire and Christendom, seventeenth-century Dutch voyagers had rather more mundane aims: their task was to add to the East India Company's profits. And if Terra Australis could be found, then its commercial potential would be more significant than whatever imperial approbation it might bring the Dutch.

To the map inherited from the Spanish and Portuguese, the Dutch first added to the coastlines of New Guinea and sketched in the northern and western coastlines of Australia.[24] Although the latter country was clearly of continental size, hopes of it being Terra Australis were quickly shattered by its bareness and its strange, inhospitable people. Jan Carstensz thus described it in 1623:

> *The land appeared very dry and barren . . . we have not seen one fruit-bearing tree, nor anything that man could make use of: there are no mountains or even hills, so that it may be safely concluded that the land contains no metals, nor yields any precious woods. . . . In our judgment this is the most arid and barren region that could be found anywhere on the earth; the inhabitants, too, are the most wretched and poorest creatures that I have ever seen in my age or time . . . .*[25]

On his voyage of 1642, Abel Janszoon Tasman saw nothing of the Australian mainland though he sighted Van Diemen's Land (Tasmania) and his course to Batavia via his 'discoveries' of New Zealand, Tonga, Fiji, and around northern New Guinea at least showed that Australia did not fill the entire South Seas. Apart from Tasman's island discoveries, other Dutch findings in the Pacific were made by Jacob le Maire and William Cornelisz Schouten in 1616. They rounded the Horn, skirted the Tuamotus, passed through the northern Tongan islands, touched at Futuna and Alofi, and reached New Ireland and New Guinea.

Dutch experiences

Relations with those few Islanders the Dutch met were not usually so marked with brutality as those of the Spanish had been. Dutch visits were generally fleeting and there was simply not enough time for sailors to pose a threat to local economies. The Dutch were also rather less concerned to interfere with island communities. As befitted the newer European mentality, they paid more attention to reprovisioning, recording what they saw, and then getting on with the voyage. They were not in the business of trying to Christianise or colonise, at least not on small islands that appeared to offer little. Perhaps more to the point, their ships, unlike the Spanish, were not filled with soldiers.

Nevertheless relations with Pacific Islanders were usually tense and sometimes violent. When Le Maire and Schouten put a boat ashore at Takapoto in the Tuamotus, a group of Islanders tried to disarm the crew and had to be shot at; and later, off Niuatoputapu in the northern Tongan islands, a visit from a chief bearing gifts degenerated into an attack on the Dutch. The cause was probably Le Maire's refusal to drink the offered kava since he suspected it might be poison. The first encounter between Maoris and Europeans was similarly inauspicious. In spite of what seemed like a friendly welcome for Tasman, a canoe rammed a Dutch cockboat and four sailors were clubbed to death, all without apparent provocation. On the other hand, Tasman spent a most pleasant time in Tonga. At Tongatapu he recorded gratefully that no one carried weapons—'it was all peace and amity here'—and his barber and surgeon remarked that some of the women 'felt the sailors shamelessly in the trouser-front' and clearly 'desired fleshly intercourse'.[26]

These Dutch voyages, though cartographically significant, brought little joy to the East India Company officials at Batavia, concerned as they were with trade. They withdrew support from any further Pacific ventures. The period of Dutch exploration ended as abruptly as had the Spanish after Quiros. It was another eighty years before a Dutchman again crossed the Pacific in search of Terra Australis. He was Jacob Roggeveen, sponsored by the West India Company. In 1722, following Le Maire and Schouten's route, he 'discovered' and landed on Easter Island, and saw Borabora and some other islands in the leeward Society group, as well as Samoa.

British and French entry

The British first became interested in the Pacific late in the sixteenth century, mainly because of the opportunities to plunder the Spanish galleons plying between Acapulco and Manila.[27] Exploration was, initially at least, an important though not major consideration and the trans-Pacific adventures of Francis Drake (1577–1578) and Thomas Cavendish (1586) added nothing to European knowledge of the islands since their routes went well north of the equator. However Drake did chart further south and north on the west coast of the Americas than any other European explorer to that time. After these forays, almost a hundred years went by before the English once again turned their attention to the Pacific Ocean, and again their interest was primarily in Spanish gold. The most well known buccaneer-turned-explorer was William Dampier with his voyage to northern Australia, along the northern New Guinea coast to New Britain. Although the latter island was his only discovery, his book *A New Voyage Round the World* published in 1697 was a best-seller and helped to stimulate British interest in the South Seas. Partly as a result, there followed a series of British circumnavigations—by Dampier again in 1703, Woodes Rogers 1708–1710, and George Anson 1741–1744. Because they were eager to plunder the Spanish all these men continued to follow the galleon routes which took them through some of the emptiest ocean wastes, well north of most islands.

Even by the 1760s, some 250 years after Magellan first crossed the ocean, vast stretches of it were quite unknown to Europeans, particularly waters to the far north and almost all the southern half. Save for Tasman, no European had sailed in southern Pacific temperate latitudes at all, except when rounding the Horn. Terra Australis, though somewhat smaller than it had been at the beginning of the sixteenth century, still covered a huge area of the globe, that space between the west coast of New Zealand and South America. Apart from the inhabitants of Guam and other Islanders in the Marianas who had been 'colonised' by the Spanish, most Pacific Islanders had had no contact at all with Europeans. In spite of 250 years of periodic European voyaging across the ocean, only a few Islanders saw canvas sails, and even fewer actually met, and usually fleetingly, those who worked them. To all intents and purposes Islanders still had no inkling of the worlds beyond their own. However the British and French scientific voyages of the 1760s, though fleeting in themselves, were soon to lead to a much more substantial European presence and influence in the South Seas.

Once the Seven Years War ended in 1763, both Britain and France could turn their attention to other matters, including attempts to solve the major geographic riddles of the Pacific. For the first time in the era of Pacific exploration the quest for scientific knowledge in itself was a major concern, though hopes for trade and new lands to rule were not entirely forgotten. The British Admiralty first sent out John Byron to search for a passage through the north American continent. Failing to find it he crossed the Pacific in 1765 on his way home, sighting some of the Tuamotus, Tokelaus, and Gilberts. Samuel Wallis and Philip Carteret went out in 1767 to look for Terra Australis, becoming separated in storms in the Magellan Straits. Carteret came across Pitcairn then went on to the Solomons, New Britain, and New Ireland. Wallis became the first European to land on Tahiti, where he stayed for a month, before going on to Guam. At the same time, the Frenchman Louis Antoine de Bougainville was in Pacific waters. He landed at Tahiti nine months after Wallis, then continued via Samoa, the New Hebrides, the Solomons, and New Ireland.

Of all the islands seen, none excited the imaginations of explorers and their reading public as much as Tahiti, which soon became a focal point for European ventures in the South Pacific. The island's earliest practical significance, from a European point of view, was as a base for James Cook. He, more than any other single explorer, brought the Pacific islands to popular European notice, and finally dispelled the myth of the mighty Terra Australis.

Cook in perspective

The British Government and the Royal Society sent Cook to Tahiti in 1768. There, as instructed, he observed the transit of Venus across the sun (in the hope of helping to calculate the sun's distance from earth) and then sailed toward Tasman's New Zealand landfall, proving that the coastline belonged to two islands rather than a continent. Continuing westward, Cook came to and charted Australia's east coast—so cartographically completing that country's outline. Cook's second Pacific voyage (1772–1775) criss-crossed the entire southern Pacific Ocean with probes even beyond the Antarctic Circle, removing once and for all the possibility of there being a Terra Australis. His third voyage (1776–1779) concentrated on finding the long-hoped-for North West Passage, but his explorations beyond Bering Strait proved that too to be a figment of imagination.[28]

Cook has the reputation of being the greatest of all Pacific explorers, especially in English minds. Yet such praise is often misplaced. Cook actually discovered very little in the strictest sense of the term. Except for Australia's east coast, New Caledonia, and Hawaii (and some minor islands), every island group he came across had been sighted previously by Europeans. Only in fairly recent times has due consideration been given to the non-English triumphs of people like Magellan, Mendaña, Quiros, Tasman, and others. Ironically Cook's greatest 'discoveries' were of what did not exist—Terra Australis and the North West Passage. This is by no means to belittle Cook's achievements, but merely to put them in a wider perspective. Cook was undoubtedly one of the foremost European seamen and explorers. One of his most significant contributions was to fix meticulously the positions of so many islands that had hitherto been cartographically vague, and to survey much of the hazardous coastline of Australia and northwest America. In addition, his voyages made an invaluable contribution to the budding sciences of Pacific ethnography and anthropology, biology, meteorology, and a host of others. There again, acclaim for the man must be kept in perspective. In one sense, comparisons between Cook and those who had sailed the Pacific before him are misleading. Cook belonged to a very different age from that of Quiros and others, one that had different preoccupations and supplied him with vastly improved navigational techniques and technical and moral support generally. Neither should Cook's achievements be highlighted at the expense of some of his contemporaries and travelling companions. For too long, men like Alexander Dalrymple, Joseph Banks, and John and George Forster have taken a back seat when their work is valuable both in its own right and as an influence on Cook.[29] Historians now in the process of demythologising Cook also point out that some of his other alleged virtues and triumphs cannot be substantiated. His long-held reputation for kind humanitarianism—treating everyone alike with equanimity and generosity—is now somewhat tarnished. His dealings with both his crew and the Islanders were rather more ruthless than some of his earlier biographers would dare admit. Nor was he always the cool, rational, even-tempered hero standing unflinchingly on the quarterdeck. There were times when he was a raving madman, especially on his third voyage, when his once iron-hard constitution was stricken by what is now believed to be a vitamin B deficiency. This perhaps helps explain his senseless outbursts of violence, the last of which led to his death on Hawaii's dark shores.[30]

Even his long-trumpeted success at preventing and curing scurvy is shown to be another myth. Instead, it is argued that Cook's views on the treatment of scurvy were quite erroneous and retarded for decades the experiments that finally produced an effective antiscorbutic. In the meantime, thousands of sailors continued to die from the disease. Nor was the general level of health on his ships as high as is frequently claimed. Close scrutiny of the records of his three voyages indicates that mortality and morbidity were far worse than anyone had previously suspected.[31]

All this is not to say that Cook is now discredited by scholars. He and his achievements have simply been reassessed and he is now seen in a more human context.[32] As befits our age, there are no more heroes.

After Cook, all that was required on the Pacific map was some 'tidying'.[33] By the end of the eighteenth century, virtually every island and island group in the ocean had been placed more or less accurately on the charts. It remained the task of nineteenth and even twentieth-century explorers to find out what lay beyond the foam-fringed coastlines.

Tahiti: femmes and firearms

Dealings between Islanders and late-eighteenth-century explorers tended to follow the usual pattern—at best a hesitant, nervous exchange of greetings and goods, at worst misunderstandings, provocations and bloodshed. But the more intensive, systematic European presence from the late 1760s onward added a new element for some Islanders—return voyages by these strangers. The first people to experience several visits at relatively short intervals were Tahitians. Wallis, Bougainville, and Cook rapidly followed one another, and from then until the end of the century Tahiti probably received more visitors than any other Pacific island.

The most common view of early culture contact in Tahiti is that European visitors were welcomed rapturously, their ships loaded to the gunwhales with mouth-watering produce, and sailors frolicked with erotic Tahitian maidens in a setting of tropical luxuriance. There is considerable evidence from early records for this opinion, as witness several choice, and oft-quoted passages. When Bougainville first approached the island, his vessel was immediately surrounded by canoe-loads of young women most of whom 'were naked, for the men and old women that accompanied them had stripped them of the garments which they generally dressed themselves in'. These young ladies appeared a little uneasy, but the men

> soon explained their meaning very clearly. They pressed us to choose a woman, and to come ashore with her; and their gestures, which were nothing less than equivocal, denoted the manner we should form an acquaintance with her. It was difficult,

> *amidst such a sight, to keep at their work 400 young French sailors, who had seen no woman for six months. In spite of all our precautions, a young girl came on board, and placed herself upon the quarter-deck, near one of the hatchways, which was open, in order to give air to those heaving at the capstern below it. The girl carelessly dropped a cloth, which covered her, and appeared to the eyes of all beholders, such as Venus showed herself to the Phrygian shepherd, having, indeed, the celestial form of that goddess. Both sailors and soldiers endeavoured to come the hatch-way; and the capstern was never hove with more alacrity than on this occasion. At last our cares succeeded in keeping these bewitched fellows in order, though it was no less difficult to keep the command of ourselves.*[34]

After the Frenchmen landed, some of them were invited into a house, where the 'civility of their landlords' did not stop 'at a slight collation':

> *They offered them young girls; the hut was immediately filled with a curious crowd of men and women, who made a circle round the guest, and the young victim of hospitality. The ground was spread with leaves and flowers, and their musicians sang an hymeneal song to the tune of their flutes. Here Venus is goddess of hospitality, her worship does not admit of any mysteries, and every tribute paid to her is a feast for the whole nation. They were surprised at the confusion which our people appeared to be in , as our customs do not admit of these public proceedings. However, I would not answer for it, that every one of our men found it impossible to conquer his repugnance, and conform to the customs of the country.*[35]

Such was the stuff of South Sea paradise for eighteenth century sailors. For Bougainville, Tahiti was La Nouvelle Cythère: 'The very air the people breathe, their songs, their dances . . . all conspire to call to mind the sweets of love, and all engage to give themselves up to them.'[36] Such descriptions by Bougainville, and similar ones by Cook and Banks, took the reading public of Europe by storm, fascinating those who were predisposed to see such people as Noble Savages, and horrifying those with a narrower moral outlook.[37] But whether such apparent eroticism was applauded or considered depraved, early relations between Tahitians and Europeans were most frequently portrayed (as they still are in popular literature) in terms of sexual trystings featuring lusty sailors and willing maidens.

Such views, for all their obvious readership appeal, imply that the Tahitians were little more than sex-obsessed creatures, warm and generous maybe, but at the same time naive and unsuspecting in their dealings with these newcomers to their shores. W H Pearson has suggested that the Tahitian response was far more complex than that.[38] The friendliness and sensual delights (or depravities) that greeted Cook's and Bougainville's sailors and those who came after them, had, said Pearson, rather more subtle origins. To understand these it is necessary to examine briefly the way in which Tahitians and many other societies in Polynesia received strangers in the days before European presence. Storm-tossed castaways or weary travellers could usually expect a welcome, providing they posed no obvious threat. They would be met with long speeches and various other customary greetings. The newcomers then surrendered what possessions they had, such as their canoe, fishing gear, and remaining food (if any) to their hosts as a sign of humble acceptance of and token compensation for the food and shelter they would be offered. If later they wished to leave they might be supplied with a canoe and provisions, and given a send-off. Such rites of reciprocity and the guests' acknowledgment of their hosts' authority were never understood by European explorers. Furthermore, in order to comprehend Tahitian reactions to Cook and Bougainville more fully, their responses to the first Europeans to come to their island need close scrutiny.

Captain Wallis's *Dolphin* was met by over 800 men in 100 canoes off Tahiti's east coast in 1767. They 'paddled all round the ship and made signs of friendship ... by holding up Branches of Plantain trees, and making a long speech of near fifteen minutes'. Several of them finally ventured on board after making 'Long talks' and throwing leaves. The sailors then offered knives, beads, and ribbons in exchange for fresh food.

> *The method we took to make them Understand what we wanted was this, some of the men Grunted and Cryd like a Hogg then pointed to the shore—oythers crowd Lyke cocks to make them understand that we wanted fowls, this the natives of the country understood and Grunted and Crowd the same as our people, and pointed to the shore and made signs that they would bring us off some.*[39]

So far so good, for the newcomers, strange as they and their vessel might be, appeared to be acting in a manner acceptable to the Tahitians. Then the Islanders started taking nails and other items lying about the deck, as their protocol allowed. But the sailors, who interpreted this action as theft, became very angry and drove the Tahitians off with a 'nine pound shot over their heads'.[40] From the Tahitian point of view, this was an outrage. Their welcome had been abused, and the newcomers were acting as enemies rather than submissive friends. New tactics were required to counter the now very real threat posed by the *Dolphin* and her 180 crew.

The vessel moved around the coast, as did news of her presence. A cutter sent to sound for an anchorage was attacked and the Islanders were again fired upon. As the vessel stood off a likely anchorage in Matavai Bay, a few canoes came out and there was some tense trading.

> *The country people behaved very insolently, non of them would trust any of our men with any of their things until they got nails or toys from them, then several of them would push off and keep all and oythers caried their insolence so high that they struck several of our men.*[41]

Wallis spent several days sounding for a safe anchorage. He was unwilling to send a party ashore since the heavy surf would doubtless have wet their

4   *Captain Wallis of the Dolphin clashes with Tahitians at Matavai Bay, 1767.*
(*Hawkesworth* An Account of the Voyages for Making Discoveries. . . . *Alexander Turnbull Library*)

muskets, while on the beach had gathered several thousand Islanders, all jeering and looking decidedly hostile. The English were tense. On several occasions they fired at and killed Islanders who ventured too close in canoes. But the *Dolphin* was now critically short of fresh water. Wallis risked sending a boat into the shallows. Six water barrels were handed across to the Islanders to fill in return for nails and hoop iron. They filled only four. This was the occasion when Tahitian women were seen for the first time, some four days after the *Dolphin* had first reached the island. A number of young girls were brought to the water's edge:

> *This new sight Attract our mens fance a good dale, and the natives observed it, and made the Young Girls play a great many droll wanting tricks, and the men made signs of friendship to entice our people ashoar.*[42]

The following day, Wallis took the *Dolphin* into Matavai Bay and some Islanders ventured out to trade. Most canoes now had young girls aboard who made 'all the Lascivious Motions' and played 'all the Wanton Tricks imaginable'. Clearly those Tahitians in authority were testing to see if naked females could divert the sailors and enable the Tahitians to regain some initiative in their dealings. For, while the sailors rivetted their attention on the girls 'Pulling up their cloaths', the Tahitian men suddenly showered the *Dolphin* with 'stones lyke hail'. The ship's crew replied with rounds of musket fire, cannon-balls and grape shot 'which struck such terror amongst the poor unhapy croad that it would take the pen of Milton to describe'.[43] This withering fire smashed canoes and forced those still afloat to flee. The Tahitians regrouped their fleet more than a kilometre away from the *Dolphin*, thinking they were safe, until cannon-fire again smashed into them. Only then did the Islanders realise the great range and destructive capacity of the ship's big guns. The hundreds of people who had manned canoes and the thousands of spectators on shore vanished from sight.

The following day a few canoes ventured out, their occupants waving banana leaves as an apparent sign of submission. When the English landed that afternoon a crowd of several hundred gathered 'every man careing the bow of a Plantain Tree in his hand as an Emblem of Peace'.[44] Trading commenced again, though it was tense. The Tahitians planned another attack, but the sailors were ready and again caused havoc with their cannon. The final straw for the Tahitians came when they retired to what they thought was the safety of a nearby hilltop, only to have a cannon-ball lobbed neatly in their midst. This last devastating shot finally convinced them that they had no match against these weapons and they were prepared to concede defeat, at least on this score. Although their subsequent friendly behaviour toward the sailors was tempered by their fear of firearms, they still tried to gain some initiatives. On the day after the hilltop massacre, Tahitian leaders openly engaged in sexual politics:

But our Young men seeing several very handsome Young girls, they could not help feasting their Eyes with so agreeable a sight this was observed by some of the Elderly men, and several of the Young Girls was drawn out, some a light coper colour oythers a mullato and some almost White. The old men made them stand in Rank, and made signs for our people to take which they lyked best, and as many as they lyked and for fear our men hade been Ignorant and not known how to use the poor young Girls, the old men made signs how we should behave to the Young women, this all the boats crew seemed to understand perfectly well, and begd the Officer would receive a few of the Young Women onboard, at same time they made signs to the Young Girls, that they were no so Ignorant as the old men supposed them, this seemed to please the Old men Greatly when they saw our people merry, but the poor young Girls seemd a little afraid, but soon after turnd better aquanted.[45]

Thus began a flourishing trade in prostitution, much to the delight of the *Dolphin's* crew.

A Dear Irish boy one of our Marins was the first that began the trade, for which he got a very severe cobing by the Liberty men for not beginning in a more decent manner, in some house or at the back of some bush or tree, Padys Excuse was the fear of losing the Honour of having the first.[46]

Tahitian chiefs, intimidated by English firepower, had discovered an effective way of placating the strangers. Tahitian women were not nymphets clamorous for sailors; rather, some women of low birth were ordered to prostitute themselves as a political strategy. Not only did this ensure the goodwill of the English, it also brought considerable economic advantage to the chiefs. Sexual relations between Tahitians and Europeans soon became as much a commercial enterprise as a political tactic. Women's favours initially cost sailors a nail, but the interplay of supply and demand soon had the price hiked to large metal spikes. The *Dolphin* was soon denuded of every piece of metal capable of being prised loose.

When Bougainville arrived nine months later, and then Cook after him, Tahitian leaders were careful to display what appeared to be a grovelling servility, and to make sure Tahitian women kept sailors happy. Hence the early appearance of naked maidens above opened hatchways.

Cook especially, said Pearson, similarly built on precedents established by Wallis, making a point of displaying his firepower when he thought it appropriate. Chiefs, well aware that cannon were trained on their villages, had no intention of giving the strangers the slightest excuse to use them. 'The basis then of relations between European and Tahitians in the first ten years of contact was fear of European fire-power, and Tahitian behaviour to the Europeans can be seen as a series of strategies by which the threat posed by the visitors could be diminished or controlled, or, finally, converted to the political purposes of the host *ari'i* [chiefs]. Amiable as Tahitians no doubt were, their celebrated benevolence to the intruders was exacted at gun-point.'[47]

Tahiti: the early consequences

Since Europeans regularly visited Tahiti over the last three decades of the eighteenth century, the island provides examples of some early consequences of Western contact.

Like most Pacific Islanders, Tahitians were instantly fascinated by various European goods. Initially they wanted those items that were novel and sometimes more efficient substitutes for their own, such as nails and any pieces of metal that could be used for cutting and scraping. Wallis and Cook (on his first voyage) could purchase pigs, fowls, and whole breadfruit trees with such items, though Cook noted that some prices had inflated since Wallis's time. On Cook's second voyage (which included two visits to Tahiti), nails were no longer in such demand. Instead the people wanted cloth, trinkets, and hatchets. Cook also offered red parakeet feathers, collected in Tonga, which the Tahitians prized highly. By his third voyage, nails, trinkets, and the like could buy little (though red feathers were still in vogue). Some chiefs had so many of these items that they asked for wooden chests to store them in. By now the Tahitians showed a preference for tools rather than simple nails and spikes.

The introduction of these goods marked the beginning of a long and complex process of technological and social change. Steel tools, metal fish-hooks, and cloth were eagerly desired, not necessarily because they were always more effective than Tahitian equivalents, but because they came ready made. The laborious fashioning of a stone adze, the delicate, painstaking working of a shell fish-hook, the pounding of mulberry bark to make tapa all became unnecessary. Soon an element of cultural dissatisfaction crept in. With the increasing arrival over the remainder of the century of such labour-saving devices, the greater became Tahitian dependence upon them. On his last visit, Cook commented:

> *It seems to me, that it has become, in a manner, incumbent on the Europeans to visit them once in three or four years, in order to supply them with those conveniences which we had introduced among them, and have given them a predilection for.*[48]

Some years later, in 1791, Vancouver bore out Cook's prediction.

> *The knowledge that they have now acquired of the superiority and the supply with which they have now been furnished of more useful implements, have rendered these, and other European commodities, not only essentially necessary to their common comforts, but have made them regardless of their former tools and manufactures which are now growing fast out of use .... it manifestly appears that Europeans are bound by all the laws of humanity, regularly to furnish those wants which they alone have created.*[49]

Crews from visiting ships also fathered a large number of children in Tahiti (and elsewhere). Statistically, at least 1 per cent of all nonpregnant women having sexual intercourse with sailors could expect to conceive on the first day of contact. If that vessel stayed for a month 36 per cent of these women could (statistically) be pregnant. From this one month's visit it is theoretically possible to have some 3000 surviving descendants today. Given the considerable number of ships visiting Tahiti in the late eighteenth century (some 23 between 1788 and 1808), not to mention all the nineteenth-century contact, the number of mixed births must have been very high, even if the above theoretical figures are a gross overestimation.[50]

Other more immediate demographic and social consequences resulted from the introduction of the European diseases. Tahiti, and most other islands contacted from the 1770s onward, had gonorrhoea and venereal syphilis infect their inhabitants.[51] Introduced epidemics of influenza and dysentery were also common. Whether the Tahitian population had declined dramatically by, say, 1800 as many contemporaries claimed is still open to debate, since calculations of depopulation depend on just what the population had been in 1768. There is no general agreement about that figure.[52]

It is too easy to overestimate European impact on Pacific island communities before about 1800. No island, not even Tahiti, was changed overnight. Until the last few decades of the eighteenth century, most Pacific Islanders had little or no contact at all with the itinerant strangers from the other side of the world.

Overall, some three hundred years of European exploration in Pacific waters had minimal or no immediate effect on Pacific lifestyles. The impact was far more noticeable in Europe itself. As well as providing geographic enlightenment, the European discovery and exploration of the Pacific Ocean made a major contribution to political, economic, and intellectual developments in the Old World. Yet the explorers, especially those after the 1760s, ultimately influenced island societies in a most profound way. Their discoveries, their accounts of the exotic South Seas, were responsible for the sudden and steady stream of European commercial and religious interests to their shores from about 1800. The islands were soon to remain islands only in the literal sense. Figuratively they were islands no longer. They had became part of a wider world, one which introduced new ways and new ideas, offered new opportunities, and imposed new demands.

5

The wealth of islands

There was no Terra Australis. Instead there were numerous small scattered islands and not a trace of Ophirean wealth on any of them. But they did offer the merchant something, even if it was rather more mundane than diamonds and gold. Cook's widely read journals told of timber and flax in New Zealand, of sea otter and seals on the northwest American coast, of whales throughout the ocean, of pigs, breadfruit and other provisions in Tahiti. Apart from these attractions for the would-be trader, a handful of people saw the possibility of founding settler colonies in various parts of the Pacific. Yet the most immediate follow-up to Cook's voyages was the British government's decision to dump convicts, who could no longer be sent to former colonies in North America, on Australia's east coast at Botany Bay in 1788. It is possible that naval strategic considerations also played a part in establishing such a presence on the other side of the globe.[1] From there early commercial penetration of the Pacific islands commenced.

Trading from New South Wales

The economic basis for the new penal colony of New South Wales was tenuous in the extreme. The colony could not produce enough food for its own requirements, and the British East India Company's monopoly prevented any merchants there from trading directly between New South Wales and the Asian mainland. However, the South Sea islands were considered within the colony's domestic jurisdiction and, thanks to the Pacific explorers' accounts, far more was known about these islands than about the interior beyond the New South Wales coast. The Pacific Ocean was the colony's first frontier, not the continent's vast inland expanses, which remained for decades hidden beyond the seemingly impassable Blue Mountains.[2]

By the beginning of the nineteenth century, vessels radiated out from Sydney Harbour, travelling halfway across the ocean to Polynesia and beyond in search of food and other basic commodities for the colony, as well as the luxury items—sandalwood, bêche-de-mer, pearl shell, seal skins—for sale on the lucrative Chinese market. Not all these ships were based in Sydney, for the harbour also became a major port of call for vessels out from England as well as for the 'country' ships from India seeking goods to sell to the Chinese in return for sugar, tea, coffee, and silk.[3]

The first shipment of island produce to New South Wales consisted of 80 pigs from Tahiti in 1793. Then from 1807 until the mid-1820s an average of three vessels a year plied the 11 000-kilometre route carrying in all some three million pounds of salt pork to the hungry colony. Although this was an 'appreciable, but not large' volume of trade by New South Wales standards, and one which gave a relatively low net return of some 20 per cent, the Tahitian pork trade offered considerable security since there was a reliable source of supply and demand.[4] Pork traders also periodically supplemented their salty cargoes with more lucrative commodities such as pearl shell from the Tuamotus from 1803 and sandalwood from the Marquesas about 1816. Other traders also flocked to these localities but the risks were high. Ubiquitous and uncharted reefs were a constant danger. Sometimes Islanders were hostile. By 1817 a depletion of supplies at these islands, coupled with a New South Wales duty on both items (but not applicable to pork), made promoters and speculators lose interest.

There were also potential riches on islands closer to Sydney than those of eastern Polynesia. In 1804 Sydney traders learnt of sandalwood stands on Fiji's Vanua Levu and gathered there especially during the boom years 1808–1810.[5] At Canton the excellent Fijian sandalwood offered Sydney merchants a high return which outweighed the dangers of collecting it and the steep duty they were forced to pay when it was transhipped into Company vessels at Sydney. Some tried to bypass the Company monopoly by sailing directly from Fiji to Canton, but if caught they faced ruinous fines. By about 1810 the timber was becoming depleted and the Fijians, never as tractable as the Tahitians, proved increasingly unreliable as labourers and were frequently hostile. There were several more 'sandalwood rushes'—at the Marquesas 1815–1816 as already mentioned, at Hawaii from 1815 to 1828, and finally at New Caledonia and the New Hebrides in the 1840s and 1850s. With the exception of Hawaii, all of them attracted Sydney traders, and especially the last, by which time the Company's monopoly had been abolished.[6]

The other main locality that attracted vessels from Sydney was New Zealand. Sealers and whalers worked its southern shores sporadically before 1800, though the boom in sealing came about 1810 and whaling not until the 1830s. New Zealand's kauri timber and flax that so impressed Cook became much sought after in the later 1820s and 1830s. This commerce led to tiny pockets of Europeans settling at a few harbours, where passing vessels could hire Maori labourers, restock with provisions, and rest crews. The Bay of Islands became one of the main 'port towns' in the South Seas, a haven for Sydney vessels and, later, for New Englanders.[7]

Trading from North America

New South Wales merchants were soon rivalled by their North American counterparts who ranged further and wider through Pacific waters and eventually dominated the 'luxury' trade and whaling. The official account of Cook's third voyage, which explored the northwest American coast and the Hawaiian islands, was published in 1784. Within twelve months English vessels were scouring the wild Pacific coastlines of North America in search of the sea otter colonies described by Cook. The skins were sold at Canton, where prices reached record levels. Yet again British company monopolies bedevilled the private English entrepreneur. The South Sea Company tied up British trade on America's west coast, while the East India Company controlled the Chinese market. Boston merchants who were unfettered by such restraints moved in and from 1787 until 1825 the fur trade was dominated by the Americans. While sea otter pelts were the richest prize, other fur skins, such as beaver, ermine, fox, or seal, were also shipped to Canton. The Hawaiian islands were strategically situated on the route and became an important stopover where vessels were reprovisioned and repaired, and where Hawaiians were hired for shipboard duties and for work on the North American frontier.[8] Hawaii soon became more than a stopover. From about 1815 until 1828 sandalwood was heavily exploited by American merchants in conjunction with the Kamehamehas, Hawaii's kings. But American involvement was not confined to the northerly reaches of the ocean. From the 1790s, New Englanders were making frequent calls at Sydney and numerous South Sea islands in search of sandalwood and pearl shell, and they dominated the Fijian bêche-de-mer trade of the 1820s and 1830s. But of all their commercial ventures, the one most popularly associated with them is whaling. Again, Cook's writings had attracted English and American whalers to the Pacific from the now-depleted whaling grounds of the Atlantic. Lasting from 1789 until the 1850s, whaling was the longest lived, largest, and most profitable of all Pacific commerce, especially in the boom years of the mid-thirties to the fifties. English whalers, who first operated out from Sydney and in Chilean waters, soon dropped out of the race. Australian whalers continued to play a small role, concentrating on the less expensive bay whaling around the coasts of southern Australia and New Zealand. But the New Englanders dominated. They had the capital, technology, and experience needed to mount deep-sea ventures on the other side of the globe.[9] In the 1840s the American whaling fleet numbered almost 700 vessels and was crewed by 16 000 hands. In the words of Commodore Charles Wilkes, 'Our whaling fleet may be said ... to whiten the Pacific Ocean with its canvas'.[10]

The first whaling grounds in the Pacific were off California, Chile, and New Zealand. By the 1820s new grounds had been discovered off Japan and in equatorial waters generally. Major whaling bases were established at

Honolulu and Lahaina for the northern Pacific, Tahiti for equatorial regions, and the Bay of Islands for the south. In the heyday of whaling, in the thirties and forties, literally hundreds of vessels visited these ports each year. In addition, there were smaller bases in Tonga, Rarotonga, Fiji, Marquesas, Samoa, Pitcairn, and elsewhere.

Patterns and profits

By the 1840s, European commercial penetration had reached virtually every island of consequence in Polynesia, and was fast approaching the fringes of the still commercially unknown islands of Melanesia and Micronesia. The products the islands and surrounding seas had offered by this time had been exploited rapaciously, with various commodities replacing each other in importance according to market prices until supplies were eventually depleted altogether. Many a vessel went out one year after timber and flax, the next after sandalwood, then bêche-de-mer, pearl shell, and so on. Because trading venture was only as good as the profits it returned to its promoters, secrecy and subterfuge were part and parcel of organising expeditions and the eagerness with which the cargo was gathered. No consideration was or could have been given to conservation in the free-for-all competition from both sides of the ocean. When trees were all cut and lagoons cleared, the race was on to the next island. Every product, every quarry was the same, from pearl shells to sea otters to the mighty whales.

Tales of fabulous profits in the markets of China and Europe are legion. Certainly there were those who made huge profits by being in the right place at the right time, but more often than not they were exceptions rather than the rule. Equally possible for promoters was having their ships wrecked on some distant reef, or their crews involved in a bloody fracas with Islanders, or some cargo landing on a glutted market where prices might not cover investment. As usual, the smaller investor or company was more likely to suffer such vagaries. The larger concerns could more easily carry losses and wait for better times.

For those crewing the vessels, the financial rewards were not very great. Whenever there was the (anticipated) opportunity to make more money elsewhere, such as in Australia during the gold rushes, labour throughout the islands could become scarce. Crews on the New England whaling vessels were perhaps worst off financially for they received a percentage of the profits from the sale of oil at the end of the voyage. After expeditions lasting up to four years they could end up in debt to their employers if they returned without a full load, or if current oil prices were then depressed. Expenses for their clothing and bedding were deducted from any final amount owing them. Captains or masters and those with positions of responsibility on whaling and trading vessels usually did better than common seamen, though even the most resourceful, like Peter Dillon,[11] could suffer from wildly fluctuating fortunes.

Islanders as traders and labourers

Pacific traders and whalers have usually had a bad press, often being typified as the forces of mammon. Whalers have been described as 'lusty fellows' who had a 'quite stupefying' effect on Islanders. Traders are alleged to have 'chalked up a record of chicanery, violence, and evil to equal the blackest chapter of colonial history .... Whatever these aliens touched they altered or destroyed ... most islanders lost more than they gained'.[12] There are numerous instances of bloodshed and barbarity when trader and Islander met. Yet overall relations between them were relatively harmonious. Both sides, sooner or later, realised the mutual advantages to be gained by cooperation rather than confrontation. Islanders could indeed react aggressively, kill traders, even capture their vessels. Yet this might well scare away other Europeans, so cutting off any further opportunities to get European goods, and it might bring swift retaliation with cannon fire from other ships. As far as traders were concerned, they were seldom in any position to force their demands upon unwilling Islanders, especially since they were invariably outnumbered by these people, and frequently on strange territory thousands of kilometres from the safety of home ports. Moreover, most traders in island produce were totally dependent on local communities to supply them with what they wanted. All of the trading ventures mentioned so far were maritime based, as opposed to the land-based enterprises such as plantations and mining that were developed later in the century. Maritime-based trading at most Pacific islands, except where there were port towns, was of a fairly transient nature, and a major consequence of doing business from a quarterdeck, or from a longboat hauled up on the shore, was reliance on the Islanders' cooperation. Without the voluntary participation of Pacific Islanders as labourers, most European commercial ventures would have been impossible. This active, cooperative role of island communities has usually been overlooked by those writers who have seen early culture contact as a clash between dominant, initiative-taking Europeans, and passive, helpless Islanders reeling backward from the 'invasion'. But culture contact throughout much of the Pacific was not a one-way process so much as a more subtle and complex interaction.

Most Islanders were keen to do business with traders in return for trinkets, tools, utensils, cloth, tobacco, firearms, and any other goods they desired. Yet despite this keenness, not all Islanders were equally enthusiastic to work, especially if someone else got the benefits. Sometimes the Islanders' reactions were determined less by trader initiatives than by their own authority structure. For example, in the most rigidly stratified societies like Hawaii and Tahiti, the leading chiefs were in a position to order their subjects to work for them—for little or nothing in return. Commoners on Tahiti owned no land and had to raise and care for thousands of pigs that belonged to the landed and ruling classes, to whom most of the profits from the pork trade with Sydney merchants went, rather than to those who did all the work. But pig breeding on Tahiti was a lot easier than cutting and carrying sandalwood for Hawaii's rulers. One traveller contrasted Tahitians, whom he believed 'do not know what it is to subsist upon the fruits of their labour', with the 'less pampered, and more aristocratically-oppressed Sandwich [Hawaiian] Islander'.[13] Leading Hawaiian chiefs, some of whom developed an obsessive greed for western goods, forced their followers to gather ever-larger amounts of sandalwood.

On one occasion we saw two thousand persons, laden with faggots of sandalwood, coming down from the mountains to deposit their burthens in the royal store-houses, and then depart to their homes, wearied with their unpaid labours, yet unmurmuring at their bondage.[14]

The commoners' apparent acceptance of their lot amazed European travellers.[15] Nevertheless, it came as some relief to the workers when Hawaiian sandalwood was depleted, by the late 1820s.

In other societies where there was less social rigidity, leaders were unable to force unwilling masses to labour for them, and were in no position to monopolize any profits. Because there was much more opportunity for everyone to get at least some share of the offered booty, spontaneous enthusiasm for working for Europeans was more apparent. There was seldom a free-for-all, since work was still usually organised by chiefs in conjunction with traders, but the workers cooperated willingly. Maoris, for example, were considered amongst the more commercially aggressive Islanders. They joined sealing and whaling gangs, scraped flax, cut down and pit-sawed timber.[16] Wherever Europeans set up temporary or permanent bases around the New Zealand coast, Maoris flocked to become labourers and providers of pigs, potatoes, fish, and vegetables. The New South Wales authorities quickly realised that any profitable trade depended on Maori cooperation and did all they could to foster good relations. Maoris visiting Sydney were invariably given a warm welcome. Te Pahi, a chief from the Bay of Islands, spent three months in 1803 as Governor King's guest. In the early 1800s King made a point of sending certain chiefs pigs, goats, and potatoes as gifts. These were added to existing stocks, nurtured, then in turn sold back to traders. Maoris had always been good horticulturalists. The introduction of the English potato (by Cook or Surville in 1769), which grew more easily than the sweet potato, coupled with the traders' demands for food, saw Maoris cultivate it on a grand scale. Even by 1803, vessels arrived in Sydney from New Zealand with up to eight tonnes of potatoes on board. Whalers calling in to New Zealand spoke

of the 'abundant supplies of potatoes, and the assistance they have constantly received in procuring wood and water, as well as the hospitable reception and protection'.[17] One Captain's wife described Maoris

> *flocking to the shore, extending their arms to receive the white men from a distant country, bringing with them the fruits of their agriculture in great quantities, at the lowest prices. A quarter of a dollar here, I am positive, would purchase more than could be had in the New York market for two dollars.*[18]

Maoris soon began to export their produce to New South Wales on a regular basis. In later years, the 1840s and 1850s, their agriculture helped feed the tens of thousands of settlers who poured into New Zealand. Maoris also planted thousands of hectares of wheat, not only supplying the city of Auckland with food, but exporting large quantities to New South Wales.[19]

Fijians were mobilised in their hundreds for collecting sandalwood and bêche-de-mer. As individuals, they were perhaps more under their chiefs' thumbs than Maoris, though they were probably not as much at the mercy of chiefly despotism as were the Hawaiians. There was a sense of eager participation:

6 Bêche-de-mer drying house, Fiji. (*Wilkes* Narrative of the United States Exploring Expedition, *vol III*)

Our manner while here of obtaining the sandal wood, was thus:—On concluding a
bargain with the king (the whole of this article being royal property) for a certain
quantity, to be delivered by a stipulated day, at the landing place, on the bank of the
river, he would direct a chief to take his men, fifty, more or less in a gang, as the case
required, proceed up the mountain, cut down such trees as should be selected by our
men from the ship, and bring them trunk and limbs to the landing. The chief dared
not for his life but be punctual in performing and accomplishing his task by the time
agreed on. With this gang is sent one of the ship's crew, to select the large and sound
trees, and, in charge of the saws, axes, and grind-stone, and to direct the sawing
down the trees as close to the ground as possible. This sawing off the body with the
cross-cut saw, bringing the tree down from the stump, was a highly favourite part of
the work, and was frequently severely disputed for between the natives, owing to the
exquisite and delightful music to them, in the ringing of the saw. In fact, at times,
they would dispute so earnestly about whose turn it was, as to come to a raging
grapple with each other. It frequently required the authority and interference of
their chief to quiet them, and restore harmony. The tree being thus sawed down, it
was then trimmed of all its limbs, and the top cut off where, after all the bark and
sap should be shaved off, it would leave the heart part of the diameter of about one
and a quarter inches. All the limbs were trimmed out in this manner, and the gang
continued working on the mountain, sawing down, and trimming out until a
sufficient load for the whole gang to carry down to the landing was obtained. Several
days were spent at work in the mountain woods at each excursion, before a full load
of body and limbs for all the gang, was prepared; they then collected it all at one
spot, the chief set off the load for each one, or for three, or five, or more as required;
they then shouldered it, and all in Indian file proceeded down the mountain with their
burdens to the landing place. The ship's men under the directions of the carpenter,
and his mates, with some natives to assist, saw and cut the body and limbs to proper
lengths of between four and five feet, and then shave off, with the drawing knife, all
the bark and sap. It is then in merchantable order for shipping on board, and the
king is paid for the lot, as has been previously agreed. He then sends it off alongside
the ship, and immediately divides the purchased articles with the chief, who has with
his gang performed the task with his men in procuring the wood.[20]

Activity on Fijian bêche-de-mer stations was even more intensive. The
stations themselves were impressive. There was a huge drying house, 30
metres or more long and 6 metres wide. A ditch ran the entire length of the
floor, filled with burning timber, which smoke-dried the bêche-de-mer
hanging in racks above it. There was also a house for the trader and his
goods, and huge iron pots for cleaning and boiling the slugs before
smoking. Fijians came from kilometres around, sometimes building makeshift villages in the neighbourhood so as not to miss anything. From each
station, scores of canoes with up to 100 men scoured the reefs and lagoon
shallows for the quarry. Another 50 or so stayed ashore cleaning and
boiling the bêche-de-mer, arranging it in the smoke-house, and tending the
huge fire. Another 100 or more were employed in the never-ending task of

collecting firewood to keep the smoke billowing. As well as these labour requirements, traders needed substantial quantities of food for their vessels' crews and the station workers. Small boats travelled around the Fiji group buying yams and pigs which Fijian communities raised just for this purpose.[21]

While such mobilisation of labour was not typical of all trading enterprises on the islands, it is indicative of the Islanders' (and certainly their chiefs') willingness to reap what rewards they could. Nowhere in the Pacific islands then visited by European commercial vessels was there any sustained refusal to supply goods and services, from Hawaii in the north to New Zealand in the south. It was the same from the Marquesas in the east to Futuna in the west:

> *The boat [at Futuna] was filled in about half an hour, the natives having rushed off to their gardens the moment they saw the boat leaving the ship's side—with pigs, turtle, ducks, turkeys, fowls, and vegetables of every description ... besides a multiplicity of various descriptions of fruit which happened to be in season.*[22]

> *But few ports in the Pacific offer greater facilities for the refreshment of ships than Resolution Bay [Marquesas]. Supplies of hogs, poultry, and vegetables, are abundant, of excellent quality and may be obtained on very easy terms. Wood and water are equally available.*[23]

Islanders and overseas travel

Just as Pacific Islanders participated vigorously in trading with Europeans on their own islands, so too did they show considerable eagerness to sail on ships as crews or labourers for distant lands or just as tourists. Early maritime commerce not only brought Europeans to Pacific islands, but also enabled large numbers of Islanders to travel far beyond their own shores.

Much has been made of the very first Islanders—like the illustrious Omai—who were taken to Europe by the explorers and paraded before 'society'.[24] Yet the impact these few people had when they returned to their islands (if indeed they survived the ravages of smallpox and other diseases) was minimal. Omai meant far more to Europe than he did to Ra'iateans and Tahitians. Yet within a few more decades large numbers of Islanders were in the habit of sailing away, and their return had much more significance for their communities.

Hawaiians were among the first to travel in any numbers, on the fur trading vessels plying between northwest American coasts and China. By the late 1780s some Hawaiians had visited Canton, and Nootka Sound on Vancouver Island. Soon thousands of them were keen to go, lured by the excitement of travel and the prospect of gaining wealth that distant chiefs would find difficult to wrest from them.[25] The more venturesome became involved in the inland fur trade, especially along the Columbia River, where they were employed as labourers, canoeists, and trappers. Some travelled as far east as Lake Superior. Hawaiians eventually formed a 'sizable proportion of any given trapping party'; a typical party in 1818 was described as consisting of 'twenty-five Canadians, thirty-two Owhyhees, and thirty-eight Iroquois'.[26] Most of these eventually returned from the cold lands to their home islands, where they inspired still more Hawaiians to go away.

> *The Sandwich islanders ... frequently make voyages to the north-west coast of America, and thereby acquire sufficient property to make themselves easy and comfortable, as well as respected among their countrymen; to whom, on their return home, they are fond of describing, with great emphasis and extravagance, the singular events of their voyage.*[27]

Sandalwood and whaling vessels calling at Hawaii provided further opportunities for those eager to see new lands for themselves. They were in some demand as seamen and labourers because of both their alleged amiability and their willingness to work for minimal wages. Even by the 1820s, groups of Hawaiians were to be found in Nantucket, causing editorial imaginations to run wild. The *Boston Recorder* noted under the heading 'Heathen Society at Nantucket':

> *The place has long been the resort of youths from pagan countries .... There reside there twenty Society or Sandwich Islanders who on stated evenings when the sky was clear, assembled in the streets, erected ensigned idols, and in frantic orgies paid their homage to the Host of Heaven.*[28]

By the 1840s over 1000 Hawaiians left annually for employment and adventure. In 1844, some 400 were employed by the Hudson's Bay Company in Oregon, and in the same year over 600 were reported sailing on American whaling vessels.[29]

Maoris also began to travel from the earliest days of European commercial shipping. Many reached Sydney on sealing and whaling ships before 1800, and from then on there were few such vessels calling regularly at New Zealand that did not hire Maoris as crew or labourers. Some Maoris visited London early in the century.[30] American captains became particularly keen to have them, since 'most of them have been brought up in English whale ships'.[31] 'They make excellent sailors', commented one master, 'after a short course of training; as I can vouch from experience, having had several of them at sea with me'.[32] Everywhere that traders and whalers called regularly, Islanders seemed eager for adventure and captains ready enough to sign them on because of their cheapness, reliability, and skills. A typical crew was on Dillon's *Calder* in 1825: a Chinese cook, a Bengalee steward, and equal numbers of Europeans and Polynesians. 'The latter were mainly Tahitians, of whom several appeared in the ship's muster under exotic names clearly devised by Dillon—"Governor Macquarie", "Major Goulburn", "Buckgarow Riley", and "Salt Fish".'[33]

Early culture contact in the Pacific was not just between Westerner and

Islander: Hawaiians, Maoris, Tahitians, Tongans, Fijians, and a host of others visited each other's countries, and travelled far beyond, to a hitherto quite unprecedented extent. John Turnbull's voyage round the world, 1801–1804, provides an early example of some Islanders' mobility. He first took a Tahitian crew to Hawaii where because 'language, complexion, and manners, bore a strong resemblance' they and their Hawaiian hosts 'were too highly delighted with each other, to be prevailed on to part until after midnight'.[34] At Tonga, Turnbull's Tahitians found that one of their countrymen had been living there for three years. When Norfolk Island was reached, one of the Tahitians found another

> *of his countrymen, of the name of Oreo, who had lately arrived from England in the ship Albion, smartly dressed in the style of an English sailor .... It was easy to see that, from the knowledge which this man had acquired travelling, he conceived himself far superior to any of his countrymen. He shewed the youth the riches he had amassed by such an adventurous enterprise; this wealth consisted of a musket, two pistols, a few axes and scissors, with some European clothing. The sight of this immense treasure had an evident effect upon the young Otaheitean; he now treated his countrymen with more distant respect, apparently acknowledging him as a far superior man to himself.[35]*

In Sydney, which the Tahitians at first thought was England, they met Maoris who had been to London.[36]

Meetings of Islanders from different parts of the Pacific frequently amused Europeans. One described the arrival at Tahiti of

> *a whale-ship from New Zealand, with a party of natives of that country on board, whom the master permitted to exhibit their war-dance for our diversion .... the effect upon the peaceable Otaheitans was such that long before they came to charge some of them ran away through fear, and all, no doubt, congratulated themselves that there was so wide an expanse of water between their country and New Zealand.[37]*

Beachcombers

Just as commercial shipping enabled Pacific Islanders to travel, to experience new lifestyles, and perhaps to escape from the demands or boredom of their everyday living, so too did it offer certain Europeans the same prospects. These were the beachcombers, men who deliberately chose to live in an island community, accepting or at least tolerating its customs. Initially, some had a beachcombing life forced upon them as a result of shipwreck, being marooned, or, in some cases, being kidnapped. A few of these came to like their new situation and chose to stay on even when an opportunity to leave presented itself. Yet others, whether they had arrived deliberately or involuntarily, could not wait to get away.[38]

The first beachcomber was Gonçalo de Vigo who deserted Magellan in the northern Marianas in 1521 and was picked up from Guam by Loaysa in 1526. During the sixteenth and seventeenth centuries a small number of European castaways ended up living on islands astride the main trans-Pacific sailing routes, for example in the Tuamotus, or more commonly in Micronesia. The beachcombing era proper began with the commercial shipping that radiated out from Sydney and North America from the late eighteenth century. Beachcombers were henceforth most likely to be found wherever trading was busiest. Hawaii was a favourite haunt from the 1790s to the 1820s, during the fur and sandalwood trades and the early days of whaling. There were as many as 200 beachcombers in this period, though relatively few stayed for any length of time. Tahiti was another early beachcombers' mecca during the pork trade with Sydney, though there were probably no more than 30 or 40 altogether, from the 1790s to the 1810s. Tonga was not the focus of any commercial activity, and was as well racked with civil wars, yet still hosted some 20 to 25 beachcombers from the 1790s onward. Samoa, despite having a bad reputation since the massacre of La Pérouse's crew in 1787 and being off the commercial routes, had a similar number of beachcombers. Rather more were to be found in Fiji—some 50 or more—during the years of the sandalwood and bêche-de-mer trades, and in New Zealand during timber and flax trading operations, when estimates put the number of 'pakeha-Maoris', as they were called, at about 150. Indeed, virtually everywhere in the central and eastern Pacific islands there were beachcombers, from the Tuamotus and Marquesas (150) through to the Cooks and Rotuma (70). And as traders and whalers ventured further afield, so too did beachcombers, to Nauru, to Ocean Island, to Ponape. By the 1840s and 1850s there were probably 2000 beachcombers scattered throughout Polynesia and Micronesia. There were relatively few in Melanesia. Around New Guinea and the Solomons there was little shipping at this stage, and their inhabitants had a reputation for great hostility toward newcomers. Beachcombers who lived to tell their tales had some horrendous experiences, such as Leonard Shaw who suffered the most extreme tortures and privations on Kilinailau in the northern Solomons.[39] Further to the south, in New Caledonia and its dependencies and in the southern New Hebrides there were rather more beachcombers, both because of the sandalwood trade in the forties and fifties and because many of the island communities were less hostile to strangers.

Probably a quarter of all beachcombers were escaped convicts from New South Wales and Van Diemen's Land. Given the brutalising conditions of prison life, the islands must have seemed, initially at least, a paradise to these men. The remaining beachcombers were usually sailors who similarly saw island living as a pleasant escape from the rigours of shipboard discipline. As one captain remarked:

Indeed, there does not occur a greater difficulty to European ships in the South Seas, than that of keeping their crew together; such is the seduction of that life of indolence and carelessness which the several islands hold out. The beauty of the country, particularly that of Otaheite; and still more, the facility with which the necessaries of life may be procured, are, in general, temptations too powerful to sailors exhausted with the fatigue of so long a voyage: add to this the women; then the difficulty of retaining our seamen against so many attractions will excite no further surprise. [40]

But seldom was the promise of an idyllic existence under swaying palms fulfilled. The image of beachcombers as philosophical hedonists, so often portrayed in popular accounts of life in the South Seas, has little basis in reality. The reception and treatment a would-be beachcomber received could never be predicted with certainty. Some were killed outright when they landed on a beach, others were tortured first. This form of welcome was more likely in parts of Melanesia and sometimes in Fiji before the inhabitants had much experience in dealing with Europeans. But the majority of intending beachcombers in Micronesia and Polynesia were generally permitted to land and stay, though the treatment they received varied greatly according to local customs, current politics, and what the newcomer might have to offer. Most island communities quickly sized up their would-be guests and ranked them accordingly:

Most of the ships that visit Feejee are Americans, and the cooks generally negroes. Cooks are the meanest people in the Feejees, a number of them having to cook for one man or chief; and they say that, if they themselves get something blacker by sitting occasionally over the pots assisting to dress and cook for one chief, no wonder that the "Kaisi papalangi" (foreign slave) should get black entirely by having to cook and prepare the food for a number of chiefs continually, as they term all white people "turanga" (chief or gentleman), for the sake of politeness. [41]

Many runaway sailors and convicts had neither the personality nor the material possessions to impress Islanders. Typical were three deserters from an American whaling ship who found themselves on Futuna:

The natives looked upon these somewhat forlorn youths with anything but favour or pity! . . . These poor chaps lived in daily and hourly jeopardy lest their ship should return again, and then by the offer of the much-coveted rewards, the natives would be sure to pounce upon them and deliver them up to the captain, who would be sure to augment his tyrannical cruelty for the rest of the voyage if he once again ever got them into his clutches! [42]

Samuel Patterson on Fiji was similarly treated with scant respect:

One of them came up to me, and took off my hat, in which was my pocket book which contained my protection and other papers; but I gave them to understand that if they would let me retain my papers, they might freely have my hat and pocket book; but they took the papers and rolled them up and put them thro' the holes in the rims of their ears. . . . They then took from me my jacket, trousers and shirt. . . . I now was left naked.[43]

The condition of some beachcombers in Tahiti was thought to be

by no means enviable; they complained very heavily, and with great reason, of the royal family; who after having tempted them to desert their ship for the sake of their property, had left them when become poor, to shift for themselves. They were now in the most abject state, differing little from the natives.[44]

Loss of a beachcomber's possessions did not lead inevitably to misery, providing the man was not too unimpressive. In some societies it was the custom for a newcomer to be stripped of his goods and clothing and in return offered quite lavish hospitality. For example, when O'Connell and six others landed on Ponape after being shipwrecked and drifting for five days, the Islanders 'stripped us of our clothing, and took everything out of the boat, whale irons, tubs, muskets etc'.[45] Yet O'Connell was soon elevated to chiefly rank and given a wife. He was also tattooed.

One of my women produced a calabash of black liquid; another took my left hand, squeezing it in hers so as to draw the flesh tight across the back. Then a little sliver of bamboo was dipped in the liquid and applied to my hand, upon which it left a straight black mark. The third beauty then produced a small flat piece of wood with thorns pierced through one end. This she dipped in the black liquid, then rested the points of the thorns upon the mark on my hand, and with a sudden blow from a stick drove the thorns into my flesh. One needs must when the devil drives; so I summoned all my fortitude, set my teeth, and bore it like a martyr. . . . After my executioner had battered my hand awhile, she wiped it with a sponge. I hoped she had finished; but no! She held my hand up, squinted at the lines, as a carpenter would true a board. Then she commenced again, jagging the thorns into places where she thought the mark was imperfect. The correction of the work was infinitely worse than the first infliction. . . . On the next morning the gout-puffed hand of the canon of Gil Blas would not have been a circumstance in size to mine. . . . Another squad of these savage printers followed our breakfast . . . eight days were occupied in the process upon different parts of my body. My legs, back, and abdomen . . .[46]

Other beachcombers like Robarts in the Marquesas, and Lockerby and Diapea in Fiji, also achieved similar status, though often without the humiliation of being stripped of clothes and possessions (or the pain of tattooing). Such men were useful to chiefs as interpreters, traders, repairers of muskets, and providers of material possessions. In return they were held in considerable esteem and lacked for nothing in everyday comforts. Some island communities were so desirous of having a whiteman live with them that they tried kidnapping. Such was Diapea's fate on Samoa:

Two natives caught me up and carried me into a back house on a hill, and then drove the rest of the boat's crew off to the ship. . . . After the boat's crew were well off from the shore, they brought me down to the beach, stripped me of my clothing, and

7   *Castaway James O'Connell saves his life by dancing before threatening Ponapeans.*
     (O'Connell A Residence of Eleven Years...)

gave me a large tapa ... and then put me in the fresh water and washed me clean. . . .
I soon became a favourite of the natives, and especially the king's . . .[47]

Hawaii's Kamehameha I was among the most well known island chiefs for
his reception and treatment of beachcombers. Those who gained his favour
with their skills and advice, especially in military matters, were amply
rewarded. Two in particular, who became his life-long supporters, were
John Young and Isaac Davis. It was generally believed that 'from their
knowledge of fire-arms, proved of essential service in the expeditions in
which he [Kamehameha] conquered Mowee, Morotoi, and Wahoo. . . .
They were rewarded, by being raised to the rank of chiefs, and received
extensive grants of land.'[48] Young even became Kamehameha's governor
of the Island of Hawaii. One visitor, Archibald Campbell, described the

many inducements ... held out to sailors to remain here. If they conduct themselves
with propriety, they rank as chiefs, and are entitled to privileges of the order; at all
events, they are certain of being maintained by some of the chiefs, who are always
anxious to have white people about them.
     The king has a considerable number in his service, chiefly carpenters, joiners,
masons, blacksmiths, and bricklayers; these he rewards liberally with grants of
land.[49]

Campbell himself became a favourite, with fifteen servants and hectares of
land.[50] There were similarly successful beachcombers throughout the

Pacific islands—William Mariner in Tonga, Charlie Savage and David Whippy in Fiji, Frederick Maning in New Zealand. Yet for every beachcomber in this league, dozens more found island life distasteful and even dangerous. The vast majority of beachcombers stayed for only a matter of months. Only a few stayed for years, and even fewer stayed permanently. Most beachcombers sooner or later could not stand the psychological and physical stresses of living in and being dependent upon an alien community, especially if there was little or no opportunity to communicate with fellow countrymen. In particular, the constant real or imagined insecurity was generally enough to wear down even the most hardy sailor or convict. Even boredom could be debilitating.

> *Here, I at first thought, my dreams of island felicity were to be realized . . . But this could not continue. The gloss of novelty wore off in a few weeks, and disclosed the bareness and poverty of savage life, even in its most inviting forms. I grew weary of lying all day in the shade, or lounging on the mats of the great house, or bathing in the bright waters. I soon found that the quietude of Samoan life was but apparent. Petty feuds and open hostilities disturbed this small world.*[51]

Almost as many who escaped to paradise were only too keen to escape back again.

Beachcombers were mostly transient visitors. Yet some of them were significant in their host societies, especially if they stayed for any length of time, if they had goods to share or skills to impart, and if they acted as intermediaries between their hosts and other European visitors. In playing some or all of these roles, they facilitated a degree of intercultural understanding, particularly by giving Islanders a much better introduction to Western ways than they could have gained from brief encounters with passing vessels. Beachcombers were cultural brokers to a greater or lesser extent. Unlike missionaries, most beachcombers had no conscious desire to try to change island cultures; indeed, for the most part they had to live on the Islanders' terms. Yet their very presence sowed some seeds for the concessions and changes that were to come.[52]

But exchanges of cultural news were not just between European and Islander. Much information about the Western world came to island communities from other Islanders who travelled about on European vessels. Some Islanders themselves became beachcombers. The Tahitian Harraweia lived in the Marquesas for several years in the late 1790s.[53] Tama, a Hawaiian, was there also:

> *He had been to Boston In America From Owyee in one of the ships from Masafiura [Juan Fernandez Islands] going to China with seal skins, and had stopt at Boston some months. But on his return to Owyee, the ship touching at St Cristiana [Tahuata] for refreshments, his being to courteously treated by the Chief of this place and attracted with the beauty of the Ladies of the Isle, [he] had forgot his own*

native country. Of course he was left by consent. He came aboard our ship and speaking a little broken english was our interpreter. He was usefull to both ships in procuring refreshments, wood, water, etc.[54]

Tama had arrived in the Marquesas with a 'suit of regimentals, a chest of cloth, a musket and some ammunition'. In addition, his skill at throwing spears and stones so impressed the Islanders that he was adopted by Teinae, a chief of Tahuata, and elevated to the rank of *toa*—warrior chief. Tama frequently led armies of 800–900 warriors against neighbouring islands.[55] Such indigenous beachcombers had other uses too. Fijian chief Cakonauto, or Mr Phillips as the English called him,

could talk almost fluently in Spanish, Tahitian, Tongan, and all the different dialects of Feejee, there being present in his house . . . people from all those different countries. He was an extremely intelligent man for a Feejeean, and felt happy in the company of foreigners, although they were no small expense to him. After tea he ordered his steward, who was a Manilla man, to set out the grog, and it was handed out in a powder keg. . . . He had ordered about seven or eight towns to supply four Tahitian natives with bananas, sugar-cane, and ti root, and for their trouble he supplied them (the Tahitians) with wives, provisions, tortoiseshell, etc.

These Tahitians distil from the above about three or four gallons a day and send it over to Thakonauto, and he and his companions (mostly English and Americans) drink it, getting sometimes beastly drunk, and cutting all manner of capers, and playing tricks on the inhabitants, which are only looked upon as childish chief's freaks.[56]

Accounts of early commercial shipping in the Pacific islands frequently convey the impression of dynamic movement by European traders, ranging across the ocean from Sydney to Valparaiso, from New England to Canton and exploiting the islands in between. For their part, the Islanders have usually been seen as somehow 'fixed' on their beaches, passively watching this shipping come and go. On the contrary, European trading and shipping offered most island communities all sorts of opportunities to participate actively in commercial undertakings and to travel widely around the Pacific and beyond. On balance, probably more Islanders than Europeans travelled from island to island, all the time adding to the complex and substantial interchange of experiences and information amongst all peoples—European and Islander—within the Pacific region. Culture contact had many dimensions.

6

To recover the remnant

The Spanish government worried that the British might found a settlement on Tahiti after Samuel Wallis 'discovered' it in 1768. Spain still looked upon the ocean as her own even though her exploratory initiatives had long been eclipsed by other nations. In particular, Tahiti was considered too strategically close to Spanish dominions in the Americas to let the British get a foothold there. But Spanish resources were now meagre in that part of the world, and other matters were more pressing. In 1772 a Spanish vessel put in to the island and stayed for two months. Two years later the Spanish landed two Franciscan friars, a marine, and a seaman, who stayed for almost twelve months.[1] Relations with the chiefs were cordial enough, though most other Tahitians showed little more than derisive contempt for the Spaniards and especially the friars. These two men seldom left their house and spent most of their time reporting Tahitian roguery and licentiousness:

A vast number of people arrived before the sun was up, and struck terror with their disorderly voices and yelling. They did their Heyba, *which lasted an hour without drums; and brought their performance to a close by all repeating one particular word (whose meaning we did not understand) over and over again together, with such force and loud yelling that it appalled one. The greater portion of them went off, and the rest stayed a few hours. They stole five chickens from us.*[2]

The government vessel that took the grateful friars back to Callao was the last Spanish ship to call at Tahiti for a hundred years. Yet for the Tahitians, and most other Pacific Islanders, the age of the missionary was dawning. Just as island produce and fisheries attracted traders and speculators into the Pacific from about 1800, so did the prospect of hundreds and thousands of allegedly unredeemed souls attract those who wished to save them. Evangelical protestantism was on the move.

The evangelical mind

The evangelical revival in England had its intellectual roots in the sixteenth-century Reformation, and its socioeconomic roots in the industrial revolution.[3]

Revivalism in eighteenth-century England consisted of a series of movements that challenged some of the entrenched practices and orthodoxies of the established church. Many of the missionary societies that entered the Pacific emerged from the evangelical or Methodist teachings of men like John Wesley and George Whitefield. They argued that the church had lost sight of some of the more fundamental doctrines propounded at the time of the Reformation. They demanded much more concentration on 'the preaching of the atonement, the doctrine of the cross . . . emphasis on the eternal peril of the soul . . . emphasis on the propagation of the Bible.'[4]

Under the general umbrella of the evangelical movement was a bewildering array of differing, sometimes conflicting, organisations and theologies. For example there were the Calvinistic evangelicals and the Wesleyans. Both believed humans were sinners and needed to be born again of the spirit and devote themselves totally to the service of God. But the Calvinists stressed the doctrine of salvation by grace—humans were always frail, always in great danger of sinning and no matter what they did, whether it be good or evil, salvation could only come from God's will. The Wesleyans believed people's own actions counted for more—good works increased the chances that God would bless them with salvation. However some churchmen (especially Anglicans) also considered themselves evangelicals, just as some dissenting evangelicals supported certain features of the established church. Thus, several early missionary societies emanated from England—the London Missionary Society (mainly Calvinistic), the Church Missionary Society (evangelicals within the Church of England), and the Wesleyan Methodist Missionary Society. As well, from North America came the Presbyterians sent by the Church of Nova Scotia, and the evangelicals under the auspices of the American Board of Commissioners for Foreign Missions.

The doctrinal and even organisational differences between these various missionary interests were in practice sometimes far from clear cut. For example, the Anglican Samuel Marsden was a director of the London Missionary Society, helped to establish the Church Missionary Society in the South Seas, and assisted the Wesleyan missionaries to go to New Zealand.[5] A typical Church Missionary Society missionary was often socially and doctrinally indistinguishable from his London Missionary Society counterpart. Though sometimes there were detectable differences in geographic location and social background between British Wesleyans and Calvinists.[6] Overall, the various missionary organisations drew essential support from the same broad social groups—the lower-middle and upper-working classes. The evangelical revival was thus inextricably bound up with the social ethics of these people. There was an obsession with industrious living, 'respectability', a rigid and narrow moral code, and personal social and economic advancement. There was a pervasive, sometimes almost desperate aspiration to the 'middle station of life'.[7] Worth was equated with usefulness. It was very much a utilitarian outlook. Mechanic skills, especially, epitomized the honesty and decency of work and consequent economic rewards (which should not be too lavish). Such economic worth and progress went hand in hand with moral and spiritual improvement; the two were indistinguishable.

The belief was widespread amongst evangelicals (and many others) that they belonged to the greatest nation on earth. Both the English and Americans (and other European nationalities too) developed an ethnocentric world view whereby the 'white race, western civilisation, and Christianity occupied the top rungs of the racial, cultural and religious ladders of mankind'.[8] In considering other cultures, the evangelicals transformed the perceived technological gap into a social and moral distance. They assumed that their own technological 'superiority' implied moral and social superiority, whereas the further some other community was from industrial and mercantile prosperity, the less moral it must be, the less civilised, the more savage. According to the evangelicals, a country like Britain or America was materially great because it was Christian, or more specifically Protestant, such greatness being the result of hard work, Christian virtue, and divine favour. Protestantism was seen as both the cause and the justification of national vigour and temporal progress. Civilisation and Christianity were inseparably linked, being in turn the cause and consequence of each other. A people could not be properly civilised unless they were Christian, and they could not be properly Christian unless they were civilised.

> *True civilization and Christianity are inseparable, the former has never been found but as a fruit of the latter.*
>
> *In proportion as individuals receiving Christianity yield themselves to its influence, just as in that proportion they must be civilized. No man can become a Christian, in the true sense of the term, however savage he may have been before, without becoming a civilized man.*[9]

To be civilised and Christian was both a blessing and an obligation. British evangelicals spoke of their country as the new Israel, and they, like the Jews of old, were members of God's chosen race. Their task was to go out into the world and confer their alleged benefits upon the savage and the ignorant and thus usher in God's kingdom.

Ignoble savages

These evangelical beliefs coincided with and were to some extent stimulated by the discoveries of the late eighteenth century explorers. In the Pacific Ocean were innumerable islands peopled by strange new 'races'. To the evangelicals these Islanders were utterly depraved, being completely

ignorant of Holy Scripture, and still living in what was considered a most
primitive stone age. They were very far removed from Christianity and
civilisation and, by definition, had to be economically, socially, morally,
and spiritually bankrupt. As Samuel Marsden noted about Maoris:

> *The New Zealanders are a Nation who have derived no advantages hitherto either*
> *from Commerce or the Arts of Civilization; and therefore must be in a State of*
> *Heathen Darkness and Ignorance in which every nation must unavoidably be, who*
> *has no connection with the Civil Religious and Commercial part of Mankind.*[10]

This view contrasted with the popular notion of Islanders as Noble
Savages. Instead of island societies being seen as remnants of some former
golden age, as innocents living a life of primeval harmony, they were
depicted as degraded and brutish. For evangelicals, the idea of a noble
savage was a contradiction in terms—the savage could never be noble. But
evangelical revulsion was based on more than such ideological argument.
There was an overwhelming aversion to the Islanders' manners and customs as described by the explorers and those who popularised their reports.
Where some European philosophers were enraptured by the image of free-
loving Islanders, the evangelicals were horrified. The Islanders' real or
alleged sexual habits, cannibalism, infanticide, and human sacrifice were
the absolute antithesis of the 'respectability' that was so central to evangelical aspirations. Hence the evangelicals saw nothing but war between their
culture and that of the South Sea's inhabitants, a battle between absolute
good and absolute evil, 'betwixt CHRIST and BELIAL'.[11] Thomas
Haweis, one of the founders of the London Missionary Society, preached
the first sermon to it in 1795:

> *A new world hath lately opened to our view, call it Island or Continent, that*
> *exceeds Europe in size: New Holland; and now become the receptacles of our*
> *outcasts of society.— New Zealand, and the innumerable islands, which spot the*
> *bosom of the Pacific Ocean, on each side of the Line, from Endeavour Straits to the*
> *Coasts of America, many of them full of inhabitants,—occupying lands, which*
> *seem to realize the fabled Gardens of the Hesperides,—where the fragrant groves,*
> *which cover them from the sultry beams of day, afford them food, and clothing;*
> *whilst the sea offers continual plenty of its inexhaustible stores; and the day passes*
> *in ease and affluence, and the night in music and dancing. But amidst these*
> *enchanting scenes, savage nature still feasts on the flesh of its prisoners—appeases*
> *its Gods with human sacrifices—whole societies of men and women live promiscu-*
> *ously, and murder every infant born amongst them.*[12]

Yet in spite of such depravity, or rather because of it, the evangelicals felt
doubly committed to transform such horrific ways of living. As Christians
they felt a duty to save the souls that all people, even the most wicked,
possessed; and as British 'Israelites' they were obliged to impose upon
benighted savages the ways of the blessed English. 'We have but to do our

duty—to Christianize and educate—to show by our conversation and example the value of our religion and our laws'.[13] Hugh Thomas wrote of the Fijians in 1818:

> *They are in one word the very* dregs of Mankind *or Human Nature, dead and buried under the primevial curse, and nothing of them alive but the* Brutal part, *yea far worse than the Brute-Savage quite unfit to live but far more unfit to die, and yet they are the Sons and Daughters of Adam, and destined to live forever.*[14]

Civilisation and Christianity

How were such depraved people to be spiritually saved and materially civilised? For many years it was a matter for argument whether civilisation should precede Christianity, be introduced with it, or follow it. One opinion was that civilisation, or in practical terms the mechanic arts, had first to be introduced to bring the Islanders' technology and social habits to the point where they could more properly understand Scripture. An alternative view was that simply preaching the doctrine of Atonement would in itself bring about a transformation from savagery to civilisation.

It has been fashionable to see the first London Missionary Society missionaries as experimenters with the civilisation-before-Christianity strategy mainly because four of the original thirty were ordained ministers and the rest were 'Godly mechanics'—carpenters, shoemakers, drapers, tailors. Yet as Niel Gunson has remarked, 'these men were sent to preach the gospel before all else'.[15] Indeed it was the failure of their mission that convinced people like Samuel Marsden to place more emphasis on the civilisation aspect, as he did with his Church Missionary Society mission to New Zealand. And the London Missionary Society itself also for a time placed more emphasis on material works. But by the 1830s, experience had blurred the theoretical niceties as to whether civilisation was or was not a necessary prerequisite. The more common opinion then was that Christianity and civilisation should proceed hand in hand.[16] At the practical level, most evangelical missionaries came to see civilisation not as a prior requirement, but certainly as an essential ingredient in the teaching of religion. Thus did the evangelicals teach a social doctrine as well as the doctrine of the cross—or as Gunson has called it 'the social doctrine of the Cross'.[17] Evangelicals believed that there was one correct set of values and way of life which all societies, given certain conditions and opportunities, would embrace eagerly. They were unable to distinguish between the essential features of their theological beliefs and the values of their lower-middle-class backgrounds. They had 'an extraordinary faith in the power of the Evangelical gospel to affect men's minds so that they would promptly assume the social system of northern Europe'. As was observed at the time: 'Religion is strictly and essentially a civilizing process'.[18]

Attempts to civilise Pacific Islanders were based on far more than a wish to improve their technological skills and economic fortunes. Such things were a means to an end, rather than an end in themselves. Because the morally edifying and spiritually elevating power of civilisation was so important, it was necessary to try to impose the Protestant work ethic. Admirers of the Noble Savage ideal praised the fact that Tahitians appeared to have little need of work and were unburdened by the conventions of compulsive activity and guilt that plagued Europeans. But the evangelicals were horrified that anyone should not be working, worshipping, or in other ways 'usefully' employing their time.

> *We must find out the best means of employing them; we must give them something to do; we must devise what will best suit them as staple articles of production;* we must multiply their artificial wants; *by education we must elevate their minds; by the arts we must refine their manners, and multiply their comforts; by stimulating their industry, we must keep them from indolence, and mischief, and vice.*[19]

In general terms, the evangelicals saw salvation as involving 'God's service in perfect obedience to His Will, and of this industrial and commercial concerns are part'.[20] As well as spiritual transformation, the missionaries hoped for social revolution. Pacific Islanders were supposed to become brown-skinned middle-class Europeans.[21]

Evangelical missionaries

Most of the early evangelical missionaries conformed to a fairly uniform and almost predictable pattern of experience (at least before they left their homelands).[22] A typical missionary was quite young, often in his early twenties, and came from the 'lower middle and mechanic' classes. Often he was a carpenter or had similar mechanic skills. Usually he came from the city, though a larger proportion of Wesleyans came from the country. From his earliest days he was brought up in an atmosphere of strict piety, with Godliness, cleanliness, hard work, respectability, and aspirations to middle-class economic status as the predominant values. In his teens he was usually involved in church activities, such as teaching Sunday school and doing charitable work. Somewhere in his late teens or early twenties (or later) he experienced a Calvinistic conversion, a common enough phenomenon amongst people of his background. This conversion involved two stages. First came a sudden realisation of his sinfulness and utter degradation before God. No matter what good works he may have been doing, he was still a sinner. Man after all had fallen; the flesh was always weak. The young man was now 'awakening to the perils of the unregenerate soul'. This was a stage where he made much of his sins—which probably never

8   *An evangelical perception—'A village in Pukapuka [Cook Islands], under
    heathenism. . . . The same village, under Christianity'. (Gill* Life in the Southern
    Isles*)*

amounted to very much—but it was necessary to highlight sinning because only by being sinful could one experience salvation. This led to the second stage: being 'born again in the spirit'. By committing oneself totally to God one could achieve salvation through his grace.

Such a process of conversion occurred commonly enough and was probably unconsciously self-induced. In many cases all sorts of subtle and not so subtle social or family pressures could lead to such an outcome. For some young men, the experience was profoundly traumatic, for others less so, but it was always an emotionally intense event. The consequences were invariably significant for the individual, in that his outlook on life changed markedly, and for most it was a change for life.

The decision by the young convert to become a missionary required a second conversion, usually far less psychologically demanding, though nonetheless another major personal turning point. Having experienced a personal spiritual rebirth, he felt that God now called upon him to save others. But as Gunson says, 'It was not simply love of the "perishing heathen" which led men to the South Seas. It was love of God, the glorification of God'.[23] Often this second conversion was triggered off by sermons and addresses, especially from missionaries who had already been in the field. In part too, the aspiring missionary was consciously or unconsciously motivated by a desire to save his own soul and improve his social and even economic standing. The missionary vocation could be synonymous with bourgeois aspirations. The young man then approached a missionary society, where his religious enthusiasm and piety and general suitability for missionary work were assessed. If accepted, he usually, though not invariably, spent some time in one of the several missionary training institutions, where emphasis tended to be on theological instruction. More than three-quarters of evangelical missionaries were ordained pastors before they sailed, or received ordination while in the field. The earlier missionaries left for the South Seas with little or no idea of what to expect. Even in later years, after the experiences of these men were widely publicised, the intending missionary still left for the other side of the world with supreme confidence, but quite unprepared for what lay in store for him. In that ignorant confidence lay one of his greatest strengths. The budding missionary believed that he was one of God's chosen people, and that he went out as an agent of the Holy Spirit, an instrument in a divine plan. Great emphasis was placed on Isaiah's prediction (11:2):

> *And it shall come to pass in that day,* that *the Lord shall set his hand again the second time to recover the remnant of his people, which shall be left, from Assyria, and from Egypt . . . and from the islands of the sea.*

With such a divinely ordained mission, they were supremely confident. They could not fail to convert the 'heathen' Islanders. Not only were the missionaries, in their own estimation, members of a superior race possessing a superior culture, but they saw themselves as part of a holy global strategy, backed by God's assurance of its inevitable success.

Early missionaries in the islands

The London Missionary Society (LMS) was the vanguard of evangelical penetration of the South Seas. It was formed in 1795 and one year later sent the vessel *Duff* into the Pacific Ocean. On board were thirty missionaries. In keeping with early LMS policy, religious zeal and practical knowledge were seen as essential missionary qualities. Four were ordained, the rest were mechanics. Only five were married. Tahiti was chosen as their main base since more was known about that island than anywhere else. Some of the Society's founders, like Thomas Haweis and Samuel Greathead, avidly read the works of Wallis, Cook, and others, and they interviewed Bligh and other travellers returned from the islands. Although its inhabitants were totally debased, Tahiti seemed to offer several advantages. Haweis claimed that since the Tahitians were 'not harassed by labour for daily bread, or as slaves' they would have 'abundant time for instruction. Every man sitting under his cocoa or breadfruit tree is at hand, and the very sound of a hammer, a saw, or a smith's bellows will hardly ever fail to attract an audience.' Haweis also believed that the Tahitian 'government' seemed 'monarchial but of the mildest nature' and that missionaries would have 'more to apprehend from being caressed and exalted than from being insulted and oppressed.' Strangely enough he even concluded that Tahitians had 'no religious prejudices' and that their language could easily be learnt.[24] Furthermore, the climate was excellent and food readily available. Although Haweis and others had nothing but contempt for the idea that Tahitians were Noble Savages, he and others of his ilk were clearly susceptible to some of the island's much-publicised attractions.

After a 22 000-kilometre voyage via the Cape of Good Hope and out of sight of land all the way, the *Duff* anchored in Tahiti's Matavai Bay in March 1797. Eighteen missionaries set up camp on the beach, and the *Duff* sailed on for Tonga where another ten were landed on Tongatapu. The final two were put down at Tahuata in the Marquesas. The brave hopes of most of these men soon turned to despair. John Harris spent a most memorable first night on Tahuata:

> *The chief . . . desirous of obliging him, not considering any favour too great, left him his wife, to be treated as if she were his own, till the chief came back again. Mr Harris told him that he did not want the woman; however, she looked up to him as her husband, and finding herself treated with total neglect, became doubtful of his sex; and acquainted some of the other females with her suspicion, who accordingly came in the night, where he slept, and satisfied themselves concerning that point, but not in such a peaceable way but that they awoke him. Discovering so many*

strangers, he was greatly terrified; and perceiving what they had been doing, was determined to leave …[25]

The woman ran off with his clothes and Harris spent the rest of the night huddled on top of his chest of goods. At daybreak he fled back to the *Duff* at anchor 'in a most pitiable plight, and like one out of his senses.'[26] His companion, William Crook, decided to stay on the island and lasted a year there before isolation and the harsh realities of life amongst the inhabitants got the better of him. He caught a passing whaler to Sydney.

The mission on Tongatapu was equally abortive. The missionaries were plagued by several vagabond beachcombers. One missionary, George Vason, 'went native'. More seriously, civil war erupted on Tongatapu and three missionaries were killed. The remainder were in a hopeless position, surrounded by 'the most savage barbarity',[27] poverty stricken, short of food and clothing, and completely at the mercy of the Tongans who were not the least interested in what the missionaries had to say. Early in 1800, the dejected band gratefully took passage on a vessel bound for Sydney.

The mission on Tahiti fared little better. John Cock quickly succumbed to carnal delights. The Tahitians treated the missionaries kindly enough but, like the Tongans, seemed totally unmoved by missionary preaching. Twelve months after the missionaries had arrived, the trading vessel *Nautilus* put in for supplies, and they persuaded the captain not to sell firearms to the Tahitians. When the Islanders found out they stripped the missionaries naked. Eleven of them sailed with the *Nautilus*. Shortly afterward, two more missionaries, Thomas Lewis and Benjamin Broomhill, went off to live with Tahitian women. By 1800, only five of the original eighteen remained as missionaries on the island.

For the next fifteen years, a small band of missionaries tolerated the rigours of life on Tahiti. Fortunately they chose to support chief Pomare II who, after a series of military defeats, eventually gained paramountcy over the whole island. From then on the mission flourished and by 1820 most Tahitians were nominally 'converted' to Christianity. Missionaries moved onto neighbouring islands and by the early 1820s were established throughout the Society group.

Meanwhile, other mission societies had entered the Pacific. Marsden's Church Missionary Society (CMS) mission was established at the Bay of Islands in New Zealand in 1814. The Wesleyan Missionary Society (WMS), with Marsden's assistance, also began operating in New Zealand in 1819. Both the LMS and the WMS then headed for the central Pacific islands— the WMS with its European missionaries and the LMS experimenting with its 'native teachers'. Just as traders depended upon the cooperation and labour of Islanders, so too did the spread of missionary influence depend very considerably on the assistance they could gain from their Island supporters. The idea of sending 'native teachers' as pioneers to new islands

9   *Renegade missionary—the Rev. George Vason turns Tongan warrior.*
(Orange Life of the late George Vason*)*

had several advantages. A Tahitian going to Rarotonga, for example, would live as the Rarotongans did and eat the same food. He would not require the impressive houses and the usual paraphernalia associated with European missionary stations. He would be familiar enough with the language (at least throughout eastern Polynesia) and would, in practice, explain certain Christian ideas (or his interpretation of them) in terms that other Islanders could comprehend. In short, there would be none of the obvious cultural barriers that existed between European missionaries and their potential converts. The use of these teachers had other advantages too. They were much more numerous than European missionaries, hence mission resources could be expanded quickly and cheaply, and they were also much more expendable in the eyes of the LMS. In spite of these potential advantages, the LMS (and later other mission societies) became aware of the scheme's weaknesses. Many teachers had only the most rudimentary knowledge of Christianity and the overall nature of their task as conceived by their European overlords. Many teachers slipped a little too easily into some of the 'unchristian' manners of those they were supposed to be reforming. Yet they were never meant to be more than shock troops. They were supposed to begin introducing new ways and to start breaking down existing beliefs. Then it was the task of European missionaries to enter, take over, and complete the job of civilising and Christianising the Islanders. For all the practical difficulties the scheme encountered, it was successful enough, though usually only in Polynesia.

The LMS first sent teachers from Tahiti and other parts of the Society Islands to the Tuamotus, Australs, Marquesas, Cooks, and Tonga in the 1820s. In 1830 they landed in Samoa and Fiji. Permanent European missionaries from both the LMS and the WMS followed them quickly (except in the Marquesas, Tuamotus, and Australs). There was some conflict between the LMS and the WMS over jurisdictions. The Wesleyans eventually stayed in Tonga and Fiji and Rotuma—building on the work of the LMS teachers—while the LMS became predominant in Samoa, the Cooks, and the Society Islands. By the 1840s, LMS missionaries and their 'native teachers' were moving into southern Melanesia—the New Hebrides and New Caledonia. Presbyterian missionaries from Nova Scotia and Anglican missionaries from Bishop Selwyn's Melanesian Mission soon followed. In 1820, the American Board of Commissioners for Foreign Missions (ABCFM) landed in Hawaii missionaries who were assisted by the LMS missionary William Ellis and his Tahitian teachers. In the 1850s the ABCFM turned its attention to Micronesia. A local Hawaiian missionary society also sent Hawaiian missionaries to the Marquesas in 1853.

The bickering between WMS and LMS missionaries, and between LMS missionaries and the Melanesian Mission, was nothing compared to the outright hatred between Protestant and Catholic missionaries. Not only were there major doctrinal divisions, but national ones as well. Protestant missionaries were in the main English and American; Catholic missionaries were mainly French. Such religious and national conflicts were perfectly tailored to many of the Pacific Islanders' own political struggles. An all-too-familiar theme in many islands was rival chiefs supporting rival faiths. Overall, however, Catholic missionaries tended to arrive later than most Protestant missionaries (at least in Polynesia) and consequently their converts tended to be numerically fewer and their geographic areas of influence smaller. Their influence on islands already settled by Protestant missionaries was usually limited to those Islanders disenchanted with the existing (Protestant) sociopolitical order.

The Picpus Fathers arrived in Hawaii in 1827, Mangareva in 1834, and Tahiti in 1841. From there they established outposts in the Tuamotus and the Marquesas. The Société de Marie (Marist) missionaries chose to start in 1837 with two small yet strategically placed islands that the Protestants had not yet reached—Wallis and Futuna. The following year they opened a mission in New Zealand.

By the 1840s and 1850s, most of the inhabitants of Polynesia were considered Christians, and the mission frontiers had shifted to Melanesia and Micronesia. Protestant evangelicals could claim with some justification that the 'conversion' of Polynesia was a remarkable achievement given their rather shaky beginnings. Virtually everywhere a traveller might go in Polynesia there were huge churches and mission stations. The Islanders seemed devout enough, being clothed, able to read and write, fastidiously observing the Sabbath, and generally obeying all the requirements of Christian lifestyles. Yet such apparently extensive social and religious changes were not simply imposed by missionaries. Rather, they resulted from a much more complex process involving the interaction of Islanders, missionaries, and commercial concerns. The nexus for these various protagonists was the issue of control of island affairs.

Conquering kings

Feathered helmet, Hawaii

7

Pomares of Tahiti

Three island kingdoms emerged in the early nineteenth century. Their monarchs were men who exploited customary status and authority structures within their own societies and the presence, techniques, and ideas of Europeans. Ambitious chiefs and Westerners both had vested interests in the aggrandisement and centralisation of political power. Chiefs sought status, power, and wealth, missionaries desired dutiful Christian populations obeying law and order, and traders wanted security, a reliable supply of produce, and labour, all of which could come from an entrenched monarchical government. Some or all of these aims found expression in the kingdoms that were formed in Tahiti, Hawaii, and Tonga.

Background to Tahitian politics

At the time of first European contact, Tahitian society was among the most stratified of any in Oceania. There were three main social divisions, the *ari'i* (chiefs), *ra'atira* (lesser chiefs or landed gentry), and *manahune* (commoners). These divisions were by no means as clear cut as their European translations and connotations might suggest. Within each broad division were complex and subtle categories. The *ari'i* were roughly divided into *ari'i nui* (or *ari'i rahi*), the great chiefs, as opposed to the chiefs of lesser rank called *ari'i ri'i*, though the situation was in practice much more complicated depending on whether any of the various *ari'i* also had kin titles or other status attributes. In general, the *ari'i nui* usually ruled over the more powerful and prestigious localised kin groups, and over tribal groups encompassing large numbers of people over a broad area. Of particular significance was the position of the *ari'i* as intermediaries between the people and the gods—they were religious as well as secular rulers. Rather less is known about the *ra'atira*, beyond the fact that they were the 'landowners' and provided valuable economic and administrative assistance to their *ari'i*. Within the *ra'atira*, ranks ranged widely, from what missionaries called the 'gentry' through to the 'middle-classes' and even

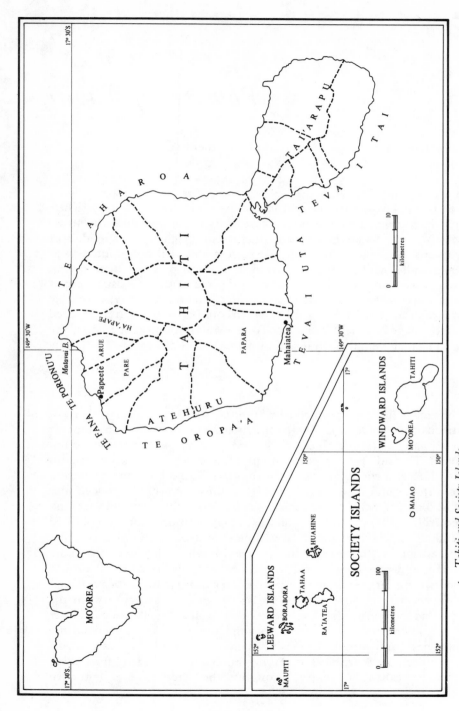

4   *Tahiti and Society Islands*
(*Tribal boundaries based on CW Newbury's map in Davies* The History of the Tahitian Mission)

lower to the (blurred) social boundaries with the *manahune* who formed the bulk of the population. The *manahune* were in turn ranked, from the more respected commoners down to the servants, war captives, and sacrificial victims.[1]

In the 1770s the island of Tahiti was divided into six or seven tribal coalitions, forged by conquest, marriage alliances, and diplomacy.[2] There was a shifting balance of power amongst them with no one *ari'i nui* able to dominate too many others. If one did become too ambitious in Tahitian territorial politics, the combined strength of other leading *ari'i nui* would be used against him. Such a political equilibrium seems to have been fairly long lived. There is no evidence that pre-European Tahiti ever paid homage to a single ruler, at least in remembered genealogical time. The number of tribal coalitions probably varied between three and eight in the seventeenth and eighteenth centuries. From 1815, however, the island was ruled by one man, Pomare II, 'King' of Tahiti. Explanations for this political revolution are varied. One view is that Tahitian society was 'immutably multitribal' and the emergence of a single overlord came about only because of European contact.[3] A contrary argument is that the hierarchical and status-conscious nature of Tahitian society eventually would have produced some form of political centralisation without European presence.[4] Both views are probably overstated. The Pomare family's rise to political paramountcy can be explained in terms of both indigenous and exotic influences. European presence and actions could never have given Pomare II kingship had he not possessed the necessary rank-status in Tahitian terms, yet this rank-status in itself could not have enabled him to establish a centralised government—that needed European assistance at certain crucial times and in particular ways.

The emergence of the Pomares

Eighteenth century Tahitian politics were more dynamic than the first European visitors imagined. European influences followed significant developments already underway. Ironically, events on neighbouring islands had considerable effect on the course of Tahitian politics, and Tahitian history may well have to be reinterpreted in the light of further research, especially on the Leeward Islands.

The island of Ra'iatea, one of the Leeward Islands 160 kilometres to the northwest of Tahiti, had long been of special political and spiritual significance to the Society Islands as a whole, a mecca of Eastern Polynesia.[5] There, in the seventeenth century, the cult of Oro emerged as a powerful force. Oro was a deity who rapidly became one of the most powerful in the pantheon of gods in Society Islands cosmology. Oro was sexually aggressive, supreme in war, and a devastating tyrant to those who refused to believe in him. The development of the Oro cult, with its rituals and demands, was probably a political strategy of those chiefs who saw it as a way of increasing and legitimising their authority. The cult has long fascinated European ethnographic imaginations, mainly because of its special sect, the *Arioi*, who were members of a privileged group devoted to the worship of Oro. The *Arioi* were usually young, virile men and women noted for their overt sexuality and their killing of certain of their offspring, both to limit the cult's numbers and as a sacrifice to Oro. Their main task was to travel about in groups providing ceremonies and various entertainments such as plays and satires all within the context of Oro worship. The cult employed powerful symbols and sacred regalia, in particular images of Oro himself and a number of feather girdles known as *maro*. The possession of these artefacts conferred great prestige, and they were vigorously sought by those who claimed the highest rank-status titles. Early in the eighteenth century, the Oro cult (and the *Arioi*) arrived in Tahiti, whereupon tribal groups fought amongst themselves either to adopt or oppose it. By the later eighteenth century, Oro was dominant throughout the island and on offshore Mo'orea.[6] Tribal fighting at the time of first European contact was probably one of the long-lasting legacies of Oro's arrival, though by this time conflicts were less to oppose his presence and more to gain access to and monopoly of his alleged powers, particularly by capturing as many of the most significant *maro* as possible and depositing them in tribal *marae*.

At the same time as the Oro cult spread through Tahiti and Mo'orea, several marriages were contracted between chiefly families on Tahiti, Mo'orea, and Ra'iatea and were consecrated under Oro. From these marriage links, and others with the Tuamotus, came the Pomare family. Pomare I (or Tu as he was known) was born about the middle of the eighteenth century and his son, Pomare II, was born in the early 1780s, by which time the family was one of the highest ranked on the island. Pomare I, with his close links to Ra'iatean royalty and the Oro cult and his high-born status, had great prestige in the northwest of the island, especially in the district of Pare-Arue, tribal homeland of the Te Porionu'u.[7] The story of the Pomares' rise to political prominence over all Tahiti is essentially a story of how they turned their high status into effective power. Both Pomare I and Pomare II were quick to see the possibilities of exploiting Europeans and European influences to that end. They had excellent opportunities to do so since part of their territory encompassed Matavai Bay—one of the few safe deep-water anchorages and hence the place most visited by Europeans.

Explorers and politics

European explorers had at best only the most superficial understanding of the intricacies of Tahitian politics. Moreover their readiness to interpret the

10   *Tu or Pomare I.*
      (Painting by John Webber, on Cook's third voyage. Alexander Turnbull Library)

hierarchical nature of Tahitian society in European terms could be most misleading. A common assumption was that the island had, or should have had, a supreme ruler. There are many references in explorers' accounts to kings and queens, with the rest of the population variously graded along feudal lines featuring nobles, serfs, and the like.

When Wallis arrived in Matavai Bay in 1767 he thought that the island was governed by 'Queen' Purea, a woman of imposing stature who seemed to command utmost respect from her subjects. Some of the *Dolphin*'s officers visited her 'palace' where they described the grovelling servility that surrounded her and the way in which she was hand fed by selected maidens.[8] Purea also dined on board the *Dolphin*. Wallis took the reputation of her sovereignty back to Europe, but he was quite mistaken. She certainly had respect in the Matavai Bay region because of high family ties there, and she was married to Amo, tribal chief of Papara in the Teva-i-uta tribal coalition, who also had kin ties in the Matavai area. Purea therefore had influence amongst Te Fana, Te Porionu'u, and Teva-i-uta but was by no means a queen of the island. Shortly after Wallis's visit, Purea met her downfall. In order to advance her son's political prospects she imposed a *rahui* (food taboo) in his favour and ordered the construction of a huge *marae* for him at Mahaiatea in Papara. This was to be the final repository of one of the three main Oro images (the *to'o*) then located in Atehuru, the neighbouring rival district. Tutaha, chief of Atehuru, immediately organised an army and in December 1768 defeated Purea's forces. She and Amo fled inland and later took refuge with her family in Ha'apape, adjacent to Matavai Bay. There Cook and Banks saw her in 1769: 'She appeared to be about 40, tall and very lusty, her skin white and her eyes full of meaning, she might have been hansome when young but now few or no traces of it were left.'[9] Cook remarked that she no longer had 'authority over the rest of the Inhabitants whatever she might have had when the *Dolphin* was here'.[10] Banks stumbled upon the battleground in Papara where he found the 'numberless human bones cheifly ribbs and vertebræ' of her fallen warriors.[11] The victor in this war, Tutaha, was described by Banks as a 'hercules', and as 'a great king'. Cook referred to him as 'the Chief man of the Island'.[12] Little can be gleaned from these explorers' journals about the young Pomare I. Wallis never heard of him. Cook and Banks did hear that there was a 'sovereign' called 'Otou' (Tu),[13] Tutaha's great nephew, but they never saw him. By Cook's next visit in 1773, the situation had altered. Tutaha had fought against chief Vehiatua of the Teva-i-tai. Just before Cook arrived, however, Tutaha was killed in battle, and Vehiatua died. Pomare I now assumed the mantle of Tutaha. With his family connections, combined with his political fortunes since the rout of Papara, he now had a rank-status higher than anyone else in Tahiti and Mo'orea,[14] and significantly he made much use of Oro symbolism. Yet his actual control as opposed to his status was still limited, mainly to the northwestern section of the island. This discrepancy between his status and his actual power lasted throughout his lifetime.

Just as Wallis saw Purea as queen in 1767, and Cook and Banks saw Tutaha as king in 1768, so did Cook in 1773 see Pomare as another king, though not, it seemed to Cook a particularly brave one: 'all his actions shew'd him to be a timerous Prince'.[15] Nor, in Cook's opinion, did Pomare's style befit a monarch: 'he seems to avoide all unnecessary pomp and shew and even to demean himself, more than any other of the Earee's' (*ari'i*).[16] When Cook called at Tahiti for a third time, in 1774, Pomare and his allies were attacking Mahine, the paramount chief of Mo'orea. Mahine had no children to succeed him and rival factions were endeavouring to secure the chiefship for their own candidates in what became known to Europeans as the Mo'orean wars of succession. Cook was amazed at the size of the navy Pomare and his supporters were preparing to send against Mahine. By Cook's reckoning there were some 330 canoes and almost 8000 men.[17] Pomare justified this campaign to Cook by explaining how Mahine had 'revolted' against him—or as he put it 'his Lawfull Sovereign'.[18] This is the first recorded time that Pomare used such a fiction in the hopes of gaining European sympathies, and it was not to be the last. Cook readily accepted this interpretation since he assumed Pomare *was* king of Tahiti and Mo'orea.

When Cook returned to Tahiti for the last time, in 1777 on his third Pacific voyage, he found that Pomare's wars with Mahine had been largely ineffectual. This time, those at Matavai Bay who were eager to continue the fight (Pomare was not among them) asked Cook directly, as he said, 'for my assistance and all of them wanted to know what part I would take'.[19] Cook diplomatically declined to get involved. Whilst Cook was there, a truce with Mahine was finalised though apparently on terms seen as un-favourable by his more ardent opponents on the mainland. Some of these chiefs turned on Pomare and accused him of being cowardly. Te To'ofa, described as Pomare's 'old Admiral', was, said Cook, 'Irritated to a Degree of Madness, he Abused him [Pomare] Everywhere and was very glad to get any of us to Listen to him He would Curse Ottou for an Hour to gether and Foam At the Mouth with rage'.[20] Cook heard rumours that Te To'ofa and his supporters planned to attack Pomare as soon as Cook sailed away: 'This called upon me to support my friend by threatening to retaliate it upon all who came against him when I returned again to the island'.[21] For the first time Pomare received open support from foreigners. No one dared attack Pomare whilst Cook's vessels lay at anchor, their cannons trained onshore. The Tahitians remembered only too well Wallis's visit and the damage he had caused.

Pomare clearly saw the potential advantages to be gained by cultivating friendship with visitors like Cook. Not only were there obvious economic gains from presents and payments for goods and services (including prosti-tution), but there were political benefits as well. The regal treatment he received from Cook and others doubtless helped to increase his status in the eyes of his followers. Increasingly he came to see how foreigners could be powerful allies in his conflicts with other chiefs. Yet all these actual and potential advantages could also be counterproductive. Chiefs who had no similar access to European goods became jealous, as well as fearful of Pomare's ambition. Even some of his allies became uneasy. Te To'ofa eventually joined forces with his old enemy Mahine and in about 1782 soundly routed Pomare's warriors and ravaged the districts of Pare and Arue.

When Captain Bligh arrived in the *Bounty* in 1788, he found Pomare 'a Man only nominally possessed of power, or otherwise he has not abilities to govern, which may be the case, as the Chiefs revile him upon all occa-sions'.[22] A forlorn Pomare related to Bligh how the 'People of Imeo [Mo'orea] and those of Atta-hooroo under Tettomah [Te To'ofa] now being master of all their property, destroyed every thing they could get hold of, among which were the Cattle, Sheep, Ducks, Geese, Turkeys and Peacocks left by Captain Cook in 1777'.[23] Bligh had no qualms about supporting this dejected 'monarch':

There is a great deal due from England to this Man and his Family; by our connections with him and them we have brought him numberless Enemies. Their elligble situation for our Ships has brought us intimately connected with them, and by this perhaps we have not only sown the seeds of discord but of revolution.[24]

Bligh argued that if Pomare's enemies were to attack him again 'it is the business of any of his Majestys Ships that come here to punish any such attempt'.[25]

Shortly after leaving Tahiti, Bligh found himself at the wrong end of a revolution, cast adrift by the *Bounty* mutineers. Sixteen of them eventually decided to live on Tahiti; the remainder went to Pitcairn. The mutineers were warmly regarded by the Tahitians and were given privileged positions. Thirteen of them settled in the Matavai Bay area, one went to Papara, and two went to live with the powerful chief Vehiatua III in Tai'arapu. One of the latter men—Churchill—was elected to the chiefship when Vehiatua died, but then the other man—Thompson—turned on his colleague and killed him, whereupon the Tahitians killed Thompson. Those Englishmen who stayed at Matavai Bay became closely associated with Pomare. Some took part in his battles, where their firearms and tactics tipped the balance Pomare's way. As one of them said, 'We Now informed the Chiefs that they must alter their mode of Fighting and bring their people under some Command'.[26] Hitihiti, one of Pomare's friends, who had accompanied Cook to Antarctic waters 1773–1774, led a military expedition supplied with arms provided by the *Bounty*'s crew, and rapidly defeated Mahine's successor on Mo'orea. The seventeen-year-long Mo'orean 'war of succession' thus came to an end, and Mo'orea became a residency for Pomare and a place of refuge from any mainland enemies.[27] Then the Te Oropa'a were defeated, again with English support. Such victories meant further titles for Pomare. In particular he transferred one of the most important *maro* and an Oro image from a *marae* belonging to the defeated Te Oropa'a to a *marae* in Pare. The possession of these sacred items further enhanced Pomare's already supreme rank-status, though his temporal power, boosted by the recent military victories, was still potentially fragile since it was based on the vagaries of tribal alliances and the presence of a few Englishmen. The loss of the *Bounty* mutineers when they were taken away by HMS *Pandora* in 1791 was doubtless a severe blow to Pomare. When George Vancouver arrived in HMS *Discovery* a short time later, Pomare begged him for firearms and military assistance. Vancouver had previously visited Tahiti with Cook, and noted that Pomare's former timidity had vanished. Now, remarked Vancouver, his character was 'marked with an evident superiority expressive of the exalted situation he filled'.[28] Pomare was even claiming the Leeward Islands among his domains and

requested that I would have the goodness to conquer the territories on which they meditated a descent, and having so done, to deliver them up to Otoo; *and as an excuse for their subjugation, insisted that it was highly essential to the comfort and happiness of the people at large, that over the whole group of these islands there should be only one sovereign. On satisfying them that the islands in question were out of my route, and that I had no leisure for such an enterprize,* Pommurrey, *in the most earnest manner requested, that on my return to England I would, in his name, solicit His Majesty to order a ship with proper force to be immediately sent out, with directions, that if all those islands were not subjected to his power before her arrival, she was to conquer them for* Otoo; *who, he observed, I well knew would ever be a steady friend to King George and the English. This request was frequently repeated, and he did not fail to urge it in the most pressing manner at our parting.*[29]

The 'Otoo' referred to was Pomare's son who was gradually being invested, according to custom, with his father's titles. Vancouver described him as 'a boy of about nine or ten years of age. He was carried on the shoulders of a man, and was clothed in a piece of English red cloth, with ornaments of pigeon's feathers hanging over his shoulders'.[30]

Pomare was also keen for Vancouver to supply him with 'Ava Britarne'—British kava. He swigged down a whole bottle of brandy, went into 'such violent convulsions, that four strong men were required to hold him down', fell asleep, and awoke an hour later as refreshed 'as if he had retired perfectly sober'.[31]

By the turn of the century, the Pomares' political fortunes seemed favourable enough. They had exploited kin ties and tribal alliances and had accumulated the major symbols of authority which legitimised their claims to the highest rank-status in Tahiti. In large part this had been achieved within a customary Tahitian context, though at several crucial points moral support provided by visiting Englishmen as well as the firearms and tactical support some of them provided boosted the emergence of the Pomare dynasty. But such visits by late eighteenth century explorers were too infrequent to enable the Pomares to turn status into permanent power. There were constant challenges to them by jealous or ambitious chiefs, especially from Atehuru, who were eager to capture items of the Oro regalia. What the Pomares needed, they believed, was regular trade with the outside world and permanent, supportive European presence. The arrival of LMS missionaries and Sydney pork traders promised just such assistance.

Hogs and evangelicals

Pomare I (who died in 1803) and his son, Pomare II, sold their pigs for muskets and ammunition. 'Nothing', wrote one visitor, 'was so acceptable to them as fire-arms for they consider every thing else as useless trifles.'[32] Hence the embarrassing fate that befell the early LMS missionaries who tried to stop the captain of the *Nautilus* from selling guns.[33] The Pomares badgered every ship's master for arms and had messages of appeal sent to the directors of the LMS in London and to Governor King in New South Wales. King received this letter in 1801, probably drafted by missionaries:

> *May it please your Excellency,*
> *Your letter and present I kindly accept. I love King George and his subjects, and will, while I live, be a protector to those who put themselves under my care; but I must tell your excellency, I at this time stand in fear of the commonality, many of them being disaffected towards me, and their disaffection, I fear, is encouraged by some seamen who are on the island; and therefore I wish your excellency to present me with a few fire-arms, whereby my authority may be maintained, and the peace of my kingdom preserved.*[34]

Governor King immediately sent the *Porpoise* under a lieutenant to Matavai Bay. Pomare was regally fêted, given some muskets, and the Tahitians were awed by a display of the vessel's firepower. The lieutenant made it clear that Governor King 'declared himself the Friend of Pomare' which apparently 'intimidated both the Natives and Seamen'. The missionaries believed that the arrival of the *Porpoise* was a 'very providential interference, as the affairs of this country was brought to such a crisis, that a few days, if not hours, would certainly have either dethroned Otoo, or established him in his authority'.[35]

King also inserted a clause in contracts with some private Sydney traders who supplied Tahitian pork to New South Wales to the effect that they were to land only at Matavai Bay and give arms only to the Pomares. Most pork traders did so since they had a vested interest in supporting this family to ensure protection and a regular supply of pigs. On several occasions when the Pomares were in a sticky situation, men from these trading vessels helped them out by fighting so-called rebels. For example in 1802, when there were several trading ships in the bay, some twenty or thirty well-armed sailors 'all accustomed to the use of firearms' went into battle against 'rebels' from Atehuru.[36] As the Pomares became increasingly dependent on European assistance, so did they become more vulnerable whenever there was an absence of shipping. Between 1803 and 1807 only one trading vessel arrived, causing Pomare II (who had finally become leader in his own right after Pomare I died in 1803) great consternation.

The five LMS missionaries who remained after the rest of their brethren fled for Sydney following the *Nautilus* affair, or went native, were totally ineffective in evangelising the Tahitians. Providing they did not antagonise the Pomare family they were safe enough physically in the local communities, though they had to put up with continual pilfering. And they certainly were fearful enough of attacks from Atehuru to convert

> *their dwelling-house ... into a sort of fortress, having procured the guns of the Norfolk, which ... had been wrecked on the shore. With these guns being planted on*

*11   An optimistic rendition of 'missionary house and environs', Matavai Bay, 1797.
(Wilson* A Missionary Voyage to the Southern Pacific Ocean. *Alexander Turnbull
Library)*

*the upper story of the house, and having laid in a large supply of bread-fruit, cocao
nuts, and other necessaries, they were able to withstand a more vigorous siege than
that of the Attahoorians.*[37]

The missionaries' greatest dangers, however, probably came from
within—continued horror at Tahitian lifestyles, combined with an overwhelming frustration at their inability to understand the language sufficiently to get their message across or to find out about tribal politics. But at
least they maintained a presence and their meagre numbers were augmented by a second contingent of missionaries who arrived in 1801. All the
same, the mission remained totally ineffective in its aims. Even when some
missionaries became more familiar with the language the results of their
teachings were scarcely encouraging. For the Tahitians, the missionaries'
opinions were totally irrelevant and generally treated with contempt or

ridicule. A mood of pessimism settled over the alien community. One missionary wrote in 1806:

> *They are peaceably inclined towards us, and the king is kind and generous; but we are sorry to say he has not the least inclination to embrace Christianity; he is very inimical to receive religious instruction, and whenever the subject is introduced either in conversation or writing, he artfully puts it of....*
>
> *The poor natives remain as before: no success has attended our labours, so as to terminate in the conversion of any, and there is no apparent desire after being instructed in the blessed truths of the Gospel; the news of salvation is an idle tale to them, and tho' they are visited as a nation with sore afflictions, they still reject and despise our message.*[38]

Yet the mission made an impact in other respects. From their first days ashore, missionaries associated themselves with the Pomares mainly because they believed they were the island's kings. It soon became apparent that the Pomares had few of the powers kings were supposed to have, and the truth soon dawned that the Pomares were not the leaders of an island nation. The missionaries also found much in the characters of the Pomares to revolt them. Like his father, Pomare II had frequent violent fits of intoxication.[39] Even worse, from the missionaries' point of view, Pomare II associated with *mahu*:

> *They assume the dress, attitude, and manners, of women, and affect all the fantastic oddities and coquetries of the vainest of females ... the encouragement of this abomination is almost solely confined to the chiefs. Otoo himself is a monster of debauchery. Their pollution in this respect beggars all description.*[40]

Nevertheless, missionaries had a vested interest in seeing the Pomares achieve political paramountcy. If a king could be created and the missionaries gain his support, there would be a good chance of exploiting the king's influence over his subjects. For their part, the Pomares recognised that missionaries could be useful allies in their political ambitions. So began a mutual exploitation that lasted for decades. While the Pomares and the Tahitian people ignored missionary preaching, they did not ignore other influences and attributes missionaries possessed. As well as trying to play a religious role, missionaries were unavoidably playing a role as Western agents. Their very presence in Matavai Bay stimulated trade with the outside world. Traders tended to equate mission settlement with 'civilisation'. Furthermore, missionaries acted as interpreters and guides for ships' masters, they 'made Matavai the safest port in the South Pacific, and ships began to call frequently'.[41] Missionaries themselves also supplied the Pomares with various Western goods. One missionary referred to 'the vast acquisition of wealth that he [Pomare I] gained at our first coming, and at different periods since, [which] served to bind him to us'.[42] The missionaries' technical knowledge (remembering that they were skilled trades-

12   Pomare II, about 1819. (Ellis Polynesian Researches, vol 1)

men) clearly impressed Tahitians. As early as 1804, the missionaries had built Pomare II a 50-tonne vessel. They also taught him to read and write a little in English.[43] All this, combined with the overt political support they gave the Pomares, meant that they were far from uninfluential, even if their Christian message did fall on deaf ears.

The Pomares were especially keen for the missionaries to help supply them with firearms and 'engage in war'.[44] The missionaries' response in 1801 was a little less dogmatic than it had been several years earlier when the *Nautilus* was in the bay. This time they were, they said, 'men of peace, and would have nothing to do with war, except in self defence'.[45] This was a significant qualification, for helping to arm the Pomares could be interpreted as assisting in the defence of the mission against 'rebels'. As already mentioned, Pomare's letter to Governor King in 1801 asking for firearms was probably drafted by missionaries and the missionaries were clearly delighted when colonial vessels provided military assistance for the Pomares. Missionaries no longer wished to prohibit the musket trade; rather they welcomed it since it would strengthen the Pomares' rule and contribute to political stability. Thus did self-professed men of peace support war as a means of promoting peace. They did not directly supply arms, nor did they fight themselves, but they tried to ensure that only the

Pomares got firearms from trading vessels, and they supported those Tahitians and Europeans who did battle for the royal family. Writing about the expedition led by twenty to thirty armed sailors against Atehuru in 1802, one missionary observed:

> *The sight of the Europeans overpowered the rebels; their spirit failed them, and they now fled in different directions.*
>
> *This circumstance proved highly advantageous for Pomarre, as God gave into his hands seventeen of the rebels, who were killed on the spot; all fighting men, and among them one of the principal ringleaders of the rebellion. . . . Upon the whole, this short campaign, through the mercy of God, has tended very much to destroy the strength of the prevailing commotion.*[46]

In missionary eyes, the Pomares' victories were blessed by God, and, in the longer term, this point was not unnoticed by Pomare II.

Thus were the missionaries very significant in Tahiti in the early days, but in ways which, only a short time beforehand, they could never have conceived.

Pomare II: fluctuating fortunes

In spite of Pomare II's unparalleled rank-status in Tahitian terms, and in spite of the support of his European allies, his power remained tenuous and limited. This inability to hold sway over the whole island, or indeed even over his own district at times, was explained in various ways by contemporary Europeans: that Pomare was a poor warrior, that he was a drunkard, and that European shipping was not regular enough to supply him with the arms he thought he needed. These opinions were all valid enough, though Pomare's relative political impotence must also be seen in a wider context. Pomare and his missionary allies had not been able to monopolise completely European goods, including firearms, that arrived on the island. The more widespread these became, the less awe Pomare could command. More important, Pomare II pushed harder than his father had to try to establish his temporal or administrative supremacy. Under Pomare II's rule there was renewed emphasis on ceremonies employing the *maro* and Oro images as he attempted to legitimise his aspirations. These ceremonies usually featured human sacrifice on a scale not often seen on the island. He also exacted huge tributes in food and artefacts, tried to redistribute land, and continued to manipulate kin relations in heavy-handed ways. He placed much more emphasis on direct means of influence rather than on the more indirect methods that were customary in local and district affairs. While Tahitians had no qualms about acknowledging his paramount rank-status, which was quite legitimate, they opposed his attempts to turn this into arbitrary power. In short, Pomare II was seen as going beyond the bounds of what, in Tahitian terms, was acceptable. Indeed while Pomare constantly complained about those who 'rebelled' against his authority, it was he who was the revolutionary in trying to impose unprecedented controls over the population by exploiting both Tahitian and outside ways.[47]

Major opposition to Pomare II flared in 1808. The missionaries became so concerned for their safety that most of them shipped out for Huahine, and later New South Wales. Four unmarried missionaries chose to remain with Pomare. When he was defeated in battle and his lands plundered, they fled with him to Mo'orea. Three of the missionaries sailed on to Huahine, but Henry Nott remained with Pomare—an act of loyalty that Pomare never forgot. Pomare's quest for kingship and the LMS mission to Tahiti appeared finally to have foundered, yet by 1815 both Pomare and the LMS missionaries had the Tahitian population firmly under their control.

After Pomare's defeat no single individual on the island had sufficient status to keep tribal coalitions together. Once the common enemy of the moment departed, intertribal discord quickly emerged. The lack of any overall strategy by Pomare's enemies was well attested by several impulsive acts which severely disadvantaged them. The most significant was their sacking of the schooner *Venus* in Matavai Bay soon after Pomare had left for Mo'orea. Not only did this result in retaliation from another English vessel, but it ensured that Sydney traders kept well away from the bay and continued to trade instead with Pomare on Mo'orea. Pomare's enemies thus deprived themselves of their hoped-for commercial advantages. Such were the divisions and rivalries on the island after Pomare's departure that concentrated anti-Pomare policies could not be sustained. Pomare himself was allowed to spend some time back in Pare providing he kept a low profile, and during the period of his so-called exile on Mo'orea he in fact managed to divide his time between that island and Pare.

Pomare's continued friendship with Sydney traders assisted his preparations to reestablish his supremacy in Tahiti. Furthermore, he was able to invoke kin and diplomatic ties with chiefs on the Leeward Islands who sent him several hundred warriors. Most of these were transported to Mo'orea on pork-trading ships.[48] In 1811, Pomare landed on Tahiti with a large force of Leeward Islanders and local supporters. There was no opposition. Shortly afterward LMS missionaries rejoined Pomare and their colleague Nott. Pomare retained Mo'orea as his main base, but made more frequent trips to the mainland.

In 1812 Pomare publicly declared his 'conversion' to Christianity and asked to become a candidate for baptism. Exactly why he did so can never be determined. Perhaps it had to do with his gradual disillusionment with Oro, who had brought him as many defeats as victories. Might the new Christian god alter his political and military fortunes? Perhaps too Pomare's changed stance was a logical consequence of his close association with missionaries over the past decade. Nott's personal loyalty to him must have counted for something. Furthermore, by this time Nott and other missionaries had a much greater understanding of both the language and local politics and became increasingly more useful as advisers. Whether Pomare's motives were purely expedient or otherwise made little difference to the LMS missionaries. This was the breakthrough they had been working for ever since 1797. Pomare's very interest in Christian teachings, together with his declared support for Jehovah and rejection of Oro, gave the missionaries a new aura of respectability. Some of Pomare's close supporters as well as some of the Leeward Islanders began to conform to at least the outward requirements of Christian behaviour. Thus began the first few public repudiations of Oro and the burning of his images.

Pomare's standing on Tahiti was still tenuous. His presence was accepted but his governance had yet to be established. Although he had a potential military superiority this was by no means permanent. There was always the possibility of further tribal coalitions against him. Indeed small-scale fighting intensified as the island was gradually divided among those who still supported Oro and those who supported Jehovah. The latter arrived at Pomare's base on Mo'orea in ever-increasing numbers. Eventually Pomare and his troops once again crossed from Mo'orea to the mainland en masse and in the name of Jehovah, their new war god, defeated their opponents in the battle of Fei Pi, in 1815. European firepower again played a significant part in Pomare's victory.

By all accounts it was not much of a battle yet it marked a turning point in Tahitian history. From a military point of view, Pomare had at least a momentary supremacy, but he had been in this situation several times in the past. What made his win in 1815 different were the changing political circumstances. By now his longstanding diplomatic strategies and status hunting had effectively removed any potential rivals. More important, Pomare had won in the name of Jehovah, and the switch in allegiance from Oro to Jehovah was to have quite unprecedented consequences for political life in Tahiti. Pomare claimed himself 'King of Tahiti' after Fei Pi. Immediately he asked the missionaries 'if two could come over to Tahiti [from Mo'orea] to instruct the people how to proceed in the present new state of things'.[49] Pomare and the missionaries then set about creating a new administrative structure for the rule of a unified Tahiti.

Legitimising the kingdom

Before Pomare's 'revolution', the *ari'i nui* were both spiritual and temporal authorities. They traced their family links back to the ancestor gods. Much of their day-to-day authority, their social control, was maintained by spiritual sanctions, especially the use (and abuse) of the *tapu* system. In short, Tahitian religion provided both legitimacy for its chiefs and sanctions for controlling the population and harnessing its productivity. In this context Pomare I and Pomare II (at least until 1812) tried to establish themselves as the legitimate intermediaries between Oro and the people in the hopes of achieving a temporal supremacy over the island. But Pomare II eventually rejected Oro, and his victory in 1815 was essentially a victory over Oro. After Fei Pi there was, in simple terms, no government and no 'state' religion to support one. There was just Pomare in a position of (probably temporary) military superiority. He was a king without a constituted kingdom. As one missionary shrewdly commented:

> *The intimate connection between the government and their idolatry, occasioned the dissolution of the one, with the abolition of the other; and when the system of pagan worship was subverted, many of their ancient usages perished in its ruins. They remained for some years without any system or form of government, excepting the will of the king, to whom the inhabitants usually furnished liberal supplies of all that was necessary for the maintenance of his household, and the accomplishment of his designs.*[50]

If Pomare were to justify and consolidate his new position he needed some form of divine justification or legitimacy—which could hardly come from a god he had rejected—and some new administrative structure also justified by laws or sanctions of some kind. Pomare's relationship with the LMS missionaries was therefore crucial. He saw that he could gain a new spiritual legitimacy from the Christian god and that he could exploit certain missionary ideas and teachings to provide rules and regulations for government. In the strength of the LMS mission lay the strength of Pomare. The advantages for the missionaries in supporting a constituted Christian king ruling a law-abiding Christian community were likewise most attractive. In the strength of Pomare lay the strength of the mission.

The missionaries at first wanted Pomare to call together 'the chiefs of the several Districts, that he might propose, and in conjunction with them, after consultation and agreement, settle certain laws and regulations, for the general good of the people, and the better ordering of their civil affairs'.[51] Pomare strongly objected since he wanted to organise his administration without being seen to take advice from or defer to any other chief. Besides, he feared such consultation might enable some of his more ambitious rivals to challenge his authority. A compromise between the missionaries and Pomare was finally achieved and in 1819 a simple code of laws for the kingdom was promulgated.[52]

The code began with a statement about the source of Pomare's legitimacy:

> *Whom God has given as king to Tahiti and Mo'orea and to all the surrounding islands.... Safety to all his loyal subjects in the name of the true God.*

Then followed a list of the 'Laws of Tahiti' which were a mixture of Tahitian custom such as the 'Law of Pigs', and evangelical morality, such as the 'Law of observing the Sabbath'. Some of the laws illustrate a compromise between these two views whenever they were incompatible and touched on sensitive matters. The missionaries knew just how far they could go without alienating the population. Such was the case with Law Nine:

> *Of two wives for one man:*
>
>   *It is not right that there be two wives for one man, no more than two men for one woman, which should not agree with the new law to be observed. However, for the man who already has two wives, according to pagan custom, let us leave him; the law will not see any crime in that. But should one of his wives die, and the other remain alive, he should not have two again.*

These laws placed great emphasis on defining wrong-doing, and in more than just a moral sense. Any opposition to Pomare was declared seditious, and the definition of opposition was all-embracing. The 'law of troublemakers' listed 71 offences which ranged from breaking wind to armed rebellion. Some 707 judges were to be appointed. These were 'the second class of chiefs, having above them the great chiefs' in the 23 territorial divisions of Tahiti and Mo'orea. There were to be some 30 courthouses.

   The code was designed to give Pomare a 'constituted' authority to rule in a manner more or less acceptable to the LMS missionaries, and to provide for an obedient, God-fearing, and Pomare-fearing population. In practice, Pomare and his missionary allies were far from satisfied. Pomare was opposed to the notion that he should not be above the law himself; the missionaries were concerned that Pomare's predilection for arbitrary power might not be held in check. In their view, the code was a step in the right direction.

Conversion

The political unification of Tahiti under Pomare II in 1815 coincided with the conversion to Christianity of the majority of the population. By the early 1820s most Tahitians were considered Christian. They had publicly abandoned the practices of their former religion and its material trappings. Missionaries wrote excitedly about Tahitians gathering in their frenzied hundreds to destroy their idols. Having renounced their past ways, the Islanders flocked to church services, sang hymns, and recited catechisms. They did not frolic or work on Sunday. They covered their nakedness with cloth. Thousands went to school and were eager for instruction. Generally they acted, according to missionary accounts, with due decorum and respect.

   The rapidity and extent of this apparent change in a whole population's outlook and behaviour overwhelmed the LMS missionaries. For years they had tried to evangelise the Tahitians with no success at all. Now they were caught quite unawares. Yet the conversion was not a random phenomenon. Pomare's 'new state of things' from 1815 and the Tahitian conversion were closely related. As mentioned earlier, Pomare himself took the initiative when he opted for Christianity in 1812. His interest aroused a spirit of curiosity amongst his closest followers. The missionaries, still on Mo'orea, noted: 'There is a stir among the people many doubt and waver, some examine and enquire.'[53] Defiance of Oro and even desecration of his images sometimes followed, though on a very small scale. But Pomare's victory in the name of Jehovah at Fei Pi in 1815 opened the flood gates. The Tahitian population as a whole became caught up in the excitement of opting for the new religion. Many explanations are possible. Perhaps the Tahitians were tired of endless fighting and were prepared to accept a new leader who had a novel and apparently all-powerful deity.[54] Perhaps too the conversion resulted from years of missionary influence. Some missionaries were now fluent in the Tahitian language and far more knowledgeable about Tahitian society and politics. Certainly they were seen to be amongst the most loyal and useful of Pomare's supporters. According to this argument, missionary opinions and teachings were seen to have more relevance. In this context the role of literacy was very important. Tahitians, like most Pacific Islanders, were fascinated by European books and letters, which were interpreted initially as wondrous objects that could somehow speak. Not only was writing novel, even magical, it could clearly be of great use. Pomare I and Pomare II had been among the first Tahitians to realise this and had managed, with missionary assistance, to write letters in English to the likes of Governor King. But instruction in written English proved far too difficult for most Islanders. Missionaries were on a much firmer footing when they learnt Tahitian, drew up an alphabet, and began to translate Biblical texts into the vernacular, which they taught people to read. The Tahitians' fascination with this process was a prelude to a fascination by all Pacific Islanders, and perhaps one of the missionaries' most significant legacies was to turn island societies from a state of nonliteracy to literacy. Most of this was accomplished by the Islanders teaching each other. On Tahiti and elsewhere, once missionaries had taught a few people how to read and write their language, the movement snowballed. Lamps burned late into every night as Islanders instructed one another. The passion for owning and reading translated and printed Gospels, hymn books, catechisms, or anything with words on it was frenzied. Even before a printing press arrived at the Tahitian mission in 1817, the missionaries had large numbers of books and pamphlets printed overseas:

> *700 of the spelling books printed in London, catechism printed in Sydney 1000, N. Test. history 400 Old ditto 400, hymns 100, spelling books 2000 making in all 4600. These were scattered thro' all the islands.*[55]

13   *The 'conversion' to Christianity—Tahitians destroy their idols.*
(Missionary Sketches, *VI, 1819*)

No sooner had the mission press arrived on Tahiti than 2300 copies of
Tahitian spelling books were run off. Over the years missionaries translated
and printed tens of thousands of religious texts of various kinds.

G S Parsonson has argued that Tahitian interest in literacy and the arrival
of the printing press were largely responsible for the conversion of the
island to Christianity.[56] Literacy and all the excitement it generated was
certainly a major feature of the conversion phenomenon, though it was less
a cause than a symptom of the surge in interest in missionary teachings and
skills at this time. More than this, literacy was also a key to full acceptance
into the church. The LMS requirements for baptism at this stage were
relatively strict and often took two years to complete. Some Tahitians
could obviously parrot answers to endless catechisms, but it was much
easier to learn by reading. In this sense there was some relationship between
the introduction of the press, the attainment of literacy, and church membership in the period 1817–1820.

But it would be going too far to say that literacy and the press were
responsible for the Tahitian acceptance of Christianity. Literacy provided a
means by which Tahitians could, with some excitement, accept elements
of the new religion, but it could not cause them to do so. Their acceptance
of Christianity was ultimately motivated by Pomare's unification of Tahiti
in 1815 in the name of Jehovah, and by his deliberate attempts to use the
missionaries and their teachings to justify and sustain his new authority as

supreme ruler of the island. In the final analysis, the Tahitians' conversion was a political phenomenon—just as was the Christianisation of Spain by Charlemagne, or Ireland by St Patrick. The doctrine of *cuius regio, eius religio* (as the King, so the religion) has universal, not just European application. Whatever attractions Christianity and association with missionary activities might have had for the Tahitian population, the initial decision for most Tahitians to begin to participate was the inspiration, example, perhaps even orders from their new king. Pomare's success at Fei Pi and the mass conversions which followed soon after were intimately related. And once the movement started it gained its own momentum. If at first it was obligatory to attend church, it soon became fashionable and even pleasurable, as well as appearing to offer various advantages.

But the conversion cannot be interpreted in evangelical terms. Most Tahitians did not experience an overwhelming sense of their own sin and become reborn of the spirit as had the missionaries themselves. Tahitians, and other Islanders in these early days of European contact, could not simply embrace the evangelical world view with its obsessions about sin and guilt, its work ethic, its middle-class mores—all products of Western intellectual and socioeconomic environments. The conversion Tahitians exhibited was more outward conformity than inward spiritual rebirth, as the missionaries were only too ready to document. Tahitians who became Christians did not suddenly reject their age-old beliefs, even if they might have abandoned their outward forms. Rather there was a blending of old and new concepts. While missionaries saw nothing but an absolute contrast between the evils of paganism and the blessings of Christian living, Tahitians made no such intellectual or moral distinctions. Indeed, Christian beliefs and rituals, as the Tahitians understood them, were not so very different from their own beliefs and rituals. Both Tahitians and missionaries had deities who wielded supernatural powers; both had rules and regulations based upon these powers; and their respective deities were represented by symbols—Oro had his images, Christ his cross. There was no difference between a *tapu* on some act and Christian prohibitions such as not working on the Sabbath. One set of rituals was not unlike the other. Christian prayers, hymns, blessings all had equivalents in Tahitian religion. Both had sacred places—Tahitians their *marae*, missionaries their churches. Tahitians were certainly converted in the sense that many aspects of their day-to-day living and outward modes of behaviour altered when they adopted Christianity. But this is not the same as the intellectual, emotional, and spiritual conversion experienced by the evangelicals. Just as the conversion of the missionaries themselves must be explained in terms of religious, social, economic, and political currents in eighteenth-century Europe, so must the conversion of Tahitians be explained in terms of religious, social, economic, and political currents in early nineteenth-century Tahiti; and these revolved around Pomare's political centralisation.

Pomare II: toward an empire

Interest in Christianity quickly spread beyond Tahiti. It caught on rapidly in the Leeward Islands, from which many men had been with Pomare since his exile on Mo'orea. The LMS had again augmented the numbers of the Tahitian mission, enabling missionaries to settle on Huahine, Ra'iatea, Borabora and Tahaa by the early 1820s. These missionaries began training Tahitians as teachers and sending them to other islands in the Society Group, the Tuamotus and Australs, and beyond to the Cook Islands and Tonga. The LMS was on the march.

Pomare took advantage of the spread of Christianity in the Leeward Islands because of his long-held ambition (and indeed that of his father) to establish a political hegemony there.[57] While the missionaries were keen to have his support on these islands, they were sceptical about his motives. Considerable rivalry existed between Pomare and the LMS missionaries as to who should have jurisdiction over the native teachers. The missionary Threlkeld believed that Pomare's intention was to 'endeavour to make Christianity subservient to his politics in worldly aggrandisement' and to 'use the ministers of the gospel resident in the Islands as instruments for his purposes'. Threlkeld thought that Pomare's ultimate goal was 'to become the universal monarch of the Islands in the Pacific Ocean and through the profession of faith in the King of kings to make himself a King of kings'.[58] For the most part, the missionaries were able to keep the teachers and the church in the Leeward Islands from falling under Pomare's direct command. Although Pomare's rank-status was widely acknowledged as paramount over the Leeward Islands, in practice chiefs there, with mission support, retained much of their authority. The missionaries organised separate but similar law codes to Pomare's of 1819 for Ra'iatea, Tahaa, and Borabora in 1820 (known as the Tamatoa Code) and for Huahine in 1822. Both the Tamatoa and Huahine codes ostensibly placed the governance of these islands in the hands of their leading chiefs, but Pomare's symbolic supremacy was still paid lip service. In brief, the Leeward codes were an attempt to maintain the existing political organisations. Unlike Tahiti, the adoption of Christianity in the Leeward Islands was not accomplished by political revolution.[59]

Pomare remained undaunted and tried to reestablish his old monopoly over the pork trade. He increased his demands on his Tahitian subjects for tribute by imposing *rahui*.

> *All without exception ... must serve the King, members with broken backs some bent quite double, very many with a scrotum the size of half a gallon to that of a bushel measure, and several with Elephant legs or arms, all are employed in getting pigs for the King or making his oil or building his store houses etc.*[60]

He bought his own vessel, the *Governor Macquarie* skippered by Samuel Henry (son of missionary William Henry), which ranged far out to the

Tuamotus and Australs after pearl shell and sandalwood and any other cargo that could be shipped to New South Wales. Pomare became more and more in debt to Samuel Henry, owing over £6000 at one stage. But he was not after just wealth for its own sake; he saw the island produce he gathered as a form of tribute that justified, in his view at least, his position as monarch over these far-flung islands.

The death of Pomare II

The LMS missionaries on Tahiti continued to give the king every public support, though in private they had serious reservations about his greed and his increasingly arbitrary rule, not to mention his personal appearance and habits. William Ellis described Pomare as

> *tall, and proportionately stout, but not corpulent, his person was commanding, being upwards of six feet high. His head was generally bent forward, and he seldom walked erect. His complexion was not dark, but rather tawny; his countenance often heavy, though his eyes at times beamed with intelligence. . . . his habits of life were indolent, his disposition sluggish, and his first appearance was by no means adapted to produce a favourable impression on a stranger's mind. . . . The habits of intemperance which Pomare was led to indulge . . . threw a stain on his character. . . . He was also reported to be addicted to other and more debasing vices . . .* [61]

Even though Pomare became a candidate for baptism in 1812, the missionaries held out until 1819 before they finally agreed to baptise him, such were their reservations about his morality.

Pomare died in 1821. The missionaries paid their champion handsome tribute in public, but their private assessments varied. Davies claimed that the King's death was to the 'great loss of the Islands in general and the keen regret of the miss, particularly the elder ones, whose steady friend he had been for many years'.[62] Nott, perhaps his closest missionary friend, tactfully left an assessment of his character to 'him who judgeth righteously' and added that all should remember 'with gratitude to God now the King is no more the countenance, protection and favour their mission long enjoyed under his government'.[63]Other missionaries were less charitable. Williams and Threlkeld on Ra'iatea thought that 'not one native in this Island, whose conduct is at all consistent with the Gospel, lamented his loss, but rather consider it interposition of God in removing him, in short his whole aim was to grasp at all the Islands under the pretence of Christianising them'.[64] An even more cynical though not totally inaccurate opinion came later from Orsmond:

> *The King, who was indeed head and tail, root and branch, the Alpha and the Omega, the first and the last, in all religious affairs, to whom the Missionaries paid great obsequiousness and deference, was a beastly sot. . . .*

The King changed his Gods, but he had no other reason but that of consolidating his Government. After his conquest it is true he went by short stages to shew his authority, receive presents from his newly acquired subjects, drink the abundance of native spirits, and then in their inebriety cast down their Marae and destroy their Gods, thus by stratagem taking away from any future rebellion thro the power of the idols which were always leaders in war.[65]

The missionary kingdom

The missionaries 'crowned' Pomare II's infant son Pomare III. Ari'ipaea Vahine (sister of Pomare I) and a chief of Porionu'u acted as regents. Whatever Pomare II's weaknesses as leader, in missionary eyes, those of his heirs were even greater. Davies believed the Vahine brought political affairs to a 'wretched state' and was grateful that other 'principal chiefs' provided some checks to her meddling and bossing.[66] Another cause of concern to missionaries was 'backsliding' amongst sections of the population. As the initial excitement and novelty of Christianity wore off, and its imagined benefits failed to eventuate, there was more open reversion to former habits (which probably had always been practised privately anyway). Church attendance declined. Public drunkenness seemed more common than usual.

The missionaries needed to put the monarchy on a firmer footing and to have a greater say in its running. Ironically, Pomare II's death gave them just such an opportunity. As long as he was alive, many chiefs had kept up an undercurrent of opposition to his rule, or at best had accepted his authority in a grudging and not overly cooperative manner. With Pomare II out of the way, these chiefs were more likely to support a less arrogant and arbitrary and more efficient monarch, especially if they could be incorporated into the administration of the kingdom in a way that would enable them to regain some of the former status that Pomare had denied them. Even the Pomare family had a vested interest in such reform, if only to give the monarchy what it now sorely lacked—a firm financial basis. Because the tributes which Pomare II tried to exact had been too arbitrary and provoked too much opposition, they were not an efficient means of raising sufficient revenue. Some form of regular taxation was needed. The outcome of discussions amongst missionaries, the royal family, and leading chiefs, was the constitution of 1824, drafted mainly by Nott.

This constitution provided for a parliament that consisted of all adult male members of the Pomare family and of the families of principal chiefs of Tahiti and Mo'orea. In addition, these two islands were divided into districts, each one sending two male representatives, elected by male suffrage, for a three-year term in parliament. The parliament was to meet each year and pass laws, which the king could veto. When the parliament first met, Nott was chosen as its 'President' (or Speaker) and new laws were introduced and passed. As in 1819, the laws were a mixture of evangelical-inspired regulations and Tahitian practices, though they were theoretically stricter and more embracing than those of 1819. The system of judges and courts was also revamped. Significantly, the administration was given a firmer financial footing, with provision for fixed revenues not only for the king but for important chiefs and others who helped run the kingdom. In practice, the parliament was far less democratic than it appeared on paper. The royal family and missionaries remained the dominant influence. Nor was the system of government as efficient as was anticipated. Those chiefs who managed to become a part of the system were often just as keen to advance their own interests as was the royal family. The Pomares had no monopoly over greed, and as usual the burden fell on the commoners.

In one sense this constitution marked the high point of the missionary kingdom in Tahiti. For the royal family, it represented the rationalisation of the power they had been accumulating for several generations. The kingdom had become enshrined in a new politico-legal orthodoxy. For the LMS mission on Tahiti, it represented perhaps the height of their influence. In theory at least, Tahiti had a sound central government under a Christian monarch ruling over an outwardly Christian population. Similarly, the constitution symbolised the changes that the missionaries' role had undergone since those first traumatic years when a handful of godly mechanics eked out a cheerless existence at Matavai Bay. Far from being simple tradesmen content to preach the gospel to the heathen, missionaries over the years had had to become deeply involved in the high politics of the island. As well as their purely evangelical role, they had become military strategists, economic advisers, political sages, and legal and constitutional draughtsmen.

Tahitian life

Just as a history of English kings can no longer claim to represent a comprehensive history of England, so interpretations of Tahitian history that concentrate on the emergence and consolidation of the monarchy tell only a small (though significant) part of the story. The great mass of the Tahitian population, while not unaffected by the political centralisation of their island, saw relatively little change in their everyday lives. They may have witnessed a political revolution amongst those at the top of the social pyramid, but there was no social revolution. The leaders had changed, but they still ruled in much the same way. The minority at the top still exploited the masses below. The commoners' obligations remained fundamentally the same—providing food and labour to those whom they owed obe-dience. To be sure, the population dressed differently on occasions, used different tools and utensils, no longer fought battles, and outwardly adopted new customs such as church going and drinking alcohol. And there was more prostitution and new diseases and more opportunities for sailing away. But their existence was still essentially unaltered. As Beechey reported in 1825:

> *Though their external deportment is certainly more guarded than formerly, in consequence of the severe penalties which their new laws attach to a breach of decorum, yet their morals have in reality undergone as little change as their costume.... Their dwellings, with the exception of doors to some and occasionally latches and locks, are precisely what they were when the island was first discovered.... Their occupations are few, and in general only such as are necessary to existence or to the gratification of vanity. In our repeated visits to their huts we found them engaged either in preparing their meals, plaiting straw-bonnets, stringing the smallest kinds of beads to make rings for the fingers or the ears, playing the Jew's harp, or lolling about upon their mats.... The indolence of these people has ever been notorious, and has been a greater bar to the success of the missionaries than their previous faith.... a more lively, good-natured, innoffensive people it is impossible to conceive....*[67]

> *Considering the advances the country had made toward the formation of a government by the election of a parliament, and by the promulgation of laws, we certainly expected to find something in progress to meet approaching events, yet in none of our excursions did we see any manufactures beyond those which were in use when the island was first discovered, but on the contrary, it was evident that they had neglected many which then existed.... nor did there appear to be any desire on the part of the people to improve their condition; but so far from it, we noticed a feeling of composure and indifference which will be the bane of their future prosperity.*[68]

Whether the Tahitians believed themselves to be better or worse off than formerly can never be known. All we have are impressionistic and subjective accounts by various European travellers, and these tell as much about the authors as the Tahitians. On the one hand, anticlerical observers like the Russian navigator Otto von Kotzebue described how

> *by order of the Missionaries, the flute, which once awakened innocent pleasures, is heard no more. No music but that of psalms is suffered in Tahaiti.... Every pleasure is punished as a sin, among a people whom Nature destined to the most cheerful enjoyment.*[69]

Yet other visitors saw a different side of life:

> *The abundance and indiscriminate sale of ardent spirits, as well as the laxity of the laws which permitted the sensuality of a sea-port to be carried to a boundless extent, caused scenes of riot and debauchery to be nightly exhibited at Pápeéte that would have disgraced the most profligate purlieus of London.*[70]

Denouement

From a constitutional point of view, the Tahitian monarchy was at its height in the mid-1820s. Yet in practice it never worked as well as it did in theory. Leadership remained arbitrary and weak and ever prey to the various and often conflicting pressures from the LMS missionaries and district chiefs. The young Pomare III died in 1827 and sovereignty passed to his fourteen-year-old sister Aimata (Queen Pomare IV), noted for her 'wild' and 'disorderly' living. Whatever missionaries might have thought about Pomare II's character, they acknowledged that he had an authority lacking in his successors.

Beneath the superficial veneer of respect for the monarchy and the missionaries was considerable disaffection by the mid-1820s. There was a noticeable lack of enthusiasm for Christianity, and deference was given grudgingly by more and more commoners. Usually, opposition to missionaries, monarchy, and the bureaucracy was more clandestine than overt. Public compliance went hand in hand with private grumbling and covert disobedience. However, there were some instances of open opposition, especially from members of the *Mamaia* cult that emerged in 1826.[71] *Mamaia* was the creation of two Tahitians, both well versed in Christian teachings, who claimed that they were prophets and foretold of a coming millennium when all Tahitians would have exactly what they wanted. The cult was a mixture of Christian ritual and Tahitian custom. Missionaries reacted with horror. They saw its beliefs as heretical, and regarded cultist behaviour, (which included a good deal of sexuality) as pagan in the extreme. Both missionaries and the royal family feared the cult's political implications—if Tahitians believed a second coming was imminent, then kings and constitutions were irrelevant. *Mamaia* was seen as a direct threat to the state and the state religion. Open conflict between the royal forces and the cultists broke out periodically in the late 1820s though the cult was never a serious military threat. It usually remained underground, and eventually spread throughout the Society Islands, surviving at least until the 1840s.

Far more serious for the monarchy was the growing interest in Tahiti shown by Great Britain and France. As naval commanders became increasingly involved in Tahitian affairs and resorted to gunboat diplomacy in the late 1830s, the monarchy and its LMS allies lost their initiative. In 1842, France declared Tahiti a protectorate. The Tahitian monarchy survived in a nominal capacity until 1880, when King Pomare V transferred Tahitian 'sovereignty' to France and the island became a French colony.[72]

8

Kamehamehas of Hawaii

At the same time as Pomare I and Pomare II were trying to establish their political supremacy and construct a centralised state, Kamehameha I was doing exactly the same. Like Tahiti, Hawaii evolved a 'constitutional' monarchy in the early decades of Western contact.[1]

Background to Hawaiian politics

Hawaiian society was organised in much the same way as Tahitian society, with a relatively small number of chiefs (*ali'i*) of various rank together with an administrative nobility ruling over the bulk of the population, the *maka'ainana*. As on Tahiti, there were numerous gradations within these three broad social groups, especially amongst the *ali'i*. The most important chiefs, the *ali'i nui* were those who had the highest rank-status and who were the most able in war and peace. They traced their ancestry to the most powerful gods. Again in common with Tahiti, the various deities not only provided legitimacy for leadership but their alleged powers were exploited by chiefs to provide all manner of restrictions and prohibitions for social control known as the *kapu* system. To outsiders Hawaiian 'religion' was most obviously manifest in giant stone constructions called *heiau* (equivalent to *marae* on Tahiti), various religious festivals, and in the *kapu* which prohibited such activities as women eating with men.[2]

These superficial similarities between social systems in Tahiti and Hawaii are not surprising given the common ancestry of their peoples. But their histories were separated by 1000 years by the time of first European contact, as well as by thousands of kilometres of ocean. There were also differences that had developed as the respective populations gradually adapted to local conditions. These differences were less marked in the features of social organisation just outlined, but more marked in terms of how government operated in practice. Political control in Hawaii was rather more formalised or institutionalised than in Tahiti. By the time the first Europeans arrived at Hawaii, in the late 1770s, the islands were divided into a series of chiefdoms each ruled by a high chief of a family dynasty.

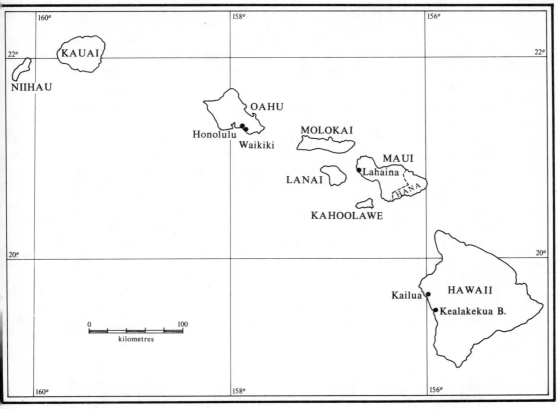

5 Hawaiian Islands

Kalaniopuu ruled the island of Hawaii and the Hana district of Maui; Kahekili's lands were Maui (except Hana), Kahoolawe, Lanai, and Molokai; Peleioholani controlled Oahu; and Kaneoneo held sway over Kauai and Niihau. Each of these leaders had high ranking officers to assist him, in particular the *kahuna nui* or priest, who advised on spiritual and ceremonial matters, and the *kalaimoku*, whose concern was with secular affairs. There was a complex bureaucracy for administration. This formalised machinery of government seems to have given Hawaiian chiefs rather more direct power over their people than Tahitian leaders had. Certainly many Hawaiian chiefs, and especially the high chiefs, appeared to act in a much more authoritarian and haughty manner. In the words of the Hawaiian historian David Malo:

> *The condition of the common people was that of subjection to the chiefs, compelled to do their heavy tasks, burdened and oppressed, some even to death. The life of the people was one of patient endurance, of yielding to the chiefs to purchase their favour. ... the people held the chiefs in great dread and looked upon them as*

> gods. . . . *Only a small portion of the Kings and Chiefs ruled with kindness; the large majority simply lorded it over the people. . . . The* ma-ka-aina-na *were the fixed residents of the land; the chiefs were the ones who moved about from place to place. It was the* ma-ka-aina-na *also who did all the work on the land; yet all they produced from the soil belonged to the chiefs; and the power to expel a man from the land and rob him of all his possessions lay with the chief.*[3]

Yet there are some examples, certainly not common, of a community striking against the more extreme tyranny of their overlord and killing him.

Just as no Tahitian leader was able to gain paramountcy, so no one Hawaiian was able to conquer his fellow leaders. In part this was because several of them were able to band together to prevent one of their number from achieving too much territorial power, and in part because while family dynasties could rule an area for generations, there was no strict lineal succession. On his death, a great chief's lands and accumulated powers and responsibilities were divided amongst his kin. This usually resulted in some instability as various individuals jockeyed for position and tried to accumulate for themselves the various powers held by the previous leader. Even the most potent chiefdom could, on the death of its high chief, be reduced to warring factions. But, as in Tahiti, Hawaii became politically united under one leader and the principle of lineal succession was introduced in the early decades of European presence.

Warrior kings

High politics in Hawaii were characterised by a continual struggle as the high chiefs sought to defend and extend their domains by diplomacy and military strength. Nowhere were relations more strained than on the island of Hawaii where Kalaniopuu was engaged in a campaign against neighbouring Maui. When Cook saw him in 1779, Kalaniopuu had a foothold in the Hana district of Maui but was unable to push further into Kahekili's lands. Kalaniopuu was in any case now physically feeble. He was described by Clerke as the

> *drunkenest fellow we saw in the Kingdom, he was I believe about 50 years of Age totally debilitated and destroyed, he tottered upon his limbs like an infant, his eyes were continually full of Rheum and his hands shook to such a degree that it was with the utmost difficulty he could put anything into his Mouth, indeed he was generally fed by his people, but I have seen him in my Cabbin in endeavouring to drink a glass of wine lose its every drop before he could convey it to its channel, and then as the more convenient vessel take the Bottle to his head; he has sometimes come on board the Discovery in the Forenoon so tipsy he could scarcely stand and as soon as he got into the Cabbin laid down to sleep whilst two or three of his People continually rubbed and chaf'd his Limbs to give the blood the better circulation.*[4]

Soon after the *Discovery* and the *Resolution* sailed from Hawaii, leaving Cook's grisly remains behind in Kealakekua Bay, Kalaniopuu passed some of his authority to his son Kiwalao. But the war god of Hawaii—Kukailimoku—he entrusted to his nephew Kamehameha. Kamehameha was much more aggressive and ambitious than Kiwalao, and had obvious designs on the island's leadership. Even his countenance bespoke a forceful personality, as Cook's men noted: 'savage a looking face as I ever saw, it however by no means seemd an emblem of his disposition which was good naturd & humerous; Although his manners shew'd somewhat of an over-bearing spirit'.[5] Kamehameha is reputed to have received Cook's hair after his body had been divided up amongst the leading chiefs.[6]

Kamehameha soon fell out with Kiwalao, though matters came to a head only when Kalaniopuu finally collapsed and died in 1782, and according to custom, his lands were to be redistributed. Leading chiefs on the island aligned themselves with either Kiwalao or Kamehameha and went into battle against each other. Kiwalao was soon killed. Others took over leadership of his faction. Kamehameha was unable to win a decisive victory. Fighting dragged on for several years with neither side able to conquer the whole island.[7]

By far the most powerful chief in the Hawaiian islands in the early 1800s was Kahekili, ruler of Maui, Kahoolawe, Lanai, and Molokai. He was a tough and successful warrior, described on Cook's visit as 'a middle aged Man ... rather of a mean appearance, the Hair on each side of his head ... cut short & a ridge left on the upper part from the forehead to the Occiput ... each side of his head where the Hair was off was tattawed in lines forming half Circles'.[8] Taking advantage of Kalaniopuu's death, Kahekili had driven those from the island of Hawaii from their foothold on Maui. He made advances on his western flanks too. Exploiting rivalries following the death of Peleioholani of Oahu, Kahekili conquered that island. Meanwhile his half-brother, Kaeo, with whom he was on good terms, gained control of Kauai. Kahekili needed to defeat only the rival chiefs on the island of Hawaii to complete his rule over the entire island group. But the task was too great for him. When it came to the test, his resources and warriors were not sufficient to conquer that large island, especially since the warring factions there were prepared to settle their differences temporarily and present a united front against such external aggression.

Both Kamehameha's and Kahekili's ambitions were stimulated by the potential use each could make of European traders, who by the 1790s were calling in to the islands in ever-increasing numbers. In 1790, Kamehameha's supporters were involved in a fracas with one trader and resolved to capture the first European vessel that next came along. This was the *Fair American*. Five of her crew were beaten to death. The sixth, Isaac Davis, was protected by Kamehameha. At the same time, Kamehameha detained a crew member from another vessel—John Young. Davis and Young made one unsuccessful attempt to escape from Kamehameha's clutches, but soon became agreeably resigned to their fate and ended up as Kamehameha's life-long friends. Kamehameha was quick to appreciate how useful Young and Davis might be to him, especially in conjunction with the *Fair American* and her guns. He gave them wives, land, and every possible comfort.[9] The two of them were soon put to work. Kamehameha, allegedly impressed with their skills with muskets, decided to attack Maui.[10] Kahekili's forces found themselves driven into Iao valley where Davis and Young lobbed cannon balls into their midst, though it is not clear whether this outside assistance was the only reason for Kamehameha's victory: his skills in traditional tactics should not be under-rated.[11] Kamehameha was unable to follow up this rout since his enemies back on Hawaii had taken advantage of his absence to ravage his lands. Kamehameha returned to deal with them and the island was plunged into civil war. Once again, no faction could gain the upper hand and settle the question as to who was the paramount chief of the island. Ironically it was an act of treachery that finally saw this position go to Kamehameha; one of his henchmen slew Kamehameha's main opponent.[12]

Meanwhile Kahekili decided to take advantage of the unrest on Hawaii and sent a small naval force under the command of one of his Europeans, Mare Amara, complete with cannons. Kamehameha sent out his gunners, Young and Davis, and both sides pounded each other on the high seas. The result was inconclusive, but at least Kahekili withdrew for the meantime. For the next three years there was a lull in the fighting while both sides concentrated on building up their military strength, particularly by dealing with Europeans.

The rise of Kamehameha

Just as the Pomares on Tahiti were fortunate to have Matavai Bay, so was Kahekili fortunate to have his main residence on Oahu close to Honolulu harbour. The fur trader William Brown 'discovered' this anchorage in 1792 or 1793 and soon vessels made a point of calling in. Brown and Kahekili came to a mutually misunderstood arrangement. Brown believed the chief had ceded the island of Oahu to him; Kahekili on the other hand probably believed that he had given Brown the right to use the harbour in return for support against Kamehameha. For his part, Kamehameha also assiduously cultivated the friendship of potential allies, the most notable being George Vancouver who visited the Hawaiian islands three times between 1792 and 1794. Vancouver had of course been there earlier with Cook, and he noted how Kamehameha's personality had altered in the meantime:

> *I was agreeably surprised in finding that his riper years had softened that stern ferocity which his younger days had exhibited, and had changed his general deportment to an address characteristic of an open, cheerful, and sensible mind; combined with great generosity, and goodness of disposition. An alteration not unlike that I have before had occasion to notice on the character of* Pomurrey *at* Otaheite.[13]

But Vancouver considered Kamehameha presumptuous in his plans to conquer all the Hawaiian islands, and tried unsuccessfully to arrange a peace settlement between Kahekili and Kamehameha. He did manage to have Kamehameha 'cede' the island of Hawaii to Britain.[14] Kamehameha doubtless saw the arrangement in slightly different terms—namely that British naval vessels would support him against Kahekili.

Although Vancouver tried not to take sides in the dispute between the two chiefs, and refused to supply any of them with firearms, he did much to give Kamehameha's morale a boost. He provided canvas sails and a flag for Kamehameha's largest double-hulled canoe. Kamehameha sailed it in delight and 'observed, that she would make a much better appearance with a few swivels properly mounted; I agreed with him in this opinion [said Vancouver], but the words "*Taboo* King George" were sufficient to prevent a syllable more being urged on that subject.' Vancouver also had his carpenters build Kamehameha a small vessel—the *Britannia*. To John Young he gave some sky rockets and hand grenades 'for the sole purpose of Tamaahmaah's protection'. Vancouver approved of the role Young and Davis were playing, not in their efforts to conquer other islands for Kamehameha, but in defending Hawaii against 'foreign invasion' and 'in maintaining his authority against domestic insurrection.' Vancouver also promised Kamehameha, on behalf of the British government, a fully armed man-of-war loaded with European goods.[15] Such a vessel eventually arrived decades later, during the reign of Kamehameha's son. The clamour for firearms amazed Vancouver,[16] though he noted that the muskets warriors did possess, supplied by 'North-west American adventurers', were usually in a poor condition: 'Many very bad accidents had happened by the bursting of these fire-arms'.[17]

Yet Kamehameha's greatest opportunity came not from such outside support, but with Kahekili's death. Kahekili's kingdom of Maui, Lanai, Molokai, and Oahu (plus Kauai, which he controlled through his half-brother Kaeo) was divided up between his sons Kalanikupule and Kaeo. As was almost inevitable after such a division, fighting broke out amongst the ambitious, the jealous, and the dissatisfied. The outcome was that Kalanikupule, with the assistance of William Brown and his sailors, defeated and killed Kaeo. Flush with success, Kalanikupule decided to attack Kamehameha. But instead of soliciting Brown's aid again, he planned to capture Brown's ships and use them against Kamehameha. In 1795 he took the *Jackall* and the *Prince Lee Boo*, killed the two captains—Brown and Gordon—and held the crews hostage. Then the plan went wrong. No sooner had the vessels put to sea on their way to Hawaii than the captive crews overpowered their new masters, ignominiously put Kalanikupule in a canoe off Waikiki, and set sail for Hawaii where they informed Young and Davis what had happened. Kamehameha saw his chance. Kalanikupule was humiliated and had lost his European allies. Kamehameha marshalled his fleet, embarked his 10 000 warriors, and smashed the forces of Oahu, Maui, and Molokai.[18] Some would have it that his military successes depended on European firepower and the services of Young and Davis,[19] yet Kamehameha's superior numbers combined with his undisputed skill as a military tactician were probably more instrumental in bringing him victory. What reliable accounts there are of the fighting suggest that it was of a customary not innovative nature.[20] In any case, Kamehameha by no means had a monopoly on firearms.

Kamehameha then turned his attention to the more distant Kauai, now ruled by Kaumualii, but storms drove his fleets back. Kauai could wait. In the end, Kamehameha never did invade the island. In 1804 he once again amassed his forces on Oahu for a seaborne assault, but the invasion was postponed because of an epidemic. The two leaders hedged for some years. Finally in 1810 they made their peace. Kauai was to be a tributary kingdom under Kaumualii's governance, with Kamehameha the acknowledged sovereign. The Hawaiian islands were finally united under one ruler, King Kamehameha I.

In some respects, Kamehameha by 1810 (or even 1795 leaving aside the question of Kauai) was in a similar situation to Pomare II in 1815. His rise to paramountcy, like Pomare's, had been achieved mainly by customary means. For Kamehameha this meant exploiting changing political alliances, especially on the death of high chiefs, and using military prowess, all age-old strategies of Hawaiian leaders. Similarly, both Pomare and Kamehameha had European assistance at certain times, though Kamehameha was probably less dependent on outside help than the Pomares had been. There are other parallels between Pomare II and Kamehameha I. Pomare in 1815 and Kamehameha in 1795 were in positions of paramountcy that were inherently unstable. Their military superiority of the moment was likely to be short-lived, especially as political alliances were likely to change at any time as various factions were forever manoeuvring themselves into the potentially most advantageous positions. However, Pomare needed both to legitimise his leadership since he had rejected the old gods and to organise a stable government. Missionaries and Christianity were his salvation. Kamehameha's position was different in this respect. His supremacy was quite legitimate in Hawaiian terms. All that was new was the size of his empire. He needed no new divine justification, and there were no missionaries anyway. What he needed, as did Pomare, was an effective means of controlling his new subjects, but not, as in Pomare's case, by requiring new sanctions. The existing ones would do. He simply needed a system of administration to make sure the customary sanctions operated effectively. Kamehameha's solution was to place emphasis less on military strength and more on efficient bureaucratic management and trade with Europeans.

14   Kamehameha I, about 1816. (Kotzebue A Voyage of Discovery, *vol 1)*

Kamehameha's kingdom

Pomare II was a revolutionary in Tahitian terms. He based his monarchy
on a new divine legitimacy and ruled through new sanctions based on a
mixture of Tahitian and missionary values. Kamehameha I was more of a
traditionalist. He imposed his rule by exploiting and modifying the existing
institutions of government.[21] In particular, where Pomare II attempted to
keep leading chiefs out of his administration, Kamehameha skillfully
involved his potential rivals in his government. He employed the techniques of successful feudal monarchs everywhere, giving the ranking
nobles integral roles within the kingdom. He granted them lands and
delegated them powers, thereby increasing their status and authority in the
eyes of their followers. These chiefs came to have a vested interest in
supporting Kamehameha. By becoming the source of much of their wealth
and influence he underwrote their loyalty. He also made a point of keeping
a close eye on their activities. He frequently required them to live and travel
with him, thereby getting to know their strengths and weaknesses as

supporters and advisers. And the more lavish and attentive his hospitality, the more the chiefly recipients became not only dependent on Kamehameha but also isolated from potential sources of political opposition. As one European visitor explained:

> *It is the wise policy of this chief, that all those who possess any authority or influence in the country, should accompany him in his progress through his dominions, that he may have them constantly under his eye, and not leave them exposed to the seductions and conspiracies of his rival chiefs.*[22]

Kamehameha also appointed governors as his personal representatives on each island. In 1796 and from 1802 until 1812, Young was his governor on Hawaii.[23]

Kamehameha was shrewd enough to realise that administrative efficiency alone, especially in the earlier years of his rule, was not necessarily enough to entrench his regime. He kept a standing army of some 6000 men,[24] and had some 200–300 bodyguards who, like 'regularly disciplined troops, go on duty not unfrequently with drum and fife, and relieve each other as in Europe, calling out, "all is well" at every half hour.'[25]

The most radical change for the population at large was the cessation of large-scale fighting. No longer were the *maka'ainana* required for military service but their freedom from this demand made them more available as labourers for the chiefs. The chiefs were now less dependent on their subjects' loyalty, since chiefly status and authority now came from the King, and they could increase their exactions from the people. Furthermore, Kamehameha's policy of keeping the more important chiefs with his retinue increased land-holding absenteeism. The sometimes close bonds between these chiefs and their people were weakened; chiefs felt that their responsibility now lay more in pleasing Kamehameha than in bothering about the well-being of their communities. This changed nature of responsibility was highlighted by the role of the agents whom chiefs appointed to oversee their lands during their absence. These agents often had no interest in carefully managed cultivation, but simply got as much work and produce out of the commoners as possible. Overall the lot of the *maka'ainana* probably worsened as a result of Kamehameha's unified monarchy.[26] Not only were they at the mercy of lesser chiefs acting as agents, but also they had to foot the bill for the king's government. On top of this Kamehameha's own passion for trading with foreigners, especially when the sandalwood rush began, imposed unprecedented demands on his more lowly subjects.

From the late eighteenth century trans-Pacific fur trade vessels had called at the Hawaiian islands for provisions, repairs, and recreation. Some traders realised that there was also a market for sandalwood in Canton, and in the 1790s small quantities of Hawaiian sandalwood were shipped there. The ventures failed because these particular samples of wood proved of poor quality and traders who specialised in sandalwood went elsewhere, especially to Fiji. But by 1815, after the Fijian boom was over, there was renewed interest in exploiting the large stands of sandalwood now known to be in the Hawaiian islands. The trade boomed and quickly became the kingdom's main source of revenue.[27] Kamehameha was the main bene-ficiary since he placed a royal monopoly over all the wood. All trading had to be done through him or his most trusted agents. Often he demanded a brig or a schooner as payment. All his life he never lost his obsession with acquiring European vessels. Within two years of the sandalwood trade's operation he had at least six to add to his already impressive fleet. Nor did his passion for possessing any other item of European manufacture dimin-ish, and, to outsiders, Kamehameha's tastes seemed quite undiscriminat-ing. In addition to collecting table silverware, crystal, porcelain, and large amounts of foreign money, he just as avidly sought old shoes and handkerchiefs.[28]

Kamehameha made the most of displaying the material trappings of his position. He surrounded himself with European tradesmen of every kind, up to 50 or more at any given time. He was particularly proud of his navy, which consisted of some 30 sloops and schooners, most built by Hawaiians under the direction of European carpenters. Kamehameha's flagship was a 200-tonne vessel. His 'palace' on Oahu was a collection of large huts and stone storehouses filled with European tools, utensils, and anything else that had caught his fancy. He flew British colours on his flagpole and had a battery of sixteen carriage guns.[29] Kamehameha himself usually dressed in European clothes, a blue coat and grey 'pantaloons', and to foreign visitors he was generally charming: 'stout, well-made ... rather darker in com-plexion than the natives usually are, and wants two of his front teeth. The expression of his countenance is agreeable, and he is mild and affable in his manners, and possesses great warmth of feeling'.[30] The warrior had become the entrepreneur, but was just as formidable. Bills of lading replaced battles as his principal instruments of power. He encouraged European shipping to 'enter his ports not only without the least fear, but with the certainty of obtaining, on the best terms, everything the place they may anchor at is capable of furnishing.'[31] His skills at bargaining became legendary.[32] He developed a highly efficient commercial intelligence net-work, employing some

> *chiefs of lower rank who speak some English, whose duties consist of visiting foreign ships and finding out from the sailors the type and amount of cargo and the number of people aboard, so that Tameamea may set his prices for goods and provisions accordingly.*[33]

There were various harbour and port dues. Kamehameha imposed a sales tax on products his people sold to foreigners, and furthermore, set a minimum price on such goods for sale. A visiting Russian naval commander explained:

> *As a result, warships which need provisions but do not carry trade goods have to pay*
> *very high prices for everything they buy from the islanders. The Americans, on the*
> *other hand, who constantly trade in these waters, bring great amounts of various*
> *European knickknacks, usually trying to select something the islanders have not yet*
> *seen.*[34]

Although much of the wealth from trade with passing vessels ended up in Kamehameha's storehouses, and in those of his trusted Hawaiian and European henchmen, considerable amounts of European goods such as clothes, tobacco, liquor, tools, and utensils found their way into most sections of society, mainly from the earnings of prostitution and Hawaiian labour on foreign vessels. Visiting Europeans who invariably equated the intelligence of other peoples with the extent to which they adopted European goods and technology rated Hawaiians relatively high on the scale of 'temporal advancement', higher than Tahitians anyway. But contrary to what many commentators claimed, the use of such European items did not mean that Hawaiian society was changing into a (slightly comic) replica of European society. The fact that many Hawaiians wore some European clothing (often just a hat), or that they had a king, a palace, a flag, a navy, a prime minister who called himself Billy Pitt after England's William Pitt, Honolulu streets and pubs named after English ones, all had much more symbolic significance for visiting Englishmen than for Hawaiians labouring in taro plantations and carrying sandalwood from the mountains.

Most European travellers through Kamehameha's lands stressed the absolute nature of his rule and believed that he was a much-respected monarch. But whether such respect came through fear or affection was debated. Archibald Campbell argued that the people now 'enjoyed repose and prosperity',[35] whereas a more common opinion was expressed by Commander Golovnin:

> *If Tameamea would only devote as much attention, or even half as much, to the*
> *interests of his subjects as he does to the interests of the Europeans living with him,*
> *he could greatly relieve the miserable condition of the common people, whose life and*
> *property are entirely at the mercy of the Chiefs.*[36]

The death of Kamehameha I

In 1819 at the age of seventy, Kamehameha died. The islands were plunged into public mourning. The key question was whether the kingdom could survive without its founder.[37] In the past, the death of rulers had frequently led to civil strife as contending factions fought to gain the various responsibilities and powers. Kamehameha himself had been well aware of this possibility and had tried to ensure that the monarchy continued after him. His son Liholiho, now twenty-two and crowned Kamehameha II, had been groomed for this position since childhood. The real power behind Liholiho was Kaahumanu, Kamehameha's favourite wife. She was an imposing woman, some 190 kilograms in weight, and soon asserted her authority. When her son was crowned king she is reported to have proclaimed 'Behold these chiefs and the men of your father, and these your guns, and this your land, but you and I shall share the realm together.'[38] No one dared contradict her and she became *kuhina nui*, a new position which meant that she was the leading administrative officer of the kingdom.

A Frenchman visited their 'straw' palace not long afterwards. Kamehameha II, whom he thought 'large fat, dirty, proud', received him dressed 'like a colonel of hussars, wearing a hat like a marshal of France.' At the king's side was Kaahumanu, 'a stout half-naked woman, who allowed herself to coquette with every stranger'.

> *She is prodigiously fat, but her face is interesting: her eyes were heavy from slight indisposition, her manner very engaging, and, after longer observation, I am not surprised at the strong attachment Tammeamah had for her. Her legs, the palm of her left hand, and her tongue, are very elegantly tattooed; and her body bears the marks of a great number of burns and incisions she inflicted on herself at the death of her husband. She offered us some beer with much kindness, drank to us, striking her glass against ours....*[39]

The kingdom did not collapse, though there were some tense moments in the early months when several chiefs tried to assert themselves and gain concessions that Kamehameha I would never have countenanced. In particular, they managed to force Kamehameha II to break the royal monopoly over the sandalwood trade and give them a share. But it was Kaahumanu who made the biggest change to the existing order of government by leading the overthrow of the *kapu* system.[40]

The abolition of kapu

The *kapu* system was a complex series of prohibitions, allegedly designed by the gods, that chiefs used to maintain social controls. To all intents and purposes the *kapu* system appeared to be a central feature of Hawaiian sociopolitical organisation. One of the more obvious *kapu* was that men and women could not eat together, and it was Kaahumanu's deliberate breach of this prohibition that symbolised the abolition of *kapu*.

Kaahumanu planned this act of defiance with Kamehameha II's mother—Keopuolani. They were also supported by Kalanimoku, a lead-

15   Kaahumanu, about 1816.
(Choris Voyage Pittoresque Autour du Monde. *Alexander Turnbull Library)*

ing adviser of both Kamehamehas, and several leading priests.
Kamehameha II was rather hesitant, but finally went along with them. He
and Kaahumanu sat down and ate voraciously together. As soon as they
had finished, the king ordered the destruction of all the tangible signs of the
Hawaiian religion—the *heiau*, idols, and images. All the major religious
ceremonies such as the *makahiki* were immediately abandoned. Virtually
everyone in the Hawaiian islands willingly followed these directions. The
only serious opposition came from Kamehameha's own war leader—
Kekuaokalani—but he and his small band of warriors were quickly defeated in battle. The Hawaiian population apparently instantly and with no
great concern abandoned what seemed to outsiders to be an integral part of
their culture.

That the *maka'ainana* (commoners) should so readily have accepted these
changes is not surprising. Many assumed, quite unrealistically as it turned
out, that they might gain some relief from the demands of their overlords.
As a missionary later explained:

*They seemed to think it was well that idolatry had been prohibited by the king; said
its frequent requisitions kept them very poor, and occasioned them much labour.*[41]

16   The Hawaiian kapu *system in action—'A delicate and ingenious method of execution'. (Arago* Narrative of a Voyage. *Alexander Turnbull Library)*

It is less easy to understand why such a revolution should have been inspired by those at the pinnacle of society. Why should the royal family itself have wanted to destroy 'the religious and supernatural foundations of the Hawaiian political structure'?[42] In doing so they seemed to outsiders to be destroying the basis of their own positions. But in fact the *kapu* system itself had become a hindrance to their potential political and economic advancement.

By 1819 the Hawaiian islands had experienced some twenty years of regular European contact. The introduction of new ideas and technology, commercial dealings with Europeans, and overseas travel by Hawaiians had all combined to produce a degree of secularisation in Hawaiian society. Chiefs especially were inclined to break *kapu*, particularly when in the company of Europeans. Kaahumanu herself broke various *kapu* in private by eating pork and shark as early as 1810. For the population at large, attitudes toward *kapu* changed gradually and subtly. They were still generally obeyed in public but obedience increasingly sprang from fear of getting caught and brutal punishment by priests and others, rather than from fear of annoying supernatural authorities. So *kapu* were often privately ignored, but only if there was no chance of getting caught. By 1819 the letter of the law was more important than its spirit, and its imposition on the *maka'ainana* and especially the women was as rigidly enforced as ever. People were put to death right up until the *kapu* were abolished. Missionaries who arrived in 1820 saw a five-year-old girl who had had her eyes pulled out for eating a banana. This was a common punishment, and one vividly described by Arago:

> *The executioner, gave . . . a violent blow with his fist over each eye, and almost at the same instant plunged his fore-finger into the lachrymal angle, and pulled out the ball; the other eye was taken out in the same manner.*[43]

Strangulation or the smashing of heads and limbs with a club were other common punishments. Golovnin, visiting Hawaii just before the *kapu* were abolished, noted:

> *The more important the chief, the less he observes these regulations, and . . . these free-thinkers, so to speak, are more friendly to Europeans and get along with them much better. A woman, however, no matter how noble her rank, may not break a single one of the prohibitions imposed upon her sex.*[44]

The underlying scepticism and secularisation had a more specific effect on the kingdom's rulers. Kamehameha I's military conquests of the islands, his administrative structure, and his exploitation of commerce with Europeans all meant that the former tribal basis of political authority in the Hawaiian islands was in the process of transformation. A centralised state had become all important and it was necessary for its rulers to streamline it. Hawaiian religion, they perceived, had to serve the state, not the state serve or be hindered by religious constraints. Kaahumanu and her close associates had a vested interest in weakening or abolishing the divine sanctions that underpinned the old systems of administration. They especially wanted to do away with the customary (unpredictable) processes of succession whereby on the death of a leader political authority became a matter of contention between rival factions. Kaahumanu was very worried about what designs Kekuaokalani, who inherited the war god on Kamehameha I's death, might have in mind. This was the very position that Kamehameha I had inherited when his father died, and from it he managed to defeat Kiwalao (Kamehameha II's equivalent) and gain supremacy. Such a process was quite legitimate and, unless the rules were changed, Kekuaokalani could similarly and quite legitimately eclipse Kamehameha II. Kaahumanu saw the abolition of the *kapu* system as a means of preventing Kekuaokalani from claiming any divine sanction or justification for such a political ambition. In effect the abolition introduced a concept of succession by heredity alone.[45] It is no coincidence that the man who most opposed the abolition of *kapu* and who led a small rebellion was the person who had most to lose—Kekuaokalani.

The new royal rulers also saw economic advantages in abolishing *kapu*.

Not only were they spared the considerable expense of helping to maintain the priesthood and its paraphernalia, but if the *maka'ainana* were freed from the demands of building *heiau* and taking part in huge festivals then their labour and produce would be free for more profitable exploitation by the monarchy. Thus Kaahumanu and her associates' abolition of the *kapu* system was a 'deliberate political response' that enabled the monarchy to ensure hereditary succession and 'to reorganise its administrative structure for a more efficient allocation of its economic resources.'[46] What it lost in terms of spiritual backing it gained by administrative effectiveness.

If the monarchy benefited from the abolition of *kapu* so too did the chiefly élite as a group. Many restrictions, which could considerably limit their activities, were removed. Kotzebue in 1816 described some of the demands on their time made by *kapu*:

> *At sunset, this evening, a* taboo *is to begin for Kereimoku and his* jerris, *which is to last one night and two days. The higher the people are here in rank, the more holy duties they have to perform, and every full and new moons they have each a* taboo; *as soon as the sun approaches the horizon, they enter the* murai, *which they do not leave again till the appointed time is over.*[47]

Now the chiefs had a much freer hand and more time to accumulate wealth, usually by working their underlings harder. To some extent Kaahumanu and Kamehameha II bought off potential opposition from the chiefs by letting them participate in the sandalwood trade and giving them the right to redistribute their lands on the death of one of their number rather than depend on the king to do so. In general, like the royal family itself, the chiefs felt emancipated from the economic and political demands of the *kapu* system, and this seems to have far outweighed the theoretical loss of their divine legitimacy.

The abolition of *kapu* has sometimes been called a 'cultural revolution' but it was nothing of the kind. As in Tahiti, there was no basic change in society. At most the abolition represented a tinkering with relationships amongst the élites. For the population at large, the *maka'ainana*, things remained the same, or indeed got worse. Demands by the priesthood diminished but those of secular rulers increased.

A main difference between Pomare II's kingdom in Tahiti and Kamehameha II's was that Kamehameha did not have missionaries and the spiritual sanctions that their god could offer. These were not necessary in Hawaii, mainly because of the nature of the new administration. The Hawaiian monarchy had an administrative and military strength (which had precedents in pre-European times) that the Tahitian monarchy could not match. But this raises the question as to whether there was any religious 'vacuum' in Hawaii immediately after 1819. There was certainly no state religion though for all practical purposes there was no need for one. Most people seemed glad to be freed from restraints and demands. Those who ruled the state felt more secure, and ordinary individuals did not suddenly lose any spiritual comfort they might have relied upon. To destroy the church is not necessarily to destroy the faith, which in fact existed for generations afterwards. As one missionary later put it:

> *From the oppression of idolatry, the people feel themselves emancipated.... But though they approved of the destruction of the national idols, many were far from having renounced idolatry.*[48]

Another commented:

> *The worship of images was prohibited, but the* private belief *of the people and their superstitious regard to the genius of the volcano, to the spirits of the departed, to the bones of their kings, and their* kini *of gods, the 40,000 deities on whom they had vainly called, were left to die a natural death, or to live on.*[49]

The rule of Kamehameha II (Liholiho)

Kamehameha II was a far less effective ruler than his father. He was dominated by Kaahumanu on the one hand and constantly badgered by leading chiefs on the other. Frequently he took refuge in getting drunk. Rumours of rebellion were rife, but invariably unsubstantiated. The main preoccupation of those chiefs who might conceivably have attempted a coup was with commercial exploitation of the masses. They had more to gain by supporting the monarch than by trying to overthrow him, especially since the abolition of *kapu* gave them more control over their own activities, and since they had been given a share in the sandalwood trade. For many of them the prospect of civil war was unthinkable. As one visitor reported in 1822: 'instead of a divided and lawless aristocracy, the King and his Chiefs compose a united corps of peaceable merchants, whose principal object is to become rich by the pursuits of trade.'[50]

The years 1821–1823 saw the greatest amount of sandalwood ever shipped overseas. Demands upon the *maka'ainana* became extreme. As coastal sandalwood was depleted, workers were sent further into the mountains to cut and drag out the precious wood.

> *There were between two and three thousand men, carrying each from one to six pieces of sandal wood.... It was generally tied on their backs by bands made of ti leaves, passed over the shoulders and under the arms, and fastened across their breast. When they had deposited the wood at the store house, they departed to their respective homes.*[51]

These carriers were known as *kua leho*, callous backs. Parties of 3000 or more sometimes spent weeks gathering the wood for their demanding chiefs, and subsistence agriculture was often neglected. Serious regional famines occurred periodically. Then, while sandalwood trading was at its height, whaling vessels began calling at the islands. Again the *maka'ainana* were exploited by their rulers.

> *Many vessels, principally whalers, resort to the Sandwich Islands for fresh provisions, etc—we have seen upwards of thirty lying at anchor off Oahu at one time. The farmers in many places dispose of the produce of their land to these ships; but in Oahu, and some other harbours, this trade is almost entirely monopolised by the king and chiefs. There is, indeed, a public market, in which the natives dispose of their stock; but the price is regulated by the chiefs, and two-thirds of the proceeds of whatever the natives sell is required by them.*[52]

For all their apparent wealth, the king and chiefs were usually in debt to foreign traders. Such was their concern to fill store houses with European goods that Hawaiian leaders frequently struck bad bargains with merchants. It was all too easy to accept on-the-spot payments in return for signing promissory notes for amounts of sandalwood or other produce that in effect they had no hope of gathering. By the mid-1820s Hawaiian debts to merchants amounted to hundreds of thousands of dollars. Although sandalwood had been depleted by the end of the 1820s, commercial activity in Hawaii was sustained at high levels with the advent of whaling during the 1830s. Honolulu became one of the largest port towns in the Pacific, with a population of up to 1000 Europeans and 9000 Hawaiians.[53]

> *Owing to the number of foreigners now settled on this island [Oahu], exercising various trades and keeping well-stocked shops, supplies of almost every description can be obtained at Honoruru with the same facility as at a second-rate sea port in England; while several hotels, or boarding houses of different grades, a well-equipped billiard-room, bowling alleys, lotteries, auctions, and amateur theatricals, afford much accommodation and amusement to the foreign resident.*[54]

The missionaries

After a five-month, gale-lashed voyage via the Horn, the first party of missionaries from New England, under the auspices of the American Board of Commissioners for Foreign Missions (ABCFM), put in to the royal homelands on Hawaii's western shore in 1820. Their unofficial leader, Hiram Bingham, was as gratified at reaching land as he was horrified at its inhabitants:

> *The appearance of destitution, degradation, and barbarism, among the chattering, and almost naked savages, whose heads and feet, and much of their sunburnt swarthy skins, were bare, was appalling. Some of our number, with gushing tears, turned away from the spectacle. Others with firmer nerve continued their gaze, but were ready to exclaim, 'Can these be human beings!'*[55]

There was one great consolation for these unhappy travellers. They listened with wonder to tales of the abandonment of the *kapu* system.

The images are destroyed,— the heiaus of idolatrous worship are burned .... The hand of God! how visible in thus beginning to answer the prayer of his people, for the Hawaiian race![56]

Kamehameha II received them cordially enough, though he typically referred their requests to Kaahumanu. After much discussion amongst the royal family the missionaries were given permission to settle at the king's residence at Kailua on Hawaii and at Honolulu. Kaahumanu was intensely interested in what the missionaries had to offer. Whether she placed any store on Bingham's argument that no ruler could govern successfully 'a nation without any public recognition of religious obligation'[57] can never be known. But it was certainly possible, and Kaahumanu was careful to give the missionaries twelve months' probation.

The missionaries in Hawaii were in a much more favourable situation than had been their London Missionary Society (LMS) counterparts in Tahiti. The Hawaiian islands were united under one leader, the state religion was abolished, and the Islanders had had a great deal of contact with the West. None of these conditions had existed in Tahiti when missionaries first arrived there. The missionaries in Hawaii were also somewhat better prepared than the Tahitian ones. They had less initial difficulty communicating with Hawaiians, mainly because many Hawaiian's had a smattering of English, even if the missionaries considered it 'barbarous English ... acquired by intercourse with sea-faring men'.[58] Also, these missionaries brought with them four Hawaiians who had earlier found their way to America and had eventually been 'educated' at the Foreign Mission School in Connecticut. Furthermore, missionaries in Hawaii knew something of the LMS experiences in Tahiti. In particular, LMS missionary William Ellis who had been on Tahiti since 1817, visited Hawaii in 1822 and stayed for two years. His fluency in Tahitian enabled him to pick up the Hawaiian language easily and he was the first European to preach to the Hawaiians in the vernacular. Ellis was also instrumental in organising a written form of Hawaiian and translating the Bible. The American missionaries' early concentration on learning the local language, preaching and teaching, and encouraging literacy amongst the population at large readily gave them advantages that the LMS missionaries had not had in Tahiti for years. Furthermore, from their first days ashore the missionaries in Hawaii were materially far better off than the travellers on the *Duff* had ever been.

On the other hand, the conversion of the Hawaiian population was far more gradual than the relatively instant conversion of the Tahitians, reflecting the respective political situations. The Pomare regime after 1815 urgently needed legitimacy and an effective system of government. Hawaiian rulers in the early 1820s had no such pressing requirements. They had only just abandoned a state religion—to no apparent ill effect—and they had a fairly efficient administration bequeathed them by Kamehameha I. While members of the royal family were courteous to the missionaries, they were not exactly encouraging from the evangelists' point of view. Some said they supported what the missionaries preached, but everybody waited for the king to give a lead one way or the other. Kamehameha paid their teachings only scant attention. He was more concerned with touring his kingdom, to the great annoyance of the missionaries who thought his 'disposition to range about seemed to us hardly less than that of the aborigines of America'.[59]

This incessant roving affecting large classes, greatly hindered his own improvement and that of his wives and friends, and the missionaries felt that so far as they were bound to educate them, they were like the Israelites when required to deliver the full tale of brick, and find their own straw where they could.[60]

Kamehameha's constant drunkenness and 'rebellious lusts' also caused great anguish in the missionary camp, but they were forced to suffer the man with deference and good humour (just as the LMS missionaries had had to tolerate Pomare II). After all he was the king, and, as Kaahumanu said to William Ellis, no one could serve the missionary god 'unless the king does. If he embraces the new religion, we shall all follow.'[61]

As well as trying to win friends in high places, the missionaries appealed to the masses. They conducted open air services and schools. At times hundreds of Hawaiians attended, mostly out of curiosity.

Christianity and politics

In 1823 Kamehameha II and an impressive entourage set out for London to visit King George III. No sooner had he left than Kaahumanu and Kalanimoku came out in support of Christianity. They declared 'their determination to adhere to the instructions of the missionaries, to attend to learning, observe the Sabbath, worship God, and obey his law, and have all their people instructed'.[62] Proclamations to this effect were read out in Honolulu, Lahaina, and on Kauai and Niihau. News then came from London that Kamehameha II and his wife had died of measles. Their bodies were returned to Hawaii. Kamehameha II's young brother Kauikeaouli succeeded him, but since he was a minor the kingdom was entrusted to Kaahumanu as queen regent and Kalanimoku. Almost immediately after Kamehameha II's funeral, Kaahumanu and Kalanimoku, along with other leaders, asked to be baptised. The missionaries were torn between wanting to accept such influential people into the chuch at once (as Bingham said 'That laws, tabus, and commands given by Hawaiian rulers should always have some influence on the multitude, was a matter of course.')[63] and wanting to see signs of some spiritual motivation on their part. In a reversal of situations, the missionaries requested that the leaders spend six months' probation as candidates for baptism. At the end of 1825 they were admitted to the church.

Like Pomare II on Tahiti, Kaahumanu had seen the political advantages of Christianity. A new state religion could, after all, help entrench the ruling élite, and the time was certainly propitious. There was no charismatic monarch, just a minor, which raised the possibility (however remote) of some rebellion. Ironically, the abolition of the *kapu* had been a means of preventing such strife on the death of Kamehameha I in 1819. Now, with the death of Kamehameha II, the reimposition of new *kapu*—Christian ones—might ensure a peaceful succession and further entrenchment of the monarchy. Kaahumanu spearheaded her campaign with schooling in literacy. Her own house was sometimes crammed with people 'who under her Majesty's own superintendence, were reading from spelling-books, and writing on slates.'[64] She ordered missionary-trained Hawaiian teachers to all the islands. District chiefs were instructed to supply them with huts, food, and schools 'immediately, and to order all the people in her name to attend to the *palapala* [prayers], and the *pule* [writing].'[65] And 'as soon as these [teachers] had taught a number to read, they were expected to divide their districts, and thus to multiply the schools, until at length the land became full of them.'[66] By the 1830s there were almost 1000 schools and some 50 000 pupils, most of whom had at least some inkling of reading and writing their own language.

The purely religious advances were, on the missionaries' own reckoning, far less spectacular. In their view there was too much outward observance and not enough spiritual commitment. Church membership, as opposed to participation in church affairs, was denied to all but a few. Between 1825 and 1837 only 1300 Hawaiians were baptised. Nevertheless Kaahumanu and her missionary advisers imposed a rigid programme of public worship. Kotzebue, admittedly a stern critic of missionary 'tyranny' described accurately enough the changes that had occurred in Honolulu between his first visit in 1816 and his second in 1825. Where 'carousing', billiards, horse racing, model boat racing, and whist had been the order of the day, now

> *the inhabitants of every house or hut . . . are compelled by authority to an almost endless routine of prayers. . . . The streets, formerly so full of life and animation, are now deserted; games of all kinds, even the most innocent, are sternly prohibited; singing is a punishable offence. . . . On Sundays, no cooking is permitted, nor must even a fire be kindled: nothing, in short, must be done; the whole day is devoted to prayer, with how much real piety may be easily imagined. . . . Kaahumanna . . . will hear of no opposition; and as her power extends to life and death, those who would willingly resist are compelled to bend under the iron sceptre of this arbitrary old woman.*

A short time before our return, a command had issued, that all persons who had attained the age of eight years should be brought to Hanaruro, to be taught reading and writing. The poor country people, though much discontented, did not venture to disobey, but patiently abandoning their labour in the fields, flocked to Hanaruro, where we saw many families bivouacking in the streets, in little huts hastily put together, with the spelling-books in their hands. Such as could already read were made to learn passages from the Bible by heart. Every street in Hanaruro has more than one school-house: they are long huts, built of reeds, without any division. In each of these, about a hundred scholars, of both sexes, are instructed by a single native teacher, who, standing on a raised platform, names aloud every single letter, which is repeated in a scream by the whole assembly. These establishments, it may be supposed, are easily recognised afar off; no other sounds are heard in the streets; and the human figure is seldom to be seen amidst this melancholy stillness, except when the scholars, conducted by their teachers, repair to the church. Every sort of gaiety is forbidden.

Lord Byron had brought with him from England a variety of magic lanterns, puppet-shows, and such like toys, and was making preparations to exhibit them in public, for the entertainment of the people, when an order arrived from Bengham to prevent the representation, because it did not become God-fearing christians to take pleasure in such vain amusements.[67]

Kotzebue was convinced Bingham was the root cause of such 'entire change' and that he had made Kaahumanu 'the instrument of his will'.[68] If anything it was the other way around. Bingham was certainly in no position to dominate Kaahumanu, though both personalities did gain advantages from the mutual exploitation of each other's attributes. Furthermore, neither Kaahumanu nor Bingham could enforce such changes on a totally unresponsive and unwilling populace. While there was obviously initially a good deal of dragooning of the *maka'ainana* into church going and behaving as Christians, these activities could also have their appeal. As in Tahiti, the attainment of literacy and the novelty of new rituals, could offer some pleasure and even excitement to Hawaiians in the 1820s. On the whole, however, the conversion of the Hawaiian population—a phenomenon not completed until about 1840—can ultimately be explained in terms of the political control it offered the Hawaiian monarchy, especially Kaahumanu.

The monarchy and law and order

Pomare II and his successors, in conjunction with missionaries on Tahiti, attempted to formalise government and its relationship with the people in the law code of 1819 and the constitution of 1824. Hawaiian rulers needed equivalent mechanisms not only to improve and consolidate their rule but also to regulate relations between Hawaiians and foreigners. Hawaii, unlike Tahiti, became a major commercial entrepôt in the Pacific and the vested and often conflicting outside interests caused Hawaiian rulers and missionaries much concern. They were particularly worried about the Great Powers who were in the habit of sending warships to try to sort out the conflicts involving their nationals. A key theme in the development of the monarchy from the 1820s was its attempts to maintain initiative in the affairs of its islands.

The first laws attempting to regulate the behaviour of sailors ashore were published in 1822. Throughout the 1820s visiting British and American naval captains urged Kaahumanu and Kalanimoku to formulate more comprehensive regulations, not only pertaining to foreigners but for more efficient government administration generally. But Bingham and some of his fellow missionaries seem to have had more influence on the royal family. From 1825 a series of proclamations forbad such crimes as gambling, drunkenness, 'debauchery', violating the Sabbath. *Kapu* were also placed on Hawaiian women at Honolulu and Lahaina to stop them meeting sailors. This particular law almost got Bingham lynched at Honolulu, along with his colleague William Richards at Lahaina, when mobs of angry sailors descended on them.[69] The heavy puritanical hand of missionaries and government reached its peak in the early 1830s when Bingham, Kaahumanu, and her brother Kuakini—the newly appointed governor of Oahu—cracked down hard on the residents of Honolulu following a minor rebellion led by the wife of the previous (runaway) governor. Kuakini organised a police force which persecuted both Hawaiians and foreigners found drinking, gambling, and generally enjoying themselves. Several Catholic priests who had lived in Honolulu since 1827, to the absolute horror of most Protestant missionaries, were bundled downtown and forced to take passage on a government schooner. Never had the Protestant missionaries had more influence in Hawaiian affairs, a situation attested to by their now very comfortable living conditions.

> *In worldly matters they are particularly well favoured; few of the foreign residents possess better dwellings, or more available comforts; their supplies from their native land are liberal and regular; a schooner packet runs between the islands at their command; and a physician resident on each island, has the charge of their health.*[70]

But it was not all plain sailing for the comfortable clerics. Their all-powerful patron Kaahumanu died in 1832. Kauikeaouli—Kamehameha III—was now old enough to rule in his own right. Free from Kaahumanu's domineering personality, Kauikeaouli reacted spectacularly to his puritanical upbringing. With a group of wild young men he went about drinking, carousing, fornicating, and ridiculing the church. Some of the strongest opposition to such behaviour came from other leading chiefs who felt their own authority in danger of being undermined. They saw their strength in the continued imposition of the Christian *kapu*. So entrenched was support for these laws amongst large sections of the chiefly élite that Kauikeaouli soon found that he could not sustain what was essentially a one-man rebellion. As one perceptive visitor explained:

> *It is probable, however, that the degree of absolute power vested in the throne depends much upon the talent and disposition of the monarch. Kamehameha I and Riho-riho [Kamehameha II] reigned with very despotic sway; while the comparative inefficiency of the present king, the effects of a protracted regency, and the increasing influence of a powerful church-party, have now tended greatly to throw the reigns of government into the hands of the principal chiefs.*[71]

By 1835, Kauikeaouli was obedient to their wishes and new moral laws were proclaimed. The errant king virtually retired from public life and quietly indulged his pleasures—billiards, horse riding, and playing cards with foreigners.[72] This marked the beginning of what the Protestants called the Great Awakening or the Revival. Catholic priests came again and were persecuted. Protestant church discipline was reimposed with increased vigour. The number of baptisms shot up dramatically, some 20 000 after 1837, which can be accounted for not just in terms of increased church activity but a more liberal policy for accepting candidates by a new missionary, Titus Coan. By 1840, the Hawaiian islands were considered Christianised.

Denouement

In 1839 the French warship *L'Artemise* anchored off Honolulu and threatened to bombard the town unless Catholics were given religious freedom.[73] The captain also demanded, and received a $20 000 bond for surety, and the right for French products to be imported. Another moderating influence was Bingham's departure from the islands in 1840. Protestant missionary influence remained strong, but with Bingham gone, lacked much of its puritanical fervour.

Now more than ever it became apparent that the monarchy needed to put its own affairs more firmly in order, and more in keeping with popular wishes, if only to ensure that foreign powers would have no excuse to interfere. From the Hawaiians' point of view, far too many British, French, and American warships were arriving in their ports. The *L'Artemise* affair was by far the most serious, but it was only one in a long series. Throughout the late 1820s and 1830s many warships had called in and their commanders had investigated complaints about Hawaiian debts to European merchants or the treatment of their nationals, and had imposed demands or 'treaties' of various kinds.

The Hawaiians needed to show that they were a sovereign and well-organised state. One result was the formulation of a Hawaiian constitution, drawn up by a number of the king's more intelligent advisers, both Hawaiian and European. Missionary influence was relatively strong, but far less so than in the drawing up of Tahiti's constitution.

The constitution had been prefaced in 1839 by a declaration—in the name of the Christian God—of rights and laws which proscribed arbitrary chiefly power and gave certain rights, such as freedom of religion, to their subjects. These rights were included in the constitution promulgated the following year—again in the name of God—which both legitimised many existing political institutions and added some new ones that were faint echoes of Tahiti's constitution. There was to be a legislative body with two sections: an 'upper house' comprising the king, the *kuhina nui*, and a council of chiefs; and a 'representative body' chosen by the people (though how they were to do so was not spelt out). Laws had to pass both houses and be signed by the king, giving him the power of veto. There was also to be a supreme court and a series of district and local courts and judges. The finances of the nation were to be regulated by tax officers. There were several modifications to the constitution in the 1840s and 1850s—for example, adult suffrage was introduced and land tenure regulations were reorganised. But the Hawaiian monarchy's attempts to organise its kingdom through constitutional arrangements were in the long run insufficient to counter foreign presence, investment, and Great Power rivalry. For decades 'national' politics were characterised by crisis after crisis. There were threats of revolution, plots for republics or annexation by Britain or the United States. The monarchy itself came to an end in 1893 when its eighth royal ruler was forced to abandon the throne. In 1898 the Hawaiian Islands were annexed by the United States.

9

Taufaʻahau of Tonga

Taufaʻahau was the most sucessful of the nineteenth-century monarchs of Polynesia. Like the Pomares and the Kamehamehas he exploited customary ways and new European influences to forge and consolidate a kingdom. But unlike the kingdoms of Hawaii and Tahiti, Taufaʻahau's still exists.

Ancient polity in Tonga

In contrast to Hawaii and Tahiti, Tonga had a long tradition of being a united kingdom.[1] As early as the tenth century AD the scattered islands of Tonga were brought under the rule of the Tuʻi Tonga. Legend has it that the first Tuʻi Tonga, ʻAhoʻeitu, was the son of the sky god Tangaloa and a human mother, hence the justification of the Tuʻi Tonga's absolute authority in both sacred and secular matters. A long succession of Tuʻi Tonga maintained their supremacy until the fifteenth century. By this time the population had increased substantially and the rigid social stratification that so marked Tongan society by the time of European contact was already well evolved (along lines similar to Hawaiian and Tahitian). As a result the Tuʻi Tonga was less able to keep the population in check, and was more likely to be opposed by ambitious families well up in the social hierarchy. During the fifteenth century a number of Tuʻi Tonga were assassinated by aspiring rivals. Kauʻulufonua Fekai, the twenty-fourth Tuʻi Tonga, tried to end such troubles by creating a new position—the *hau*—to assist the Tuʻi Tonga by taking charge of temporal affairs. The Tuʻi Tonga could then confine himself to his sacred duties unmolested. The office of *hau* went to the Tuʻi Haʻatakalaua dynasty. Early in the seventeenth century one of the Tuʻi Haʻatakalaua created another title—Tuʻi Kanokupolu—mainly to help him control part of the populous Tongatapu. However, holders of the Tuʻi Kanokupolu gradually took over the administration of the whole of Tonga and became the effective holders of the *hau*. Tuʻi Haʻatakalaua remained only nominally in charge of administrative matters. By the eighteenth century Tonga had a tripartite form of government. The

Tu'i Tonga remained the sacred monarch, the Tu'i Ha'atakalaua was nominally head of civil matters, and the Tu'i Kanokupolu held actual administrative powers. Marriage ties helped to cement the working relationships amongst these three leaders. The eldest daughter of the *hau* (now held by the Tu'i Kanokupolu) usually became the Tu'i Tonga's main wife. Any son who would usually be the next Tu'i Tonga, was thus closely related to the *hau* (maternal cousin) and the *hau* continued to support the Tu'i Tonga. Early Europeans had no trouble relating to the various divisions, as they saw them, in Tongan society, ranging from slaves to chiefs, but they were invariably confused by the trinity of 'kings'. Nevertheless, these observers usually reported the country well run, peaceful, and prosperous.

Abel Tasman reached Tonga in 1643, the first European visit since Schouten and Le Maire's brief call in 1616. Tasman saw no-one carrying arms. Cook arrived 130 years later, in 1773. He reported that the 'art of War is not unknown to these people though perhaps they practise it as little as any nation upon earth'.[2]

> *Considering the number of islands that compose this little state, and the distance some of them are from the Capital [on Tongatapu]; one would think some of them would be for throwing of [sic] the yoke but they till us this never happens; for if there is a troublesome man in any of the island[s], Feenough [head policeman of the Tu'i Kanokupolu], or whoever hold that office, goes and kills him. By this means they crush a rebellion in its very infancy, for things cannot be carried on so privately but what they must know it before it gets to any head.*[3]

Later members of the Tu'i Tonga and Tu'i Kanokupolu dynasties who tried to assert their leadership over the islands looked back to these times as some sort of golden age. But that was mainly to try to legitimise their ambitions. Tonga was by no means as free from political unrest as they claimed it had been under the rule of their ancestors. Government in Tonga in these centuries was centralised, effective, and ruthless.

Troubled times

During the latter part of the eighteenth century Tonga's centralised authority broke down and the islands became embroiled in a series of civil wars.[4] The collapse of central government can in part be attributed to the long-standing administrative stability itself. Generation after generation had seen power monopolised by a handful of privileged families. As time went by and the population increased, more and more chiefly families became frustrated at their lack of political and economic advancement. While most of them dutifully paid homage to their overlords, the more ambitious individuals worked quietly to establish a local power base for

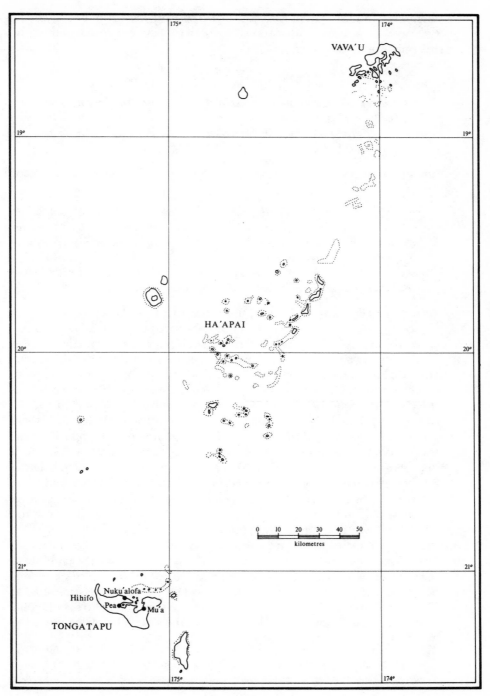

175°   174°

VAVA'U

19°   19°

HA'APAI

20°   20°

0   10   20   30   40   50
kilometres

21°   21°

Nuku'alofa
Hihifo
Pea   Mu'a
TONGATAPU

175°   174°

6   Tonga

themselves. In the eyes of early European visitors local and district chiefly tyranny was rampant. Those travelling with Cook commented on the cruel treatment of commoners:

> *The Chiefs kept the rabble in order; if they came too near the House they pelted them with Stones & Cocoa nuts & those they could reach they banged most unmercifully with Clubs, we have seen instances of their knocking a fellow in the Head with one of their Clubs which deprived him of his Senses . . . while the Chief paraded about not minding whether he was alive or dead or seeming to take any Notice of what he had done.*[5]

On another occasion Clerke saw a commoner punished for having made love to a chief's wife:

> *4 or 5 of the Indians arm'd with Clubs, rush'd thro' the Croud, fell upon him & beat him to Mummy, they sever'd his Skull, mash'd one of his Thighs & wou'd not have left a whole bone in his Skin, but our People recovering from their Consternation & being much hurt at such an appearance of Cruelty, made them desist. . . . what is very extraordinary on these Occasions, the Standers by look on with the utmost indifference, just as tho' they were Matters of course.*[6]

As local chiefly power increased, the authority of the Tuʻi Tonga and Tuʻi Kanokupolu tended in practice to become more nominal and ceremonial, especially in regions they did not often visit. Yet the more immediate causes of civil disturbance were the rows over succession amongst the chiefly families. Sometime before Cook's visit Paulaho, who apparently had tenuous claims to the position, was appointed Tuʻi Tonga. Whilst Cook was there in 1777 Paulaho's main wife—Tupoumoheofo—arranged for her son to be installed as Tuʻi Tonga while Paulaho was still alive. This was going quite against custom, but since she encountered little opposition she was encouraged to go further. She placed her supporters in a number of important offices, including the Tuʻi Vavaʻu and the Tuʻi Haʻatakalaua.[7] She herself began to dominate a succession of Tuʻi Kanokupolu, and when in 1793 one of them decided to vacate his position, Tupoumoheofo took the unprecedented step of declaring herself Tuʻi Kanokupolu. This was too much for Tukuʻaho, son of aging Mumui, who should normally have taken the title. Tukuʻaho raised an army and drove Tupoumoheofo and Paulaho from Tongatapu and they took refuge on Vavaʻu. This was a great blow to the prestige of the Tuʻi Tonga title itself and paved the way for the eventual demise of the position in the nineteenth century. Mumui was installed as Tuʻi Kanokupolu and when he died in 1797 his son Tukuʻaho assumed the position. Tukuʻaho was later described by a beachcomber as having a

> *vindictive and cruel turn of mind, taking every opportunity to exert his authority; and frequently in a manner not only cruel, but wanton; as an instance of which, he on one occasion gave orders, (which were instantly obeyed), that twelve of his cooks,*

who were always in waiting at his public ceremony of drinking cava, should undergo the amputation of their left arms, merely to distinguish them from other men, and for the vanity of rendering himself singular by this extraordinary exercise of his authority. This and many other acts of cruelty laid the groundwork for an insurrection, and a complete revolution in the affairs of Tonga.[8]

Tukuʻaho's main rival was Finau ʻUlukalala II who also lived on Tongatapu and claimed that he and not Tukuʻaho was the real Tuʻi Kanokupolu. Long gone were the days of effective central government and civil peace described by Cook. Into this turbulence came the first European residents.

Missionaries and beachcombers

When the London Missionary Society (LMS) vessel *Duff* landed its ten godly mechanics at Hihifo on Tongatapu in 1797 they found a number of beachcombers. Two of these men—Benjamin Ambler and John Connelly—were associated with Tukuʻaho, and another—Morgan Bryan—lived in the Haʻapai group.[9] All were escaped convicts from New South Wales. They immediately opposed the missionaries, not only because of their rather different outlooks on life, but because the Tongans seemed far more impressed by the evangelicals with their material possessions, which included a cuckoo clock, than by a few ragged ex-convicts. But any missionary influence with the Tongans was short-lived. Tukuʻaho gave them protection but soon paid them little attention. Within a month of their arrival, the missionaries had to put up with the insults and taunts of another half dozen beachcombers who found themselves on Tongan shores. Even more serious, from the missionaries' point of view, was the defection of one of their number, George Vason, who 'went native' and lived with three women.[10] Then the unpopular and tyrannical Tukuʻaho was murdered by Finau ʻUlukalala's men and Tongatapu was plunged into civil war as Finau and his armies went about routing Tukuʻaho's supporters. Vason threw in his lot with Finau and marched with his warriors, though by his own admission seems to have spent most of his time running away from any action.[11] One particular battle saw the death of Mulikihaʻamea, the last of the Tuʻi Haʻatakalaua line and head of Vason's Tongan family. The killers then bore down upon the mission house and clubbed to death three missionaries (Daniel Bowell, Samuel Harper, and Samuel Gaulton) and the beachcomber Benjamin Burnham.[12] Finau's men finally gained the upper hand on Tongatapu, gathered their slain opponents 'and after inflicting every brutal insult of savage cruelty [wrote Vason], roasted and ate them.'[13]

Finau then moved to Haʻapai and Vavaʻu where he similarly crushed any opposition and appointed his own 'governors'. Finau himself settled on Haʻapai, but spent much time on Tongatapu putting down periodic uprisings against his rule. Vason, who by now had been tattooed and was a trusted supporter, sometimes accompanied Finau's expeditions. He described 'enemy ravages' such as the 'large stacks of human bodies, piled up, by being laid transversely upon each other, as monumental trophy of the victory'.[14] Not that Finau's treatment of his enemies was any more subtle. He sometimes sent captives

> on board old and useless canoes, which were then scuttled, and immediately sunk; others were taken three or four leagues out to sea, and being put in old leaky ones, and tied hand and foot, were left gradually to meet their fate. Those against whom Finow entertained the greatest inveteracy were taken to the island of Lofanga, and there tied naked to stakes driven in the ground, or to the trunks of trees, and left to starve to death . . . . several of them bore their torments with the greatest fortitude, lingering till the eighth day, while others of weaker constitutions died in three or four days.[15]

The brutality and insecurity of life finally got to Vason and he fled on a passing vessel in 1801, some eighteen months after his former brethren had also escaped from Cook's Friendly Islands.

Periodic fighting, especially on Tongatapu, was aggravated by ever-increasing numbers of beachcombers. Most attached themselves to a chief for protection, but their lives were steeped in violence. Ambler and Bryan were eventually clubbed to death, Burnham was killed along with three missionaries. Some beachcombers preyed on their own kind and were encouraged in this by chiefs who were after European goods. One survivor—Doyle—from the *Argo*, wrecked in Fiji's Lau Islands in 1800, made his way to Tonga where he was responsible for the capture and massacre of most of the crew of the American vessel *Duke of Portland* in 1802.[16] Doyle was later killed by some of the survivors. Among their number were a Malay and a Hawaiian and they in turn tried to lure passing vessels inshore where they could be seized and plundered.

William Mariner and Finau 'Ulukalala II

The Hawaiian succeeded with the *Port au Prince* in 1806. Most on board were beaten to death, though William Mariner and a few others were spared, probably to assist their captors with firearms. Mariner soon found himself in Finau's household and was later adopted as his son. Finau ransacked the *Port au Prince* and added the vessel's muskets to the 2000 Mariner believed he had already amassed.[17] But the greatest prize was the *Port au Prince*'s eight carronades and 'four long guns', though the latter proved too heavy for the Tongans to take into battle. Finau lost little time in putting the new weapons to work.

17   Beachcomber William Mariner, Tonga 1806–10.
  (*Martin* An Account of the Natives of the Tonga Islands, *vol 1*)

*Mr Mariner, and those of his companions who were with him at the Island of
Lefooga, (four in number), now received orders from the king to prepare for the
annual attack upon the Island of Tonga, [Tongatapu] and to get ready four twelve-
pound carronades. They immediately set to work, to mount them upon new
carriages with high wheels, made by the native carpenters under their directions;
which being done, Finow expressed his opinion, that the gun was an instrument not
well fitted for their mode of warfare, which consisted in sudden attacks and retreats,*

according to circumstances, rather than in a steady engagement. He very readily entered into an acknowledgement of the advantages of a steady contest, but was apprehensive that his men would not easily be brought to stand it. Mr Mariner and his companions, however, promised that they and their countrymen (who were dispersed upon other islands), would remain in the front of the battle with their four guns, provided the Tonga people would agree to stand fast and support them. The king assented to this on the part of his men, and a few days afterwards, when he reviewed them, he signified his wishes, and they swore to fulfil their duty.[18]

Their objective was the fortress at Nuku'alofa, impressive and hitherto impregnable, made of three metre reedwood walls interspersed with battle towers and surrounded by four metre deep ditches.[19] Mariner and a total of 'fifteen other Englishmen' landed with Finau's warriors on the beach before the fortress under the cover of musket fire. The four carronades were slung on poles, carried from the canoes, and set up on the reef. Finau sat there himself upon a chair from the *Port au Prince* and gave the signal to open fire. The carronades bombarded the fort for an hour and though the flexible reed walls held, the shot decimated those inside. Finau's soldiers then advanced, set fire to the walls, and clubbed the survivors whilst muskets shot blank cartridges to 'intimidate the enemy'. Young boys who 'followed the expedition to be trained to the horrors of war' were allowed in to help beat the wounded to death.

In a few hours, the fortress of Nioocalofa, which had obstinately and bravely defended every attack for eleven years or more, was thus completely destroyed. When Finow arrived upon the place, and saw several canoes, which had been hauled up in the garrison, shattered to pieces by the shot, and discovered a number of legs and arms lying around, and about three hundred and fifty dead bodies, he expressed his wonder and astonishment at the dreadful effect of the guns. He then thanked his men for their bravery, and Mr Mariner and his companions in particular, for the great assistance rendered by them.[20]

However this new means of warfare did not give Finau any more control over the Tongan Islands than before. He never followed up this particular victory by launching a major assault on Tongatapu as Mariner urged. Also, effective cannon fire ultimately depended on the enemy staying in one place. As Finau had already explained to Mariner, cannon were 'not well fitted for their mode of warfare'.[21] And not many people were prepared to sit around in reed-wall forts whilst being bombarded, especially after Finau's memorable attack on Nuku'alofa. The more usual strategy was to disperse and conduct guerrilla-type skirmishes against an approaching army. An exception was the huge fort at Vava'u, built to defend the entire population of some 8000 against Finau after some of the Vava'uan chiefs rejected his authority. Unlike the fort at Nuku'alofa, this one was surrounded by a huge clay embankment.[22] Finau advanced with 5000 men and his four trusty carronades. The opening salvo lasted for six or seven hours, but there seemed to be 'little or no injury to the works, owing to the height of the place and the strength of the embankment.'[23] A long siege ensued. Eventually Finau tricked the Vava'uan chiefs into agreeing to a peaceful settlement. Later, when their fort had been dismantled, Finau treacherously had them captured and killed.[24]

Finau's control over the islands was never more than marginal, especially over Tongatapu. His authority depended on just where his army happened to be. The further away his warriors, the less assured was his supremacy. Furthermore, even his military strength was compromised. His cannons were sometimes as much a hindrance as a help. They could not penetrate clay ramparts and were very difficult to transport. Those who had to carry them 'swore heartily at all guns, and all Englishmen, and wanted to know why they were not lighter; or at least, since they had ingenuity enough to make the guns, why had not made legs for them to walk upon.'[25] But even if Finau had been more successful in battle, his control would have been tenuous. As both Pomare II and Kamehameha I appreciated, force of arms in itself was not sufficient. Paramountcy could only be maintained by effective administration, and that required—in addition to military strength—a loyal or at least dependent bureaucracy operating workable laws and sanctions. The inability of any Tongan leader to organise his rule along these lines condemned the Tongan people to decades of civil strife.

Reorganisation of rule

Finau died in 1810, and Mariner left shortly afterwards. Political intrigue and violence increased. One of Finau's sons became Finau 'Ulukalala III, ruler of Vava'u and the nominal *hau*. He died three years later and Vava'u was embroiled in succession squabbles. Meanwhile Tupouto'a, Finau II's half brother, assumed leadership of Ha'apai, intervened in Tongatapu, and through marriage alliances became Tu'i Kanokupolu. He then turned on the leaders of Vava'u and in defeating them became ruler of both Ha'apai and Vava'u, though he could never consolidate his authority over Tongatapu. When he died in 1820, rulership of Vava'u went to Tuapasi, another of Finau 'Ulukalala II's sons, who became Finau 'Ulukalala IV. In Ha'apai leadership went to Tupouto'a's son Taufa'ahau, though he did not inherit the Tu'i Kanokupolu title or the position of *hau*. Not until 1827 were these offices filled. Nor was there at this stage even a nominal Tu'i Tonga.[26]

Ironically, the lack of a Tu'i Tonga, Tu'i Kanokupolu, and a *hau* in the early 1820s marked the beginning of the end of political instability, for structural changes in island politics were taking place beneath the seem-

ingly endless succession of would-be rulers. The Haʻapai and Vavaʻu
islands had each emerged as separate political entities under the control of
the Tuʻi Haʻapai (Taufaʻahau) and Tuʻi Vavaʻu (Tuapasi or Finau ʻUlukalala
IV). Tongatapu was still divided, though Palu was ruler over most of it and
known as King Palu by visiting Europeans, who now appeared in ever-
increasing numbers. Into his patronage came the second expedition of
missionaries to Tonga.

Missionaries again

Sydney Methodist minister Walter Lawry persuaded the British Wesleyan
Conference to send himself and two artisans—Charles Tindall and George
Lilly—to Tonga in 1822. Lawry set up a post on Tongatapu with Palu's
blessing, but as was invariably the case the island patrons were interested
only in the missionaries' worldly goods. The people at large proved
indifferent or hostile to Lawry. He departed with an ill wife in 1823.
Tindall, who was sick and tired of Palu's demands, left soon after. Lilly held
out until 1827. Three Tahitian teachers trained by the LMS mission also
landed on Vavaʻu in 1822 and received protection from Finau ʻUlukalala IV.
Their mission too was short-lived. Two of them gave up their duties and
joined Finau's warriors: the third went to Tongatapu.[27]

More Wesleyan missionaries arrived in 1826.[28] This time they were
better prepared. They had more home comforts, dispensed medicine to
ailing Tongans, made a start translating and printing religious texts, and
held schools and services at Nukuʻalofa. Their new leader, Nathaniel
Turner, proved a capable man, less dictatorial than some of his brethren,
and impressed certain influential chiefs. The mission soon made a breakthrough by gaining the support of Aleamotuʻa of the Tuʻi Kanokupolu
family at Nukuʻalofa. Following Tupoutoʻa's death in 1820 no-one was
installed as Tuʻi Kanokupolu since certain high chiefs on Tongatapu were
able to defer an election, so keeping considerable authority for themselves.
But Aleamotuʻa claimed to be the Tuʻi Kanokupolu designate. If he could
gain this exalted position, the mission's influence would be much enhanced. For his part, Aleamotuʻa had his eye on the possible political
advantages that might come from supporting missionaries and their teachings. As in Tahiti and Hawaii, the prospect of mutually advantageous
exploitation brought certain chiefs and missionaries together.

Aleamotuʻa was eventually elected Tuʻi Kanokupolu in 1827 (not because of his association with missionaries, but after military victories by
Tuʻi Kanokupolu forces). In 1830 he was baptised. He then sent messages
to Finau ʻUlukalala IV on Vavaʻu and Taufaʻahau on Haʻapai suggesting
that they should accept Christianity. He explained how he still had enemies
on Tongatapu but that if they attacked him on account of his *lotu* (religion)

he would now have the British to help him.[29] Taufa'ahau needed little prompting. For several years he too had been weighing up the possible advantages of accepting missionary teachings. And it was Taufa'ahau's manoeuvrings that finally led to a unified, Christian Tongan kingdom.

The rise of Taufa'ahau

In 1820 Taufa'ahau, a member of the Tu'i Kanokupolu family, assumed leadership of the Ha'apai group on the death of his father, Tupouto'a, the Tu'i Kanokupolu.[30] Taufa'ahau's ambition, like that of his father and grandfather, was to establish the supremacy of the Tu'i Kanokupolu throughout Tonga. But at the same time the Tu'i Tonga family wanted to reestablish the Tu'i Tonga's dominance. Intense rivalry between these two families posed a serious threat to Taufa'ahau's own position in Ha'apai. He took a daring initiative which spelt the eventual demise of the Tu'i Tonga. Taufa'ahau persuaded his family elders not to give his sister as the main wife to the Tu'i Tonga elect—Laufilitonga—as was customary. In the normal run of events this couple's son would have become the Tu'i Tonga. But since the marriage would not now take place the Tu'i Tonga, should one be elected, could never have an heir. Sporadic warfare broke out between the two dynasties and Taufa'ahau finally defeated the Tu'i Tonga forces in 1826. Partly as a result of this victory, Aleamotu'a was installed as Tu'i Kanokupolu in 1827, as has been mentioned. As a concession to the losing side, Laufilitonga was installed as Tu'i Tonga. Since he had promised not to cause any trouble, and especially since he could have no heir, the Tu'i Tonga was in effect a spent force in Tongan high politics. When Laufilitonga died in 1865, the position of Tu'i Tonga was abolished.

By the late 1820s, Taufa'ahau had already achieved much through customary tactics—manipulating marriage alliances, and military strength. Missionaries and Christianity were next added to his repertoire of strategies.

Taufa'ahau made several visits to Tongatapu where he paid close attention to what Aleamotu'a and his missionary allies were doing. In 1828 he asked Turner to send missionaries to Ha'apai. Turner was shrewd enough to see that Taufa'ahau was one of the most astute and promising of all the Tongan leaders, much more so than the mission's current champion, Aleamotu'a. However, Turner could only supply him with a baptised Tongan teacher at this stage. Taufa'ahau was somewhat piqued. He wanted a European. But he grudgingly accepted his Tongan and returned to Ha'apai, where by the early 1830s most of the population had ostensibly accepted the *lotu*. Yet again on a Pacific island, rapid conformity to the outward requirements of Christianity was a political phenomenon. Once prestigious leaders like Aleamotu'a and Taufa'ahau ordered that new customs be adopted, their followers obeyed dutifully enough. There were the usual attractions, especially the excitement of literacy. A printing press arrived and by 1832 had produced over 17 000 books in Tongan.[31] The promise of stable and powerful leadership offered by Taufa'ahau also appealed to his people of Ha'apai and elsewhere who had suffered from decades of civil strife. In 1831 he was baptised. He also renamed himself King George after tales he heard from the Wesleyans of George III of England.

On Vava'u Finau too was baptised and his people became 'Christian'. A few communities objected, but the combined military forces of Finau and Taufa'ahu soon forced them into submission. In 1833 Finau died after declaring Taufa'ahau his successor. Both Ha'apai and Vava'u were Taufa'ahau's. He ruled both by customary rights and as a leader of the new religion. As a preacher of the Christian gospel he was, by all accounts, most impressive:

> *The attention of his audience was riveted.... The King is a tall and graceful person: in the pulpit he was dressed in a black coat, and his manner was solemn and earnest. He held in his hand a small bound manuscript book, but seldom looked at it. I believe, however, that his sermon was written in it. His action was dignified and proper, his delivery fluent, graceful and not without majesty. He evidently engaged the attention of his hearers, who hung upon his lips with earnest and increasing interest. I perceived that much of what he said was put forth interrogatively; a mode of address which is very acceptable among the Tongans.*[32]

Completing the kingdom

Certain chiefs on Tongatapu, especially the Ha'a Havea, viewed Taufa'ahau's northern 'conquests' with great alarm. Some violently opposed Christianity, since they accurately saw it as an important part of Taufa'ahau's strategy for dominance over the whole Tonga group. Throughout the later 1830s fighting between allegedly Christian and non-Christian factions on Tongatapu intensified. The aging Aleamotu'a—the Tu'i Kanokupolu—who led the Christian forces on the island, sought Taufa'ahau's assistance. Taufa'ahau was only too keen to send his warriors, not only to trounce the Ha'a Havea, long-standing enemies of his family, but to strengthen the Tu'i Kanokupolu—the position he coveted for himself. The Wesleyan missionaries gave every encouragement to Taufa'ahau's 'Christian soldiers' in these 'Holy wars'.[33] An engagement in 1837 saw Taufa'ahau's forces take an early victory. The missionaries were convinced that this was a sign of God's will and declared that the bones of Taufa'ahau's enemies were a 'visible mark of God's displeasure against sin'.[34] In 1840 the Ha'a Havea and the Christians were again locked in battle. Taufa'ahau organised a major military expedition and laid siege to a massive Ha'a Havean fort at Pea.[35] This time the contest was more evenly matched and was at a stalemate when Commodore Wilkes of the United States Exploring Expedition called at Tongatapu. Wilkes tried unsuccessfully to arrange a truce, then sailed away. Shortly afterward Captain Croker arrived on HMS *Favourite* and took a much firmer line than the more diplomatic Wilkes. When the 'heathen' chiefs of the fort refused to surrender to him

> *he ordered his guns to be drawn within musket shot of the fortress, contrary to the expostulations of some of his own subordinates, and then, heading the sailors, sword in hand, he said, 'Now, blue-jackets, follow me'. They did so, but the consequences were disastrous in the extreme. The captain was shot dead upon the spot.*[36]

This tragi-comedy did have some effect. So terrified were the Ha'a Havea chiefs of reprisals from other British warships that they agreed to submit to Taufa'ahau's authority, and there was relative calm on Tongatapu for a while.

Throughout the 1830s Taufa'ahau, Aleamotu'a and the Wesleyan missionaries advocated strenuously that the Tu'i Kanokupolu was the legitimate ruler over all Tonga and that on Aleamotu'a's death, Taufa'ahau should inherit the title. By the time Aleamotu'a did die, in 1845, there was widespread acceptance that Taufa'ahau would gain the position, and he did. After all his father and grandfather had held the office and in addition Taufa'ahau had proven himself capable of such leadership. His avowed enemies had, at least for the meantime, been subdued. Nor was there any alternative candidate. The Ha'atakalaua line had long since ended, and the existing Tu'i Tonga, the feeble Laufilitonga, had no heir. By right and might did Taufa'ahau call himself King George Tupou, Tu'i Kanokupolu. But the monarchy emerged was not necessarily the monarchy consolidated. While most of the Tongan population was prepared to accept that Taufa'ahau had at least the alleged blessings of customary legitimacy for his position, there was every likelihood that certain disaffected chiefs might oppose him at any time. The bitterness engendered by the past fifty or more years of civil turmoil could not be forgotten. And no sooner had Tongatapu been 'pacified' in 1840 than a new threat to Taufa'ahau's hegemony emerged. In 1842 Roman Catholic priests found a ready reception amongst the Ha'a Havea chiefs who saw the opportunity of playing off French Catholics against Taufa'ahau and his English Protestant allies.[37] The priests were equally appreciative of the potential benefits association with the Ha'a Havea might have. They also made special efforts to win over Laufilitonga—the Tu'i Tonga—in the hope of revitalising an ancient alternative to Tu'i Kanokupolu's supremacy. Laufilitonga had earlier refused to accept the Wesleyan faith and he similarly rebuffed early Marist attempts to woo him. But Taufa'ahau's assumption of the Tu'i Kanokupolu title and the kingship of Tonga in 1845 caused Laufilitonga to

think again. It was not that he had any intention of trying to overthrow
Taufa'ahau. Indeed in 1848 he publicly renounced claims to civil power.
But he wished to reinforce the separate and independent identity of the Tu'i
Tonga. In 1848 he enrolled as a Catholic catechumen and was baptised in
1851. Fighting on Tongatapu broke out in 1852. Its origins were in long-
standing rivalries aggravated now by the conflicting religions and especially the fears on both sides that British or French warships might join in.
Taufa'ahau's forces again descended on the Ha'a Havea. He starved out
one of their forts, but the great one at Pea held out. As in 1840, the arrival of
a foreign naval vessel marked the end of the Ha'a Havea. When HMS
Calliope anchored offshore, the besieged commanders in Pea felt obliged to
parley with Taufa'ahau in Nuku'alofa. Meanwhile Taufa'ahau's troops
persuaded those still behind the walls that peace had been declared and they
were let in. Pea was soon dismantled and most of its former defenders
agreed to become Wesleyans. Only at the Tu'i Tonga's residence at Mu'a
was Catholicism tolerated. However, the French warship that the priests
had sent for during the siege at Pea eventually arrived. Though months too
late to save the Ha'a Havea, the captain extracted from Taufa'ahau a
promise not to persecute Catholics again. In 1855 the French governor of
Oceania, Du Bouzet, forced Taufa'ahau to sign a treaty which gave
Catholics and French citizens in Tonga protection from discrimination.
Taufa'ahau wisely upheld these provisions, for the most part at least, and
Catholicism survived in Tonga, though very much as a minority religion.
By guaranteeing its survival, Taufa'ahau effectively rendered it neutral as a
serious political threat. If persecutions against the Catholics had been
allowed to continue, Catholicism might once again have become a rallying
point for disaffected chiefs. Besides, the French navy had always to be
reckoned with. French commanders had never been reluctant to use force
or the threat of force on other islands in the Pacific, as knowledgeable
Tongans like Taufa'ahau were only too well aware.

Codes of law

The best possible security for the monarchy in Tonga, as in Hawaii and
Tahiti, was workable laws and an effective administration. In Tonga, as on
these other islands, missionary influence played an integral part in creating
a new order.

Taufa'ahau promulgated his first code of law on Vava'u in 1839 after
long consultations with Wesleyan missionaries.[38] The code had
Taufa'ahau 'appointed' by the Christian God and with the task of convey-
ing God's wishes to everyone else on Vava'u by way of a series of
prohibitions. These included the usual mixture of customary sanctions
about obeying chiefs and not stealing pigs, and missionary-inspired rules

against adultery, fornication, drinking of alcohol, and working and playing on the Sabbath. All people, whether of high or low birth, were subject to these laws, which meant, in theory if not practice, that chiefs were bound by the same laws as commoners and answerable to their monarch. A court was established and magistrates appointed to enforce the regulations. Selling land to foreigners was prohibited. This was the forerunner of land legislation that helped prevent the growth of a large population of European residents on Tonga, and in turn meant that Imperial Powers were less interested in interfering in Tongan affairs. This 1839 code was extended to Ha'apai and then to Tongatapu after Taufa'ahau became Tu'i Kanokupolu in 1845. In 1850 the laws were revised.[39] There was also some borrowing from the LMS code for Huahine of 1823, which the Wesleyan missionaries on Tonga copied from William Ellis's *Polynesian Researches*.

The overall effect of the early laws was to consolidate Taufa'ahau's position as supreme ruler (after God). The simple judicial machinery gave him considerably increased powers over individuals including, significantly, other chiefs. Their opportunities for taking initiative became increasingly circumscribed. At the same time, they became more dependent on the king for whatever authority and prestige he might concede to them. This relationship was most clearly advanced in 'The Law referring to the King' of the 1850 code:

1. The King, being the root of all government in the land, it is for him to appoint those who shall govern in his land.

2. Whatever the King may wish done in his land, it is with him to command the assemblages of his Chiefs, to consult with him thereon.

3. Whatever is written in these laws, no Chief is at liberty to act in opposition, but to obey them together with his people.

4. The King is the Chief Judge; and anything the Judges may not be able to decide upon, shall be referred to the King, and whatever his decision may be, it shall be final.

Taufa'ahau, unlike his fellow kings on Tahiti and Hawaii, was more catholic in his choice of Western advisers. In Tahiti the Pomares were all but presented with the 1819 law code and the 1824 constitution by the LMS missionaries. Mission initiatives were a little less blatant in Hawaii, but in the 1820s and 1830s missionaries played a prominent part in drawing up the 'moral laws'. Taufa'ahau, however, took more initiative himself. While his laws were clearly influenced by missionaries, he was using missionaries rather more than they were using him. Taufa'ahau's aggressiveness in seeking advice from anyone he thought could help him, as opposed to slavish attachment to missionaries alone, was clearly demonstrated during the late 1840s. And as a consequence, some Wesleyan missionaries, like John Thomas, became annoyed. They resented his proud independence and hankered for the earlier years when Taufa'ahau had appeared more

18   Taufa'ahau, early 1860s. (West Ten Years in South-Central Polynesia)

amenable to their paternalism. Now he was their patron rather than the reverse. Tonga under Taufa'ahau was no less Christian than Hawaii or Tahiti; indeed it was more so, but missionaries themselves had less direct influence with the king. Taufa'ahau sought advice from everyone—beachcombers, ships' captains, even Governor Grey of New Zealand. In 1853 Taufa'ahau visited Sydney. There he met Charles St Julian, who was a law reporter with the *Sydney Morning Herald*. The two subsequently struck up a lively correspondence. In 1854 St Julian, who was by then the Hawaiian consul in Sydney, urged Taufa'ahau to enter 'political and commercial relationships' with the Hawaiian monarchy, and to secure from the Imperial Powers recognition of Tonga's sovereignty and independence. He advised Taufa'ahau to draw up a constitution along the lines of the 1852 Hawaiian constitution, a copy of which he sent him. Taufa'ahau was considerably influenced by St Julian's ideas, but the impulsive consul soon lost patience with what he considered the King's slowness to implement them.[40] Taufa'ahau moved at his own pace. He gained another adviser in 1860—Shirley Baker, a Wesleyan missionary, who became his most trusted associate for several decades. It was Baker the man, not Baker the missionary that impressed Taufa'ahau.[41]

In 1862 Taufa'ahau issued another code of laws which represented an amalgam of advice from foreigners like St Julian and Baker, and his own views and experiences. This code set precedents for the future shape of the monarchy by introducing several structural changes in government and in the economy of Tonga.[42] Among the most innovative provisions was the 'Emancipation Edict' (Law 34), whereby

> *All chiefs and people are . . . set at liberty from serfdom and all vassalage . . . and it shall not be lawful for any chief or person to seize or take by force, or beg authoritatively, in Tonga fashion, any thing from any one.*[43]

In theory this meant that chiefs could no longer exploit their commoners for food and labour. Instead the king was to pay salaries to all 'Governors, Judges, Rulers and Officers', and pensions to other chiefs, as compensation for the loss of the customary tributes they exacted from the commoners. To finance this scheme all Tongans had to pay a small poll tax. There were radical changes in landholding too. Chiefs had to make available to every adult male an area of land for farming, for which these tenants would pay a tiny rent. Chiefs had no rights to dispossess these land users. Once again it was clearly stated that no land could be sold to foreigners. With this 1862 code, Taufa'ahau further consolidated his centralised bureaucratic control over the country. The Tongan economy was set on a predictable cash basis instead of the usual arbitrary tribute system. This, combined with the commoners' security of tenure, saw a boom in Tongan agriculture, especially copra production from the 1870s.

Throughout the 1860s and early 1870s Taufa'ahau and Baker worked closely to give Tonga and its monarchy trappings of Westernisation. In part this was to further entrench the king's position, but it was also to demonstrate to foreign powers that the Tongan kingdom was capable of looking after its own affairs in a civilised manner, unlike neighbouring Fiji and Samoa which had no centralised governments and were now at the mercy of the conflicting demands of British, German, and United States citizens there. While Tonga did not have a large resident European population, nor a plantation economy controlled by foreign investors—all factors that contributed to the eventual annexation by Western governments of Fiji, Samoa, Hawaii, and other islands—Taufa'ahau still felt vulnerable. Too many hitherto forgotten corners of the globe were now being incorporated into the empires of European politicians.

The Constitution of Tonga, 1875

A major step toward securing Tonga's independence came with the constitution of 1875.[44] It was drawn up by Baker, in consultation with lawyers and various experts in Australia and New Zealand, and had as its model St

Julian's Hawaiian constitution. The document, permeated with Christian phraseology, began with a declaration of rights. Next came a section on government. Tonga was a constitutional monarchy with succession passing to Taufa'ahau's heirs. This was the final step in ensuring the survival of the monarchy after the king's death. Under the king came the privy council (composed of cabinet ministers, governors, and the chief justice) and the cabinet (whose members were appointed by the king). Together the king, privy council, and cabinet formed the executive. A legislative assembly was made up of cabinet ministers, twenty nobles appointed from chiefly ranks by the king, and twenty representatives of the people elected by adult male franchise. The judiciary consisted of a supreme court, circuit courts, and police courts. Finally there was a section on land: all land belonged to the king, who granted estates to the twenty nobles he appointed. Their titles and lands were hereditary. Portions of these estates were to be leased to commoners.

This constitution was the final act in the creation of a Tongan monarchy and its promulgation made it possible for Germany (1876), Britain (1879), and the United States (1888) to recognise Tonga's independence. Within the Tongan context the constitutional arrangements were not perhaps as innovative in reality as they appeared on paper. The king, though subject to theoretical checks and balances, remained politically supreme as well as sacred. The appointment of twenty nobles with estates brought back what Taufa'ahau had earlier abolished—a landed aristocracy. This meant that the commoners were in practice less emancipated than they had been under the 1862 laws. This was a calculated strategy. Taufa'ahau recognised the necessity to buy off these families to prevent any opposition they might conceivably organise in the future, had they remained too far beyond the pale of privilege. Tonga, like Hawaii and Tahiti, witnessed no social revolution in spite of apparently radical constitutional concessions to the bulk of the population. It was the upper levels of the social hierarchy that had been reorganised. One supreme family and twenty others of slightly lesser standing were now safely entrenched by rules of succession and land ownership. Other chiefly families were effectively frozen in their ranks, but since they were all members of a bureaucracy controlled by the king their standing depended on their continued loyalty and service to their monarch. To the commoners, the bulk of the population, the Tongan social order seemed largely unchanged.

So too did the way of life in Tonga for most people remain in essence unchanged from earlier generations. To be sure there was peace and order, and Christianity had permeated Tongan social mores through the Free Church of Tonga (born in 1885 after Shirley Baker declared the Wesleyan Church in Tonga independent from its Australian mission overlord). By all outward appearances Tongans were amongst the most dutiful of Christian congregations anywhere. The casual traveller saw many signs of English-inspired civilisation—the neat villages with white picket fences, cobbled streets, village church spires, well-clothed congregations, the choirs at evensong. Yet in other respects the Tongan Islands failed to experience the other consequences of European contact that were usual for Pacific islands—the port towns with their quarrelsome frontier societies, the alienation of land by planters and companies, the demands for labour, the presence of migrant workers from overseas. For some late nineteenth century travellers, Tonga was quaintly civilised, with some of the virtues of English life and few of its evils; for others, Tonga was a socially and economically stagnant backwater.

Denouement

Taufa'ahau died in 1893. Unlike those of the founding monarchs of Tahiti and Hawaii, his life spanned most of the nineteenth century, and with it the range of experience from earliest European contact to the era of European annexation of Pacific islands. Unlike the kingdoms of Hawaii and Tahiti, Taufa'ahau's still remains. In part this was due to geographical and geological accident. Tonga, in European eyes, had not the rolling fertile landscapes of Samoa, Hawaii, or Fiji to attract planters and investors. Nevertheless, foreigners would have come but for Taufa'ahau's insistence that Europeans could not buy land in Tonga. The otherwise probably inevitable progression from port town to colony was never allowed to begin. Although the monarchy survived, Tonga after Taufa'ahau was not in practice as politically and economically independent as is commonly claimed. Tonga was not annexed by any of the Great Powers, as were all the other Pacific islands, but Tongan leaders (many by inclination), and the Great Powers by agreement, saw Tonga a British protectorate early in the twentieth century, with British officials having more than a little influence in Tongan affairs.[45]

Comment: Monarchs in Oceanic context

The Pomares, the Kamehamehas, and Taufa'ahau all used customary strategies—force, exploitation of kin and family ties, diplomacy—to build up their rank-status and power. While the centralised governments they created were unprecedented on their islands, the means by which they achieved their leadership was within the bounds of legitimate and accepted behaviour: Pomare I with his *maro* and Oro images was the highest-ranked person on Tahiti by the 1790s, Kamehameha I had conquered by force most of the Hawaiian Islands by 1795, and Taufa'ahau on Tonga became the Tu'i Kanokupolu in 1845. European assistance initially was far less important than many writers have claimed. Western advice, technical expertise, and firearms may have been useful, even crucial, to the aspiring monarchs on occasion but such assistance was no guarantee of success. In particular the use of firearms in indigenous warfare did not give their owners unquestioned military superiority over others. The island kings made themselves, with the assistance of some Europeans and their ways. But Europeans and European interests did not and could not make the monarchs. The social and political organisations and processes in Tahiti, Hawaii, and Tonga provided the opportunities and sanctions for the emergence of such leaders.

European assistance became much more pronounced after a degree of political centralisation had already been achieved by customary means. Missionaries and Christianity were particularly useful for legitimising and consolidating the newly forged kingdoms. The adaptation, exploitation, and imposition of Christianity on the leaders' new subjects was a common and highly successful political strategy, and was quickly formalised. Mainly though not exclusively through missionary advice, each monarch had codes of law drawn up and these eventually became constitutions that were designed not only to consolidate the reorganisation of the internal polity, but to impress foreign powers in the hope of giving them no excuse to intervene. As it happened, the three kingdoms were Protestant and pro-British in outlook, mainly because the British navy and Protestant missionaries were among the more commonly found and influential Europeans in Pacific waters in the late eighteenth and early nineteenth centuries.

A predominant theme was of aspiring warrior kings uniting their islands, legitimising, reorganising and consolidating their rule and eventually creating constitutional monarchies. But in Hawaii, Tonga, and Tahiti constitution making had in practice more to do with reorganising relationships amongst the upper echelons of society than with changing relationships between an élite minority and the great bulk of the population—the commoners. The trappings of nineteenth-century democracy transported into these Pacific kingdoms meant little to the mass of the people, who remained more concerned with the day-to-day tasks of caring for their families and working for overlords whose demands they could never escape.

The monarchs of these three island groups were by no means the only Pacific island leaders to increase their powers and domains during the period of early European contact, but nowhere else in the Pacific were such large and united polities established. The explanation for this unique trio of kingdoms lies in the social and political makeup of Tonga, Tahiti, and Hawaii at the time of European contact. These three societies were the most stratified in the Pacific Ocean. It seems no coincidence that the most effective political centralisation under indigenous leaders of anywhere in the islands after Europeans arrived occurred in these three places.

Whatever the island contexts in which these kingdoms emerged and operated, outside influences far beyond the control of the kings and their subjects ultimately determined the fate of the royal regimes. The French took over Tahiti in 1843, mainly for strategic reasons; Tahitian kings were kept as figureheads until the fifth one finally gave up sovereignty in 1880. The eighth monarch of Hawaii abdicated in 1893, after decades of political strife amongst Hawaiians, Americans, and other nationals in the islands, and the United States annexed Hawaii in 1898. The Tongan monarchy survived, not just because of certain attributes and strengths it possessed, but because the Great Powers agreed to allow it to survive, under British protection, after Britain and Germany rationalised their respective spheres of influence in the South Seas at the end of the nineteenth century. Had any of the powers wanted to annex Tonga there would have been little the Tongan monarchy could have done to prevent it.

Monarchs manqué?

Whale-bone club (kotiate), *New Zealand*

10

New Zealand

Leaders on other islands of Polynesia were just as politically aggressive and had just as much or more opportunity to exploit Europeans and their goods and ideas as the Pomares, the Kamehamehas and Taufaʻahau. That they were unable to turn themselves into triumphant kings ruling over centralised states had little to do with their own abilities or lack of them. The real obstacles to achieving such paramountcy were inherent in their respective social and political organisations. Just as the highly stratified societies of Tahiti, Hawaii, and Tonga provided the necessary bases for successful kingships to emerge, so did the lack of such stratification inhibit these developments elsewhere, even, as in New Zealand, to the point where the very idea of unifying an entire country had not entered the concerns of chiefly politics.

Maori society

In contrast to the homelands of other Pacific Islanders, New Zealand is large as well as cold and gale blown for many months of the year. The difficulties of living in a climate that by tropical standards is often miserable, together with the demands of travelling over its rugged landscape or around its cold, temperamental seas, gave a certain rawness and harshness to the lifestyles of the first settlers. Living in the extreme south of Polynesia required rather more effort than in the tropical lushness of places like Tahiti. Most of the staple crops of the tropical Pacific were not brought to, or did not survive in New Zealand. The one staple that did—the sweet potato—required very considerable planning and hard work to enable it to survive. In many parts of New Zealand such as in the southern North Island and most of the South Island a hunting and gathering lifestyle, as opposed to a more sedentary agricultural life, was required. The first New Zealanders also devoted much more time and effort to keeping warm and dry than did their tropical cousins. Some form of clothing was essential in winter and garments woven of coarse fibres were worn. Usually only chiefs

wore cloth of fine, soft texture. Weatherproof housing was also essential.
The more nomadic or semi-nomadic groups in colder parts on the country
built rough shelters that Cook described as 'low wretched huts made of the
bark of trees'.[1] In more settled parts houses were more substantial:

> *The houses of these people are better calculated for a cold than a hot climate: they*
> *are built low and in form of an oblong square, the framing is of wood or small sticks*
> *and the sides and covering of thatch made of long grass. The door is generaly at one*
> *end and no biger than to admit a man to creep in and out; just within the door is the*
> *fire place and over the door or on one side is a small hole to let out the smook. These*
> *houses are 20 or 30 feet long, others not above half as long; this depends upon the*
> *largness of the Family they are to contain for I believe few families are without such*
> *a house as these, altho they do not a[l]ways live in them especialy in the summer*
> *season when many of them live disperse'd up and down in little temporary hutts that*
> *are not sufficient to shelter them from the weather.*[2]

The importance of even temporary shelter was well illustrated by Queen
Charlotte Sound Maoris who moved close to Cook's *Endeavour*:

> *It is curious to see with what facility they build these little temporary habitations: I*
> *have seen above twenty of them errected on a spot of ground that not an hour before*
> *was covered with shrubs & plants. . . . [They] are abundantly sufficient to shelter*
> *them from the wind and rain.*[3]

The never-ending physical labour to keep warm, dry, fed, and safe from
enemies, together with the associated high incidence of illness and degenerative diseases, contributed to a very short life expectancy by modern
standards.[4] Prehistorians are in the process of painting the now academi-
cally respectable view (though one quite at odds with fashionable romantic
and political views of the pre-European Maori) of a lifestyle which, in neo-
Hobbesian language, is characterised as 'harsh, hungry and short.'[5]

The climate and terrain not only influenced Maori habits, material
culture, and economic activities generally, but also affected less visible and
tangible aspects of life—social and political organisation. But the environment was just one of the elements that determined the shape of social and
political arrangements; the 'ideologies' of these early settlers probably
carried equal if not greater weight.

Maori society differed in several key aspects from the societies of Tonga,
Tahiti, and Hawaii. Sociopolitical units were fairly small and geographically fragmented, social divisions were less clear cut and more flexible, and
leadership was less authoritarian.

Any large-scale sociopolitical units in New Zealand would have been too
difficult to maintain since rapid long distance travel with armies was not
possible overland, and travel by sea along potentially dangerous coastlines
was too unreliable, unlike canoe-borne forays in tropical climes. Even
though most of the Maori population at the time of European contact,

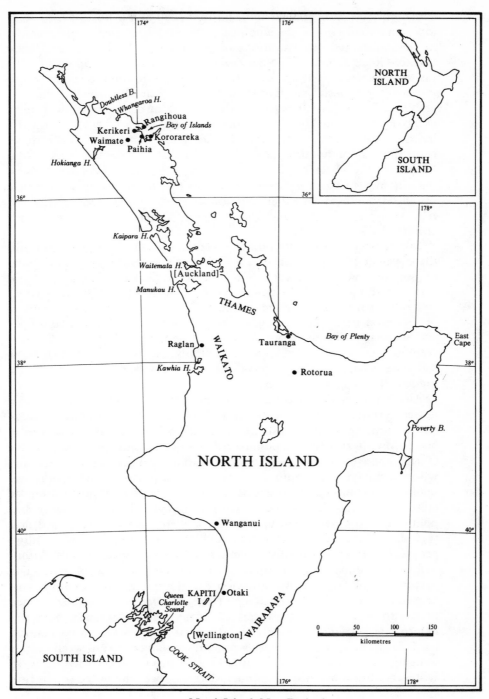

7   *North Island, New Zealand*

some 100 000–120 000, lived in the northern half of the North Island, with only some 5000–6000 in the whole of the South Island, there were very few of the substantial concentrations of population found in other Pacific islands. Given its land area, New Zealand was relatively unpopulated. This geographic fragmentation of settlement was more reminiscent of many regions of Melanesia than of most of Polynesia. Kamehameha I, Pomare II, and Taufa'ahau could impose controls on distant communities with their ability to travel quickly with sea-borne armies, but a New Zealand chief living, for example, in the Bay of Islands had no means of effectively controlling a community hundreds of kilometres to the south. As Cook explained: 'At whatever place we put in at or whatever people we spoke with upon the Coast they generaly told us that those that were at a little distance from them were their enimies; from which it appeared to me that they were very much divided into parties which make war one with another'.[6]

In contrast to the highly stratified societies of Tahiti, Tonga, and Hawaii, there was in New Zealand, to use Goldman's terminology, a traditional organisation where rank was based on birth and traced usually through the male line, though a high birth did not necessarily result in effective power.[7] Individual ability also counted for much. Society was stratified in terms of genealogical status, but not rigidly so. There were no formalised classes and social mobility was considerable for the able and ambitious. Maori communities were divided as much vertically, on a sociopolitical chart, as Tahitians, Tongans, and Hawaiians were divided horizontally into graduated social strata or classes.

All Maoris belonged to one of about fifty tribes or *iwi* which were broad descent groups tracing ancestry back to real or mythical canoe landings (either from eastern Polynesia or from within New Zealand). Each tribe had its own territory, but boundaries were constantly changing, as was tribal composition itself, as a result of warfare and migration. The tribe, whose members might number a few thousand to tens of thousands, was seldom a unified political organisation, but more often an institution for cultural and emotional identity. Within the tribe the economically and politically more active groups, or *hapu*, were also descent based and typically comprised a more manageable membership of a few hundred people. *Hapu* were in turn divided into *whanau* or extended families. Within each of these three categories there was a graduated hierarchy of status. The paramount chief of the tribe or *iwi* was called *ariki*, the chief of a *hapu* was *rangatira*, and the senior member of the *whanau* was *kaumatua*.[8] Since relationships within and between these entities were constantly expressed in terms of descent from chiefly ancestors, virtually anyone could claim to be of chiefly rank, or, as it is more commonly explained, no one would admit to being a commoner. In this sense the only groups acknowledged were aristocrats and war captives. Samuel Marsden shrewdly noted on his first voyage to New Zealand in 1814, 'From what I could learn there appears to be no middle class of people ... but that they are either all chiefs or, in a certain degree, slaves.'[9]

Maori society had not developed clear-cut social division and stratification whereby a small élite ruled over the bulk of the population, as happened to its culturally closest relatives—Tahitians and Hawaiians. In part this can also be explained by the environment. The endless drudgery necessary to ensure the survival of relatively small communities on very large islands hindered the appearance of a leisured élite. Even the most prestigious leaders sometimes had to dig gardens and defensive ditches or collect shellfish.[10] In part too there is an ideological explanation in the conceptual duality of leadership as expressed in the terms *tapu* and *mana*. *Tapu*, very roughly translated, is a measure of sacredness (though it can also refer to secular matters such as prohibitions of various kinds). The strength or amount of a person's *tapu* was dependent on birth and sex. It was 'socially ascribed' and 'inalienable',[11] and could be neither increased nor decreased. It was an expression of a hierarchy or gradation of rank-status. Persons with the highest rank-status from birth had the greatest amount of *tapu*, but their authority was ritualised, involving priestly or other religious duties. Power was not conferred by birth or office but was 'achieved and retained solely on the basis of demonstrated personal skills.'[12] The measure of a person's achievement was expressed as *mana*. The most able individuals, whose *mana* was strongest, were the effective leaders. The importance of *mana*, for most people claimed at least some measure of it, cannot be overemphasised. Its personal, achievable nature lent a particular character to Maori social and political life in at least three respects. First, it placed great importance on the role of the individual and a person's worth and self respect. Individual or private enterprise on the part of ordinary members of a community was thus far more acceptable than in the more stratified societies where individual will was suppressed in the interests of more collective or corporate activity for the benefit of an élite. Maori society was extremely competitive, both between and within the *iwi*, the *hapu*, and the *whanau*. Economic activity was, as Europeans often commented, very entrepreneurial. Individuals were permitted a degree of private property (though if they amassed too much they would be raided by kith and kin) and much chiefly activity was concerned with amassing material wealth.[13] In these respects too, Maori society had much in common with many of the Big-Men communities in parts of Melanesia.

Second, the concept of *mana*, in its justification of leadership, was a further limit to the development of authoritarian and arbitrary rule. Since those people who achieved secular power, as distinct from those having ritualised authority, were not holders of any constituted rights or office, they were in no position to coerce and command their followers. They had to rule by example and with consensus. The chief and his followers, within *iwi* and *hapu*, were mutually dependent on each other. In the strength and prestige of the one lay the strength and prestige of the other, and this shared or integrated *mana* could result only from mutual respect.

Third, the central importance of *mana* (and *tapu*) to all individuals meant that any insult or affront whether at domestic or tribal level could not be countenanced. Vengeance, or *utu*, was demanded. This helped to make Maori society seem particularly violent and war ridden. The need to avenge insults seems to have intensified the more universal motives for conflict— the control of resources and ambition. As Cook explained:

> *New Zealanders must live under perpetual apprehinsions of being distroyed by each other. There being few Tribes that have not received some injury or a nother from some other, which they are continually upon the watch to revenge and perhaps the idea of a good meal may be no small incitement. I am told that many years will sometimes elapse before a favourable oppertunity happens, and that the Son never losses sight of an injury that has been done his Father. There method of executing these horrible designs is by stealing upon the party in the night, and if they find them unguarded (which however I beleive is very seldom the case) they kill every soul that falls in their way, not even sparing the Women and Children, and then either feast and gorge themselves on the spot or carry off as many of the dead as they can and do it at home with acts of brutality horrible to relate. If they are discovered before they can put their design into execution, they generally steal off again, some times they are persued and attacked by the other party; they neither give quarter nor take prisoners, so that the Vanquish'd can only save their lives by flight. This method of makeing War keeps them continually upon their guard so that one hardly ever finds a New Zealander of his guard either day or night.*[14]

In general, Maori communities did not have the potential for a supreme leader to emerge and rule over a politically united populace as happened in Tahiti, Hawaii, and Tonga. Maori settlement patterns and social and political organisation worked against such a process. Even the idea of centralisation did not exist. No-one in New Zealand had ambitions and advantages equivalent to those of a Tu'i Kanokupolu in Tonga, or of a *maro* holder in Tahiti, or even the military and bureaucratic controls that Hawaiian rulers could exploit. Again this is not a deterministic argument. A Maori strong man or king could have arisen in the period of early European contact, but the possibility was more remote than in the highly stratified islands of Polynesia, and, in effect, went unrealised.

Explorers' experiences

Early Maori-European relations were marked by considerable violence. Four of Tasman's sailors were killed by Maoris in 1642 and, as a result, the Dutch explorer never dared set foot ashore. Cook, who visited New

Zealand more often than anyone else in the 1770s, admired Maori bravery and industry and willingness to trade and their 'intelligence' generally; indeed he attributed them with many of the qualities of the Noble Savage, yet he also highlighted the constant warfare, cannibalism, and overall violence of their lifestyle. Cook certainly took no chances, and though he claimed it grieved him to have to do so, he shot to kill whenever a situation proved threatening. His men killed four, perhaps five Maoris within the first few days of making landfall in Poverty Bay in 1769. Then Tupaia, the Ra'iatean on board, almost lost his 'Indian Boy' servant when Maoris tried to kidnap him. Another two or three Maoris were shot. Although Cook did all he could to encourage friendly relations, and often succeeded, several more Maoris were killed, and many felt the sting of grapeshot, as he made his way up the east coast of the North Island. In the South Island, and in particular in Queen Charlotte Sound, where he spent most of his time on his New Zealand visits, relations with Maoris were usually more friendly. Yet on the second voyage, Cook's accompanying vessel, the *Adventure*, under Furneaux, had one of her boat crews killed and mutilated in the Sound. If there was any treachery in Maori-European dealings, it was certainly not all one-sided.

The French explorer Surville, on the North Island's northeast coast only months after Cook sailed past, repaid Maoris who had assisted him when his ship was in danger of being driven ashore by high seas by kidnapping and clapping in irons a chief—Ranginui—with the intention of taking him to France. He died of scurvy before reaching South America.[15] Some years later, in 1773, another Frenchman, Marion Du Fresne, spent what seemed to be a most enjoyable month in the Bay of Islands. But without warning Du Fresne and some of his men were ambushed and killed on a fishing expedition. The attack was premeditated, but the motives remain unclear. The presence of so many foreigners who stayed for such a long time and perhaps unintentionally transgressed sanctions of various kinds doubtless began to concern local Maoris. Certainly a few tensions had developed. The surviving French officers took violent revenge, killing about 250 Maoris.[16] To Julien Crozet, Du Fresne's second in command, the massacre of his leader was the work not of a calculating people but of primitive and terrible passions that inevitably welled in the uncivilised mind.

> *We had become so familiar with these men that nearly all the officers had particular friends amongst them, who served them and accompanied them everywhere; had we departed about this time, we would have brought to Europe the most favourable accounts of these savages; we would have painted them in our relations with them as the most affable, the most humane, and the most hospitable people on the face of the earth. From our accounts philosophers fond of praising primitive man would have triumphed in seeing the speculations of their studies confirmed by the accounts of travellers whom they would have recommended as worthy of belief. But we would all*

of us have been in the wrong. . . . For my part I maintain that there is amongst all the animals of the creation none more ferocious and dangerous for human beings than the primitive and savage man, and I had much rather meet a lion or a tiger, because I should then know what to do, than one of these men. I speak according to my experience. . . . I have traversed the greater part of the globe, and I have seen everywhere that when reason is not assisted and perfectioned by good laws, or by a good education, it becomes the prey of force or of treachery, equally as much so among primitive men as amongst animals, and I conclude that reason without culture is but a brutal instinct.[17]

Back in Europe, Crozet's tirades against the popular notion of the Noble Savage did much to introduce the contrary idea of the ignoble savage[18] that soon coincided with and was reinforced by the evangelical view.

The future course of New Zealand history was substantially affected by such arguments. As a result of Tasman's, Furneaux's, and Du Fresne's bitter experiences with Maoris, New South Wales was chosen in preference to New Zealand as Britain's new penal colony. There Aborigines posed no threats, whereas Maoris, it was argued, were altogether too fearsome.

Early trading contacts

Such fears were probably more prevalent in Europe than in the South Seas. The authorities in the struggling penal colony of New South Wales after 1788, as well as American traders from the other side of the ocean, were keen enough to gather the New Zealand resources Cook had detailed— whales and seals around the coastlines, and timber and flax ashore.

American and British whalers were plying New Zealand's offshore waters by the early 1800s. Sealers discovered vast colonies of the hapless creatures in the southern reaches of the South Island, and in the first decade of the century ruthlessly depleted their numbers before moving on to sub-Antarctic islands.[19] Attempts to gather flax and timber were initially far less successful. The first forays date from the 1790s. Lieutenant-governor King at Norfolk Island was having trouble preparing the local flax for making fabric and decided to kidnap some Maoris, who were known to be skilled in the art of flax dressing, in order to learn their techniques. Tuki and Huru subsequently found themselves abducted from Doubtless Bay and put to work scraping flax on Norfolk Island. Though they were well treated and became firm friends with King, the experiment was a failure. Tuki was a priest, Huru was a warrior, and flax scraping was women's work.[20] The occasional cargo of New Zealand flax arrived in New South Wales, but not until the late 1820s did a regular and substantial trade in New Zealand flax get under way. It was a similar story with timber. A few vessels took spars from the New Zealand bush in the 1790s and early 1800s but the timber trade did not flourish until the 1820s. The reasons for the slow growth of these trades had little to do with New Zealand conditions and more to do with the vagaries of British and colonial economies and world markets generally; the attraction of other island products, such as Fijian bêche-de-mer, Tahitian pork, Hawaiian sandalwood; and the shortage of investment capital, ships, and labour in the region.

Maori responses

Most Maoris were isolated from and unaffected by the early trading ventures. Only a very few Maoris lived near the wild southern coastlines frequented by sealers. In the more populous North Island only those around the Bay of Islands, which became a popular port of call for whalers, had much to do with Europeans. This was the tribal homeland of the Ngapuhi. Early culture contact in New Zealand was, however, highly localised; generalisations for New Zealand as a whole drawn from the example of the Bay of Islands are untenable.

Where there was contact between Maoris and traders, Maoris proved eager participants, a reflection of the economically competitive nature of Maori society. Those few who lived in the southern South Island provided food for sealers, joined their gangs, and sailed on their vessels. Whalers in the Bay of Islands reported a similar response. By the early 1800s Maoris there were growing quantities of English potatoes (brought by explorers as well as by Tuki and Huru from Norfolk Island), selling them to vessels, and even exporting them to New South Wales. King, now governor of New South Wales, encouraged such trade by sending seeds, plants, and pigs to local chiefs.[21] As he wrote in 1805:

> The many vessels that have put into the Bay of Islands and other parts of that coast have never, as far as I have learn'd, had any altercation with the natives, but have received every kind office and assistance....[22]

Surgeon John Savage, who spent two months at the Bay of Islands in 1806, wrote in glowing terms about Maori friendship with Europeans, even if Maoris fought fiercely amongst each other. He took a young Maori, Moehanga, back to London with him.[23]

Numerous Maoris travelled to Sydney, Norfolk Island, Fiji, and beyond on whaling or sealing vessels. Governor King befriended in Sydney one young Maori who turned out to be the son of Te Pahi, a leading Bay of Islands chief. Te Pahi and his son later visited King, who insisted they lodge with him and enjoy viceregal comforts and honours. King was indefatigible in his efforts to ensure the favourable reception of European vessels in the Bay of Islands. As he had with Pomare at Matavai Bay in Tahiti, King hoped to have valuable allies in the Bay of Islands. After three months Te Pahi returned to New Zealand loaded with presents and even enjoyed the prestige of a European house which King had erected for him on his island in the Bay of Islands. The chief made several trips to New South Wales and seemed to revel in the attention and respect paid to him. He was once described thus:

> *He was dressed in certain robes of state presented to him when on his former visit by Governor King. They were covered with tinsel, and in some measure resembled those worn by a merry Andrew, with some improvement, emanating from his own invention. He was lame of one leg, on which he wore a black stocking, and on the other a white one. He appeared a man of considerable gravity, displaying an easy consciousness of his own dignity. Upon the whole, he showed himself a man of some observation, and was by no means deficient in intellect, but the most prominent features of his character were a certain shrewdness, and low cunning; from what I had an opportunity afterwards of observing, he was much inferior to several of his countrymen of equal rank. Being the first of his nation of any consideration who appeared at Port Jackson, he obtained unmerited distinction among Europeans, and eventually amongst his own countrymen, who were equally dazzled by the riches he brought back, and the attentions which were shown him by men so much superior to themselves.*[24]

His son, Matara, visited England with King.

Another Bay of Islands chief who travelled widely was Ruatara. He first shipped for Sydney on the whaler *Argo* in 1805 and spent twelve months on board. To return to New Zealand he served six months on another whaler. He then decided to visit the king of England, shipped on the *Santa Anna*, and found himself (along with another Maori, two Tahitians, and ten Europeans) left on remote Bounty Island to catch seals. The *Santa Anna* sailed away and did not return for the half-starved party until three months later. The vessel then sailed for England. However, Ruatara was seldom permitted ashore when the vessel reached London and never got to see the king. Miserable and ill, he was put on the convict vessel *Ann*, bound for Sydney, and cared for by Samuel Marsden, with whom he lodged after they arrived.[25]

Marsden's mission

Samuel Marsden arrived in New South Wales as chaplain to the colony in 1794.[26] He was one of the leading evangelical administrators who played an influential role in the London Missionary Society (LMS) and the Church Missionary Society (CMS)—and also later in the Wesleyan Missionary Society (WMS). A man of unbridled self-righteousness and ruthless determination, he enthusiastically combined his religious duties with more worldly activities and soon became a wealthy landowner and magistrate, earning a deserved reputation as the 'flogging parson'. He was unmerciful to convicts, and despised and ignored Aborigines (considering them to be cursed descendants of Cain), yet as a result of his meetings with Maori chiefs in Sydney he became passionately concerned for the welfare of Maoris in particular and Pacific Islanders in general. He was appointed foreign agent for the LMS, and CMS agent in Sydney.

Marsden saw Maoris as living 'in that State of Heathen Darkness and Ignorance, in which every Nation must unavoidably be, who has no connection with the Civil Religious and Commercial part of Mankind'. Nevertheless:

> *The natives of New Zealand are far advanced in Civilization, and apparently prepared for receiving the Knowledge of Christianity more than any Savage nations I have seen. Their Habits of Industry are very strong: their Thirst for Knowledge great, they only want the means. . . .*
>
> *The more I see of these People, the more I am pleased with, and astonished at their moral Ideas, and Characters. They appear like a superior Race of men.*[27]

Marsden even concluded that Maoris may have been 'Jews of Old',[28] so laying the basis for the popular and long-standing view (which persists today in some quarters) that Maoris were one of the Lost Tribes of Israel.

The chaplain visited England in 1807 to organise a CMS mission to New Zealand. Unlike the existing LMS mission in Tahiti, argued Marsden, the New Zealand mission should be firmly based upon the strategy of introducing civilisation *before* Christianity. Thus, in 1808 he embarked on the *Ann* (where he found Ruatara) with missionaries William Hall, a carpenter, and John King, a shoemaker and twine spinner, bound for New Zealand via Sydney. A third missionary, Thomas Kendall, a school teacher, shipped out shortly afterward.

When Marsden and his men reached New South Wales in 1810 they heard of the terrible massacre of the crew of the *Boyd* in New Zealand the previous year. Maoris, it seemed, were not the trustworthy people Governor King and others had believed; rather their earlier reputation for ferocity and treachery was reaffirmed. No one in New South Wales was prepared to take Marsden to such a dangerous country, at least not for the money the parsimonious chaplain was prepared to pay. Not until 1814, when he bought his own vessel, could he get his mission to New Zealand.

The Boyd incident

With a growing volume of shipping around the Bay of Islands, the opportunities for tension between sailors and Maoris increased. Reports filtered to Sydney of instances of violence. In 1808 the *Paramatta* put into the bay. Her crew took on supplies from the local Maoris and then threw their provisioners overboard. The vessel put to sea but a storm blew up and it was beached near the bay's entrance. All eleven of the crew perished at the hands of the waiting Maoris.[29]

The following year the *Boyd* entered the recently discovered Whangaroa Harbour, north of the Bay of Islands. All on board, with the exception of a woman and two children, were killed—about forty in all. The ship was looted and burnt. Explanations were numerous. One opinion was that a previous European master in the harbour had dropped his watch overboard, which caused great alarm amongst the Maoris for whom the incident presaged doom. This, it has been claimed, took the form of an epidemic that struck soon before the *Boyd* arrived. Another view is that a chief, Te Aara (otherwise known as George), had been flogged by the *Boyd*'s master—a great insult that had to be avenged. Of more significance to the Maoris was not why, but who attacked the *Boyd*? European sailors in and about the Bay of Islands blamed Te Pahi, organised a convoy of six whaling vessels, destroyed his settlement, and shot some sixty of his followers in the Bay of Islands.[30] Te Pahi was wounded and escaped to Whangaroa. He was later killed in tribal fighting.

Whether Te Pahi had anything at all to do with the attack on the *Boyd* is unknown. Whangaroa chiefs Te Aara and Te Puhi probably had a lot to do with it. It is possible that Te Pahi was confused with Te Puhi or another chief, Te Pere, or was framed by rival Whangaroa chiefs. Whatever the case, Europeans in the vicinity certainly thought Te Pahi was the culprit, and he was an obvious and easy target for men craving vengeance and determined to make an example of someone prominent as a lesson to all Maoris.

The occasional whaling vessel continued to call in to the Bay of Islands over the next few years, but Whangaroa was given a wide berth.

CMS missionaries arrive

Meanwhile Marsden pressed ahead with plans to cross the Tasman Sea. He eventually had Ruatara shipped back to New Zealand, some four years after the hapless chief had left his shores to visit the king of England, with wheat and agricultural tools. In 1814 Marsden purchased the *Active* and sent Hall and Kendall on an exploratory voyage to the Bay of Islands. There Ruatara and other chiefs welcomed them, not least because of the presents, and for six weeks the missionaries were treated kindly. They then returned to Sydney with chiefs Ruatara, his uncle Hongi Hika, Korokoro, and several other Maoris, and with news that there was no apparent obstacle to founding a mission.

Until this trip Hongi Hika had been known to Marsden and others in New South Wales only by name. In Sydney Hongi was regarded as handsome—in spite of extensive tattooing—and having a quiet disposition, though it was appreciated that he was a 'chief of superior rank, and more extensive power than Duaterra [Ruatara].'[31] What distinguished him from Ruatara, who was interested in 'the pursuits of agriculture', and from Korokoro, who in telling tales of his military conquests displayed 'an impatient avidity and wild enthusiasm that sometimes assumed the aspect of ungovernable violence', was Hongi's devotion to 'mechanics' and especially muskets.[32] He brought with him a musket for which he had built a complete stock, and was often found carving cartridge boxes. His love of firearms was to have a profound effect on the future of the Christian mission in New Zealand.

Late in 1814 the *Active* returned to New Zealand with Marsden, the three chiefs, Hall, Kendall, King, and their families, and various convict assistants. The three chiefs had second thoughts when they saw the thirty-odd Europeans bound for their land and talked about how 'ruinous' to their 'independence' and 'influence' these settlers might be.[33] But when Marsden self-righteously offered to turn the vessel back for Sydney, Ruatara begged him to continue to New Zealand, and offered his 'protection and fidelity'.[34] But he could not, he said, speak for Hongi and Korokoro, who might be harbouring evil plans, and so Marsden should stay on his lands at Rangihoua on the northern tip of the Bay of Islands. Unfortunately for the missionaries, they were in this way forced to set up camp in an isolated region with steep, treeless hills rising immediately from a tiny beach. This made it impossible for them to establish an economically self-supporting farm, although they had with them cows and horses. Their subsequent dependence upon the local Maoris for food, timber, and other supplies seriously inhibited what they hoped would be their civilising and Christianising influence on the New Zealanders.

The mission in travail

When Marsden sailed for Sydney (with the boat loaded with Maoris) the depressing physical and psychological effects of isolation descended upon the tiny Christian community on the side of their steep hill. Their supposed protector, Ruatara, died soon afterward, but since economic survival rather than physical protection was the real problem the chief's death meant little. Life was thoroughly miserable for the next few years. Although the missionaries and their families were not seriously threatened, they were not exactly overwhelmed with hospitality either. They eked out a most tenuous existence and bickered amongst themselves and with Marsden, who made irregular visits and sent inadequate supplies and who seemed to want to keep them economically dependent upon himself.[35] Even when the missionaries did eventually establish a second station on much better land at Keri Keri in 1819, they were still in dire economic straits. Furthermore at Keri Keri they came under the 'protection' of Hongi Hika who exploited their weakness. As a traveller explained:

> *They considered themselves safer under the protection of Shungie . . . than under any of the other chiefs.*
>
> *It is, however, a protection at all times precarious, and maintained at the expense of much forbearance and humiliation. The natives, knowing too well that the missionaries are in their power, commit extensive depredations upon them, not unfrequently aggravating their extortions by acts of gross insult.*[36]

The missionaries were forced to trade with and give things to Maoris not only to have any relationship with these people—as late as 1829 attendance at the mission's schools 'was determined by the amounts of food on hand'[37]—but to survive. Hongi was particularly eager to get tools and utensils and especially muskets. Whether they approved of it or not, the various members of the Christian community became quietly involved in the trading and repairing of firearms,[38] just as had their counterparts at Matavai Bay in the early 1800s. Within a month of the mission first being founded at Rangihoua, Kendall complained that Maoris had offered them no food for four weeks:

> *We have procured some flax, but the natives like muskets much better than they do axes. Ships which come here and with spare muskets, will have a great advantage over us in point of trade.*[39]

By the early 1820s the demand for muskets in the Bay of Islands was so great that one could not 'barter a fresh meal' without them.[40] A missionary wrote:

> *The great and grand cry of the natives is who will supply us with muskets, lead and powder. . . . For a musket a New Zealander will make great sacrifices, he will labour hard and fare hard for many months to obtain his musket, in fact it is his idol he values it above all he possesses, he will not only part with his slaves for one, but even prostitute his children to diseased sailor for one of those instruments of destruction.*[41]

The missionaries' involvement in the musket trade brought bitter recriminations from Marsden. Although he had on earlier occasions presented muskets as gifts to certain chiefs, he now condemned the 'accursed traffic . . . [in] the instruments of death'.[42] But as Judith Binney has commented, 'the Christian community existed in the Maori world on Maori terms'.[43]

Hongi Hika

The missionaries' association with Ngapuhi chiefs and their muskets provided some of the first glimpses into tribal relations within and beyond the

19   *Waikato, Hongi Hika (centre) and missionary Thomas Kendall, 1820.*
     (Painting by James Barry. Alexander Turnbull Library)

Bay of Islands. Fighting with tribes to the south was an age-old process. Muskets had been used by some of these chiefs from as early as 1800, though quantities were very small until about 1815.[44] In 1818 Te Morenga and Hongi led two separate raids on tribes in the Bay of Plenty and East Cape to avenge the capture and subsequent death of two leading Ngapuhi women in 1806. The warriors had about 35 muskets and claimed to have killed hundreds of their southern opponents.[45] It is not clear in these earliest 'musket raids' (and indeed in later and larger ones) whether the actual firepower of the muskets was responsible for the seemingly overwhelming victories. Perhaps possession of muskets gave a psychological advantage not just because of their noise and strangeness but because they symbolised the Ngapuhi association with Europeans, whereas tribes to the south had extremely little if any contact as yet with traders. The very size of the Ngapuhi war parties may also have been important. Te Morenga led 600 and Hongi 800 in the 1818 raids. Chiefs normally had no power to compel men to join their armies. The most successful warrior chiefs were those who could lead and inspire by example and 'the check on shirking was provided by public opinion rather than by force.'[46] The Ngapuhi chiefs' possession of firearms and their association with Europeans generally was an exciting inducement for large numbers of young men to join campaigns against long-standing enemies who enjoyed no such advantages. Nothing inspires fighting men like the expectation of easy victories. In 1819 other Ngapuhi chiefs, Patuone, Moetare, and Tamati Waka Nene—from the Hokianga region—led a major and successful military expedition down the west coast of the North Island. They joined with Te Rauparaha from Kawhia and swept south to the present-day Wellington region and the Wairarapa.[47] These and other lesser raids made Hongi more determined than ever to build up his arsenal of muskets.

In 1820 Hongi accompanied the missionary Kendall to England. Kendall went to be ordained and to collaborate with the Cambridge linguist Professor Lee on a grammar and vocabulary of Maori. He took Hongi and a lesser chief (Waikato) with him in order that they might purchase firearms. Kendall believed that playing to Hongi's military ambitions would cement the relationship between the CMS mission and the chief.[48] In common with early missionaries throughout the Pacific islands, Kendall hoped that mission influence could be enhanced by supporting the political ambitions of an up-and-coming warrior chief. Hongi and Waikato were given the usual treatment reserved for visiting South Sea Islands 'royalty'. They visited the House of Lords, the Tower of London, and even had an audience with the king, who presented Hongi with a coat of chain mail and some guns. But Hongi seemed unmoved by most of the sights of civilisation. Only an elephant and the Woolwich Arsenal excited him. He and Kendall soon returned to Sydney. There Hongi sold all the presents he had received in London, except for his armour, and bought some 300 muskets.

On his arrival in New Zealand in 1821 he laid his new weapons in rows,

> *giving each its name, saying:*—'E mara ma! O friends! O Te Horeta! and Te Hinaki! Behold! this gun is "Te Wai-whariki," this is "Kaikai-a-te karoro," this is "Wai-kohu," this is "Te Ringahuru-huru," this is "Mahurangi,"' *thus naming all the battles in which Nga-Puhi had been defeated.*[49]

Within a few months Hongi had organised a force of 2000 warriors with at least 1000 muskets. Fifty canoes carried the army southward. It rampaged through the present-day Auckland area slaying, it is claimed, some 1500 Ngati Paoa. Then it was on to Thames where the Ngati Maru lost 1000 of their number. Hongi returned with some 2000 prisoners whom he intended to labour on his potato plantations so that he could buy more firearms. But this was only the beginning for Hongi. Each summer, when the weather was more likely to be settled, his canoe flotilla was paddled southward.[50] In 1822 with 3000 warriors he attacked the Waikato tribes. He took his canoes into the Waitemata Harbour, then overland to the Manukau Harbour, then overland again to the Waikato River, which he followed upstream for months until deep in Waikato lands where he captured several major *pa*.

The following year he sailed to Tauranga, and again hauled his canoes overland to the Rotorua lakes, where he decimated the Arawa tribe. In 1824 Hongi was preoccupied with Bay of Islands matters and 'quite missed the fighting season'.[51] But he was back again in 1825, this time ravaging the lower northland regions—between the Bay of Islands and the Auckland area—seeking out the Ngati Whatua. These people however, by virtue of their geographic location, now had a few firearms themselves and Hongi's warriors did not have easy victories. Hongi's eldest son was shot dead in one battle. Hongi then pursued remaining pockets of Ngati Whatua at Kaipara and also followed up those who had fled right through to Waikato lands. But by now the warrior was aging and tired, and suffered a succession of personal misfortunes. In 1827 he was shot in the chest in a skirmish near Hokianga. Apparently he was not in armour at the time. The wound did not kill him immediately, but left a hole right through his body. Miserable and paralysed, he died a year later.

Te Rauparaha

There were other famous warrior chiefs, like Te Rauparaha of Ngati Toa at Kawhia.[52] He had joined the Ngapuhi raid to the southern reaches of the North Island in 1819, probably to look for new lands to move to. His Ngati Toa in the Kawhia region were increasingly threatened by their much more numerous enemies close inland—the Waikato. In addition Te Rauparaha was impressed with Ngapuhi muskets. He dreamed of new lands where he might have not only protection from enemies but contact with European traders. The South Island had great appeal for him. There were whalers about and there was also a minor resurgence in sealing there in the 1820s. Besides it was the source of the much-valued greenstone. But there was no time for a dignified migration. In 1822 the Waikato tribes and allies descended upon the weak Ngati Toa and drove them southward. Te Rauparaha turned the humiliating retreat into eventual victory. He began restoring Ngati Toa fortunes by capturing Kapiti Island, an excellent fortress and a stepping stone between the North and South Islands. From this new base he encouraged what little European shipping there was in the area and exchanged pigs and potatoes for muskets. He soon felt bold enough to make forays to the nearby mainland and gained toeholds of influence. So successful was Te Rauparaha as a trader that by the mid-1820s only the Ngapuhi had more guns per fighting man.[53] As the flax trade began to boom in New Zealand in the later 1820s Te Rauparaha's commercial fortunes soared. By 1830 the flax trade from Kapiti represented about one-eighth of the total amount exported from New Zealand. 'Saturation level'—one musket to every fighting man (which the Ngapuhi had achieved by the early 1820s)—was reached by Te Rauparaha in the late 1820s.[54]

20   *Te Rauparaha, 1847. (Sketch by W. Bambridge. Alexander Turnbull Library)*

The chief then turned to the South Island which he had long coveted, and some of whose chiefs had long been insulting him and daring him to cross the strait and attack. From 1828 onward he launched a series of raids that were allegedly as devastating as Hongi's earlier musket raids. By the early 1830s, Te Rauparaha had successfully ranged over most of the northern half of the South Island, as well as the southwestern sections of the North Island, where he paid off old scores from the days when the Ngati Toa had been expelled from Kawhia. However, just as Hongi found that his enemies eventually armed themselves with muskets, so did Te Rauparaha. Within a few more years his raiding parties were sometimes getting as good as they gave, and his allies, often former enemies whom he had defeated, could never be trusted too much since they both feared and were jealous of his successes. The chief gradually turned to more peaceful, diplomatic ways to protect his *mana*.

Throughout the 1820s there were numerous intertribal battles all over the North Island, but perhaps none on the scale of Hongi's and Te Rauparaha's largest campaigns. Fighting continued well into the 1830s (and beyond) in many interior regions though on smaller and probably more normal levels. By this stage, thanks to the presence of flax traders and European vessels that began visiting more North Island harbours, most warriors owned a musket. This equalisation of firepower meant that the days of one-sided musket raids were over. Indeed by the 1830s the tables had even been turned in some instances—the Waikato soundly beat the Ngapuhi in several engagements.

The new warfare and new politics?

New Zealand historians were inclined to see the musket raids of the 1820s as evidence of the devastating influence of European contact in general and firearms in particular. They pointed to the tens of thousands of Maoris allegedly killed and the dislocating consequences of the enforced migrations that followed in the wake of the great campaigns.[55] Certainly there is a causal link between the introduction of muskets, starting with the Ngapuhi in the north in the early 1820s and gradually becoming available all down the North Island in the later twenties and early thirties, and a corresponding movement southward of defeated tribal groups.[56] Yet while all this was new and horrifying to Europeans, warfare and migration were quite usual (though no less horrific) for Maoris. It is problematic how many people were actually killed in the musket raids. Numbers may not have been greater overall, though at least some of the Ngapuhi raids probably caused unprecedented killing if only because the number of warriors involved was abnormally large. Even then, however, claims of a high kill rate due to muskets remain unsubstantiated. Certainly muskets were instruments of terror for those who did not possess them, but even a cursory examination of what evidence there is suggests that most people died by more usual means—being hit with clubs (and axes), and suffocating or being trampled to death when large numbers of panicking people tried to negotiate defensive ditches and avoid palisades.

21   '*A New Zealand war speech*', *1827. (Earle* A Narrative of a Nine Months'
Residence in New Zealand. *Alexander Turnbull Library)*

One thing remains clear. Whatever new means of war there might have
been, the motives, strategies, and consequences were unchanged. As one
historian has concluded, 'The role or function of warfare ... did not alter at
any time in the period [1800s–1840s].'[57] Indeed, what is striking about the
leading warrior chiefs in New Zealand, in contrast to those of Tahiti,
Hawaii, and Tonga, was their pursuit of what to Europeans seemed very
limited and customary goals, namely the desire for *utu*. It is possible to
interpret the careers of Hongi, Te Rauparaha, and others as nothing more
than an endless quest to avenge some insult.[58] Every campaign had specific
and stated objectives which invariably were to redress a particular 'outrage'. And as every expedition produced further insult and injury so the
process continued. As Marsden explained (echoing Cook's comments of
the 1770s):

> *When they have lost a near relation in battle their minds continually dwell upon the
> death of their friend, having nothing to occupy them. If they are able to revenge the
> death of their friend, they will attempt it as soon as possible; if not, they will think
> of their loss for years, and mourn over it, and if, at any future period, they can
> obtain satisfaction during their life, they will never lose an opportunity. Their
> wounded feelings never appear to be healed, and they feel it a sacred duty which they
> owe to their departed relatives to punish those by whose hands they have fallen....*[59]

John Owens has argued that the *utu*-only argument is misleading and that the more successful chiefs were also after security and economic benefits, and points to their attempts to monopolise European anchorages and amass slaves to grow their potatoes and scrape flax.[60] Yet such 'economic competition was no new phenomenon in Maori society',[61] and often a basic reason for it was to enable some aggrieved party to be better able to seek redress for some past wrong. Many 'wars were still being fought over issues which had no relation to the presence or technology of Europeans.'[62] Men like Hongi and Te Rauparaha were different from their counterparts in Hawaii, Tonga, and Tahiti. They did not seek to forge and control any empire. Their aims were, by European standards, extremely limited and had far more to do with establishing their *mana* than with amassing the material trappings and power of monarchs. As one European commented on hearing of Hongi's death:

> The natives of New Zealand pay the greatest respect to courage and warlike talents: these were the only distinguishing characteristics of Hongi; yet, by possessing these, he was more feared, and had a greater number of followers, than any other chief in the island. His hereditary possessions were but small, and his name was little known; yet his undaunted courage, his skill, and success in many sanguinary battles, made him, at length, a most powerful chief, and obtained for him that which is considered wealth in this country, namely, an immense number of slaves. In his last moments he was attended by more men of rank than had ever before assembled to witness the dissolution of a warrior, and this is considered the greatest proof of attention and respect one chieftain can show towards another.[63]

More latterly, Gordon Parsonson has said of Hongi,

> For all his military success he left nothing, neither lands nor dominion. These he had not sought nor indeed would he have understood them. He had in consequence not so much failed; he could not have acted other than he did.[64]

It was the same for Te Rauparaha. Though he conquered large areas of New Zealand he had no sense of claiming them as his own property or domain, if only because had he done so he would have been 'fiercely resisted by every single allied chief'.[65]

Maori chiefs presumably knew what was happening in Tahiti and Hawaii, since Maoris visited these places on whalers and Tahitians and Hawaiians also came to New Zealand. But there is no evidence that the leading warrior-chiefs seriously thought of emulating the Kamehamehas or the Pomares. Whitoi, a Bay of Islands chief who visited Sydney, did call himself Pomare after hearing about the exploits of the Tahitian king,[66] but this seems to have been little more than a name change. Maoris commonly adopted names of prominent foreigners. Korokoro, another Ngapuhi chief who visited Sydney, insisted on being called Macquarie after the governor there.[67]

Given the geographically fragmented and small-scale nature of Maori social and political organisation, together with its particular ideologies, any quest for a centralised empire (that leaders elsewhere in Polynesia considered a perfectly normal ambition) was alien to Maori chiefs. Europeans in New Zealand often lamented this fact and sincerely believed that it was in the best interests of the Maori to have a single government under a king. They often discussed these matters with chiefs.

> *The New Zealanders themselves are very sensible of the want of a protecting Government, and would rejoice if anything could be done to prevent the strong from crushing the weak. The New Zealanders want a head. I had many conversations with the chiefs on this subject when I was in the island last year. They told me no chief would be willing to give up his authority to another, and they could not agree amongst themself to nominate any one chief as king. I am afraid this desirable object will never be effected by persuasive means. If it is done, it most probably will be done by force. Shunghee [Hongi] has conquered many tribes, to the extent of more than two hundred miles, but he has no means of retaining his conquests. Shunghee was wont to tell me the conquered tribes would behave very well while he was in their districts, but when he left them they respected him no longer. He had not the means of leaving a force to keep them in subjection.[68]*

Missionaries and Maoris

The essential irrelevance to leading Maori chiefs of any attempts to centralise their power had a major bearing on the Maori response to missionaries and Christianity. In short, missionaries and their ideas would not be exploited by any paramount chief out to legitimise and provide new sanctions and administrative strategies for a unified regime, as happened in Tahiti, Tonga, and Hawaii. The Maori response to Christianity was far less orchestrated and had more to do with local situations. Just as Maori political life was fragmented in both a geographic and an organisational sense, so were the responses to missionary teachings fragmented in time and space and dependent upon local as opposed to 'national' circumstances. Christianity in New Zealand was not something imposed on a people by a ruling élite, as was the case in many other islands of Polynesia; rather it was adopted and adapted from below over a period of time.

While the Maori conversion to Christianity was slow and geographically untidy compared, for example, with Tahiti, there was a broad pattern: missionaries in New Zealand made very little headway in converting Maoris until the 1830s, though by the 1860s most Maoris were considered Christians.

Until the early 1830s mission activity was centred around the Bay of Islands. The CMS had stations at Rangihoua (1814), Keri Keri (1819), Paihia (1823), and Waimate (1830). Wesleyan missionaries settled further north at Whangaroa in 1823. For years Maoris treated them with considerable contempt and were interested in the missions only insofar as they were a source of muskets, axes, blankets, and other goods.

The CMS mission had its own problems as well. Kendall became obsessed with his studies of Maori language and beliefs and ended up living with a Maori girl. Marsden expelled him in 1823.[69] An early reinforcement, John Butler, the first ordained missionary to settle in New Zealand, was expelled for drunkeness at the same time. The problems caused by the mission's economic dependence on Maoris, and the rows amongst themselves and with Marsden over the musket trade and other matters, made life very difficult. The CMS mission began to get its house in order with the arrival of its new leader, Henry Williams, in 1823. Williams, with a naval career behind him, proved a capable and inspiring figure. First he stopped the mission arms trade. This was not such a difficult task because Ngapuhi demands for muskets were on the wane, all warriors having at least a musket each. Blankets were now the rage. Williams also built a 55-tonne schooner, *Herald*, which, after its launching in 1826, enabled missionaries to trade further afield for supplies and break their total dependence upon the Bay of Islands Maoris, who as a consequence had to treat missionaries with rather less disdain. The opening in 1830 of the station at Waimate, where there was good farming land, further enhanced the mission's self-sufficiency. Then Williams altered Marsden's strategy by emphasising the teaching of Christianity at the same time as, rather than after, introducing the 'useful arts of civilisation'. This meant that more effort was put into learning Maori, translating religious texts, and disseminating the printed word. More emphasis was placed on holding schools, with attention now given to adults as well as children. The mission was also strengthened by the arrival throughout the 1820s of more missionaries, men who were usually a little better prepared for life in New Zealand than had been Marsden's first unhappy 'mechanics' left at Rangihoua. By force of his personality Williams was also able to gain a hitherto unprecedented measure of respect from many Maoris, and by the later 1820s he was able to mediate successfully in several disputes between Maori groups. His dogmatic insistence on peace rather than war gradually attracted the attention of more and more Maoris who had suffered from or were merely tired of the musket campaigns.[70] Where in Tahiti, Hawaii, and Tonga, missionary strength lay in the military supremacy of their warrior protectors, the reverse became the case in New Zealand. Since missionaries there were not beholden to any warrior patron, they could adopt a stance of neutrality in indigenous fighting and relate to both victors and vanquished without compromising their chances. Yet while all this was essential groundwork for the CMS mission, and while it developed a mood of some confidence, born of growing economic security, it still looked in vain for any signs of conversion amongst the local communities. What really mattered in processes of conversion was not how missionaries acted in island situations but how Islanders reacted to missionaries.

The CMS missionaries' Wesleyan counterparts at Whangaroa, still a region isolated from much European contact, experienced no similar improvements in their outlook and situation. Instead they were constantly plagued by both economic and physical insecurity, and in 1827 local Maoris who had never welcomed mission presence sacked the station. The missionaries fled to New South Wales, but came back later in the year and set up a post on the Hokianga River.[71]

From about 1830 Maoris in the north began to show a definite interest and even enthusiasm for missionary teaching. Both the CMS and WMS missions became major centres of attraction. Hundreds and eventually thousands of Maoris went *mihanere*—that is, attended services and schools and became candidates for baptism. The missionaries then began to extend their operations southward. In the 1830s the CMS set up stations in the Thames-Waikato region, the Bay of Plenty, and Rotorua. Wesleyans, after arguing with the CMS over their respective domains eventually went to Raglan and Kawhia. The Maori response in these regions, hitherto little contacted by Europeans, was immediately enthusiastic. CMS missions were founded in other North Island locations—Wanganui, Otaki, East Cape. A Roman Catholic mission arrived in the Bay of Islands in 1838 and though it was always relatively small it too established some outposts in various parts of the North Island. By the later 1850s most North Island Maoris were Christian, or more specifically Protestant. Missionaries also went to the South Island and in the 1840s and 1850s Christianised most of those few Maoris who lived there.

The causes of conversion

There has been considerable debate amongst historians as to the reasons for the Maori conversion to Christianity. Harrison Wright first stimulated discussion with his argument that by the 1830s Maori society had been dislocated by European impact, particularly with the introduction of diseases and firearms. Maoris who were initially dominant and confident were by the 1830s reduced to a state of severe cultural disruption resulting in massive depopulation which expressed itself in bewilderment and depression. Thus, said Wright, Maoris looked to Christianity for comfort and solutions.[72] Wright, and those who supported his interpretation,[73] based their studies mainly on the Bay of Islands. Those historians who have examined other regions have usually offered alternative explanations. In looking specifically at Maori responses to Wesleyan missionaries, John Owens claimed that there was no specific turning point from Maori dominance to bewilderment, from rejecting Christianity to accepting it.

Rather, there was a continual 'exchange of ideas' and while 'social context' and 'social processes' were important they did not totally determine this exchange: 'What counted most was the nature of the ideas themselves and the manner in which they were brought to bear upon each other: content and communication mattered more than context.'[74] This view can be supported by studies in other areas, for example the Thames-Waikato region, where Maoris were anything but bewildered yet instantly responded to Christian ideas, as they understood them. They saw them as novel, exciting, and appearing to offer both material and other benefits.[75]

There is considerable agreement amongst historians that certain developments contributed to the conversion processes. Missionary techniques were getting better all the time. Missionaries' knowledge of the Maori language was now more sophisticated. They had an economic independence from the Maori communities in which they lived. They could exploit the apparently insatiable Maori desire for literacy and possession of books with the arrival of printing presses.[76] Their medical skills sometimes attracted Maoris.[77] Missionaries also trained Maori teachers who were effective in introducing notions of Christianity to areas where missionaries had not yet gone. The missionaries' role as peacemakers also became more prominent. Yet all these factors refer only to the European side. There is still no agreement as to why Christianity eventually became so relevant to Maori communities—was it because Maoris were suffering from culture shock, or was it because they chose to accept potentially beneficial ideas and practices from a position of relative strength and cultural vigour?

The search for an answer has proven futile and the debate has rather unsatisfactorily fizzled out. The problem is that this question implies that there *is* an answer, that there is at least a general monocausal explanation which in turn implies that some historians are right and others wrong. However, if one looks at these possible explanations within the wider context of Pacific islands history, and in particular by comparing the New Zealand experience to that of Tahiti, Tonga, and Hawaii, the lack of an acceptable monocausal explanation should not be a problem. Given the nature of Maori society and politics there could not be a single or general Maori response. Rather there were innumerable responses at different times and in different places for different reasons depending on local circumstances. In other words, all the explanations offered by various historians may be valid, if only for the area they studied, and no attempt should be made to generalise for New Zealand as a whole from particular case studies. Indeed, even within a single community where all members were subject to the same social context, responses sometimes varied widely.[78] This is only to be expected given the fragmented, small-scale, individualistic, and competitive nature of Maori society compared with the more stratified societies controlled by a ruling élite elsewhere in Polynesia.

The significance of the diversity of Maori motives for an interest in Christianity, at least from a comparative point of view, has been over-looked by most historians. Since the Christian standard in New Zealand was not held aloft by a few leading chiefs out to create empires, as it was on some other Pacific islands, missionaries in New Zealand could be apolitical. They had no need to tie their fortunes to those of a warrior patron. To have done so would have proven pointless anyway since such warriors were not out to establish kingdoms. Hongi consistently rejected Christian teachings. Late in his life, long after his military career was over, Te Rauparaha had some sympathy for some missionary ideals but he was never converted. In New Zealand in the 1820s and 1830s the message of Christ as Prince of Peace had substance in contrast to those islands of the Pacific where missionaries were often blessing and actively supporting their 'Christian Soldiers' marching into battle against 'heathens' and 'heretics'. The early CMS missionaries, with the possible exception of Kendall, who was im-pressed with what he heard about Pomare II and perhaps saw Hongi following suit,[79] traded in muskets to survive, not to assist Hongi to impose some sort of hegemony over the tribes to the south. In contrast to missionaries in Tahiti, Tonga, and Hawaii, those in New Zealand could stand aside from indigenous politics and relate to both winners and losers.

A major consequence of this, again from a comparative point of view, was that Christianity in New Zealand moved upward through society, with 'ordinary' individuals responding first, rather than being imposed from above by some ruling élite. Chiefs often accepted Christianity after many of their followers had done so. The fact that in New Zealand there was no unified state and therefore no state religion meant that individuals were much freer to experiment with ideas. They did not have to fear the wrath of an entrenched priesthood whose job it was to enforce religious sanctions as a means of social control on behalf of the rulers. Europeans constantly expressed admiration for what they considered Maori 'intelligence' and 'eagerness to learn'.[80] Maoris were in fact no more 'intelligent' than any other Islanders but they could experiment far more openly and without fear[81] than could, say, Hawaiians who were so rigidly controlled by the *kapu* system.

Yet if Maoris had essentially different reasons from Tahitians, Tongans, and Hawaiians, for accepting Christianity, the nature of Maori Christianity was similar to that throughout the islands, ranging from 'model' Christian decorum to applying aspects of Christianity to 'heretical' cults.[82]

Whose New Zealand?

From a European perspective the 1830s was a crucial decade in New Zealand's history. There was an upsurge in commercial activity with large-scale timber and flax trading and bay whaling. This led to a substantial increase in the number of European settlers especially in the Bay of Islands by the end of the decade. The British and New South Wales governments were inevitably drawn into matters of trade and the real or alleged problems of relations between Maori and European. The all-powerful humanitarian lobby in Britain and others also painted a picture of Maori society being ruined by unregulated European presence. The result was the annexation of the country by Britain in 1840.[83]

This overview may be a valid interpretation of the preliminaries to colonial rule and hence to a history of Europeans in New Zealand, but it tends to misread the realities of the culture contact situation, if not leave out the Maori side of things altogether. This can be understood in that New Zealand, unlike other Pacific islands considered here, became a major settler colony. Where, for example, a history of Tonga must necessarily be concerned with the indigenous peoples of that island group, the history of New Zealand has often been written as a history of Britons overseas.

It should be emphasised that the European presence in New Zealand before 1840 was very small—less than 1000—and highly concentrated in the Bay of Islands. Even most of these people had arrived only a year or so beforehand. Elsewhere in New Zealand there were a few tiny pockets of traders living in Maori communities, usually at anchorages around the North Island and in some parts of the South Island. In spite of substantial migration from Britain after 1840, Maoris kept their numerical superiority until well into the 1850s and even then much of the North Island was still 'Maori country'. It took the wars of the 1860s to begin to change this situation. Even so the remote, central regions of the North Island were not opened to European settlement until toward the end of the century. Therefore, to write about the early European colonisation of New Zealand is to write about a minority group. It is anachronistic to assume that the position of subservience that Maoris everywhere found themselves in by the end of the nineteenth century had existed at earlier times.

When Maoris have been considered in immediate pre- and post-annexation times, the tendency has been to assume that 'Maori society' was a homogeneous entity relative to *pakeha* or 'European society' and that Maoris were reeling tragically after the body blow of European contact. Both these assumptions need considerable modification if only because Maoris could not have been affected uniformly since European presence was highly localised. The majority of Maoris in 1840 were not in direct contact with Europeans.

However, the situation was more complex than this. While Bay of Islands Maoris were clearly more exposed to European influences than more distant Maoris, European presence could still have indirect effects far from the Bay, especially via muskets and epidemics, which, it is often claimed, led to substantial depopulation.[84]

It has already been suggested that muskets probably did not result in unprecedented mortality in battle and that the reasons for fighting and the consequences of it were little different in the 1840s from the 1770s. There is certainly no evidence of any widespread war weariness. Intertribal conflicts in many parts of the North Island continued well into the 1850s, and the wars between colonial forces and central North Island Maoris in the 1860s were used by other Maoris to engage in further civil war.[85] This suggests a considerable degree of cultural confidence and continuity in Maori thought and action in many parts of the country.

The effects of introduced epidemic diseases are more open to question, but whatever miseries these may have caused the case for early and massive depopulation is difficult to sustain. The Maori population by about 1840 was estimated at 115 000,[86] which is about what it was in 1769. Only if, as was once believed, the 1769 population was much higher is the case for depopulation arguable.

Rather than stress the negative and destructive consequences for Maoris of European contact, and the passive nature of Maori responses, many historians are now emphasising the adaptability and creativity of Maori lifestyles—in particular their adoption of European tools, plants, and animals, their exporting of agricultural produce overseas, their willingness to trade with Europeans and labour for them (for a price) scraping flax, cutting, hauling and sawing timber, and chasing whales.[87] They were similarly responsive to new ideas—Christianity, reading, and writing—which they vigorously applied to their own customs.

The case for cultural disruption came from a few Europeans, like James Busby, the British Resident appointed in 1833, and the humanitarian lobby, who painted a picture of savage anarchy between and amongst Maoris and Europeans. Those who took this line either generalised from incidents in the Bay of Islands, or were arguing a case to suit their ends, or else genuinely, though misleadingly, contrasted their view of civilisation with behaviour in New Zealand which they could not understand. As John Owens has written, 'The "fatal impact" theory had more to do with British interests than the state of New Zealand society at the time.'[88] Life in New Zealand in the 1830s was far from being all peace and tranquillity, but the picture of lawlessness and depravity painted back in Britain was not a fair assessment, especially beyond the Bay of Islands. If anything characterised Maori-European relations on the broad front it was mutually exploitive cooperation. Dieffenbach's description of Cook Strait could be applicable to many other parts of New Zealand.

> *The natives inhabiting both shores of Cook's Straits were at the time of my arrival placed in a position which could not fail to awaken my deepest interest. Although their number is not large, taking them as a whole, yet they live so much dispersed in small tribes that they occupy a long coast-line. For the last fifteen or twenty years*

they have associated with Europeans, who have lived amongst them as traders or as whalers; and they were annually visited by many whaling-vessels. Mutual advantage, and the connection of almost all these Europeans with native women, from which connection a healthy and fine-looking half-caste race has sprung up (about 160 in number), kept the white men and natives in harmony with each other, and has cemented their union. Thus we find Europeans arrayed against Europeans in the combats of the different tribes amongst whom they lived, or emigrating with them to another locality, or following the hazardous chase of the whale with a crew of natives.[89]

By the late 1830s there were two parallel traditions in New Zealand—dominant Maori, and minority European.[90] In terms of social and political organisation and aims and values, especially with regard to the pursuit of *mana*, Maoris were unchanged.[91]

Denouement

It is tempting to argue that Maoris had very little to do with the steps leading to annexation in 1840, and that this event resulted from the activities and perceptions of sections of the European minority. Yet Maoris unwittingly contributed to the loss of their sovereignty in that they provided strong support for the cases put by the two main lobbies—commercial and humanitarian—for annexation. Maori commercial enterprise and willingness to cooperate with traders made trading and settlement in New Zealand viable in the first place. And for the humanitarians, the fact that Maoris seemed to be accepting the two fundamental ingredients of civilisation—agriculture and Christianity—meant that Britain had a duty to press on with the grand scheme of assimilating Maoris, that is, making them brown-skinned Englishmen.[92] This was all the more urgent, the humanitarians argued, because Maoris as a race were in danger of destruction by unregulated white presence. Even here, Maoris unwittingly strengthened the humanitarian case because it could be argued that in having no centralised government of their own they were a hopelessly divided and anarchic people in need of Imperial guidance, protection, and regulation. What could not have been understood was that Maori chiefs had not failed to unite their country politically—it had not occurred to them to do so. Even after decades of colonial rule, when some Maori communities tried to organise a united front against the onrush of settlement, such as the King Movement in the Waikato in the late 1850s, support was still tribal and localised. There could be no such thing as a Maori nation.

11

Samoa

Samoans, like Maoris, did not create for themselves a politically centralised country as did Tahitians, Hawaiians, and Tongans. But the Samoan experience during the period of culture contact differed considerably from that of the Maoris in that Samoan leaders did eventually see the need to unite politically to protect themselves against foreigners. However, they achieved little success, mainly because their social and political organisation was too inherently localised and factionalised—a situation that various European interest groups exploited to Samoa's disadvantage.

Society and politics

At first glance Samoans seemed to display some of the characteristics of the Tahitians, Hawaiians, and Tongans, with their élitist and hierarchical organisations having all the paraphernalia of status and status seeking on an island-wide level. Yet at the same time some particular features of Samoan life were in some respects closer to New Zealand models than others in eastern Polynesia. Whereas in Tonga, Hawaii, and Tahiti settlement was commonly non-nucleated and areas of political control (in pre-European times) could be fairly large, incorporating regions or whole islands, Samoan settlement patterns were highly nucleated. Just as villages were physically well defined, so was the political authority of the country clearly localised within them.[1] As missionary George Turner explained 'The village communities of from two to five hundred people, consider themselves perfectly distinct from each other, quite independent, and at liberty to act as they please on their own ground, and in their own affairs.'[2] In New Zealand such small-scale settlements resulted from relatively few people living in a large and diverse country, but in Samoa, with its greater density of population relative to landmass, social and political philosophy or ideology exercised a greater influence on where and how people lived.

Each village consisted of a number of extended families. Relationships among these families were carefully defined in terms of kinship and social status and were constantly reinforced by formalised renditions of the village's history as reflected in accounts of titles and genealogical connections. Each family was headed by a *matai* who was chosen or elected by his family. This elective principle was a significant feature at most levels in Samoan society. Again like New Zealand, Samoa had no rigid class structure, and people of ability could achieve positions of status. Each village had a principal or head *matai*, chosen or elected from the most able candidates. There were two types of *matai*—the *ali'i* and the *tulafale*. *Ali'i* can be loosely translated as a chief whose status derived from real or proclaimed lines of descent. The closer the *ali'i* was to the major genealogical branches leading back to Samoa's ancestor gods, the greater his (or much less frequently her) status. But *ali'i* could also be self-made. The successful warrior chief could reinterpret history to give him the necessary genealogical status, and this is where Samoa differed most notably from New Zealand. Where Goldman has New Zealand in the Traditional category, he has Samoa in the Open one.[3] The *tulafale* was the *ali'i*'s spokesman and executive officer, and his standing resulted from his skills in oratory and knowledge of oral tradition. The *tulafale* could be a most influential figure, especially since Samoan politics revolved around the issues of status, and status was very much derived from genealogical background. Those who controlled the knowledge and interpretation of the past could influence the present. Some *tulafale* had customary rights to confer the highest chiefly titles in Samoa upon those candidates deemed most worthy.

Family and village *matai* were usually influential and highly respected persons, yet they seldom wielded autocratic powers. Their decisions were usually taken after extensive consultations.[4] Those *matai* who became oppressive were often exiled or killed. Each village had a *fono*—a council consisting of all the family *matai* who took their seating positions and speaking order according to the relative importance of their titles. Council protocol was rigidly determined by convention. As Wilkes of the US Exploring Expedition explained:

> *In all such meetings, a rigid order of precedence, that seems well understood by everyone, is established; all conversation is carried on in a whisper; no one is seen standing in the presence of a superior, and sitting with outstretched legs is considered indecorous.*[5]

In Tonga the *fono* met to be told what to do by the most powerful chiefs, and woe betide its members if they disobeyed. But the Samoan *fono* was an assembly for deliberation in which no-one had the right to impose a particular decision. All members were given a say with the intention of reaching consensus.[6] Once such consensus had emerged, all *matai* were obliged to comply or face banishment from the village.[7]

This principle of consultation and consensual policymaking permeated

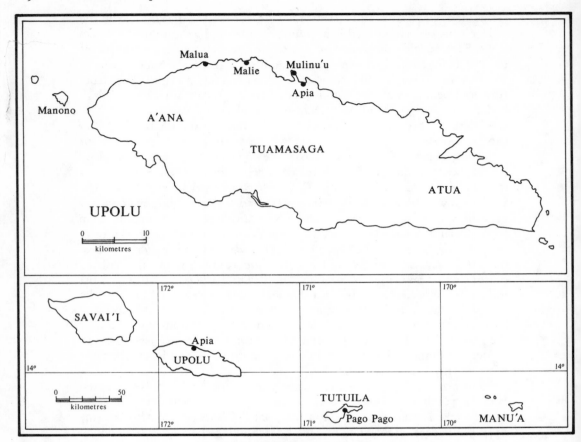

8   Upolu and Samoan Islands

all levels of Samoan society and would have been a major impediment to any Samoan aspiring to be the equivalent of a Pomare, a Kamehameha, or a Taufa'ahau. As Turner said, their political system was more 'patriarchal and democratic ... than ... monarchical'.[8] This system was of course far from perfect. When disputes arose that could not be solved by peaceful discussion, people might leave, or be forced to leave a village, or the village might divide itself into two, each section forming its own *fono*. Physical violence and warfare were also resorted to, but for the most part social, economic, and political relations were regulated at the village level in a way that did not usually require and indeed did not usually permit personal political aggrandisement beyond acceptable levels. Missionaries were to find in Samoa a level of social control which, in their view at least, made Samoa seem less disordered than many other places.

Villages did not operate in isolation. Individuals and families had all manner of kin and other relationships with people far and near, and there was a constant coming and going of friends and enemies.[9] These relationships had administrative counterparts. Several contiguous villages might form a subdistrict, which like its component villages had a historical identity and a *fono*. Subdistrict functions were rather different from those of the village, where day-to-day issues were decided. The subdistrict represented any common interests of the component villages, particularly in relations with similar outside groups. Subdistrict meetings were especially important in matters of diplomacy and warfare, or in any general crisis. But in most other respects subdistrict organisations were not very effective, or nonexistent. Because a village very jealously guarded its own interests where these clashed with those of its neighbours, the possibility for conflict in any joint organisation was high. Subdistricts worked effectively only when their supporting villages faced some common threat.[10] There was little administrative machinery above village level that could be exploited by some would-be autocrat.

A subdistrict belonged to a district which also had a *fono* whose functions were even further removed from the day-to-day business of the bulk of the population. This *fono* was more concerned with relationships amongst those powerful families or dynasties which claimed the most important lineages in Samoa as a whole. There were three main districts on Upolu, each with a capital, and each with a supreme title or titles and titleholder. The titleholders were elected by certain élite orator groups when the purity of the candidate's line of descent, according to genealogical interpretation, could be agreed to. But there were also candidates who through success in warfare could force the élite orators of the conquered side to confer major titles. In recent pre-European times members of the Sa Tupua (or Tupua family) had a preemptive hold on the titles from two districts, while the titles from the third district were normally the preserve of the Sa Malietoa. These two great families—Sa Tupua and Sa Malietoa—were to play a central role in nineteenth-century Samoan politics. The island of Savai'i was divided into six districts, each with its capital, supreme titles, and élite orators. The Sa Malietoa had important connections with many of these districts and also with equivalent ones on more distant Tutuila.[11]

The holders of these impressive titles enjoyed great status but little power though they were sometimes expected to be successful in battle. On the whole these were ceremonial positions of the most exalted kind, far removed from the mundane matters of everyday living at village level. All the districts could act in concert in which case a *fono* representing the two main islands would be called together by certain élite orators. More common was division and conflict. By the early nineteenth century the A'ana and Atua districts of Upolu, led by Sa Tupua, were usually aligned against the third district, Tuamasaga, and most of Savai'i, led by Sa Malietoa. One of the most common causes of warfare at these levels was competition for the various supreme titles. In particular anyone who by genealogical connection and/or success in war could gain the four main titles of Upolu (one each from A'ana and Atua and two from Tuamasaga) became *tafa'ifa*, or ruler of Samoa. But such a position was extremely difficult to attain since it cut across both Sa Malietoa and Sa Tupua lines. The ascendancy of the one family necessarily meant the military conquest and humiliation of the other. The position was empty for far longer than it was ever held. Furthermore, if an individual did manage to become *tafa'ifa*, his powers were largely ceremonial and not executive.[12] There was no associated bureaucracy that could have given any holder the secular controls enjoyed by the kings of Tahiti, Hawaii, and Tonga. Furthermore, there was no way in which the *tafa'ifa* could hand his position on to a successor, as those other monarchs could. When a *tafa'ifa* died the four key titles became scattered since the various orator groups could never agree to handing them en masse to some unproven person. The long and difficult process of someone putting himself forward as a candidate for the titles through diplomacy and conquest, and the necessary conferring of them by the orators, would have to start all over again.

The idea of a king was thus certainly present in Samoa, unlike New Zealand, but the position was rarely filled and entailed no administrative or executive powers. Unlike Tahiti, Hawaii, and Tonga, Samoa had no bureaucracy, no priestly class, and no state religion which a king might exploit to create a kingdom.

Samoan social and political organisation displayed both strengths and weaknesses in the face of European presence. On the one hand the nature and importance of village-level activity provided a high degree of stability and cohesiveness yet also allowed for creative modification as circumstances changed. This was displayed most notably in the Samoan response to missionaries and Christianity. On the other hand, because Samoan organisation at a 'national' level was far removed from the temporal running of the country, the people encountered many major problems when they tried to create an effective central government to cope with certain other consequences of European settlement.

Early European contacts

Samoa remained out of the mainstream of European activity in the Pacific until the 1830s. Roggeveen made brief contact in 1722, as did Bougainville in 1768, though neither landed. Bougainville thought the Samoans who came out to his ship less 'gentle' with features 'more savage' than Tahitians.[13] La Pérouse did land in 1787 and was staggered at what he considered the 'colossal proportions' of the Samoans, who, for their part, mocked the Frenchmen's smallness, 'laughed at our threats, and made a jest of our genitels'. A boat party of twelve was soon cut to pieces. The terrified sailors had tried to ward off their attackers with muskets. Each shot of their first volley killed a Samoan 'but there was no time to reload.' La Pérouse left Samoa singing the praises of its natural beauty and condemning its inhabitants for their savagery.[14] The Samoan reputation for treachery seemed confirmed when some of them unsuccessfully attacked HMS *Pandora* during her search for the *Bounty* mutineers in 1791. Most early traders gave Samoa a wide berth, choosing safer places like Tahiti and Hawaii, and even New Zealand. Even in 1824, navigators like Kotzebue still argued that Samoans were 'perhaps the most ferocious people to be met with in the South Sea'.[15] The ubiquitous beachcombers were also absent from Samoa in these times. One was found living there in 1802, and even in 1830 there were still relatively few.[16]

Life in Samoa was little affected by direct European contact before the 1830s, yet there was a considerable amount of indirect European influence. Samoans who travelled to Tonga and Fiji in the 1820s returned with some knowledge of European ways, including missionary teachings.[17] A small party of London Missionary Society (LMS) converts from Raivavae drifted to Samoa in 1829. One Samoan, Siovili, travelled to Tonga on a whaler in the mid-1820s and then went on to Tahiti where he had some contact with *Mamaia* cultists. He may have returned via New South Wales. Once back in Samoa he began making prophecies and telling strange tales about someone called Jesus, and the dead coming alive, and the imminent arrival of the white man's riches, but only for those who believed in the white man's god.[18] Siovili began a form of cult and these ideas became widespread throughout Samoa and were apparently given additional credence with the arrival of European missionaries.

John Williams

John Williams was one of the LMS's most aggressive pioneers in the South Seas—a man whose innermost drivings found the perfect vehicle of expression in attempts to spread the Christian message far beyond Tahiti.[19] Williams first introduced Christianity to the Cook Islands and there built himself a 70-tonne ship—the *Messenger of Peace*—and set his sights on the far more numerous benighted souls known to exist in the central Pacific islands and Melanesia. Tonga was his first port of call where he met Fauea, a Samoan chief who persuaded him to visit Samoa; there, he assured Williams, the leading chief Malietoa Vai'inupo would welcome him.[20] Williams duly arrived off Malietoa's village on Savai'i in 1830. The occasion was extremely significant for the LMS mission on at least two counts. First, Fauea's speech to his fellow Samoans confirmed what many of them, and especially the Siovili cultists, were anticipating—that the acceptance of the European god would bring endless prosperity. Other Samoan chiefs took up the argument.

> *I look . . . at the wisdom of these worshippers of Jehovah, and see how superior they are to us in every respect. Their ships are like floating houses, so that they can*

traverse the tempest-driven ocean for months with perfect safety; whereas, if a breeze blow upon our canoes, they are in an instant upset, and we sprawling in the sea. Their persons also are covered from head to foot in beautiful clothes, while we wear nothing but a girdle of leaves. Their axes are so hard and sharp, that, with them, we can easily fell our trees, and do our work, but with our stone axes we must dub, dub, dub, day after day, before we can cut down a single tree. Their knives, too, what valuable things they are; how quickly they cut up our pigs, compared with our bamboo knives! Now I conclude that the God who has given to his white worshippers these valuable things must be wiser than our gods, for they have not given the like to us. We all want these articles; and my proposition is, that the God who gave them should be our God.[21]

Williams and others declared themselves to be just a little abashed at such crude sentiments yet they were delighted enough at the effect.[22] Williams himself was a master at exciting Islanders' cupidity in order to make a favourable impression. Christianity was thus initially introduced to Samoa with the promise that believers would inherit great wealth.

Second, Williams's arrival coincided with the rise to pre-eminence of Malietoa Vai'inupo. Williams hoped that the acceptance of Christianity in Samoa, as in Tahiti, would be associated with the emergence of a king. Samoa had been racked with civil war for some time. A chief of Manono who was allied to Sa Malietoa had been killed by Sa Tupua followers just before Williams arrived. Malietoa Vai'inupo was in the process of successfully avenging this death and in doing so was now close to gaining the four titles that would make him *tafa'ifa*. Malietoa returned from a successful campaign to find Williams waiting for him. In return for Williams's gifts and promise to send him European missionaries, Malietoa agreed to protect the eight native teachers Williams wanted to leave. He also promised to give up fighting after he gained a final victory.[23] Williams sailed away delighted since he was convinced he had found another Pomare or Kamehameha.

When Williams returned in 1832 he found that Malietoa had won the war, that there was peace, and, more amazingly, that

Malietoa, his brother, the principal chiefs, and nearly all the inhabitants of their settlement, had embraced Christianity; that their chapel would accommodate six or seven hundred people, and that it was always full; and that in the two large islands of Savaii and Upolu the Gospel had been introduced into more than thirty villages.[24]

Williams believed that Maleitoa was now king, but not until 1836 were the various orator groups persuaded to bestow all the four titles upon him, making him *tafa'ifa*. Even in 1832 Williams was beginning to appreciate that a Samoan king's powers were greatest in times of war, and that at other times the position was mainly ceremonial. Nevertheless Williams still felt

22   *Malietoa Vai'inupo, 1839.*
     (*Wilkes* Narrative of the United States Exploring Expedition, *vol II*)

that the LMS needed Malietoa's support and accordingly gave him a virtual monopoly over where teachers should be placed in Samoa, in the hope that Malietoa might gain influence in areas not normally his preserve. The mutually advantageous association that Williams expected between the Samoan monarch and the LMS mission never eventuated. As Williams himself soon had to admit 'There appears to be no principal chief exercising kingly authority over the whole group.'[25]

Shortly before the LMS landed resident European missionaries in Samoa in 1835, the Wesleyan mission in Tonga landed Peter Turner and some Tongan teachers. In contrast to Williams, Turner was prepared to ignore powerless kings and work at village level throughout Samoa. He found himself operating at the level where important decisions were made in Samoan life and where endless divisions between and amongst villages could be fruitfully exploited. Samoans had the choice of either *lotu taiti* (LMS) or *lotu toga* (Wesleyans). Villages selected one or other or neither depending on various political and diplomatic considerations. Some feared Malietoa and opted for the *lotu toga*. Within two years Turner claimed that one third of the Samoan population was Methodist. The LMS landed two missionaries just months after Turner arrived, and the following year increased the number to nine. But even with more personnel at their disposal, the LMS acknowledged Turner's head start. Taking a leaf out of Turner's book they rejected Williams's strategy of concentrating on Malietoa and plunged headlong into village politics all over the islands. Samoan factionalism was inflamed by mission rivalry.[26] Relations between the LMS and Turner became bitter. Much diplomatic activity back at the relative mission headquarters soon resulted in Samoa being 'given' to the LMS and a most disgruntled Turner departing for the Wesleyans' Tonga in 1839. However Wesleyan influence did not cease altogether. Taufa'ahau continued to send Tongan teachers to Samoa, and visited Samoa twice in the 1840s to encourage their mission. The Wesleyan Methodist mission was reestablished in 1857—this time under the auspices of the Australian Conference of the Wesleyan Methodist Church, but it remained a minority church in Samoa. Another challenge to LMS dominance came in 1845 when Marist missionaries arrived. But only a handful of Samoans supported them, most being piqued Wesleyans together with Siovilians (whose cult lasted until the 1860s), who hoped they might be better off in the political squabbles with LMS supporters. For the most part, the LMS had Samoa to itself.

Conversion

By 1840, only ten years after missionaries landed in Samoa, most Samoans were Christians and some 10 000 could read their language.[27] Unlike events in Tahiti, Tonga, and Hawaii, this development had not been inspired by conquering kings imposing Christian doctrine as part of a political strategy. The Samoan response to Christianity had more in common with the Maori response in that decisions to accept or reject missionary teachings were made at a local level and for local reasons. However, in Samoa, with its relatively small size and more uniform settlement patterns and social and political organisations, the overall conversion to Christianity was easier, quicker, and relatively more homogeneous than in New Zealand.

Both LMS and Wesleyan missionaries always made much of the material benefits association with the church would bring Samoans and entry into their villages was invariably accompanied with lavish gift giving. At the same time Williams and Turner were not particularly demanding in their requirements—both asked of Samoans little more than a public profession of Christianity rather than any radical change in outlook or even action. Williams told Malietoa that God forbad war and 'rude' songs and dances, which was a rather short list of sins compared with those other missionaries elsewhere were compiling. Williams believed that those attracted to Christianity by its material trappings should not have all their habits condemned for fear 'they take a total dislike to a religion that prohibited that in which their whole life and comfort consisted'.[28] He believed that they would eventually learn for themselves from the Bible what was right and wrong.[29] He and other LMS missionaries still required a period of testing before candidates were actually baptised, but the Wesleyan practice was far less rigorous. Turner baptised Samoans as soon as they professed themselves Christians.

This relatively undemanding process of conversion required by the missionaries in the 1830s was complemented from the Samoan side (as it was in New Zealand) by the lack of any state religion. Williams wrote that

> *the religious system of the Samoans differs essentially from that which obtained at the Tahitian, Society, and other islands with which we are acquainted. They have neither maraes, nor temples, nor altars, nor offerings; and, consequently, none of the barbarous and sanguinous rites observed at the other groups.*[30]

In Samoa (and New Zealand) people could decide to become Christians unconstrained by the demands of an institutionalised religion (as distinct from religious beliefs), an entrenched priestly class, or even a supreme ruler. This may be one reason why Samoans (and Maoris) seemed to be so interested in new ideas as well as new technology. There was an aggressive experimenting with new concepts, as the Siovili cult had demonstrated before missionaries arrived. Tahitians or Tongans were not necessarily less interested initially, but they were more likely to keep their intellectual questioning private so as not to upset the authorities.

Individuals in Samoa did not have complete freedom of choice. Decisions about accepting teachers and missionaries, and whether to opt for the *lotu taiti*, *lotu toga*, Marists, or Siovili, were generally taken by family *matai* and then the village *fono*. Overall there was a political element in that villages made such decisions according to village–subdistrict–district relations. The *matai* played a key role in the conversion of Samoa. They quickly saw the political and other advantages that might accrue by accepting teachers and missionaries. They might increase their prestige by having access to new wealth and new skills such as literacy, not to mention a whole new genealogical interpretation of the cosmos. *Matai* could in fact become, to missionaries, meddling nuisances in their enthusiasm:

> *The undue interference of native chiefs with religious affairs has to be guarded against, particularly in the early stages of missionary work. Having been accustomed to take everything of importance into their own hand, and legislate accordingly, it comes quite natural to them to wish to have their say in the arrangements made by the missionary for schools and other services. Thinking, no doubt, that it would please me, the chiefs in one part of my district made a law that every man who did not appear at the six o'clock morning-school for reading and prayer should be fined in a quantity of cooked taro, fish, and other eatables. The chiefs like anything of that sort that bring in a fine; some are sure to transgress, and*

then the old senators are quite in their element feasting over the fines. Whenever I heard what had been done, I sent a message to the chiefs, begging them to confine their legislation to other matters, and leave all at liberty to search the Scriptures and worship God, or the contrary, just as they pleased, as it was to God and not to man all were at length to be called to give an account of their reception or rejection of the gospel.

It was the same in building a chapel, viz., a disposition to impose fines and penalties on all who did not assist. We begged, however, in this case also, to claim an exception; adding, that we wished it to be said in the erection of our churches, as was said of old in the days of David, that the chiefs and people 'offered willingly'.[31]

Village *fono* decisions were considered binding, and as was customary, those who disagreed were punished or exiled.

Missionaries were deeply impressed with the rapidity of the evangelisation of Samoa, yet not so naive as to be unaware of the reasons for it:

How different were the circumstances of the brethren at Tahiti! what years of toil and anxiety they endured before this desire was created; and at New Zealand, also, to what privations, labours, and perils, were the devoted Missionaries of the Church Missionary Society called for nearly twenty years, before anything like a general desire for instruction was evinced by the inhabitants. At the Navigators, on the contrary, in less than twenty short months, chapels were erected, and the people anxiously waiting for instruction. Our Saviour has taught us to appreciate the importance of this state of a people, under the beautiful similitude of a corn-field "white unto the harvest". I would by no means affirm that many, or even that any, of the Samoans had experienced a change of heart, neither do I believe, that, in the majority of the people, the desire for Missionaries arose from a knowledge of the spiritual character and supreme excellency of the Gospel; for, doubtless, they were actuated by various motives. Some thought that, by their embracing Christianity, vessels would be induced to visit them; others imagined that thus they would be preserved from the malignity of their gods; many hoped by adopting the new religion to prolong their lives; and a few valued it chiefly as a means of terminating their sanguinary and desolating wars. Some were undoubtedly convinced of the folly and superstition of their own religious system; and a few had indistinct ideas of the soul and salvation.[32]

Samoan Christianity

Where Christianity was imposed upon a people by a paramount leader like Pomare II, Kamehameha II, or Taufa'ahau the nature of the subsequently established Christian church took on a particular character.[33] It was marked by fairly rigid controls over the population through laws and a bureaucracy manipulated by a royal family and a few missionaries. However much mission organisations might have opposed theoretically the coming together of church and state, in practice this union was essential for mission success in many islands of Polynesia. Evangelical missionaries argued that their job was not to interfere with indigenous government yet they justified their obvious political influence with such governments by saying that they had a legitimate role as advisers.[34] The charge that they supported theocratic policies in Hawaii, Tahiti, and Tonga was not entirely unjustified. However, in Samoa as in New Zealand there was no indigenous state. Missionaries could not work through paramount chiefs and advise them to promulgate law codes and constitutions and other trappings of a centralised government. Whatever hopes some LMS missionaries might still have harboured that Malietoa the *tafa'ifa* would assist their cause were finally dashed when the chief died in 1841, his titles were scattered, and warfare in pursuit of them broke out and continued sporadically for another two decades. The Christian church in Samoa reflected far less missionary dominance and far more Samoan characteristics than missionaries would have liked. As individuals, missionaries in Samoa had little of the direct influence over congregations that they enjoyed on islands where political authority was centralised. For example, the contrast between missionaries on Tonga and Samoa was often cause for comment. As Erskine said,

> *I am, indeed, bound in justice to remark, that, in respect to their treatment of the people [of Tonga] . . . the gentlemen of this mission do not compare favourably with those of the London Society in the Samoan Islands. A more dictatorial spirit towards the chiefs and people seemed to show itself.*[35]

Samoans were far too emotionally and socially tied to their village to want to settle near any mission headquarters—a problem missionaries often encountered when working with nucleated as opposed to non-nucleated settlements. If missionaries wanted to influence Samoans they had to go to their villages. But the LMS and other missions simply did not have the resources to station a missionary in each village. Even on a small island like Tutuila, with a population of less than four thousand, the problem was acute for the missionaries. As one of them explained,

> *A great part of it [Tutuila] is very difficult of access, and the people are widely scattered. There are over thirty villages. Thus it could only be embraced, and the population brought under Christian instruction and influence, by the employment of a numerous staff of native teachers.*[36]

These teachers were Samoans whom the missionaries trained. In 1839 there were eleven European missionaries in Samoa and 138 teachers.[37] There was certainly no problem in attracting teachers.

> *Great anxiety was exhibited by the candidates; and I have never seen a more proper state of feeling, or listened to more correct sentiments than were expressed on this occasion. All appeared devoted to their calling and some of them were quite*

eloquent. After the choice was announced, those upon whom it had fallen manifested a cheerful but not unbecoming triumph, while the rejected candidates were evidently grieved and disappointed. The former were now invested with their new apparel, which, although no more than a striped cotton shirt, gave them an air of consequence among their brethren.[38]

Teachers were deliberately sent to villages other than their own and hence were strangers and totally dependent upon their hosts for food, shelter, and whatever status they might or might not be accorded. In particular they were subject to the authority of *matai* and *fono*. They could not simply barge into a village and begin preaching, as missionaries were wont to do all over the Pacific. Instead the teachers spoke only when occasion and custom permitted. In addition to these limitations, the teachers had to cope with missionary concern that teachers in villages were beyond supervision. Missionaries deliberately kept 'religious' authority to themselves. Teachers were not permitted ordination or allowed to administer the sacraments. But this put the missionaries in a contradictory position. They were totally dependent on the teachers to take the Christian message out to the villages, and indeed established a large seminary at Malua in 1845 to train these men, yet at the same time they feared that the teachers far away in the villages might build up rather too much personal and 'Samoan' influence. This stance was ultimately untenable. Teachers became increasingly disgruntled and began to demand a degree of religious authority as well as an allowance for books and clothing, and a salary. Not for long was a shirt considered adequate recompense. The teachers believed these rights and goods would raise their status and therefore their influence in the villages. Sometimes their congregations supported them. General dissatisfaction came to a head in 1850 when the Tutuila teachers 'revolted' and demanded books, clothing, and that the missionaries' salaries be paid by British donors so freeing local Samoan contributions for paying the teachers' salaries.[39] LMS missionaries in Samoa had no option but to give in, for without the teachers there could be no mission, especially now that LMS headquarters in London began reducing the number of missionaries in Samoa (and elsewhere) as a cost-cutting measure. The teachers thus got their books, clothes, and a salary—paid for by a reorganisation of the annual contributions to the church. Instead of one collection there were two—one for the missionaries, the other for the teachers—and the latter, to the missionaries' chagrin, was always the largest. Yet the missionaries had to support this system of finance and they managed to put church finances in a most healthy situation because of it. They exploited the Samoans' competitive spirit by publishing lists of contributors together with the amounts offered. Samoans went all out to get their names at the top of the lists. As Gilson nicely reflects,

Whereas the Samoans had once expected to receive lavish material gifts through the London Missionary Society, they were now reversing the relationship, and doing so with 'delight and enjoyment', not so much to support the mission as to seek the favour of God and the respect of men in the volume of their sacrifices.[40]

Church activity was increasingly becoming a Samoan affair, and as the years passed the teachers' standing within the villages gradually increased, especially when the LMS made its first concessions to them. A teacher's oratorical skills when preaching were appreciated, as was the ability to read and write. As a teacher's status within the village increased so too did the *matai*'s if he associated himself with the teacher. The teacher became an important example to many in the village of how a missionary education promised social advancement. It was a great honour to go to the training college at Malua. An aristocracy of education was being grafted onto Samoan social organisation. The more influential the teachers became the more the missionaries were forced to grant them further privileges. At first a select few were ordained and permitted to administer the sacraments, but by the mid-1870s most had gained that status and right. Whatever the missionaries did, the church became more Samoan in character. Even its very administrative shape reflected Samoan influence. The LMS accepted that one day Samoa would have an independent church and while this was in effect rapidly developing, many missionaries in Samoa quietly opposed it all the way and only gave in when they had no alternative. By the 1870s the fears of the first missionaries in the 1830s had been borne out—Christianity as a doctrine and the church as an organisation had been assimilated into village life and, to missionaries, this meant that there was far too much local interpretation. This might not have happened had there been an effective church authority and bureaucracy transcending individual villages. What missionaries ideally wanted (in practice if not in theory) was some centralised state onto which could be grafted a national religion. But in Samoa there was no such institution. Missionary attempts to build a church hierarchy for the country as a whole were doomed before they started. Samoan teachers and pastors wanted to or were obliged to reflect the interests of their village. The village was so central to Samoan social and political life that these men could not support policies of some organisation beyond the village where these conflicted with their *fono*'s opinion.

Samoans were Christians, as outwardly devoted to their church as any other peoples of Oceania. But their Christianity was not something imposed on them; rather it had been absorbed, adapted, and given a uniquely Samoan expression. Yet Samoan society handled other Western influences far less successfully. If the lack of centralised authority gave them the upper hand over LMS missionaries, it bedevilled their attempts to come to terms with European settlers and their metropolitan governments.

23   *Classroom and students' cottages, LMS seminary at Malua, 1850s. (Turner Nineteen Years in Polynesia)*

Warfare and high politics

High politics in Samoa remained relatively unaffected by European presence and influence for far longer than in most other Pacific islands. This was mainly because the priorities of the leading families long continued to be concerned with customary dignity and status—attributes which in the Samoan context had more to do with ceremonial occasion than executive power. The highest-ranked Samoan chiefs were not initially concerned to exploit the new European influences to establish centralised controls as were their counterparts on some other islands. They were more interested in gaining the titles that constituted the *tafa'ifa*. When Malietoa Vai'inupo—*tafa'ifa* since 1836—died in 1841, his titles were scattered and twenty years of warfare ensued. There were two main camps—that of Sa Malietoa (led by Taimalelagi who succeeded Malietoa to the Malietoa title) and Sa Tupua.

Most of the fighting was inconclusive and, from a European point of view, not very warlike at all. Erskine on HMS *Havannah* visited Samoa in 1849 and was singularly unimpressed with the military tactics he witnessed. On one occasion he watched what promised to be a major naval engagement. Some 800–1000 men in war canoes went 'through a kind of exercise':

> *The paddlers . . . were dressed up with red caps or turbans, whilst one, the warrior of the canoe, went through a variety of antics in the bow, occasionally squibbing off a musket, with which he alone seemed to be armed. We saw this ridiculous kind of manoeuvring occasionally repeated during our stay, but never anything like concerted or general movements among the fleet. Indeed, we were told that such were never practised, any fighting which may take place being confined to one canoe on either side, the party of that in which the first man is killed or badly wounded, taking to flight immediately.*[41]

Land battles were seldom more bloody. Erskine reported one incident where 100 men were killed, though he believed this was 'an immense number, according to Samoan notions'.[42] Fighting usually consisted of ambushing and small-scale skirmishing. Firearms seem not to have been widely used and certainly no one side had any monopoly of them.[43]

The longer fighting for titles continued, the more some Samoans began to doubt the point of it all, especially when contact with Europeans increased. War sometimes interfered with a village's trading with Europeans, or its desire to keep on good terms with missionaries. As in New Zealand, missionaries in Samoa had no warrior patron and thus could oppose war without compromising their interests. Similarly, Samoan chiefs could use Christianity as an excuse for not going to war. On Tutuila in 1849 'the whole of the seven ruling chiefs' were Christian, so that *some pagan villages exist on the east coast, the chiefs of which are pagan, the general policy, as determined by the great council, must be according to the principles of the Christians. This great council having determined that no part is to be taken in a civil war now raging in Upolu, and a passed a law prohibiting all intercourse during its continuance, the pagans, although solicited by their friends in that island, and desiring to render them assistance, are obliged to submit to the prohibition. No one has ventured as yet to infringe it; and the penalty of doing so would probably be the burning down the house of the offender in his absence.*[44]

Nor, as was also the case in New Zealand, did indigenous warfare embroil Europeans. Just as chiefs like Hongi fought for uniquely Maori reasons, so did Samoan chiefs. Europeans were outside these concerns. Erskine believed that in no other country in the world could a European live with 'such a sense of security'. Fighting in Samoa, he continued, 'operated very prejudicially to Christian interests' but 'no animosity has been shown against either the missionaries or the white residents'.[45] The missionary Turner remarked

Throughout the struggle we observed as much neutrality as we conscientiously could.... This, however, did not make us their enemies. They always appeared friendly. They would say to each other, "These missionaries are from a foreign country; they do not understand our Samoan politics...."[46]

However, at least some of the goals of political life had eventually to be modified to cope with changing circumstances.

The growth of Apia

During the late 1830s and throughout the forties and fifties whalers called at Samoa in large numbers to rest crews and take on fresh provisions. Apia, sited on one of the more reliable anchorages, rapidly took on the characteristics of port towns that had already developed elsewhere—Honolulu, Papeete, and Kororareka. By the 1860s there were over one hundred European residents, though depending on shipping movements European visitors could far outnumber them. Small businesses multiplied. Boarding-houses, stores, and grog shops sprang up on the foreshore.[47] The growth of port towns like Apia eventually had major consequences for island communities. Hitherto beachcombers, castaways, itinerant traders, and the like had been widely and thinly scattered throughout island societies and were dependent upon their hosts. But the new generation of commercial men who grouped themselves in the tiny port towns were more economically and socially independent and so less subject to the restraints of the Islanders in whose midst they lived. European settlement in Apia, as elsewhere, posed two basic problems that were to bedevil political life in Samoa for the remainder of the century: how to regulate the activities of Europeans in the town itself, and how to regulate relations between Europeans and Samoans.

Until the 1850s or even 1860s there were essentially two Samoas—Apia (and to a lesser extent Pago Pago) and the rest, just as in the 1830s there were two New Zealands—the Bay of Islands and the rest. Most Samoans remained relatively unaffected by, though not unaware of, what was happening in Apia.

As early as 1837 a British naval captain attempted to draw up port regulations at Apia (and Pago Pago) in conjunction with LMS missionaries and some local *matai*.[48] In 1839 Wilkes of the US Exploring Expedition and missionaries promulgated a more comprehensive 'Apia code' designed to provide port services and ensure friendly relations between European visitors and Samoans. Wilkes and other naval personnel—both British and American—had no doubts about their authority and its extent in Samoa. Any 'depredations' committed by Samoans against Europeans that were not satisfactorily dealt with by Samoan chiefs were punished by 'naval justice'. The powers—Britain and America—then proceeded to keep a closer watch on affairs at Apia by appointing consuls. But if European authorities were clear as to their rights in Samoa, the position of Samoans was far less clear. The problem, as Europeans saw it, was to know where and in what institution lay Samoan sovereignty. For a while it was assumed that Malietoa Vai'inupo as *tafa'ifa* might embody this sovereignty, but his death in 1841 put an end to that. Samoans, involved as they were in their own affairs, gave no thought to such concepts, and Europeans in practice were more concerned with the problems of life in Apia than with the country as a whole, though they were not reluctant to send the odd gunboat to avenge 'crimes' committed elsewhere along the coast. A Foreign Residents' Society was formed in the late 1840s and tried to conduct 'town-meeting' government for the port, and in 1857 a court consisting of Europeans and Samoans was established to sort out any difficulties between the two communities.[49] Such institutions were at worst totally ineffective; at best they provided some semblance of order and (often rough) justice around Apia. Invariably rules and proceedings were inspired by one of the consuls, especially the American J B Williams.

The beginnings of Samoan concern

Some Samoan concern about what Europeans were doing around Apia became apparent after the wars ended inconclusively in 1857, though it was Consul Williams who took the initiative. He wanted administrative and legal 'reforms' to reach beyond Apia and proposed the acceptance of codes of law and the appointment of various executive and judicial officers in the Samoan subdistricts and districts. Several chiefs on Upolu agreed and for several years the laws were administered successfully in a few places. But two inevitable problems prevented any widespread acceptance of the system. When European and Samoan interests could not be reconciled in Apia, Europeans resorted to threats of naval bombardment. And Samoans in villages were generally unwilling to accept rulings from outsiders, especially if those outsiders were supported by a rival Samoan group. There was great fear of losing village independence or being seen as submissive.

The unlikely combination of bad weather and the American Civil War forced more Samoans to consider seriously the idea of a more centralised administration. In the mid-1860s a series of severe storms followed by drought left many Samoans short of food, and, without it to sell to whalers, cash. But they found ready riches in selling land to those Europeans who were now flocking to Samoa and elsewhere in the Pacific to plant cotton. The war in America meant that British textile factories lost their usual supply of cotton and alternative sources were urgently needed. The Pacific islands cotton boom got underway. Among the most aggressive buyers of land for cotton plantations in Samoa was the German firm J C Godeffroy & Son, and for the first time European economic interests moved beyond the immediate environs of Apia and into the very heartland of Samoa.[50]

Both European businessmen and Samoans now had good cause to want some sort of regulative administration, but for different reasons: Europeans were primarily interested in being protected from Samoans in the bush and ensuring security of tenure for the land they bought; Samoans needed to protect their interests on a broader front now that Europeans appeared to be pouring into the country and moving to its very corners. The Samoans most immediately affected were those of the Tuamasaga district who made serious efforts to create a form of district government in 1868. However conflicts over the Malietoa title not only ruined prospects for a united Tuamasaga but plunged the whole of Samoa back into a period of war.[51]

Renewal of civil war

After Malietoa Vai'inupo died in 1841, his half-brother Taimalelagi was appointed in his place by the appropriate orators. When he died in 1858 Vai'inupo's eldest son, Moli, was given the title but died two years later. Talavou, Vai'inupo's younger son, and half-brother of Moli, seemed the most likely person to take over. But he was very much out of favour with the LMS missionaries who supported one of their star pupils and one-time teacher, Laupepa, Moli's son. The Malietoa title was usually conferred by nine leading orators from the village of Malie in Tuamasaga in consultation with certain orators on Manono and Savai'i. The missionaries persuaded the Malie orators to support Laupepa, but others still held out for Talavou. This is the first recorded instance of mission involvement in such delicate matters and is indicative of the growing part played by the church, particularly in Samoan rivalries. Eventually there was an uneasy compromise. The title was split and two Malietoas were appointed. But this arrangement did not last long. In 1868, when there was talk of setting up a district government for Tuamasaga, Laupepa's supporters took the opportunity to declare him king of Tuamasaga and sole Malietoa and they set up a 'government'. In retaliation, Talavou was declared king of Tuamasaga by his supporters and they established a rival 'government' across the bay from Apia on the Mulinu'u peninsula.

Also in 1868 a number of chiefs and orators from several districts in Samoa decided to form an administration that was to be a confederation of participating districts. Mulinu'u was chosen as its headquarters. There seems to have been widespread agreement that Talavou should represent Tuamasaga in the new administration, but Laupepa opposed such a move. In 1869 Laupepa's forces drove the district government from Mulinu'u and warfare between the two sides continued until 1873.

By the time the fighting ended, Samoans were acutely aware of the state of their country. Whilst they had been warring amongst themselves, European interests had become more firmly entrenched. Vast areas of the country had been sold to them. In their eagerness for money and firearms during the war, Samoans had been only too willing to sell their lands (and those of their enemies) with little apparent regard for the consequences. European planters and businesses, seeing in Samoa a fine future for a plantation economy based on cotton and copra, were eager to buy land. Godeffroy & Son allegedly purchased some 10 000 hectares between 1869 and 1872. A San Francisco company—the Central Polynesian Land and Commercial Company—claimed to have bought some 120 000 hectares or about half of Samoa. The 140 000 hectares supposedly bought by Europeans during the war was probably an overstatement, but nevertheless many Samoans on Upolu found themselves landless or nearly so.

This war was a turning point for many Samoans. There was a growing awareness that such fighting achieved little and indeed placed Samoans at a considerable disadvantage in the changing circumstances of their country. Now more than ever they realised the necessity to organise some sort of central government to try to take political and economic initiative out of the hands of foreigners. For perhaps the first time in Samoa there seems to have been a widespread willingness, born of fear, to support some administrative machinery that would look after the interests of the country as a whole. Samoans' livelihood and even the very sovereignty of their country seemed at stake.

But the irony was that at the very time when Samoans were prepared to contemplate what had always seemed unacceptable, their hopes of creating a centralised administration were to be dashed by the economic and political interests of rival European concerns. In earlier days when the European population was small and consisted of British and American settlers, their political aspirations had been relatively simple—to have law and order in Apia and to protect their small investments. But now the population was much larger, and there were Frenchmen and Germans too, as well as large companies. The overall economic needs of the white population were much more demanding and much more complex. Samoa was needed for its land; Samoans were needed as plantation labourers. The Europeans wanted a strong government which could recognise their land claims, guarantee them rights to buy more, and generally sanction and protect their interests and property. But since the English, American, German, and French communities were riven by religious, national, and commercial conflicts they could never agree on how such a government should operate. Various European interest groups could divide and rule the Samoans, which was easy enough given Samoan factionalism, yet in doing so they quarrelled bitterly amongst themselves. The Europeans were less united than the Samoans.

The Steinberger government

In 1873, when the war ended, the Samoans established a provisional government at Mulinu'u. This time they avoided the sensitive issue of who was to be the titular leader and formed instead a council of seven highly ranked chiefs—the *Ta'imua*—none of whom were contenders for the titles comprising the *tafa'ifa*. Their job was to draft a constitution, conduct relations with European governments, and enact a code of laws that would be uniform throughout Samoa, though they did not claim the right to impose decisions on village authorities. Just as constitution drafting in Tahiti, Hawaii, and Tonga was a product of many minds, so it was in Samoa. The Samoans' key adviser was Albert B Steinberger, a so-called special agent of the US State Department.[52] For reasons unclear, President Grant recommended that the State Department send Steinberger to report on affairs in Samoa. Grant probably had in mind rather more than a report, and Steinberger, for his part, had some links with the Central Polynesian Land and Commercial Company and an interest in a trans-Pacific shipping line.[53]

Steinberger arrived in Samoa in 1873. With his natural charm and a dignified respect for Samoan custom, he quickly became a popular figure. He was soon advising the *Ta'imua* in their deliberations and suggested that he could convince President Grant to establish Samoa as a US protectorate which would guarantee Samoans their internal autonomy and protect them from the now frequent interference from the warships of other powers.

The *Ta'imua* thought this a good idea. Steinberger returned to consult with the president. In his absence the *Ta'imua* organised a government consisting of itself and a lower house (*Faipule*) with up to 40 *matai* from each district, or some 200 in all. The idea was that virtually every village could thus be represented in the central government of the country. But such a large *Faipule* was too cumbersome to operate in practice. However, the attitude of the Great Powers was now crucial. Steinberger could not get the United States to take on Samoa as a protectorate, though it did agree to consider the new government favourably. Britain recognised the government. Germany did not. In 1874 a German warship intervened forcibly on Godeffroys' behalf in a dispute over land. Steinberger went to Germany and arranged a rather dubious and secret deal with Godeffroy & Son. The company was to encourage the German government to recognise the Samoan government (to be led by Steinberger), and in return the Samoan government was to recognise the company's land claims and allow it to import labour, to use it as its banker, and to impose a tax in kind on copra and fibre that it would then channel through the company. Steinberger was also to get a commission on various Samoan government contracts with Godeffroy & Son.

In 1875 Steinberger arrived back in Samoa where, riding high on his claimed (though illusory) influence with the US government, he set about solving some of the major difficulties that had unfolded with the new Samoan government. The question had arisen as to whether the *Ta'imua* should have some sort of executive officer, which immediately raised the issue of kingship. To prevent such *tafa'ifa*-type conflicts, it had been suggested that there be two kings—one representing Sa Malietoa, the other Sa Tupua. But the two families were even internally divided as to who should represent them, and war seemed likely. Steinberger's clever solution was that there should be just one king, chosen, for a four-year term, alternately from the Malietoa and Tupua families. This king would have status but little actual authority (which accorded well with Samoan ways) and the alternation would, it was hoped, prevent the usual squabbles. Malietoa Laupepa was given first turn. Other government institutions were modified by Steinberger. The *Faipule* or lower house was reduced to a more manageable 20 *matai* representing districts rather than 200 different villages; and the *Ta'imua* or upper house consisted of 14 chiefs. Both houses had equal powers. Steinberger was declared premier.

For the first time Samoans had what looked like a workable central authority. They had achieved, it seemed, their own particular version of a state government just as the Tahitians, Hawaiians, and Tongans had variously done. But there was a crucial difference. Unlike the Tahitians, Tongans, and Hawaiians when they had first unified their countries, Samoans faced entrenched European commercial and political interests. Within a matter of months the Steinberger regime was rendered powerless.

It angered certain settler interests when it attempted to control the liquor trade. Godeffroy & Son lost faith in Steinberger when, contrary to their secret agreement, the Samoan government moved very tardily on the vexed question of land claims. Samoans continued to support Steinberger, but most of his European allies turned against him. Steinberger could not live up to his promise that he could act in the interests of both Europeans and Samoans where these were in conflict. To his former European supporters it appeared that he had sided with Samoans. Missionaries, consuls, businessmen temporarily forgot their differences and began a campaign for his removal. Early in 1876 the US and British consuls and the LMS missionaries forced Laupepa to sign a deportation order for Steinberger. The waiting HMS *Barracouta* whisked him away from Samoa for ever. The Samoans were horrified. The *Ta'imua* and *Faipule* met and dismissed the hapless yet disgraced Malietoa Laupepa. In a stroke there was neither king nor premier.

Denouement

Until the 1870s Samoans had not really wanted a central government. When they decided that they did need one, and with Steinberger created one that seemed appropriate, they were doomed to failure because the now all-powerful and conflicting European interests could never be satisfied. After Steinberger's departure, Samoan political history degenerated into one long and complex tragi-comedy. Rival European powers played with a succession of Samoan kings like puppets, which only served to fragment a society inherently riven with its own factionalism.[54]

In 1879 Laupepa's old rival Talavou was proclaimed king at Mulinu'u after a successful 'opposition' coup. On his death consuls and visiting naval officers reinstated Laupepa with a potential rival Tupua Tamasese Titimaea as 'vice-king'. In 1887 the two men quarrelled; the German consul supported Tamasese and had Laupepa exiled. Laupepa's supporters retaliated and war broke out between the rival factions. Britain and the United States sent warships to Apia to protect their nationals from threatening Samoan and German forces. The absurdity of such diplomacy was vividly demonstrated to all parties during a great storm in 1889. Six German, American, and British warships jammed into Apia harbour were smashed ashore. A semblance of international sanity prevailed temporarily as the powers held a conference on Samoa in Berlin. They recognised Samoa as an independent kingdom—yet forced trading and other concessions upon it. Apia was declared an 'international' zone. Laupepa, whom the Germans now decided to support, was again proclaimed king. But Great Power rivalry and Samoan factionalism continued unabated. R L Stevenson remarked:

24   *A Samoan army in 1899—'Lieutenant Gaunt's Brigade'.*
(Photo by T. Andrew, National Museum of New Zealand)

*There are rival provinces, far more concerned in the prosecution of their rivalry than
in the choice of a right man for king. If one of these shall have bestowed its name on
competitor A, it will be the signal and sufficient reason for the other to bestow its
name on competitor B or C.*[55]

Tupua Tamasese Titimaea's death in 1891 left the royal title of A'ana
vacant. Malietoa Laupepa and his arch-rival Mata'afa Iosefo contested the
title, and in 1893 war broke out between them. The British and Germans
deported Mata'afa. Other contenders took his place, and warships again
intervened. Malietoa Laupepa died in 1898. War followed as contenders
fought for his position. Mata'afa, recently returned, set up a government.

British and American naval forces put him down and set up Laupepa's son, who was in turn defeated by Mata'afa....

By this stage the powers had little option but to formally take over the country. Tutuila and the Manu'a group went to the United States, the remainder to Germany. In return, Britain received German recognition of her claims elsewhere in the Pacific and Africa.

Some forty years earlier missionary George Turner had prophetically written:

> *Consuls, captains of ships of war, merchants, and missionaries have done all they could to get these separate states of Samoa induced to form a union, with a house of representatives, having the higher chiefs in turn as president, or something of that kind, but, hitherto, all efforts have been in vain. Many wish a change, many more prefer remaining as they are, and it is impossible to say how long the Samoans will remain in their present political position, viz., each little community, of two to five hundred, having its own laws and form of government—uniting in districts of eight or ten villages for mutual protection—and these districts, again, combining in twos or threes, as occasion may require, in the event of insult, aggression, or other causes of war.... The missionary plods on, however, in the work of Christian instruction, in the hope that, if not in this, in some other generation, the Samoans may see the propriety of adopting some more united form of government, better suited to their social prosperity and their intercourse with civilized nations; if, indeed, they are not ere long* compelled *to give themselves up to be governed by some of the foreign powers, who, of late years, seem anxious to have possessions in the Pacific.*[56]

Fiji

Fiji in the period of early contact with the West had more in common with New Zealand and Samoa than it did with Tahiti, Tonga, and Hawaii at least insofar as no centralised monarchy emerged there. However the high politics of Fiji also differed from those of New Zealand. Unlike their Maori counterparts, certain Fijian chiefs did have a concept of political expansion and did make serious attempts to gain paramountcy over their country. Fiji differed from Samoa too in that where leading Samoan chiefs were concerned less with executive powers and more with the status and ceremony associated with title-holding, chiefs in Fiji could wield very considerable powers and were largely concerned with dominating and exacting tribute from as many people as possible.

Fijian identity

Fiji is commonly considered a genetic and cultural melting-pot, situated as it is on the supposed boundary between Melanesia and Polynesia. Certain features of Fijian society have been variously catalogued as either 'Melanesian' or 'Polynesian', an obvious though superficial example being the alleged 'Polynesian' appearance of Fijians in the east and their 'Melanesian' appearance in the west. These kinds of observations have long been used as evidence for a range of fanciful theories about Fijian origins, usually based on ideas about various waves of 'Melanesian' and 'Polynesian' migration into these islands.[1] Fijians themselves sometimes helped to create myths about their origins and prehistory that have since become gospel. A Fijian newspaper competition in 1892 for the best tale of origin led to the widespread acceptance of the *Kaunitoni* legend which had the first Fijians arriving on Viti Levu in a great canoe from the west. This story was a late nineteenth century and European-inspired creation which was 'significant of the needs, rather than the history, of the society which produced and accepted it.'[2] To be sure, Fijian society by the time of European contact was notable for elements of apparent cultural diversity, though it is no longer possible to explain this solely in terms of numerous migration theories.

Migrations to Fiji undoubtedly occurred at various times though their nature is still very imperfectly understood by archaeologists and linguists, and there are additional problems about the extent of local and regional adaptation and variation within the Fijian islands themselves. However it does seem that older views about the origins and nature of Fijian society were too concerned with the arrival of real or imagined outside influences, and too preoccupied with what appeared to be racial and cultural diversity.[3] By the time of European contact the people of Fiji had a cultural homogeneity underlying superficial variety. Even in the islands to the east, the Lau group, where there was considerable contact with Tonga, there existed a 'very real indigenous identity.'[4] Collectively, Fijians had cultural traditions that had more in common with each other than with those of Samoa, Tonga, or elsewhere. Fijian lifestyles cannot be interpreted, as they have so often in the past, as simply being a mixture of this and that. Fijians developed and shared a cultural identity and integrity just the same as Islanders in other groups.

Fijian society and politics

Fijian social and political organisation shared many of the characteristics commonly found throughout Polynesia.[5] Society was hierarchical, with chiefly élites ruling the bulk of the population. Rank was determined mainly by ancestry, with chiefly families claiming descent from major founding fathers. But a high birth alone was not sufficient to ensure leadership. Leaders had to come from chiefly families, but the elders whose job it was to decide on succession chose the candidate on ability. Those who became chiefs were those who stood out in a group of qualified contenders. To this extent they were self-made men, and perhaps Fiji could be placed in Goldman's Open category, along with Samoa? However chiefs in Fiji, while having ritual authority like Samoan chiefs, as expressed in rigid formality and elaborate ceremony, in particular in the *yaqona* (kava) ceremonies, also had great personal power. This was most obviously expressed in demands for tribute from conquered peoples and in the many human sacrifices chiefs required. To many Europeans, Fijian chiefs appeared to have the most arbitrary and ruthless powers, based on 'club-law'.

> *No eastern tyrants can rule with more absolute terror than the Chiefs do here; and few people are more thoroughly enslaved and trampled than are these islanders.*[6]

Fijians as a whole were grouped into related families called *tokatoka* (subclans) which formed the basis for village life. These were in turn members of a larger unit, *mataqali*, literally 'men who are twisted together' (a clan). Five or six of these made up the *yavusa* or tribe, which was both a

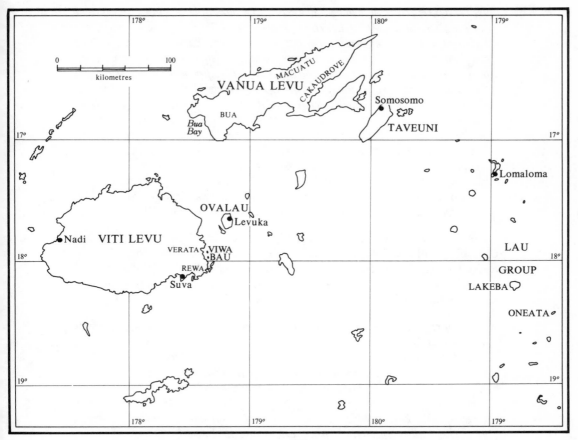

9   *Fiji*

territorial and political unit. The constituent *mataqali* often had specialised functions—some provided the tribal chief or advisers, priests, or warriors. Depending on the outcome of wars and alliances over the years the *yavusa* might be large or small, weak or strong. Some disappeared altogether, some merged with others. Some joined with others to form *vanua*, or confederations.[7]

Fijian society seems to have been in a state of considerable political flux, at least in remembered genealogical time. Each tribe had its *tukutuku raraba* or history and many of these have been collected and written down, especially for the benefit of the Native Lands Commission in early colonial times. Peter France sums up these histories as follows:

> *The original peopling of the land follows the same pattern in each story: after the first settlement the tribe grew in numbers and then the various families went off to seek land and to settle in different villages. These villages are always specified, and*

are frequently identifiable today. The rest of the story usually relates the constant movements from place to place, either at the whim of the chief, or because of the increased population, or the threat or existence of a state of war with a neighbouring chiefdom or between the tribes of their own area. The post-contact wars are related in more detail, but the constant migrations of an earlier period are remembered and the old village sites are named as evidence of the accuracy of the narrative. There is no period of calm and enduring settlement of land as far back as the traditions record. . . .

This unceasing occupation and vacation of lands is a constant feature of all tukutuku raraba. *The normal conditions in which Fijians held land, by their own accounts, in pre-contact times, were those of incessant inter-tribal skirmishing involving continuous migration and resettlement. Out of a total of over six hundred* tukutuku raraba *recorded in Viti Levu and adjacent islands, only twenty-one tell of a tribe which claims to occupy the site on which it was founded.*[8]

On the eve of Western contact Fiji was divided into at least seven relatively small *vanua*. No one chief was in a position of dominance. To rule over a large domain after military conquest was difficult for it depended upon keeping *qali* or conquered peoples under control. And as R A Derrick described,

> *The subject people gave service only so long as their chief was strong enough to enforce his demands. When they saw a prospect of success they turned, and changed masters or took the consequences. Some, no doubt, changed their allegiance merely for the sake of variety . . . and when their geographic position allowed, weak tribes played off one powerful state against another. The border people carried this policy to great lengths. They were the warriors, and paid no tribute. . . . Mutual distrust kept tribes apart. The causes of their frequent wars were disputes about land, property, or women; and the quarrels or petty jealousies of the chiefs.*[9]

Early European influence

If Fiji was fairly politically divided when Europeans first arrived, by the mid-nineteenth century most Fijians had come under the sway of one or another of a small number of rival chiefs, each intent on dominating other *vanua* and creating *matanitu* or kingdoms. This tendency toward political centralisation coincided with the presence of Europeans.

Eighteenth-century explorers who saw parts of Fiji—Tasman, Cook, Bligh—found it a dangerous place and spent very little time there, partly because of the apparent hostility of its people, but mainly because the myriad islands and reefs made navigation extremely dangerous. Fiji's first sustained contact with Europeans came during the sandalwood rush from 1804 to about 1810 which centered mainly around the western coastline of Vanua Levu.[10] There is a long-standing tradition in Fijian historiography of how the introduction of muskets by sandalwood traders together with the prodigious feats of marksmanship by beachcomber Charlie Savage led to the rise to predominance over the western half of Fiji of the tiny island of Bau, a stone's throw off Viti Levu's eastern coast. Tales abound of how the people of Bau, led by Savage into battle, decimated their vastly more numerous enemies and in the process made rivers run red with blood.[11] Yet the same arguments already rehearsed for the role of firearms in Tahiti, Tonga, Hawaii, and New Zealand, seem equally applicable to Fiji. Muskets were more psychologically important than they were technically effective,[12] and it is certainly going too far to attribute the emergence of a Bauan empire to them and a beachcomber. In any case the Bauans did not have a monopoly over the sandalwood trade—the people of rival Bua were better placed in this regard. Furthermore, Bau, under chief Naulivou, was already an up-and-coming state before Savage and muskets arrived. Naulivou's father, for example, had conquered some islands of the Lau group (including Lakeba) and southern parts of Vanua Levu.[13]

The trade in bêche-de-mer from the 1820s to the 1850s had a greater social and economic impact on Fiji than did the geographically limited and fairly short-lived sandalwood trade. Bêche-de-mer trading was more widespread, lasted longer, and involved far more Fijians as labourers. Traders too have usually been seen as revolutionising Fijian politics by introducing even larger quantities of firearms, some 10 000 from 1828 until 1850, which further strengthened the state of Bau.[14] But again any causal links between possession of firearms and political dominance must be placed in the context of indigenous politics. Bauan power came from other attributes. In these decades they had even less chance of a monopoly over firearms than formerly. Muskets were widespread throughout Fiji and at saturation levels. What political and economic advantages did accrue to the Bauans in trading were more a consequence of their improving political position than a cause of it. The real advantages in dealing with visiting traders came as much from the recognition they gave certain chiefs, which in turn increased the prestige of these leaders in the eyes of their followers. What a chief might do with a musket or a bolt of cloth or a cask of rum was less significant than the fact that he was considered worthy of such gifts. Prestige and material wealth came to those chiefs best situated and capable of supplying sandalwood or bêche-de-mer, but usually these were leaders 'who had already established themselves in positions of power' and who could therefore attract 'white men to support them and so consolidate their influence.'[15]

For all the potential rewards and advantages chiefs might gain by dealing with European traders, Fijian politics, like those of New Zealand and Samoa, were on the whole little affected by European contact at least to about the mid-nineteenth century. The vagaries of island politics, the rise and fall of aspiring kings, have to be explained more in terms of customary political ambitions and strategies than in terms of European influence.

The rise of Bau

In the late eighteenth century there were seven main *vanua* or confederations—Rewa, Verata, and Bau in southeastern Viti Levu; Lakeba in the Lau group (often controlled by Tongans); and Cakaudrove, Macuata, and Bua on Vanua Levu.[16] Bau was of recent origin. Until the 1760s this tiny island was the home of a few fishermen and traders. At about that time people of neighbouring Verata who considered these fishermen as tributaries drove some of them to Taveuni and others to Lakeba in Lau. The mainlanders then occupied the island themselves. The exiled fishermen still acknowledged a measure of allegiance to their conquerors and continued to provide their huge canoes and maritime skills as requested. The first new chief of Bau was Nailatikau and he was succeeded by his second son Banuve. Bau's influence gradually increased through these chiefs' policies of marrying into leading families of Rewa and Cakaudrove. Sons from these marriages had considerable influence in both Bau and their mothers' *vanua*. As *vasu*, or nephews, these sons had an untramelled right to take virtually anything belonging to their mothers' brothers and their people.[17] Tributes moved in both directions, but increasingly to Bau. These family ties gave Bauan leaders an essential power base from which to work, a point usually ignored by those who argue that muskets provided the key to Bauan influence. Another element of both Nailatikau's and Banuve's growing strength was their huge canoes and the sailing skills of the exiled fishermen as well as those who had been allowed to remain on Bau. Bauan chiefs ranged extensively through the whole island group on these great vessels interfering, intervening, and generally consolidating their influence. For example, Banuve successfully intervened in a dispute over succession at Lakeba and managed to get rights to tribute from central Lau. Banuve's son, Naulivou, led raids along Viti Levu coasts and along the western reaches of Vanua Levu. Eventually war broke out between Bau and Verata and Bau won in about 1808, allegedly with Savage's firepower.

In 1829, when Naulivou died, Bau was in an enviable position. It dominated northern and eastern Viti Levu, and the supremacy of Verata in the region was broken. Districts and islands once belonging to Verata became tributaries of Bau, in particular Viwa, a small island close to Bau, significant because of its influence in Cakaudrove and north Lau. Combined with Banuve's successful diplomacy at Lakeba, this meant that Bau had influence in central and south Lau as well. Rewa was Bau's greatest ally, through marriage ties, and supplied large numbers of warriors. Virtually only inland Viti Levu and Vanua Levu were free from the tributary demands of the Bauans.[18]

However the extent to which chiefly authority was personalised as opposed to institutionalised in Bau was demonstrated in 1832 when Tanoa, Naulivou's brother and successor, angered a number of Bauan chiefs by, among other things, refusing to allow them to capture some European vessels. He found himself promptly exiled: the leading Cakaudrove chief offered him refuge at Somosomo. Tanoa returned to Bau in 1837 and took a bloody revenge that was engineered by his son Ratu Seru (or Cakobau as he later became known). An aged, deaf, and snuffling Tanoa remained nominal chief until he died in 1852. His favourite sport was running down other canoes with his own magnificent vessel 'one hundred feet in length . . . its velocity . . . almost inconceivable.'[19] But the real power on Bau lay with son Cakobau, and it was he who became one of the foremost chiefs of Fiji for the next fifty years.

The rise of Cakobau

Cakobau was described as

> *extremely good looking, being tall, well made, and athletic. He exhibits much intelligence in his expression of countenance and manners. His features and figure resemble those of a European, and he is graceful and easy in his carriage.*[20]

Women and warfare appeared to be his principal interests; his ambition was to achieve total supremacy over Fiji for himself and for Bau. Arrogant, cruel, cunning, devious, bold were the adjectives commonly used by European observers. Said one missionary, he seemed 'to think about nothing else but war, and . . . to desire nothing else but power.'[21] Tales of his human sacrifices and punishments are legion in contemporary accounts, though this behaviour was quite in character for chiefs of Cakobau's stature. The lives of enemies and slaves were of little import to such deified men.[22] At times Cakobau's anger was spontaneous, as when a chief was slow to pay tribute and was immediately clubbed to death.[23] Or when one Bauan rebel was unlucky enough to be caught, Cakobau had the man's tongue cut out which he 'devoured raw, talking and joking at the same time with the mutilated chief, who begged in vain for the boon of a speedy death.'[24] On other occasions, Cakobau's cruelty was more according to established custom—eating people at feasts, crushing them under building posts, or sliding the giant canoes over staked-out human rollers.[25] Cakobau quickly became feared throughout much of Fiji.

His restless urgings for power made him dissatisfied with many of Bau's existing relations with other *vanua*, even where these were already to Bau's advantage. Bau was thus constantly at war throughout the 1840s. Conflict with Verata broke out again in 1839 with Bauan warriors once more crushing Verata's already weakened forces. The victorious Bauans sailed back to their island with 260 dead Veratans. In addition

> *many women & children were taken alive to be kept for slaves. About 30 living children were hoisted up to the mast head as flags of triumph. The motions of the*

canoes when sailing soon killed the helpless creatures, & silenced their piercing cries. Other children were taken alive to Bau that the boys might learn the art of Fijian warfare by firing arrows @ them and beating them with clubs.[26]

Cakobau also organised raids by his and his allies' warriors into the troubled *vanua* of Macuata and Bua.[27] He quarrelled too with his ally Tui Cakau of Cakaudrove. But his most challenging task was his war with Rewa. Rewa and Bau had important *vasu* links between them, and were close allies when it suited their common purpose. Yet they were also rivals and were not averse to the odd raid into each other's lands. In recent times they had been more friends than foes and any fighting between them had been more like a sporting contest. However, bitter arguments amongst Rewa's leaders led to considerable political instability and with it a mutual fear and distrust between Rewa and Bau. It is not clear which side provoked war, but probably it was Rewa led by Roko Tui Dreketi. Rewa warriors destroyed Suva, a town in their own territory but one whose chief was *vasu* to Bau. The Bauan counterattack in 1844 was far more ferocious than Rewa expected and there was general agreement that the ensuing war was much more 'fiendish than the oldest could remember.'[28] It raged on and off for the next twelve years with neither side able to gain a decisive victory though Cakobau's forces often had the upper hand. By the end of the decade, Cakobau had strengthened Bauan influence in many parts of the group and now called himself, somewhat prematurely, Tui Viti—king of Fiji. Captain Erskine on HMS *Havannah* visited the group in 1849 and described Bau's predominance over much of coastal Viti Levu, including Rewa which Erskine understood was 'completely subjugated'; and also over much of Vanua Levu, Taveuni, and the Lau group.[29] Erskine described Bau itself as

scarcely a mile in length, and with the exception of the summit, which serves as the deposit of all the dirt and refuse, is covered with houses disposed in irregular streets, reminding one, in a degree, of the poorer parts of some of our West India towns.[30]

The captain was clearly charmed by Cakobau.

It was impossible not to admire the appearance of the chief: of large, almost gigantic, size, his limbs were beautifully formed and proportioned; his countenance, with far less of the negro cast than among the lower orders, agreeable and intelligent; while his immense head of hair, covered and concealed with gauze, smoke-dried and slightly tinged with brown, gave him altogether the appearance of an eastern sultan. No garments confined his magnificent chest and neck, or concealed the natural colour of the skin, a clear but decided black; and in spite of this paucity of attire—the evident wealth which surrounded him showing that it was a matter of choice and not of necessity—he looked 'every inch a king.'[31]

A slightly more whimsical portrait was given by another visitor who found the self-proclaimed king 'amusing himself with a little pop-gun, by slyly hitting the several ladies of the court.'[32]

Opposition to Cakobau

If Cakobau appeared to be at the height of his powers, the price he paid for his wars of the 1840s was the growing resentment of Bau, either through fear or jealousy. Nowhere had he not intervened in dynastic and other disputes in the main *vanua*. Even travellers like Erskine, who were far from privy to the intricacies of tribal politics, were aware of this resentment and apprehension.[33] And it came not only from Fijians.

Levuka on Ovalau had long been a base for several European residents, most of whom had taken Fijian wives. These men acted as traders' agents, pilots, and interpreters. Among them was David Whippy, one of Fiji's more prominent beachcombers, who, when Wilkes met him in 1840 had already been in Fiji for eighteen years. In Erskine's time, a decade later, Whippy was still there along with some fifteen Englishmen and Americans and their families.[34] During the 1840s, their normally friendly relations with Cakobau deteriorated. Some openly sided with his enemies. Their town at Levuka was razed by fire in 1841, under Cakobau's orders it was widely believed, though there was no proof. Later, Charles Pickering, from New South Wales and something of a vagabond, was accused by Cakobau of spying on him for Rewa. The chief attempted to capture him but the Europeans at Levuka hustled Pickering away. Cakobau then ordered all the settlers to leave. Most went to Vanua Levu. He asked them back after a few years, and they returned, though they never forgave Cakobau. While they were in no position to pose any threat to him, they could be useful to Cakobau's enemies and they certainly could make his trading relations with other Europeans more difficult.

There were times, though, when the bêche-de-mer trade was more trouble to Cakobau than it was worth. His insistence that he controlled the trade and that traders and Fijians alike needed his permission to work particular reefs, involved him in internal factional fighting such as in Macuata on Vanua Levu, and also committed him to supplying more bêche-de-mer than he was sometimes readily able to do, without resort to arms.[35] Cakobau was beginning to appreciate that his self-proclaimed assumption of the 'kingship' of Fiji brought not just benefits but also obligations and commitments. One apparently minor incident in 1849 was to trouble him for years to come. John Williams arrived in Fiji in 1846 as the United States commercial agent. In 1849 a cannon firing to celebrate the Fourth of July exploded and Williams's two-storied house and store caught fire. 'Since among the Fijians', explained Derrick, 'a fire was always an occasion for legitimate plunder rather than for assistance in putting it out',[36] Williams's goods were looted. As Cakobau claimed that he was king of Fiji, Williams held him responsible for his subjects' behaviour. In 1851 an American warship demanded compensation set by Williams at $5000. Other incidents involved American ships and property and by 1855 the total claim for damages was assessed at $43 000. Cakobau was summoned

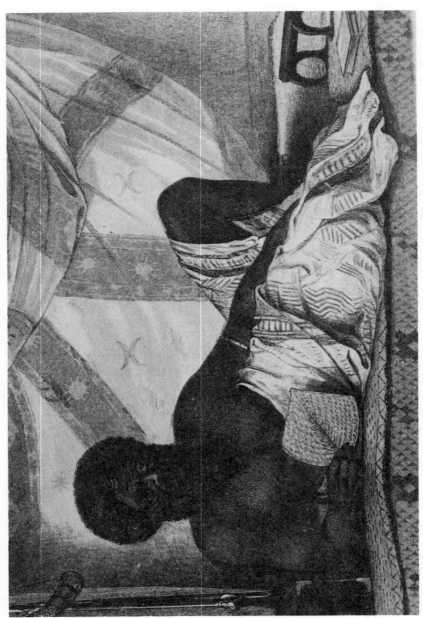

25   *Cakobau, about 1855. (Williams* Fiji and the Fijians*)*

on board a US warship and on threat of abduction signed a promissory document which gave him two years to pay.

The decline of Cakobau

The early 1850s were times of great trouble for Cakobau. Ostensibly one of Fiji's most powerful chiefs, he saw opposition amassing from almost every quarter, and, ironically, at the time when he became chief of Bau in his own right on his father's death in 1852.

The decade opened with renewed fighting against Verata, and this time the Bauan forces found the Veratans their equals in battle.[37] Then hostile forces in Rewa successfully repelled Cakobau's military expeditions into the region. European settlers at Levuka became more united in their hostility to Cakobau when again their town was burnt to the ground. Cakobau was not, as they believed, to blame. The settlers then did all they could, in conjunction with Tui Levuka, to direct European shipping away from Bau, in effect mounting a blockade of the island. Captain Denham of HMS *Herald* investigated the burning of Levuka some fourteen months later. Cakobau was again embarrassed by his alleged responsibilities if he was indeed king of Fiji. Said one settler,

> *He being king of the Fijis or so styled, the act must have been done under his knowledge, as a matter of course; until he fixes it upon somebody else.*

Denham agreed. He put it to Cakobau,

> *'Are you ready and willing to protect them and their trade in your dominions?' The King.—'Yes'* [38]

But as the missionary Waterhouse explained,

> *The title 'King of Fiji' is entirely of English origin. Thakombau has never been installed or recognised as such by the Fijian princes generally. It is questionable whether its adoption has been of any real use, as it has caused very great jealousy. 'He the king of Fiji!' said Tui Cakau in 1851: 'Why, he cannot pay for one only of the two vessels that have come for him; whilst I could pay for both. But what do the foreigners know as to who is king?' 'The king of Fiji!' exclaimed some saucy independent tribes: 'Who is he? We have heard of Namosimalua; but who can the king of Fiji he?' Still, he is unquestionably the greatest Fijian king; and, in the event of confederation, he would undoubtedly be chosen as the leader.* [39]

Cakobau's decline in authority was widely acknowledged. He became ill, perhaps as a consequence of his failing fortunes. The final straw, it seemed, was the revolt of the people of Kaba at the mouth of the Rewa River. For decades they had supported Bau, and Cakobau used their town as a vital strategic base for his raids into Rewa. He had some five hundred warriors

26   *The island of Bau in the late 1850s.* (*Calvert* Mission History)

garrisoned there, along with war canoes, sails for his own vessel, and a large quantity of arms and munitions. The loss of all these was a bitter blow to Cakobau, especially because the blockade of Bau prevented him from replacing this equipment. He seemed a spent force, with Bau in a militarily pitiful state. Yet within a short time Cakobau's position was dramatically reversed. His salvation came in the unlikely combination of Christianity and Tongan imperialism.

Missionary presence

The first toehold of Christianity in Fiji was on the island of Oneata, off Lakeba. The chief, Takai, was a descendant of a prominent Tongan who had arrived several generations previously. In the 1820s Takai went to Tonga where he met the Wesleyan missionary Walter Lawry. He also sailed with trader Peter Dillon around the Pacific and when at Tahiti requested teachers from the London Missionary Society (LMS) missionaries there. The LMS was eager to get to Fiji before the Wesleyans who were so close by on Tonga and they sent the Tahitians Hape and Tafeta back with Takai. However the teachers were detained on Tonga by Tupou Aleamotu'a. Takai returned to Tahiti and finally in 1830 arrived at Lakeba with three

Tahitian teachers. The chief of Lakeba, Tui Nayau, refused to accept Christianity. Takai and his guests then retired to Oneata where they built a church. They had a small local following.[40]

In 1835 Wesleyan missionaries William Cross and David Cargill arrived at Lakeba from Tonga. With them was an envoy for the now Christian Taufa'ahau of Tonga. Tongan presence in and relations with the Lau islands was longstanding. As well as social and political ties between these two island groups, there were important economic ones. One of the more noteworthy activities involving both Tongans and Fijians in Lau was the construction of *drua*, the huge canoes that could take up to seven years to construct, and could carry hundreds of warriors at speeds of over 30 kph. Tongan influence in Lau was substantial and could not be ignored by Lau chiefs. Tui Nayau thus had little option but to obey Taufa'ahau's envoy who directed that Cargill and Cross be kindly received. But Tui Nayau drew the line at accepting Christianity, fearing that chiefs elsewhere in Fiji might 'make war upon him'.[41] The local Tongans were not under the same restraints and several hundred became practising Christians. Tongans from elsewhere in Fiji, especially Somosomo, often came for instruction.[42] Even the aging Tui Cakau and his son Tui Kilakila paid a visit from Somosomo in 1837 to see what was going on. So impressed was the chief with the material prosperity of the mission that he asked for missionaries to live with him and even exhorted Tui Nayau to accept the new beliefs.[43] But Tui Nayau held out. In Cargill's words he was still 'a tributary monarch' and was particularly worried about how the Bauans might react if he changed his religion.[44] Not until 1849 did he finally become a Christian.

Throughout the 1840s, mission advancement was extremely slow. Cargill and Cross soon learnt that the centre of Fijian population and power lay in southeastern Viti Levu.[45] Cross visited Bau early in 1838, shortly after Tanoa and his son Cakobau had returned from exile and were vigorously purging their former enemies. So horrified was the missionary with what he saw that he decided it was no time to found a mission there. However, had Cross had more knowledge of Fijian politics and had he appreciated the implications of Cakobau's victory, he might well have settled on Bau and exploited the power that Cakobau soon achieved. Instead Cross moved on to Rewa. There Tui Dreketi, Cakobau's great rival, made him welcome and provided land for a mission, doubtless to spite Cakobau. Cakobau certainly took offence and hardened his attitude to missionaries for quite some time. The missionaries lost little time in accepting Tui Dreketi's offer, and a station complete with the mission's new press was set up in the town of Rewa.[46] The missionaries also gained the support of chief Namosimalua from Bau's neighbouring island of Viwa. Yet the missionaries made little headway in these places in any evangelical sense.[47] Less than two hundred people attended services. Most chiefs were very wary of the missionary presence. They were not opposed to missionaries themselves, but were certainly not prepared to declare themselves Christians. Wilkes explained:

All the chiefs seem to look upon Christianity as a change in which they had much to lose and little to gain. The old chiefs, in particular, would often remark that they were too old to change their present for new gods, or to abandon what they considered their duty to their people; yet the chiefs generally desire the residence of missionaries among them. I was, therefore, anxious to know why they entertained such a wish, when they had no desire for their instruction. They acknowledged that it was to get presents, and because it would bring vessels to their place, which would give them opportunities of obtaining many desirable articles.[48]

Another traveller discussed these matters with Cakobau:

'But', I observed, 'the chiefs should set the example, as the Kings of all the other islands have done.' 'What did they give them for helping them?' I replied, 'Nothing; they were induced by the superior advantages which the Christian religion offered.' As he could not be made to comprehend this part of the subject, and appeared restless, I changed the topic.[49]

The war between Bau and Rewa in the 1840s severely hindered missionary activity. Rewa had to be abandoned. The Bauans continued to reject Christianity. Even in the east mission prospects looked dim. The Tongans in Lau were supporters, but most Fijians were not. The missionaries greatest disappointment was with Somosomo. No sooner had Tui Cakau and Tui Kilakila enticed missionaries there with entreaties of support than they ignored them. The 1840 mission report noted:

The inhabitants of Somosomo are proverbial, even in Fiji, for their depraved habits, and especially for their cannibalism*: and all that we have seen of them during the past year, fully warrants the opinion which their neighbours have formed of them, and shows that they are right in considering them to be the* vilest of the vile.[50]

In 1845 the mission at Somosomo was abandoned. Small stations were subsequently established at Nadi and Bua though with quite unspectacular results. By the end of the decade, almost fifteen years of missionary activity had achieved, it seemed, virtually nothing. The Wesleyan strategy to convert any major chief had been singularly unsuccessful. And no Fijian chief had seen any real advantage in becoming a Christian. Unlike New Zealand and Samoa, people in Fiji could not accept missionary teachings on an individual basis. Chiefs were too powerful and 'the people do not dare to oppose themselves . . . in such a matter as religion.'[51] As in Tonga, Tahiti, and Hawaii, the lead had to come from the ruling élite.

Ma'afu and Tongan imperialism

During the 1840s Tongan demands in eastern Fiji intensified, probably as a result of Taufa'ahau consolidating his authority in Tonga and beginning to look further afield, just as Pomare II had tried to extend his influence beyond Tahiti via Christianity. The islands of eastern Fiji were prime targets for Tongan imperialism. By 1840 up to a third of the permanent population of Lakeba, or some 800 people, were Tongans.[52] Hundreds more lived on surrounding islands. Many more Tongans were sometimes in temporary residence when *drua* were being constructed. In 1842 more than 1000 Tongans who had been living in Lakeba for several years sailed back to Tonga in fifteen large canoes, each heavily laden with Fijian property.[53] The reputation Tongans had amongst both Fijians and Europeans was generally one of greed, arrogance, and conceit. But none were prepared to stand up against them.

By the end of the 1840s, the undisputed leader of the Tongans in Fiji, and a powerful force in Fijian politics, was Henele Ma'afu, Taufa'ahau's cousin, son of Aleamotu'a the former Tu'i Kanokupolu. One opinion is that Taufa'ahau sent Ma'afu to Fiji in order to remove someone who, as son of the Tu'i Kanokupolu, might have been a potential rival, and also to control Tongans in Fiji many of whom, it was claimed, had gone there to escape Taufa'ahau's authority.[54] But Ma'afu's rise to prominence in Fiji at this stage was largely due to his own initiative. Initially he had no special authority from Taufa'ahau, but went to Fiji in 1847 as yet another Tongan nobleman in search of overseas experience and adventure.[55] Ma'afu's own ambition soon became apparent in Fiji. Under the pretext of protecting Christian Tongan interests he involved himself in Fijian affairs. First he took sides with Tui Nayau, newly converted to Christianity, in a number of squabbles around Lakeba. Then in the name of Christianity and Tui Nayau, Ma'afu, with six canoes and eight hundred warriors, moved further afield. Exploiting political difficulties that Tui Kilakila was experiencing in various parts of Cakaudrove, Ma'afu soon controlled most of the leeward islands that formerly owed tribute to Somosomo.

> *Under one pretext or another—protecting Tongan teachers, aiding rebellious chiefs, bullying Fijians into indiscretions, and levying tribute—Ma'afu and his Tongans carried war to many parts of Lau, and the coasts of Vanua Levu. They forced their victims to abandon savage practices and turn to the* lotu; *and they plundered, massacred, and stole wherever they went.*[56]

Ma'afu's action soon gained Taufa'ahau's recognition. In 1853 he appointed Ma'afu governor of Tongans in Fiji, and in this way Ma'afu became the *de facto* leader of the Tongan, Wesleyan cause in Fiji. By the mid-1850s, his power over much of the eastern half of Fiji was unquestioned.

Cakobau, Ma'afu, Taufa'ahau, and Christianity

The implications of such Tongan power in Fiji were not lost on Cakobau, now in his hour of darkness, nor on the Wesleyan missionaries who

27   *Henele Maʻafu. (Derrick* A History of Fiji*)*

publicly deplored Maʻafu's warlike policies and privately rejoiced at his advancement of the *lotu*.[57]

The first hint of Tongan influence on Bauan affairs was in 1850 when Maʻafu and Tui Kilakila visited Bau. Cakobau was fighting some nominally Christian forces of Viwa and had them besieged in the town of Dama in Bua Bay.

> *The missionaries now appealed to a Tongan chief [Maʻafu], who was then at Bau with three hundred men. With all their faults, the Tongans invariably rally round the missionary in the hour of danger.... Thakombau saw that he would soon have them in arms against himself unless peace was established. A messenger was at once sent to raise the siege of Dama, and peace was again proclaimed.*[58]

Later in 1853, Cakobau, in desperate political straits with Bau blockaded and enemies amassing on all sides, reluctantly agreed to let a missionary live on his island.[59] His precise motive for doing so is not clear, though possibly it had occurred to Cakobau that there was now nothing to lose and possibly something to gain. What is clear is that his commitment to missionary presence was henceforth irrevocable. Shortly after his invitation to missionaries, though before they actually took up residence,

Taufa'ahau called in to Bau on his way from Tonga to Sydney. Cakobau 'feelingly referred to his present reduced position' and Taufa'ahau 'expressed his sympathy'. Cakobau then presented Taufa'ahau with a large double canoe,

> *expressing the wish that Kingly help might be afforded. George [Taufa'ahau] said,*
> *'The rebel fortress [at Kaba in Rewa] seems to me anything but impregnable.' It*
> *was evident that each king understood the other.*[60]

Taufa'ahau continued his voyage, declaring his intention to return to pick up his canoe at some future time.

Shortly afterward, Cakobau received from Taufa'ahau a copy of a letter written by the US commercial agent Williams which had been published in Sydney newspapers. In it Williams called for the annihilation of Bau.

> *Bau ought to be destroyed, and the people swept from the face of the earth. Then,*
> *and not until then, will commerce move uninterrupted in this archipelago. . . . A*
> *ship of war could lay off Bau, knock down and destroy that town, while one is*
> *smoking a cigar. If you suppose me to be severe in my remarks, I ask any man to*
> *remain here six weeks and follow the people step by step, and see the butcher-*
> *inhabitants of Bau—the human slaughter-house—a cookery of cannibals; and that*
> *observer will perfectly coincide with me in my remarks and observations herein*
> *specified. The very atmosphere we breathe is filled with the fumes of roasted human*
> *flesh; it is quite enough to fill one with disgust. The pirates that infested the Isle of*
> *Pines, in the West Indies, in its worst days, were nothing compared to this Bau: the*
> *most vivid imagination cannot describe this hell upon earth.*[61]

Taufa'ahau also sent the following advice to Cakobau:

> *Nukualofa, Feb. 28th, 1854*
>
> *To Thakombau,—I write to make known my love to you and the Bauan friends.*
> *When I arrived in Sydney, I received a letter which concerns you and the people of*
> *Bau. The letter is the writing of the consul at Rewa; and I hear that a letter has*
> *been sent to Great Britain, and another to America; and I am not certain whether*
> *Fiji will be in danger, or whether it will escape; for the consul's letter is a bad one.*
> *He says, you commanded the property of the white people to be burnt.*
>
> *I expect to visit you with the Tongan friends to bring away my canoe; and when*
> *we have finished planting, we shall come to you. It is good, Thakombau, that you*
> *should consider the thing which concerns the white people; and when the Fiji friends*
> *wish to do their minds, do not be guided by them. It is good you should be humble; it*
> *will be well for you and your land. I wish, Thakombau, you would* lotu. *When I*
> *visit you, we will talk about it; for I desire that Bau and the Fiji friends may stand*
> *well. But it will be well for you, Thakombau, to think wisely in these days. This is*
> *the end of my writing.*
>
> *I, George Tubou.*[62]

The implication was obvious enough. If Cakobau became a Christian he could call on Tongan support; if not then he stood alone to face very unpleasant consequences.

Cakobau immediately had a long session with missionary James Calvert about the possibilities of becoming a Christian. He then assembled his relatives and the principal chiefs of Bau to discuss the 'political aspect of the question.'[63] Only days after receiving Taufa'ahau's letter, Cakobau declared himself a Christian. By his command *Na Lotu nei Ratu Cakobau*, Cakobau's religion, became the new religion of Bau. Temples were destroyed, 'heathen' customs proscribed, and people thronged to the mission.

Soon afterward, Rewa became engulfed in civil strife and Cakobau intervened, though he was not in a very strong military position. Early in 1855 Taufa'ahau along with two thousand warriors from Tonga, together with Ma'afu and his men from Lakeba, arrived at Bau in 40 canoes. A combined Fijian–Tongan army of some three thousand warriors sailed in 145 canoes for Kaba in Rewa. Cakobau's opponents were crushed.

> *Thus was the authority of King Thakombau reestablished. All the rebel provinces submitted, and twenty thousand of the Fijians attested their determination to live at peace and with each other, by following the example of the king, and adopting the profession of Christianity.*[64]

Taufa'ahau played a leading role in reconciling former enemies throughout Rewa and beyond. Few dared oppose the Tongan king. He and Ma'afu then sailed east leaving Cakobau once again in a position of predominance over western Fiji. But the self-claimed king of Fiji had to live with the bitter fact that the most powerful person in Fiji was Ma'afu, a foreigner.

Almost all of Fiji was ostensibly Christian by now. The Wesleyan missionaries' difficulty was to supply sufficient teachers, missionaries, churches, and books. Yet Fiji did not become a 'missionary kingdom' in the manner of Tahiti, Hawaii, and Tonga. While conversion throughout Fiji had been imposed by a few leading chiefs, Christianity as an institution was not politically centralised because there was no political unification of the island group. Even Cakobau and Ma'afu did not have total control over conquered peoples in the manner of Pomare II, or Taufa'ahau, or the Kamehamehas. A British official in 1860, acutely aware of the great influence Cakobau and Ma'afu had, still argued that Fiji was ruled by some forty chiefs of whom twelve were prominent.[65] None of them, least of all Cakobau and Ma'afu, could ever agree to accept the supremacy of any one chief over the whole country. Furthermore, since these men were now all Christians, Christianity became far less relevant in power politics.

Cakobau and Ma'afu presented themselves as allies—an unassailable combination—though their underlying conflict of interests became increasingly apparent from the late 1850s. Fiji's internal conflicts 'were resolving themselves into a contest—almost a personal contest—between

Cakobau and Ma'afu. All minor disputes tended to fall into place in that broader rivalry, and to assume importance only in their effect upon the existing balance of power between east and west.'[66] But the outcome of such rivalry was soon affected by other considerations, namely the growing influence of European settlers and their metropolitan governments.

European settlement and consequences

Early European settler and commercial interests in Fiji soon involved European governments. There were numerous instances of arbitrary 'naval justice' by French, British, and US warships on behalf of aggrieved nationals. 'Official' representatives were also stationed there. Williams, Cakobau's *bête noir*, was the US commercial agent from 1846 until 1860. The British sent a consul in 1858, W T Pritchard, in response to an offer (which was declined) by Tui Levuka, chief of Ovalau, to cede that island to Britain, presumably on the advice of British settlers there. Shortly after Pritchard arrived, Cakobau in his proclaimed role as Tui Viti offered to cede all of Fiji to Britain. The reason was that Cakobau had been unable to make good his promise to pay the $45 000 compensation to the United States. Cakobau thought that a transfer of Fijian sovereignty should be worth British recognition of him as Tui Viti and payment of his debt to the Americans.[67] Britain declined the offer, but only after protracted investigation and not officially until 1862. British consular officials, and those of the United States government, continued to be immersed in the troubled Fijian political scene. Cakobau and Ma'afu realised that for better or worse foreign governments were going to play an increasing role in their affairs, and they each approached the various consuls arguing their cases for their respective legitimacies and the right to put the other down.

Until the 1860s, European residents in Fiji were few in number, perhaps no more than 50, living mainly on Ovalau and doing business with passing trading vessels. Most were males with Fijian wives and lived a lifestyle that was as much Fijian as European. After 1860 the nature of European settlement changed dramatically, just as it did on Samoa. A more typical settler society arrived, mainly from Australia and New Zealand, consisting of planters, graziers, and businessmen with their wives and families. Before 1862 the attraction of Fiji was the belief that Britain was about to annex it. After the British rejection of Cakobau's offer, it was discovered that cotton grew well and, given the effect of the American Civil War on English cotton supplies, Fiji, like Samoa, experienced a cotton boom. In the mid-1860s the European population was between 400 and 500, and by 1870 it was over 2000.[68] As in Samoa, tension between Islanders and the new settlers intensified and the issue of land sales became paramount. In the now familiar pattern, much land was bought and sold fraudulently. Many

Fijians sold land for firearms to use in their tribal conflicts. The absence of any defined rules and regulations acceptable to both settlers and Fijians quickly opened major issues of claim, counterclaim, and conflict that were to bedevil Fijian history for another century. There were problems too with labour. Since Fijians, like Samoans, were reluctant to labour on the new plantations, planters began importing Islanders from the western Pacific, especially the New Hebrides. Between 1864 and 1869 some sixteen hundred labourers were landed in Fiji.

Fijians soon found themselves in a similar situation to Samoans. Vast areas of their country had been alienated, and endless European settlers poured from every ship. Fijians had no means of redress since they were so divided amongst themselves. From the point of view of both settlers and Fijians, some sort of governing authority was necessary to protect their various interests, and regulate relations between and amongst Europeans and Fijians.

Fijian governments

In 1865, H M Jones, the British consul, suggested that Fiji should have a central government consisting of a confederation of the chiefs of Bau, Rewa, Lakeba, Bua, Cakaudrove, Macuata, and Nadi, all of whom duly agreed with the idea. They proposed to meet annually and pass laws for Fiji as a whole. Cakobau was elected president. Jones's intention was that such an institution might lessen conflict amongst Fijians and provide a stable, moderate government with which Europeans and European government representatives might conduct fruitful negotiations about law and order, land selling, and protection of property. The scheme soon collapsed, mainly because Ma'afu, Cakobau, and other chiefs could never agree amongst themselves. Ma'afu made a play for the presidency in 1867, lost, withdrew, and the government came to an end.[69]

If the idea of a national government sat too precariously on the foundations of entrenched chiefly rivalry, there was a better chance for regional governments to work. Among the more successful of these was Tui Bua's government at Bua. He had close links with Tonga. His mother was a Tongan, and Ma'afu and his warriors had consolidated Tui Bua's position after he became a Christian in 1855. He visited Tonga and sat in the parliament there in 1862, and returned to set up a similar institution in Bua. It had some success in regulating land sales there to Europeans. Another regional government, or attempt at one, was the Kingdom of Bau, proclaimed in 1867 with Cakobau crowned in a farcical ceremony, and modelled ostentatiously on the Hawaiian constitution. The scheme originated with the American Samuel St John, Cakobau's secretary, and was supported by European planters in Levuka who hoped it might facilitate their buying of land. When it did not, and when Cakobau failed to put down local Fijian resistance to European settlement on Viti Levu, the settlers abandoned their new King.[70] Ma'afu had more luck with his government at Lau, but his standing was initially fraught with difficulties. In consular eyes he was a foreigner. When Pritchard collected signatures on the cession proposal in 1859 he forced Ma'afu to sign a document declaring that Tonga had no claims in Fiji. Since the offer of cession had been rejected, Ma'afu believed he had free reign again. However by the late 1860s, the ubiquitous presence of British and American naval vessels in the central Pacific convinced Taufa'ahau to abandon his long cherished scheme of incorporating Fiji into the Kingdom of Tonga. In 1868 the Tongan parliament told Ma'afu that Tonga was no longer involved in Fijian affairs and ordered him to lower the Tongan flags he had flying everywhere. Ma'afu, abandoned by his royal patron, was on his own. However, with the assistance of Tui Nayau, a meeting of Lau chiefs at Lakeba in 1869 decreed that Ma'afu was a Fijian chief and gave him the newly created title of Tui Lau. Thus commenced Ma'afu's Lau government. He introduced an allotment system of landholding amongst his Fijian subjects. No land could be sold to Europeans; instead there was a very liberal system of leases. While planters and others bemoaned the fact that they could not get freehold title in Lau, they still had use of the land they wanted and, most important, they had a security not found elsewhere in Fiji. There was at least a workable system which both Fijians and Europeans had a vested interest in maintaining.[71] It was no coincidence that one of the leading merchant houses in Fiji— Hennings—was based in Ma'afu's own headquarters, Lomaloma, and had extensive cotton plantations throughout Lau.[72] The final regional government was the *Tovata* which grew out of the collapse of the 1865 confederation. Ma'afu, Tui Cakau, and Tui Bua formed their own confederation in 1867. In leaving out Cakobau they hoped to avoid conflict. But these three who formed a 'general Assembly of Chieftains' were too jealous of each other for their government to come to much.[73]

The Cakobau government

The various indigenous governments represented an acute concern with the changing circumstances in Fiji, and a willingness to experiment with new ways. But events were far beyond the control of Fiji's leading chiefs and their attempts at political reform were doomed. As happened in Samoa, chiefs increasingly lost the initiative when European influences asserted themselves in unprecedented ways. From the late 1860s the focus of Fijian power politics was in the west. During 1870 the number of Europeans increased by over a thousand bringing their total to almost three thousand. More than one thousand of these stayed in the bustling, crowded town of

Levuka which, in 1870, saw the arrival of 158 ships. Other immigrants lived on plantations and trading outposts scattered throughout Fiji, but especially in coastal and river valley regions of Viti Levu. Such a rapid rise in the European population intensified existing problems. In addition there was a desperate shortage of public amenities at Levuka, which was a wild frontier town badly in need of regulation. There were many calls for a government. The newly established *Fiji Times* noted in 1870 that Fijians controlled themselves better than the settlers: 'It is not the natives that we want the government for, but ourselves'.[74]

But out in the bush it was a different story, especially on Viti Levu, which had no chiefly governments as in Bua and Lau. Racial and intertribal violence became commonplace. Fijians killed planters and then killed each other in attempts to sell more land or prevent others from doing so. There were fears of a war between Fijians and Europeans, as had occurred in New Zealand in the 1860s. To make matters worse, the cotton boom collapsed in late 1870, then severe hurricanes destroyed crops. Widespread economic ruin amongst planters and merchants heightened the bitterness. The need for a government became acute.

The Cakobau government was proclaimed at Levuka in 1871. Cakobau, now an old man, saw his last hope of becoming Fiji's national leader by gaining the support of some of Levuka's more prominent citizens. They in turn expected him to be a figurehead in a pro-settler government that would deal with land issues and provide for security of tenure, property, and even lives. The announcement of the government's formation was initially seen in Levuka as something of a *coup d'état* by the more noted and self-interested men of affairs. After some early opposition, most settlers decided to support it. So too did a good many Fijian chiefs from all over the group, including Ma'afu. There appeared to be a genuine willingness of both Fijian and European leaders to make it work.

Cakobau became king, in theory the controller of his Cabinet, but in practice ruled by its white-only members—a retired army lieutenant, a bankrupt auctioneer, and three merchants and planters. A Legislative Assembly was elected by adult (and in practice European) male franchise. The Privy Council was the 'Native House' made up of the governors plus one high chief from each of the provinces into which the kingdom was divided. Ma'afu became viceroy, governor of Lau and commander in chief.

Denouement

The Cakobau government had a turbulent existence. Opposition soon mounted on all sides. Cakobau, J B Thurston—the British consul who became deeply involved with Cakobau—and the ministers simply could not satisfy the irreconcilable demands of merchants, planters, and Fijians.

The government became universally unpopular. Settler feeling, especially in Levuka, hardened. A ku klux klan was formed. Talk was heard of civil war between Europeans and Fijians, especially in western regions. To prevent civil anarchy Cakobau was forced to offer his country to Britain in 1873. This time the British government had little option but to accept it. In 1874, to restore order, to provide effective government, and to protect Fijian interests against the more rampant demands of some British nationals, Britain annexed Fiji as a Crown Colony.[75]

As in Samoa, customary political behaviour and organisations prevented the emergence of a paramount chief in the first half of the nineteenth century. When Fijians, like Samoans, eventually saw the need to form a centralised administration to control the consequences of European settlement, which blossomed from the 1860s, events were already beyond their control. Instead initiative lay with the conflicting interests of Europeans. The inability of Fijians and settlers to regulate matters of crucial common interest left Britain little alternative but to take control.

Western isles

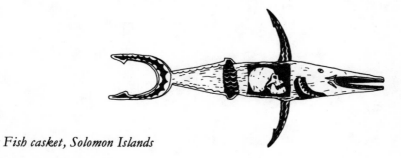

Fish casket, Solomon Islands

13

The making of Melanesia

European presence and influence was commonplace throughout the eastern and central Pacific islands by the 1840s. In the eyes of many Western observers, Polynesia was now well within the ambit of civilisation. Both European and Islander were engaged in mutually advantageous maritime commerce. European settlement was on the increase as the beachcombing era began to give way to developing port towns. The majority of Islanders were practising Christians. Tahiti, Hawaii, and Tonga had their own centralised rule. New Zealand was a British colony. Only in Samoa and Fiji was there widespread tribal fighting, but Europeans expected that these two countries would soon settle down like the others. Samoa was already Christian, and the Fiji islands, in Peter Dillon's view, 'leaving Christianity out of the scale, make the nearest approximation of civilization'.[1]

The European commercial and religious frontier that had moved progressively westward across the Pacific from Tahiti had now reached the boundaries of the Melanesian island chain—a region of the Pacific almost completely unknown to Europeans and one that proved far more difficult to penetrate than Polynesia.

Unknown regions

Some parts of Melanesia, such as areas of the New Guinea coast and some of the Solomon Islands and the New Hebrides, had been amongst the first Pacific islands ever seen by Western explorers, in the sixteenth and early seventeenth centuries. Yet their visits had for the most part been brief and apparently left no lasting effects on island communities.

Not until the latter half of the eighteenth century were there further visits by European explorers—Carteret, Bougainville, Cook, Surville, D'Entrecasteaux, and others—whose contacts were equally or more fleeting. Following the European settlement of New South Wales in 1788, several traders plying their way between there and the East Indies made minor discoveries in Melanesia. By about 1800 the coastal outlines of New

Guinea and the larger islands of the Solomons, the New Hebrides, and New Caledonia were roughly marked on maps—though there were many errors and plenty of gaps. Detailed survey work went on throughout the nineteenth century.

Although these discoveries were relatively close to Sydney, few merchants paid them much attention. Even New Caledonia and the New Hebrides, which were only a matter of days by sail from New South Wales, remained little visited until the 1840s. Vessels plied instead the many thousands of kilometres further on to better-known places such as Tahiti for pork, the Australs, Marquesas, and, slightly closer, Fiji for sandalwood. The more those islands in the central and eastern Pacific became involved with commerce and missionary activity the more hospitable they appeared. From a European point of view Melanesia remained an unknown backwater. As late as 1849, Captain Erskine of HMS *Havannah* on the eve of his exploring expedition to the 'islands of the Western Pacific' could write:

> *It is a matter of surprise that a period of time which has seen the establishment of our great settlements in Australia and New Zealand, rendering a knowledge of the western groups of that ocean an object of considerable commercial and political importance, has done little to extend our general acquaintance with them, even among our neighbouring colonies.*[2]

Even then Erskine spent more time in the central Pacific and visited only New Caledonia and the New Hebrides in Melanesia.

Images of Islanders

Erskine should not really have been surprised at the lack of interest in the islands of Melanesia. There were few detailed charts, making navigation hazardous, and moreover the inhabitants of these lands had a reputation for great savagery.

Among the first accounts known to the English was that of Carteret. In 1767 his experiences in Melanesia were similar to those of his Spanish predecessors two hundred years earlier. On Ndeni in the Santa Cruz group his men were attacked after chopping down some coconut trees.

> *Our men reported that these people fought them with bowes and arrows in as regullar a manner as Europeans could have don with fire armes, but much faster for they did shoott off 3 or 4 arrows while they could [have] loaded a musquet, and notwithstanding that they keep up a great fire with their musquets, & blunderbusses fired with 8 & 10 pistol balls at each load killing & wounding great numbers, yeat they all stood firm to it and could not be broke. Nor could our people make these brave fellows give way but like Heroick defenders of their country boldly pursued the invaders of their property, as far into the water as they could wade, the boat having got clear of those was pursued by the Canoes, but after a few shots they return'd to the shore.*[3]

There was further violence before Carteret left the island with its 'black woolly headed ... dispiretly dareing warlike people'. Off islands to the north of Malaita in the Solomons he was attacked again, as well as off the Admiralty Islands northwest of New Ireland. All these people were, he noted, 'woolly headed black ... wild, fierce, savage'.[4]

Bougainville, who followed Carteret across the ocean by a few months, made a landfall on Aoba in the New Hebrides. The inhabitants impressed him as 'short, ugly, ill-proportioned, and most of them infected with leprosy'. The French were soon driven away by a 'shower of stones and arrows'.[5] Off Choiseul in the Solomons canoe-loads of warriors 'divided very dexterously into two squadrons.... The Indians then made horrible cries, and taking their bows and lances, they began an attack'.[6]

Much the same happened off Buka, and New Ireland:

Every day there came to us canoes with thirty and forty [men] to try to capture us, and [they] were forced to return carrying the wounded and the dead, sometimes the water around their canoe was red with it, and some of their canoes sunk to the bottom with muskets and blunderbusses. They threw stones on board as big as two fists.[7]

Surville spent several days in Port Praslin on Santa Ysabel in the Solomons in 1769.[8] Early friendship with the Islanders soon degenerated into hostilities. Later, off Ulawa, between San Cristobal and Malaita, canoes full of arrow-firing warriors had to be dispersed with grapeshot.[9]

Cook too had numerous squabbles with Islanders, especially in the New Hebrides in 1774. His descriptions of the people he encountered were much fuller than those of previous explorers and drew attention to other features, apart from hostility to strangers, that were seriously to affect future generations of Europeans in Melanesia. In particular he noted the great multiplicity of languages, the lack of powerful chiefs, and the constant warfare between communities. Cook also described the different physical features of the people compared to those of Polynesia, and even apparent differences within the islands of Melanesia.[10] The Malekulans he believed to be an 'Apish Nation'.[11]

We understood not a word they said, they are quite different to all we have yet seen and Speak a different language, they are almost black or rather a dark Chocolate Colour, Slenderly made, not tall, have Monkey faces and Woolly hair.... The people of this country are in general the most ugly and ill-proportioned of any I ever saw.[12]

The New Caledonians he found 'a strong robust active well made people',[13] and the Tanese and Eromangans he classified somewhere between these two extremes.

In general Cook and other explorers painted a picture of the peoples of Melanesia as darker than those of Polynesia, with frizzy hair, and hostile—all characteristics that later made up the popular stereotype of a

28   *Cook's men skirmish with Eromangans, 1774.*
(Cook A Voyage towards the South Pole.... *Alexander Turnbull Library)*

'Melanesian'. They differed from the people of eastern Polynesia in other striking ways too. The women, wrote Cook,

> *are, so far as we can judge, far more Chaste than those of the Eastern islands. I never heard that one of our people obtained the least favour from any one of them; I have been told that the Ladies here would frequently devert themselves by going a little aside with our gentlemen as if they meant to grant them the last favour and then run away laughing at them. Whether this was Chastity or Coquetry I shall not pretend to determine, nor is it material sence the Consequences were the same.*[14]

In the eyes of ship-bound eighteenth century sailors, the women of Tahiti were never like that.

To this most unattractive picture of Melanesian islands was added the mysterious disappearance of French explorer La Pérouse, who had sailed for the Solomons from Sydney in 1788 and was never seen again. The French government sent out D'Entrecasteaux to look for him but without success. Almost forty years later Peter Dillon discovered the explorer's fate—shipwrecked on Vanikoro. Some of the survivors apparently were killed; others built a vessel and sailed away, to perish in nearby seas. Yet others had remained on the island and died of disease or old age.[15]

The nineteenth century was well advanced before anyone other than explorers or passing travellers from the Indies visited these regions. The first few who did came in search of sandalwood and souls, and their experiences were hardly encouraging either.

The first traders

Peter Dillon visited Tana and Eromanga in the New Hebrides in 1825. On Eromanga he found sandalwood. Dillon collected a cargo but never returned to Eromanga or elsewhere in the New Hebrides. The Eromangans had been unwilling to cut wood for him, 'attaching not the least value to any of our goods', and constantly attacked Dillon's crew.

> *I may safely assert without incurring the hazard of contradiction, that the Natives of the New Hebrides are by many shades further removed from civilization, and that their general disposition indicate[s] a more permanent attachment to barbarous feelings and habits than has hitherto been found in any part of the South Sea.*[16]

As was the custom, Dillon did not publicise his sandalwood discovery, though he probably told a few trusted associates. One of these was Samuel Henry, son of the London Missionary Society (LMS) missionary on Tahiti. Henry organised an expedition to Eromanga in 1829, taking 113 Tongans as labourers on the *Sophie*. The Eromangans' reaction ranged from indifference to hostility. The only time any of them showed a willingness to cooperate was after some of them had beaten their enemies and needed to take refuge from an anticipated counterattack. Their enemies then attacked the Tongans.

Henry left the Tongans on the island and sailed for Hawaii. There news of sandalwood on Eromanga leaked out and precipitated a rush to the island. The Hawaiian sandalwood boom was now over, with the aromatic timber all but depleted, and Hawaiian chiefs were desperate for alternative sources of supply. Boki, governor of Oahu, at once hired two vessels and loaded them with more than 400 Hawaiians. He took command of one, the *Kamehameha*, with a crew of 250. It reached Rotuma and then was never seen again. The other vessel, the *Becket* called at Rotuma and took on 100 Islanders to compliment her 179 Hawaiians. They reached Eromanga safely. British merchants in Honolulu also learnt of the sandalwood find, and sent another ship which picked up 130 Rotumans.

When Henry returned to Eromanga with over 200 Rotumans on board, the foreign population of Eromanga already numbered more than 500. But there was not much chance of successful wood gathering. The Hawaiians attacked every Eromangan in sight as part of a campaign to colonise the island. The Eromangans retaliated by attacking all foreigners, who in any case were rapidly depleting local food resources. Then sickness struck the foreigners—probably malaria. Henry had kept his 200 Rotumans on his vessel. The Tongans ashore, along with other Rotumans, all came on board. Many of them were sick and dying, and few lived to see their homes. Only 12 Hawaiians out of the original 179 on the *Becket* returned to Honolulu.[17]

29   *'The massacre of the lamented missionary the Rev J. Williams and Mr Harris',*
       Eromanga, 1839. (Oil print by G. Baxter. Alexander Turnbull Library)

To the explorers' list of the dangers and difficulties of operating in
Melanesia was now added disease. A few other sandalwood vessels tried
their luck in these islands in 1830 but retreated in the face of hostilities.
With good reason did merchant seafarers give this part of the Pacific a wide
berth.

The first missionaries

In the mid-1830s, LMS missionary John Williams surveyed with characteristic flair the advance of Christianity through the South Seas. He divided
all the islands into eastern and western Polynesia. In the east—the area now
known as the Polynesian triangle—the Islanders were 'a light copper
colour . . . the countenance resembling that of the Malay.' Nearly this *'whole
nation* of Polynesian Asiatics is [he wrote] now converted to the Christian
faith.' But in the west, 'from the Fijis to the coast of New Holland' lived
what he called the 'Polynesian negro'—for the term Melanesian was still
not in popular use—'having a Herculean frame, black skin, and woolly, or
rather crisped hair. . . . We have now . . . proceeded so far west, as to reach
the negro race, and our next effort will be to impart the same blessings to
them.'[18] Williams positively thrilled at the thought of entering this vast
new field, which he believed contained 'several millions of immortal

beings'. But he added: 'It will, no doubt, be attended with much danger ...'[19]

A few years later, in 1839, Williams led the first missionary expedition into Melanesia, sailing for the New Hebrides from Samoa. He landed on Tana and was received quite hospitably. Leaving behind three Polynesian teachers, he made for Eromanga and anchored in Dillon's Bay. Williams approached the beach in a whaleboat and sent ashore James Harris, a young man who hoped to become a missionary. The waiting Islanders seemed friendly enough. Williams and William Cunningham (the British viceconsul at Samoa) stepped ashore. The Islanders seemed somewhat reticent. Harris went into the bushes. Williams and Cunningham began walking along the beach surrounded by children which Williams thought was a good sign. Harris suddenly ran onto the beach, pursued by some Islanders. He tripped and was clubbed to death. Williams and Cunningham raced for the whaleboat. Cunningham scrambled aboard in time. Williams was dragged down and pulverised.[20] The news rocked the evangelical world.

The reputation of southwest Pacific Islanders in the European world had never been lower than it was by 1840. For traders and missionaries (and their reading public) there were few more dangerous places and barbarous peoples in the world. The term 'Melanesia' that was coming into currency[21] meant, literally, dark or black islands, from the Greek Melos, presumably referring to the inhabitants who were considered darker than those of Polynesia. Yet the term was far more than a literal description—it carried connotations of its Islanders' physical and cultural inferiority compared with Polynesians, and of their dark, Satanic savagery. Nevertheless, in the 1840s sandalwood traders and missionaries arrived in force.

14

Mission frontiers

John Williams in death was an even greater instrument of evangelical propaganda than he had been in life. His much-proclaimed martyrdom on Eromanga's shores allegedly highlighted the extreme barbarity of Melanesians and the great risks of going amongst them. Yet at the same time more missionaries had to be sent out, not in spite of the danger but *because* of it: people so utterly degraded, it was argued, were that much more in need of salvation. Those mission organisations—evangelical and non-evangelical—that began operating in Melanesia never expected the going to be easy. But the assumption was that Melanesians would eventually come under their influence as had the peoples of Polynesia. Sooner or later the obstacles would fall away; it was a Christian domino theory.

But the results by the end of the nineteenth century proved totally unexpected. There had been no logical progression of Christianity from one island to another as in Polynesia. Nor had missionary endeavour been so easy in some localities and so difficult in others. These paradoxes had the following geographical pattern: in New Caledonia and its dependencies the Islanders were all practising Christians—albeit of a variety of faiths—and were reputed to be among the most devout of anywhere in the South Seas. But the people of the Solomon Islands and the New Hebrides had proved indifferent or hostile to missionaries and their teachings. In short, the Islanders accepted Christianity in the south, and rejected it further north; or from a Eurocentric point of view, missionaries were successful in the south and spectacularly unsuccessful in the north. The explanations for these differences lay not as might be expected in the nature of the various missions' organisations, personnel, and strategies, but in the nature of the respective indigenous cultures and environments.

This proposition can be demonstrated by examining Islander–missionary interaction in a geographic as opposed to chronological sequence moving from north to south.

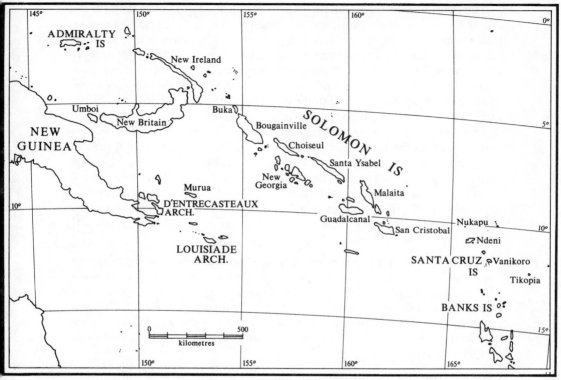

10   Solomon Islands and region

THE SOLOMON ISLANDS

The Marist mission

The first missionaries to the Solomon Islands were French Catholics, members of the Société de Marie, or Marist Fathers. Ever since 1797 missionary initiative in the Pacific Islands had been the preserve of evangelical Protestantism. The London Missionary Society was predominant in the Society and Cook Islands and Samoa, the American Board of Commissioners for Foreign Missions in Hawaii, the Wesleyans in Tonga and Fiji, and the Church Missionary Society in New Zealand. The Catholic church had been much slower off the mark mainly because its leading nation after Spain's decline, France, had been rocked by religious and political upheavals in the late eighteenth century. Not until well into the nineteenth century had the church recovered sufficiently from the consequences of the French revolution to consider missionary work on the other side of the world.

The Picpus Fathers entered the Pacific islands field in 1827 at Hawaii. By the 1840s they were in Tahiti and the Marquesas. But it seemed wherever they went that Protestants had beaten them. The most that Catholic missionaries could achieve were tiny enclaves of support more often than not surrounded by hostile evangelical missionaries and their island converts. However, the central and western Pacific islands was the sphere of influence designated by the Catholic church to the Marist Fathers and here the Protestants were not so far ahead.

The Marists were very different from early Protestant missionaries in background and outlook. They were, first and foremost, priests (or priests in training) whose long years of monastic study stood them in sharp contrast to the more worldly Protestant pioneers. The evangelical Protestant ambition of bringing social and economic as well as spiritual revolution to the benighted savages had no place in early Marist thinking. Nor, unlike the Protestants, was their own material well-being and advancement of any account.

> *The whole operation was viewed in narrow religious terms. For most the missionary vocation seems to have represented primarily a short road to sanctity. Apostolic success was secondary to and dependent on personal holiness and guaranteed by martyrdom. The only external factor considered relevant derived from the religious polemic of Europe: the emissaries of truth should reach the waiting islanders before those of Error and Mammon. The practical problems of coping with an alien world and its people weighed lightly.*[1]

One consequence of this outlook, at least in the eyes of others and especially many Islanders, was the Marists' material poverty. This often contrasted dramatically with the prosperity of Protestant missionaries with their plethora of goods and chattels, their impressive mission buildings and churches, their presses and books, and their wives who looked after them.

The Marists first established themselves on Wallis and Futuna in 1837, gaining the jump on Protestants who were just entering neighbouring Fiji and Samoa. They also established footholds in New Zealand (1838), Tonga (1842), eastern Fiji (1844), and Samoa (1845) but in all these places they, like the Picpus Fathers in the east, had little influence, mainly because of Protestant dominance. Further to the west, in Melanesia, the race was still wide open. In 1844 the Vicariate of Melanesia was created; Jean-Baptiste Epalle was its first bishop.[2]

Arrival in the Solomons

Epalle and his fellow Marists left Sydney in 1845 on a sandalwood vessel. They planned to visit the Solomon Islands having learnt of some anchorages from a Sydney whaling captain and from Dumont d'Urville's charts.

Beyond that they knew absolutely nothing of these islands and their people. Indeed Epalle together with many of his colleagues could not really be bothered with such knowledge: 'The receptiveness of the savages and infidels was thought to be guaranteed by the rightness of the Truth itself and by the missionary's relations with the Omnipotent'.[3] Epalle specifically disdained the idea of, he said, 'working . . . too much to get all possible information and [relying] . . . too much on human opinions.'[4]

After briefly visiting San Cristobal, Epalle and his party landed at Astrolabe Harbour on Ysabel. The Islanders appeared friendly. But they told Epalle that it would be dangerous for him to go around a certain point of land for that was enemy country. Epalle dismissed the warning with the comment that Islanders 'always disparaged their neighbours' and proceeded around the point. Wrote Laracy: 'Two hours later they returned, the bishop with five axe wounds in his head and several others of the party with lesser injuries.'[5] Epalle died three days later. The horrified Marists buried their new martyr and withdrew to Makira Bay on San Cristobal. Nine of them built a house and established friendly relations with the local people, the Oné, who wanted what few goods the Marists had to offer such as fishhooks. But the Marists soon contracted malaria. They erected another house further away on hopefully more healthy ground (malaria was thought to come from miasmal vapours) but this was territory belonging to the Oné's enemies. These people were only too keen to have the Marists with them, but the Oné were sorely put out. The malaria worsened. One Marist died. Two priests and a brother then tried to cross the island to find a better spot, but in doing so they went into the lands of hostile bush people and were killed. The remainder lived in constant fear of their lives as the Islanders began to harass them. An epidemic swept the island and the Marists were blamed. In 1847 they admitted defeat and withdrew from the Solomon Islands.[6]

Retreat

The Marists went to Murua (or Woodlark), an island between the Solomons and New Guinea. There they initially fared a little better. Malaria was not such a problem and the Islanders were relatively peaceful. Four of the Marists set out for a new field, this time Umboi, between New Guinea and New Britain. Two died from malaria, and the two sick survivors returned to Murua. Conditions deteriorated. There was a famine, apparently due to an epidemic in 1848 which left the Islanders too debilitated to plant and harvest crops. Interdistrict warfare broke out. The Marist superior-general decided to transfer the troublesome Murua mission to the Milan Foreign Mission Society. In 1852 a party of Italian missionaries arrived at the island. For a time the Marists stayed on, but famine, disease, and warfare drove them away for good. The Italians hung on, and also went to malaria-ridden Umboi, until they too gave up both islands in 1855. One tried to return to Murua shortly afterward. His vessel ran aground and the Muruans killed him and the rest of the crew.[7]

To add to the Catholics' troubles in the region, two Marist priests who had landed on Tikopia in the Santa Cruz Group in 1851, and a mission vessel sent to visit them in 1852, were never heard of again.[8]

The lessons?

The Catholic mission to the Solomons and nearby regions was a disaster. To some extent this was due to poor planning and reckless ignorance of conditions. The missionaries could hardly have been more ill-equipped intellectually and physically to face the rigours of strange and hostile lands. Yet many things were beyond the control of even the most well-equipped mission. Malaria was a major problem. And missionaries were helpless to stop passing vessels, perhaps even their own, from introducing epidemic diseases against which the Islanders had no immunity. The Marists were likewise at the mercy of local indigenous rivalries. In particular there were no strong leaders who could offer protection and through whom missionaries might have influenced island communities. From the Islanders' point of view the Marists had little or nothing to offer them in terms of either goods or ideas. At best they tolerated the priests, at worst they saw them as their enemies' allies and bringers of disease and death.

Not until 1898 did Catholic missionaries venture back to the Solomons. Most other mission organisations similarly gave these islands a wide berth for most of the century.

THE NEW HEBRIDES

LMS strategy

Only about six months after Williams's murder on Eromanga, the LMS returned to the New Hebrides. Since it was obviously going to be dangerous as well as a great strain on resources to place permanent European missionaries on all the numerous isles of the group, the LMS planned to use Rarotongan and Samoan teachers as pioneers. This technique had proved most successful in parts of Polynesia, especially the Cook Islands and Samoa. The advantages of employing Polynesian teachers in Polynesia were several. They were obviously more readily available than European missionaries, thus greatly and cheaply increasing LMS personnel and enabling much more ground to be covered. Their settlement on Polynesian islands was easy enough to achieve since they had the same or similar lifestyles as their hosts and did not require the same material possessions and home comforts as an LMS missionary and his family. Furthermore, there were no significant racial, cultural, or linguistic barriers between those teaching Christianity and those supposed to learn—it was evangelisation by Polynesians of Polynesians. Underlying all these obvious advantages for the LMS mission was the attitude that the teachers were far more expendable than a European missionary. As one missionary explained:

> *They are too exalted in their own estimation to labour in heathen lands—except at the* first *while they are in danger of their lives from savage men and before the natives begin to pay them deference as servants of the True God ... [The teachers were useful] not because they can do that peculiar kind of work better, or so well as European missionaries or because they are in less danger of their lives; but because to the society [LMS] their lives are less valuable than the lives of missionaries.*[9]

It seemed natural that such men should be used to spearhead the LMS advance into Melanesia. But the plan did not work as it had in Polynesia.

The LMS on Tana

John Williams had landed three Samoans on Tana shortly before his fateful landing on Eromanga. In 1840 the LMS placed two more Samoans on Tana, and believed that this island was 'decidedly hopeful'.[10] However, a visiting English naval officer soon afterward found one teacher dead and the others suffering from malaria: 'They appear to be very uneasy and unhappy, and painfully anxious to return to their native land.'[11] When the LMS vessel returned in 1841 another teacher had died and the remainder were 'entirely deserted, and ... in great straits.'[12] But the LMS pressed on. In 1842 two missionaries, George Turner and Henry Nisbet, newly arrived in the Pacific and after a crash course in 'missionary experience' in Samoa, were landed at Port Resolution on Tana.

> *We had not been twenty-four hours on shore, until we found that we were among a set of notorious thieves, perfect Spartans in the trade, and, like the ancient code of Lycurgus, the crime seemed to be, not the stealing, but the being found out. The teacher's house, in which we took up our temporary abode, was but badly shut in, with rough upright sticks from the bush, having spaces here and there which easily let in a finger or two. Before we got all these places filled up, a towel was missed here, a comb there, and a pair of scissors in another place. Nay, the very bed-quilt was caught one afternoon moving off towards a hole, by means of a long stick with a hook at the end of it.*
>
> *When we spoke to the chiefs about it, begging them to make laws; they would talk loudly, and threaten death to the thief if they could only get hold of him; but it was all a joke, the chiefs were as bad as any of them.*[13]

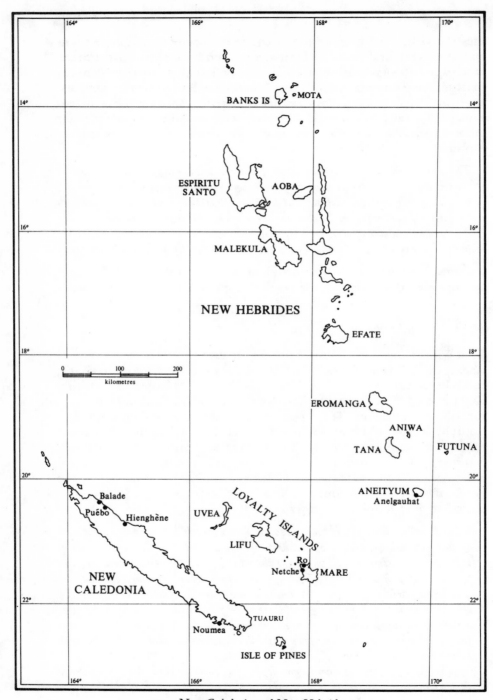

11 New Caledonia and New Hebrides

The local Tanese initially went to church services but soon the novelty wore off and 'there was no getting a congregation'.[14] The missionaries' more serious problem was lack of a paramount chief to protect them and advance their interests by advancing his own. On Tana, as in many parts of the Solomons and the New Hebrides, leaders were usually Big-Men rather than chiefs. In Turner's opinion the Tanese had 'no political constitution of any value whatsoever' and the 'authority of a Tanna chief does not seem to extend a gunshot from his own dwelling'.[15] Constant warfare between the small, scattered settlements was another great obstacle to missionary activity. Turner complained that the Tanese were 'fighting during five out of the seven months we lived among them'. The missionaries thus found themselves 'hedged in on all sides', never able to go further than about four miles from their home: 'At such distances you come to boundaries which are never passed'. Said Turner, 'We became quite familiar with the stereotyped phrase, "Don't go there, they are bad people, they will kill you."' Even if missionaries had ventured further and had not been killed, they could not have communicated with the people for 'they spoke quite a different dialect.'[16]

An epidemic of dysentery hit the island in 1843 and Turner and Nisbet, accused of being sorcerers, were held responsible. Some two thousand Tanese, urged on by the local disease-makers who feared the missionaries' supposed powers of evil to be greater than their own, angrily descended upon the mission station. Turner, Nisbet, their families, and the Samoan teachers fled from the island on a whaling vessel that fortuitously appeared in the bay.[17] The LMS landed seven more teachers on Tana in 1845. Within months a series of epidemics broke out. The teachers were blamed, one was killed, and the remainder escaped to Aneityum on a passing ship.[18]

This brief LMS experience on Tana, like the Marist endeavours on Ysabel and San Cristobal, vividly illustrated the classic difficulties (already outlined by explorers) that faced missionaries in the New Hebrides and Solomon Islands: the indifference and hostility of the Islanders, their constant warfare amongst themselves, their small, scattered communities without chiefs, their very numerous languages, combined with ever-present malaria and newly introduced epidemics.

The LMS on Aniwa, Eromanga, Aneityum and Futuna

The LMS put down teachers on other New Hebridean islands in 1840 and 1841. On Aniwa, a small island with a population of only about five hundred people, the teachers made 'little or no impression'.[19] The more populous and infamous Eromanga was a more important objective. Two teachers were landed at Cook's Bay, on the opposite coast to Dillon's Bay where Williams had been killed. Local leaders had promised the missionaries that they would look after the Samoans, but they left them destitute once the mission vessel had departed.[20] The Samoans soon came down with malaria and were in a thoroughly wretched state when the LMS called back in 1841. One teacher and a 'chief' came out to the missionaries' ship and explained that the missionaries would have to land before the Islanders would let the other teacher see them.

> *This we did not consider it advisable to do. The entrance to the landing-place was a narrow inlet between two high cliffs. These were covered with crowds of armed savages, who would have had us entirely in their power had we landed; and, with what had so recently occurred on the island fresh in our recollection, and present appearances being far from inviting, we did not feel inclined to trust them.*[21]

The Eromangan 'chief' then leapt into the sea and stroked for the shore, but the missionaries rowed frantically after him and caught him. The teacher who had been held on shore was eventually brought out in a canoe but was kept at a distance, the Islanders trying to entice the mission boat closer inshore. The teacher suddenly dived into the sea and made it to the missionaries. The Eromangan hostage was then released.[22] The mission to Eromanga was shelved for another decade.

Teachers on Aneityum suffered similar tribulations. One died of malaria, the others were sick, hungry, and often in fear of their lives from hostile Islanders. In 1846 all but two of them asked to be removed and the island was 'virtually given up' by the LMS.[23]

The two Samoan teachers left on Futuna in 1841 were less fortunate. In 1843 the same epidemic of dysentery that swept Tana and forced Turner and Nisbet to flee hit Futuna. The teachers were blamed for the suffering and, since there was no passing ship to enable them to escape, were murdered.[24]

By the mid-1840s, the LMS was disillusioned about its New Hebridean field which had yielded nothing but violence, disease, and death. Even the most arduous days of the mission's first years on Polynesian islands had been nothing like this. A few token efforts were made to keep at least some presence in the New Hebrides—a few teachers were sent to Efaté and Tana in the mid-1840s—but the story was the same.[25]

The Presbyterians on Aneityum

Scottish-born John Geddie had been agitating since 1838 for his Presbyterian Church of Nova Scotia to have its own mission to heathen lands. Eventually he got his way when his church inherited the New Hebrides from the LMS which was only too keen to be rid of these 'repulsive, forbidding' isles.[26] However the LMS continued to provide assistance where it could, especially by supplying the Presbyterians with Samoan teachers.

Geddie arrived in Anelgauhat Harbour on Aneityum with a party of LMS-trained Samoans in 1848. To his dismay he found eight Marist priests recently arrived from New Caledonia and settled on what looked like the best land in the locality.[27] However, prevailing winds blew across a nearby swamp wafting 'the invisible and impalpable malaria into their dwelling' and soon all were stricken with 'fever and ague'.[28] To Geddie's delight they were removed to the Isle of Pines in 1849. Other Europeans were there too when Geddie arrived. Sandalwood trader James Paddon had a station on a small island in the harbour and was building large storehouses and a home on the mainland.[29] Paddon and Geddie were initially the best of friends but the two soon fell out. Geddie took to criticising the sandalwood trade because of the moral and other effects he believed it was having on the Islanders: 'The conduct of the traders [he wrote] . . . is too abominable to be described.' Paddon accused Geddie of meddling with matters that did not concern him and called him a 'liar, hypocrite, and everything bad'.[30] A mutual hatred between the two men lasted until Paddon moved his station to Tana in 1852, when Aneityumese sandalwood was depleted.[31]

Geddie's first years on Aneityum were as tough as he had expected (the squabbling with Paddon apart). He was periodically very ill with malaria, as were his Samoans. Annual cyclones added to his problems. The Islanders were initially uninterested in his teachings and Geddie blamed the sandalwood traders for this. Yet by the late 1850s most of the Aneityumese population of some 3500 were 'professedly Christian': 'Hardly one can now be found who calls himself heathen. The church members number 297, and the candidates for admission to the church 110. The island is enriched by fifty-six school-houses, eleven chapels, and sixty native teachers and assistants.'[32] This was a situation quite unique in the New Hebrides.

Church hagiographers usually attribute evangelical success on Aneityum to Geddie's alleged tolerance and humanity,[33] and certainly he was one of the less arrogant and bigoted of the early Presbyterian missionaries in the New Hebrides. But factors quite independent of Geddie offer a more likely explanation.

In contrast to most islands in the New Hebrides, Aneityum had one language only (with two dialects). The problem of communicating with any one section of the population was thus very much less than elsewhere. Moreover the single language enabled the mission to translate and print pamphlets. Aneityum was politically divided into five districts and thanks to the numbers of Samoans at the mission's disposal, as well as the arrival of missionary John Inglis in 1852, each district could have a church representative. This prevented any one region from feeling left out and meant that the church was less likely to become involved in interdistrict rivalries. Warfare on the island was less prevalent than on Tana and elsewhere and there was an element of political stability. Geddie and Inglis certainly felt more personally secure than had Turner and Nisbet on Tana. In part too the

Aneityumese tolerance of missionary presence had something to do with the extent of European contact with the island through the sandalwood trade and Paddon's station. Although Geddie argued that such European presence hindered the mission, the more experience the people had with Western ways the more influence missionaries, as representatives of European culture, probably had. For example, when Paddon left Anelgauhat Harbour in 1852 some Islanders who had associated with him and who had opposed Geddie, transferred their allegiance to the missionary. Geddie believed that this was because the 'white traders ... [had] opposed ... the progress of the gospel'[34] but it is also likely that the Islanders had lost one source of contact with European goods and now looked to the mission for another.

Against this background the Islanders' attitude to missionaries and their teachings gradually changed from one of indifference or opposition to tacit acceptance.

> *The progress of the work was steady, but not rapid. On one Sabbath there would be two or three new names to be added to the roll; the next there would perhaps be only one; on the third there might be five or six, but scarcely ever more on one Sabbath. But there was hardly ever a Sabbath but there was one or more, till the whole island was Christian.*[35]

The missionaries contrasted this reaction with what they knew had happened in places like Tahiti and Tonga. Inglis continued:

> *In Eastern Polynesia, among the Malays, when a chief became Christian, every one belonging to the tribe felt that he must adopt the religion of his chief, and so became Christian.... But among the Papuans the chiefs have no such power; democracy rules. Hence religion is a personal rather than a tribal affair; every man acts on his own personal responsibility.*[36]

The Aneityumese 'chiefs' were amongst the last to declare their allegiance to the new religion. But they eventually came around. They realised that their influence might in fact be lost if too many of their followers placed faith in the supernatural forces of the Christian god. As many leaders throughout the Pacific eventually realised, they could possibly add to their own powers if they joined the Christian ranks. Some of the most ardent opponents of missionaries on Aneityum turned out to be their most zealous supporters, like 'chiefs' Nohoat and Waihit. Certainly missionaries held out the promise of an increase in their authority.

> *Had a meeting with the chiefs this morni g. Advised them to take some steps towards forming themselves into a government. In their heathen state each high chief was supreme in his own district and exercised an arbitrary power. The people viewed them with a kind of religious veneration while they lived and worshipped them after death. Their persons were considered sacred and they were greatly*

dreaded by the natives. The introduction of christianity has altered this state of things. Instead of acting independently in their respective districts we have advised them to form a united government for the suppression of crime and the good of society. The suggestion was well received and they will probably act on it.[37]

The Presbyterians on Eromanga and Tana

The success of the mission on Aneityum encouraged the Presbyterians to expand their activities in the New Hebrides. In 1857 George Gordon was landed on Eromanga, and the following year John Paton, Joseph Copeland, and John Matheson went to Tana. But hopes of emulating Geddie on Aneityum were quickly dashed. The Eromangans made it all 'up-hill work'. They were constantly at war, and far too mobile for missionary liking. 'They are scattered, and without any settled, well ordered village. They are migratory in given localities, as war and planting may require. Their chiefs are numerous, but not powerful.'[38] Gordon's wife and his Samoan teachers were afflicted with malaria. Life on Tana proved even more difficult. Paton's wife and child died, probably because of malaria. Matheson was taken off the island ill and later died. A replacement—Samuel Johnston—died of tuberculosis. Copeland was transferred to Aneityum. Paton stayed on alone, very sick with malaria. The Tanese were hostile to him, claiming he was a sorcerer. Seldom did he venture from his hut.[39]

Whatever animosity was shown to Paton, and he certainly attracted it both unwittingly by his ignorance of Tanese custom and more directly by his extreme arrogance, Tanese relations with Europeans generally were at a low ebb. Two sandalwooders had been murdered on the island's northwest coast in 1857 and two more were killed in the same place the following year. The result was a severe bombardment of the locality by HMS *Iris* only months before the Presbyterian missionaries had arrived on the island.[40] The association of naval bombardments with missionaries was made in many Tanese minds. Paton was later to convince all Tanese that naval artillery was an important part of the mission's strategy.

The measles epidemic

Early in 1861 the sandalwood vessel *Hirondelle* called at Aneityum. Some of her crew had measles.

> *The disease soon spread over the* whole *island notwithstanding the efforts made to check its progress. The population at large were laid prostrate, and I do not believe there are half a dozen of persons on the island, who did not take the sickness.... Many died of the disease itself, and many also from inattention and want of the common necessaries of life, as there were few able to help their neighbours. About*

one-third of the population were in the short space of three or four months swept into the grave.[41]

More than a thousand Islanders perished. Missionaries had unwittingly been largely responsible for the extent of the epidemic. Measles is a viral disease transmitted in minute droplets of water exhaled by an infected person. Fairly close social contact is needed for the virus to spread. In premissionary days on Aneityum there was little movement of people from one district to another and such droplet infections could not have spread very far. But by the 1860s most Aneityumese spent about an hour a day in one of the mission's fifty-six stuffy classrooms. On Sundays hundreds were crammed into churches. With the ending of what interdistrict fighting there had been, the Islanders now travelled widely around their land. There was a constant movement of people from all districts to Anelgauhat in the south or to Aname in the north. These social conditions, combined with the island's humidity early each year, ensured that such diseases spread rapidly to every corner of the land.[42] To add to the misery, three tropical cyclones bore down on the island destroying crops and villages. Food became very scarce.[43]

Some Islanders blamed these catastrophes on the missionaries' vengeful god. Geddie's showpiece chapel was burnt to the ground. But the majority of the Islanders who survived the epidemic seem to have paid 'a more than usual attention to religion.'[44] There was considerable resettlement of communities. For example those from the major inland settlement at Anumej moved to the coast, nearer the mission headquarters. As McArthur explained: 'An inevitable consequence of the more assiduous attendance at church and school was that the population as a whole became even more liable to contract droplet infections.'[45] Other diseases swept the island, including influenza in 1863, and tuberculosis. In the mid-1860s there were epidemics of diphtheria and whooping cough. The population was now half of what it had been in 1860.[46]

The 1861 measles epidemic also reached Eromanga and Tana by way of sandalwood vessels. Missionaries recorded the fearful effects.

Vast numbers . . . rushed into experiments which made the attack fatal all round. When the trouble was at its height, for instance, they would plunge into the sea, and seek relief: they found it in almost instant death. Others would dig a hole into the earth, the length of the body and about two feet deep; therein they laid themselves down, the cold earth feeling agreeable to their fevered skins; and when the earth around them grew heated, they got friends to dig a few inches deeper, again and again, seeking a cooler and cooler couch. In this ghastly effort many of them died, literally in their own graves, and were buried where they lay![47]

Yet mortality on Eromanga and Tana was probably very much lower than on Aneityum mainly because the populations had not been Christianised.

Mobility around these islands was severely limited by hostilities and even within one region social interaction was far less than on the church and school attending Aneityum. Droplet infections could not travel so far, and the cruel effects that the missionaries described were probably localised.[48] Nevertheless, the missionaries on Eromanga and Tana were to suffer far more than their colleagues on Aneityum.

When the measles reached Dillon's Bay on Eromanga, Gordon was quickly implicated by the Islanders. He may in fact have given credence to their view because he believed the epidemic was a divine retribution:

> *Were I to give you a catalogue of the crimes which this people have committed upon foreigners and among themselves for the last three years, you would be astonished; and will not be surprised to learn that God has cut off two-thirds of them in some settlements if not in all.*[49]

Gordon had little idea of what was happening beyond the confines of his station and his estimates of mortality are speculation.[50] Nor did he have any idea of how much the Islanders blamed and feared him until he saw them coming for him with axes. After his attackers had hacked him to pieces they dismembered his wife.[51]

The Tanese similarly accused Paton of bringing the pestilence to them and made several attempts to kill him. Paton once spent four days locked in his bedroom while 'armed Savages kept prowling about'.[52] News of Gordon's death on Eromanga further excited the Tanese and there were renewed threats to the mission. Paton initially refused to leave his post, but conditions became intolerable. Sickness and death amongst the Tanese near his station continued, and Paton was constantly blamed. Finally, after a hurricane early in 1862, Paton gave in and fled to Aneityum.[53]

Aftermath

After more than twenty years, mission fortunes in the New Hebrides could not have been lower. To the evangelical mind, New Hebrideans (with the exception of those on Aneityum) were just as treacherous and depraved as when John Williams first stepped ashore in 1839. Never had so much missionary endeavour in the South Seas achieved so little at such great cost in human life and suffering. The Presbyterian missionaries reacted in various ways. Some took a philosophical or rather theological view: God's will was ever mysterious and still would he save his Islanders in his good time. For others there was blinding frustration and anger and a desire to punish the New Hebrideans for their great wickedness. Of such a mind was John Paton.

In 1865 HMS *Curaçoa*, commanded by Sir William Wiseman, sailed about the western Pacific 'displaying the British flag' with instructions to in-

30   'The Curaçoa shelling the native villages at Tanna', 1865, with the mission vessel
Dayspring *nearly.*
(Liverpool Three Years on the Australia Station. *Alexander Turnbull Library)*

vestigate alleged depredations against English lives and property, including the murder of Gordon on Eromanga. Whilst at Aneityum they met a
party of Presbyterian missionaries. In the words of one passenger on the
Curaçoa:

> *Among them [were] Messrs. Paton and Gordon [brother of George Gordon*
> *murdered on Eromanga]. Both these gentlemen were bent on dangerous enterprises,*
> *in which they hoped to succeed by favour of Her Majesty's guns, that were soon to be*
> *employed in punishing and terrifying the natives of Tanna and Eramanga for their*
> *misdeeds.*[54]

The *Curaçoa* entered Port Resolution on Tana accompanied by the missionaries on their vessel *Dayspring.* The warship's cannon pounded villages
and from a cutter rockets were fired into the crowds of Islanders on the
beaches. After several hours of this treatment about 170 men were landed
'to commit such devastation as was in their power'.

> *The task, however, was not an easy one. The natives of course, incapable of*
> *resistance, fled from the coast, and concealed themselves in the bush, which presented*
> *an almost insurmountable barrier to an invading force. No guide had been found,*
> *and the advance had to be made as best it might. Taking advantage of a most*
> *unpromising path that led upwards from the beach, Commander Dent led up his*
> *men in the direction of an open space on the hill top, which the Missionary had*
> *pointed out from the ship as being the dancing ground, and which was to be the place*
> *of rendezvous. This spot, after a prodigious expenditure of creeping, crushing, and*

other fatiguing exertion in forcing a way through the intricate tangle of the bush,
was at length reached. But no sooner was this effected, than a volley from the rear
showed that the natives had been following on their track. A dash was made at
them, and they immediately vanished.[55]

Another party of sailors meanwhile destroyed 'all the canoes they could
find along the coast.'[56] The final body count was one sailor and one
Islander killed in the bush. Several more Islanders were killed several days
later as they tampered with an unexploded shell. Satisfied that the Tanese
were sufficiently contrite, Wiseman sailed away, with the mission vessel in
his wake. Some weeks later HMS *Curaçoa* anchored in Dillon's Bay on
Eromanga, and gave the inhabitants a broadside. No one, apparently, was
killed.[57]

The naval bombardment of Tana and Eromanga caused a public furore
in New South Wales. The Presbyterian missionaries who had accompanied
the warship came in for severe criticism. Paton admitted that he found
himself 'probably the best-abused man in all Australia, and the very name
of the New Hebrides Mission stinking in the nostrils of the People.'[58] The
mission argued publicly that Paton, Gordon, and others had merely acted
as interpreters and that they had not urged Wiseman to punish the
Islanders. But it was a most unconvincing case. There is every indication
that Gordon and especially Paton were only too happy to see the Royal
Navy blasting away at the treacherous heathen. There was deep division
within the Presbyterian church and mission over the affair. One result was
that it was 'not thought advisable' for Paton ever to return to Tana.[59] The
Eromangans and Tanese had little doubt that the missionaries had called
the warship to torment them.

The Presbyterian mission to the New Hebrides continued fitfully for the
remainder of the century. Islands in the south were reoccupied by missionaries and some new stations were opened on some of the larger islands
in the north. There were more naval bombardments, further epidemics,
and further killings. Like his brother before him, James Gordon was
murdered on Eromanga, in 1872. By the end of the century the mission's
evangelical impact was still minimal.[60] The exception was Aneityum, but
then its population had been reduced to only five hundred souls.

The Melanesian Mission

The New Zealand Church.of England's Melanesian Mission has become
one of the better-known missionary enterprises in the New Hebrides and
Solomons region and is popularly considered one of the most successful
missions in this difficult field. This reputation stems mainly from the
effective public relations of the dominant High Church personalities involved, Bishops George Augustus Selwyn and John Coleridge Patteson.

Their mission's self-proclaimed distinction has been endorsed by a long tradition of church hagiography. But the mission's alleged successes cannot be borne out by its impact on the peoples of Melanesia in the nineteenth century which was in the main negligible. For the historian of culture contact, the Melanesian Mission's significance lies in the fact that of all the missions operating in Melanesia in the nineteenth century this one took careful note of the particular difficulties it would encounter and adopted novel techniques to try to overcome them. That its strategies were unsuccessful is less a critical comment on the mission itself, than a suggestion that the overriding considerations as to whether people of Melanesian islands (and elsewhere) would accept or reject Christianity depended on their own initiative and interests, not on missionary intentions and tactics.

The indefatigable Selwyn was not content with the narrow confines of New Zealand for the diocese created in 1841, but saw his authority stretching into the 'dark expanse' of Melanesia and beyond (which brought him into conflict with the LMS).[61] In his early years in New Zealand he took a keen interest in the various Pacific island missions and in 1847 gained some first-hand knowledge by sailing as chaplain on HMS *Dido* to Samoa, Tonga, the New Hebrides, and New Caledonia. The rather novel strategy that Selwyn subsequently drew up was designed to overcome the difficulties, not to mention disasters, that seemed invariably to result when European missionaries and even 'native teachers' went into the Solomons and the New Hebrides. He proposed to reverse the normal proceedings by bringing some Melanesians to missionaries. This involved sending a mission vessel through the Melanesian islands each year and bringing back to Auckland a number of 'promising youths'. They would spend a summer at St Johns College being instructed in English, the gospel, and the arts of civilisation. In the autumn they would be returned to their home islands where they were expected to instruct their families and neighbours in the new truths. In succeeding years they and others were to return to St Johns for further training and eventual baptism, ending up as missionaries to their own people. Selwyn envisaged, ultimately, an independent Melanesian church 'with its own staff of clergy, its own laws, its own Bishop'.[62]

On paper the scheme was excellent. It neatly got around the problems of resident European missionaries facing diseases and hostile Islanders, coping with dozens of languages and the lack of chiefly patrons. In 1849 Selwyn set off on the first of a series of voyages which over the years took him, and his close colleague Patteson from 1858, to 81 different islands in Melanesia, with the New Hebrides and Solomons the main targets. By 1860 there had been more than a dozen arduous trips and 152 youths had been brought back to Auckland; 39 of these came for a second or third time. Yet from the mission's point of view the results were very disappointing. While fine on paper, the scheme was not so good in practice.

The mission had neither the time, the personnel, nor the resources to maintain twice-yearly voyages thousands of kilometres to all its scores of landfalls in Melanesia. Only fleeting and sporadic contact could be made with any one village, a problem that was intensified by the social and linguistic isolation any one location often had from the surrounding countryside. Selwyn's expectations of his 'scholars' were equally unrealistic. Most were very young men, enticed to Auckland in expectation of excitement and material goods. They were not generally of a temperament to want to sit and study in St Johns. Nor did these men, if they survived Auckland's much colder climate, have much wish or even authority to go about converting family and friends on returning home. For most 'scholars', a trip to Auckland was an adventure, not, as Selwyn had hoped a spiritually, morally, and socially uplifting experience filling them with reforming zeal. Most of these people fitted back into the existing order of things in their villages and were never heard of again. While Selwyn's scheme had tried to take account of the more obvious difficulties a missionary would face in Melanesia, other fundamental problems such as how to transmit ideas across cultures and how to influence small, scattered, chiefless societies were imperfectly understood.

In 1861 Melanesia became a Church of England diocese in its own right. Patteson was its first bishop. He gradually modified mission policy along more orthodox missionary lines in attempts to overcome some of the more obvious defects. The language of Mota in the Banks Group became the mission's new language for 'scholars' instead of English which, as missionaries all over the Pacific had found, never proved satisfactory. Mota was chosen because at the time there were a number of 'senior scholars' from Mota at the college. Also the mission's headquarters was moved from Auckland to Norfolk Island in an attempt to cut down on the endless travelling. There were other more radical departures from Selwyn's scheme too. Patteson planned to have a number of European missionaries reside for several months at selected locations in Melanesia itself. Patteson himself spent several months on Lifu, one of the Loyalty Islands, in 1858 conducting a school for twelve New Hebrideans. It was a failure if only because the 'scholars' really wanted to go somewhere much more exciting, like Auckland. The closer the mission moved back toward Melanesia the less material appeal and excitement value it held in young eyes. Undaunted, Patteson chose Mota as a temporary headquarters and lived there for four months in 1860. Mota and the Banks Islands subsequently became a focus for the mission. It held annual schools on Mota and became Patteson's semipermanent base. The mission extended this strategy with a handful of itinerant missionaries who periodically visited the several districts into which the region was divided: central Solomons, southeastern Solomons, and northern New Hebrides.

In spite of Patteson's reforms, the mission's impact in Melanesia was still very minimal. The high point came in 1871 when Patteson baptised some three hundred Mota Islanders, about one-third of the island's population. Yet this was small fare in view of all the years of effort since Selwyn's first voyage in 1849. The mission was in bad shape too, being short of money and personnel. To a considerable extent its ability to function at all depended on Patteson's boundless energy. But eventually he became tired and ill. More significantly, with the abandonment of some of Selwyn's key notions of taking Melanesians out of Melanesia and instead sending Europeans into the islands, the ever-present dangers to missionaries working in the region once more became apparent. In 1871 the mission vessel landed Patteson alone on Nukapu in the Reef Islands—the third time it had visited the island. An hour later a waiting boat's crew was attacked. Then the Islanders brought the Bishop's broken body out into the lagoon and dumped it. He had been killed, it was later alleged, in retaliation for the abduction of some Nukapuans by a labour-trading vessel.

Comment

Thirty years after Williams's death on Eromanga in 1839, the region of the Solomons and New Hebrides was still fertile ground for the martyr's cause. No missionary techniques, no matter how sophisticated, offered protection to missionaries or gave them any means of influencing the Islanders.

Missionaries pondered the reasons why Solomon Islanders and New Hebrideans found Christianity irrelevant. The contrast with islands in the eastern and central Pacific and even with nearby New Caledonia and dependencies, where Christianity had become an integral part of indigenous society and politics, could not have been greater. Explanations were not hard to find, and they had less to do with the missionaries themselves than with the cultural and geographic environments they found themselves in. The lack of chiefly, hierarchical societies ensured that evangelical influence would at best be halting and socially and spatially limited. As Turner complained back in the 1840s, 'We found no such thing as a king or great chief . . . No Thakombau, Pomare, or Kamehameha'.[63] Without such patrons, missionaries were at the mercy of every individual's whim and this was aggravated by the very small and mutually hostile communities. To quote Turner again:

> *In Eastern Polynesia, the rule has been that in a group of four, seven, or ten islands within sight of each other, we have found but one dialect, and the people having a good deal of intercourse, not only with each other on the same island, but also with the various islands of the group. They had their quarrels and their wars, at times, but they made up matters after a while, and went on again in harmony. In going westward, however, among the Papuan tribes of the New Hebrides, we found ourselves in a totally different region, all split up into the most hostile isolation.*[64]

In addition, wrote another missionary,

> *The most formidable obstacle to the evagelization of the New Hebrides is the great variety of dialects, if not languages, that are found. It is a very Babel.*[65]

When all these considerations are set against a background of malaria and the other diseases that were rife in the humid climates, it was no real surprise that well into the twentieth century these parts of Melanesia remained very stoney ground for those who would bring messages of salvation. Missionaries, unable to cope effectively with these conditions and situations, were seen by most New Hebrideans and Solomon Islanders as at best pathetic and irrelevant, at worst dangerous.

It seemed remarkable that in a group of islands so close to the New Hebrides missionaries met with very considerable success. By the 1860s many of the inhabitants of the New Caledonian mainland and all the people on the offshore Isle of Pines and the Loyalty Islands were practising Christians. Many of the same mission organisations and even personnel who had experienced such a difficult time in the New Hebrides and Solomon Islands found themselves greatly in demand on these neighbouring islands.

THE LOYALTY ISLANDS

A different environment

By far the most fervent Christian Islanders in the southwest Pacific were Loyalty Islanders.[66] By the 1860s the entire populations of Mare, Lifu, and Uvea—about 12 000 people—had been converted by either the LMS or the Marists. Some visitors regarded them as among the finest examples of Pacific Islanders who had embraced Christianity and civilisation, worthy of emulation even by English congregations. At the same time that Solomon Islanders and New Hebrideans were chasing or killing missionaries and teachers, Loyalty Islanders, explained one missionary,

> *spend more time in worship & religious exercises than any I have ever known . . . every Sunday these people devote seven & a half or eight hours to public worship during the whole of which time . . . they are either hearing prayer, or reading or a sermon, or being catechised, or singing. Everything is conducted with the greatest solemnity & decorum. . . . Religion has become the business of their lives.*[67]

The Loyalty Islands (and the New Caledonian region generally) lie outside the malarial zone. From a European point of view the climate is comfortable and healthy. Early missionaries there thus had a marked advantage over their sweating, malaria plagued brethren in the New

Hebrides and Solomon Islands. Furthermore, Loyalty Islanders were organised into relatively large tribal groups, by Melanesian standards. Each tribe consisted of a rigidly stratified hierarchy under a chief whose position was usually hereditary. These chiefs were not despots but were regarded with the most extreme deference. The communities as a whole placed great emphasis on status. Chiefs and the small 'nobility' they came from were usually addressed in separate respectful or 'court' languages. Such sociopolitical structures (which were similar to those on the Isle of Pines and the New Caledonian mainland) had more in common with those frequently found in Polynesia than with the fragmented, Big-Men communities typical of the New Hebrides and Solomons.[68] Missionaries were thus relieved to discover that they could have chiefly patrons once again.

> *There is one remarkable difference between the natives of these islands and their neighbours, which deserves particular notice. Throughout the New Hebrides . . . the chiefs are very numerous, and possess very little authority. Here the case is different.*[69]

In addition, Loyalty Islanders had a long tradition of accepting strangers, especially travellers and castaways blown westward by prevailing winds from the region of Tonga and Samoa. These people were commonly given positions of some status by local chiefs who treated them as favourites in return for a monopoly of whatever skills the migrants possessed. Tongans, for example, were renowned as canoe builders. The earliest European travellers all noted the prevalence of 'Polynesian' characteristics among the populace and met recent arrivals from Tonga and Samoa. A common opinion was that Loyalty Islanders had a 'less revolting appearance than the natives of the New Hebrides' and that they 'more closely resemble the Tongans, and the Polynesians generally, than the races of Melanesia.'[70] The practice of accepting migrants from Polynesia was clearly going to be of great significance when the LMS sent along its Samoan and Rarotongan teachers. Another characteristic of the Loyalty Islanders which assisted the missionaries' task was the relative fewness of languages—Uvea had two, and Mare and Lifu one each (plus their separate 'court' languages). The problem of communication on any one of these islands was thus minimal compared with islands in the New Hebrides. Finally, intertribal rivalries, the bane of missionaries in many Pacific islands, assisted in the converting of Loyalty Islanders. Once one tribal chief accepted English Protestant missionaries, his rival would immediately seek out the French Catholic missionaries and vice versa. The Christianising of Loyalty Islanders, as well as the patterns of mission settlement and influence, resulted from chiefs aggressively choosing how and where they wished missionaries to operate amongst their followers. European religious and national differences were exploited within the framework of indigenous politics on each of the three Loyalty Islands.

The LMS on Mare

The first missionaries to make contact with Loyalty Islanders were members of the LMS who in 1841 called at Mare. It was an auspicious beginning for them when a Tongan came out through the reef shouting 'I know the true God!'[71] The chief of the powerful Si Gwahma tribe into whose territory the mission vessel had sailed eagerly received the LMS teachers. During the following decade the LMS made almost annual voyages collecting and landing more and more Samoans and Rarotongans who, in contrast to their tragic lot in the New Hebrides, thrived in Loyalty Islands conditions and whose skills were eagerly exploited by the leading Si Gwahma family, the Naisilines. They used the institutions and teachings of Christianity to secure their own positions and to assume more control over the tribe than was customary. Whenever epidemics struck, Si Gwahma chiefs usually protected the teachers from any Islanders who wanted to blame them. These leading chiefs had built for themselves whitewashed limestone cottages surrounded with neat gardens and picket fences, and they ordered their people to build huge churches. The Sabbath was rigorously observed and attendance at school and church was compulsory. The Si Gwahma people took to wearing European clothing, and the men publicly gave up all but one wife. Bishop Selwyn who visited the Si Gwahma in the early 1850s thought that there were 'probably more Christians than anywhere in these seas.'[72]

But the Naisilines soon outgrew their Polynesian teachers. They wanted resident European missionaries and were very impatient with the LMS whose resources were stretched to the limit and could not provide any. The Islanders dubbed the mission vessel *John Williams* 'the no missionaries'.

> *It would seem [wrote one LMS missionary] as if the old and usual order in such matters were reversed in the case of this people—instead of our going to them to compel them to come in, they have to use their utmost effort to compel us to go to them, and teach them the way of life and salvation.*[73]

Finally, in 1854, the LMS did land two missionaries, John Jones and Stephen Creagh. The Si Gwahma had waiting for them large plastered houses and a church. The two men were amazed: 'Seldom or ever has it been the lot of missionaries to commence their labours under circumstances so favourable and among a people so prepared to receive them.'[74] Their mission was an instant success. The entire population of the Si Gwahma region, some 3000 out of the island's total of 4500, was, in missionary phraseology, clean, clothed, and reading from books. The mission stations themselves at Ro and Netche with their vast houses and workshops loaded with goods and a forge and a printing press all bore ample testimony to the mission's rapid consolidation and prosperity. But

31   *LMS missionaries welcomed on Mare, Loyalty Islands, 1854.*
(*Murray* Wonders in the Western Isles)

even the missionaries' homes were overshadowed by that of the leading Si
Gwahma chief, Naisiline Nidoish. His house was described as

> *quite a palace compared with the usual run of Western Polynesian native abodes. It
> is a stone house of two stories, with French windows which open out to a verandah
> and balcony in front. The interior fittings, such as the staircase, are not quite
> complete, and several of the rooms are still unfurnished. The furniture is of plain
> deal; and upstairs, or rather, up a ladder, is a great four-poster bed.*[75]

Such buildings which sprang up at Ro and Netche indicated to Europeans a
level of civilisation unprecedented in the southwest Pacific and English
vessels in particular flocked to northern Mare adding to the material
prosperity of the chief and his people.

Naisiline and the LMS missionaries appreciated well the benefits of
mutual exploitation. The chiefship was strengthened through association
with the mission, and the missionaries' influence amongst the Si Gwahma
was very considerable because the chief so decreed. Naisiline and his
missionaries drew up a series of laws. Such offences as theft, adultery,
failure to attend church or obey chiefs and missionaries were punishable by
hard labour and imprisonment. Young toughs were formed into a police
force. Naisiline became autocratic and the only people with the potential to
oppose him—the nobility—chose instead to support him to gain their

share of the new material prosperity and influence. They soon were amongst the more ardent advocates of the new religion and so maintained and increased their authority within the social hierarchy.

While Christianity was imposed on the population from above, it is unlikely that such dramatic changes in behaviour and lifestyle could have occurred had the majority of the Si Gwahma actively opposed them. The influence of the LMS mission and Naisiline was based on more than just political opportunism and coercion. Christianity and its trappings quickly became a dominant popular force in the north of Mare. There was a genuine and even aggressive enthusiasm for wearing clothes, church going, singing hymns, reciting catechisms, learning to read and write. Baptism and church membership added to an individual's identity and dignity, and competition was very keen for the necessary instruction. A position in the church administration was a wonderful opportunity for social advancement. The mission was also closely associated with the technological apparatus of the European world. Metal implements such as fish-hooks, saws, and axes lightened the burdens of everyday living, and were also symbols of status. Nor should the sheer entertainment value of church activity be underestimated. The missionaries organised various sports and feast days which enabled orators to show off their skills, while young men and women threw spears at targets, played cricket, marched in flag-waving processions, and at night watched magic-lantern shows and fireworks. There was an element of fun in being a Christian.

Rival chiefs, rival faiths

The new Christian ways were apparent only in Si Gwahma territory. The Si Gwahma's enemies steadfastly refused to have anything to do with missionaries since to do so would be seen as a sign of submission to 'Naisiline's religion'. And they were right, for when Naisiline had entrenched his régime in his own lands he eyed his 'heathen' opponents. Calling himself the 'Chief of Jehovah', Naisiline with mission backing led his 'Christian soldiers' on a series of successful raids from 1860. The two missionaries were delighted. 'The Christians are encouraged having *right & light* on their side.' One Si Gwahma warrior acted 'very scripturally', they said, for he emulated David and decapitated a fallen enemy. The defeated tribes rapidly opted for Christianity, as did their fearful neighbours, before Naisiline descended upon them again. The Si Gwahma Christianised most of Mare by the sword. Mission reports were wildly enthusiastic about so many 'heathens' now 'sitting at the feet of Jesus' (and Naisiline) though the missionaries were well aware that 'their hearts are not converted'.[76] The missionaries organised a coronation in 1862 and Naisiline was hailed as king of Mare. But it was a premature gesture. Some small tribal groups in the far south and east of the island called upon the Marist missionaries now settled on the Isle of Pines. The lines of battle were clearly drawn. Naisiline and the LMS ruled more than half of the island and controlled some two-thirds of its population. Their Protestant armies faced a small French Catholic–supporting force in the south and east. Naisiline trounced his enemies several times but could not make them change their newly adopted religion, and the French government now based on the New Caledonian mainland stepped in from 1864 onward to stop tribal fighting and foil the schemes of the English-supporting chief. Toward the end of the century the remaining English Protestant missionary was expelled by the French and the more troublesome chiefs were exiled.

This pattern was repeated on the two remaining islands—Lifu and Uvea. There was initial aggressive support for the LMS Polynesian teachers by some of the more astute chiefs. Their enemies were equally aggressive in their rejection of these people and sought the assistance of the French Catholic (Marist) missionaries. They arrived on Uvea in 1857 and Lifu 1858. English Protestant (LMS) missionaries hastily arrived on Lifu in 1859 and Uvea in 1864. In the 1860s all the inhabitants of these islands were practising Christians with the LMS and Marist missionaries well established in their respective tribal regions—the Protestants being numerically dominant on Lifu, and Catholics predominant on Uvea. Long-standing tribal hostilities on the two islands continued and were intensified as 'wars of religion' until the French government on New Caledonia managed to stop them by the presence of warships as well as the exiling of the more belligerent chiefs and missionaries (both LMS and Marist). If the fighting ended, religious division and rivalry did not. Even today the Islanders are still divided into (French) Protestant and Catholic spheres almost identical to the divisions created in the 1860s.

The nature of the chiefly, hierarchical societies together with pre-European precedents for assimilating and making use of newcomers and their ideas was fundamental to the success of the Christian missions on the Loyalty Islands. For most of the Islanders, the decision to become either Catholic or Protestant was initially made for them by their chief, who chose the faith he believed could best help him regain, defend, maintain, or extend his authority. But this exploitation was not solely the preserve of the Islanders. The relationship between chiefs and missionaries was a symbiotic one. Both played power politics. As one LMS missionary explained: 'Having secured the favour of the king, you were not only safe, but the gospel became popular, and multitudes attended services who would not have dared to be present, if the king had expressed his disapprobation.'[77] Both Marist and LMS missionaries made no secret of the fact that much of their political appeal lay in their mutual hatred and not in the merits of their respective theologies. The war between Catholic and Protestant Islanders, wrote one missionary, 'is not a religious one, it is an old feud, but being at enmity on land and chiefs' matters, each party has chosen to be opposite in religion also.' Another described how 'Catholics and Protestants live apart, have few relations with each other; it is less religion than questions of chiefships and territories that divide them.'[78]

THE ISLE OF PINES

The rule of Touru

The LMS reached the Isle of Pines in 1840 where they met its single ruler, Touru. The population of the island was about one thousand, all of whom spoke one language. The people had the same social and political organisation as on the Loyalty Islands; indeed Touru was a descendant of a Lifuan who generations earlier had founded a dynasty on the Isle of Pines. The Isle of Pines men were renowned as warriors and with their large Tongan-inspired canoes collected tribute from regions in southern New Caledonia. They also maintained family links with Mareans and Lifuans. The LMS saw that if they could gain Touru's support, the island would be theirs. The chief readily allowed two Samoan teachers to stay with him and when the LMS vessel returned the following year he had 'formally introduced Christianity' and his people paid due attention to the 'outward forms of religion'. However, the missionaries were somewhat uneasy about Touru's 'tyranny', his fifty wives, and the fact that he clearly supported Christianity as a means of 'obtaining property and adding to his own influence and importance'.[79]

But such influence and importance soon came from another source—the sandalwood traders who raced to the Isle of Pines in the early 1840s. When the missionaries visited the island in 1842 they found that their Samoans had left on sandalwood vessels and Touru's 'attention, and that of his people, were entirely diverted from religion to matters far more congenial to the human heart.'[80] However, it was more than simple diversion. The Samoans had enraged Touru by their refusal to kowtow to him as local custom demanded, and then, during an epidemic, they declared that Jehovah was punishing the people for their refusal to believe in him. The Samoans fled for their lives on a passing ship. Touru was also not very happy with the 'bad' behaviour of some of the sandalwood traders. To vent his rage he captured the vessel *Star*, ironically on its way from Sydney to Samoa with the two refugee Samoan teachers on board. Everyone on the ship was killed.[81] Other vessels were then attacked and the traders and the LMS kept away from the island for some time.

Coming to terms

Touru died in the mid-1840s. His successor, Watchioum, decided that Europeans should be accommodated rather than attacked and he once again established friendly relations with the sandalwood traders, especially James Paddon. Paddon now made regular visits to the Isle of Pines from his station at Aneityum. His rival, Robert Towns, maintained a permanent wood-collecting base on the Isle of Pines from 1849 to 1854.[82] Paddon was responsible for bringing missionaries back to the island. First he offered to reconcile the LMS missionaries visiting Aneityum with the new Isle of Pines chief but they were still too wary. Next, Paddon introduced Bishop Selwyn, then chaplain on the *Dido*, to Watchioum. Selwyn was impressed with the prospects for a mission but was in no position at this stage to take advantage of them. Paddon approached the Marists, who were suffering so badly from malaria, near his station on Aneityum. They did not hesitate and in 1848 Paddon landed some of them on the Isle of Pines. Paddon introduced them to Watchioum who agreed to accept them.[83] Free from the scourge of malaria, a small mission led by Prosper Goujon quietly and carefully cultivated his friendship, and, after his death in 1850, that of his successor Kaua Vendegu. The Marist's position was further strengthened after France annexed New Caledonia in 1853 and French warships became a common sight around the Isle of Pines. The French then raised their flag on the island in 1854. Vendegu was converted to Catholicism on his deathbed in 1855.

One of Vendegu's uncles, opposed to the priests and the French, took advantage of a weak regent and organised a small rebellion. A French corvette soon put it down and mass conversion to Catholicism followed soon afterward. From then on there was never any question that the island with its small, homogeneous, and politically unified population would become thoroughly influenced by Catholic and French concerns.

NEW CALEDONIA

Early LMS ventures

Mainland New Caledonians were rather less easily converted to Christianity than their neighbours on the Loyalty Islands and Isle of Pines, and the story of missionary endeavour and New Caledonian responses is much less clear cut. The mainland was a more populous place—perhaps thirty thousand people lived there—and divisions between and amongst tribes were extremely complex. In addition the mountainous terrain and some fifteen or more languages made missionary operations more difficult.

The ubiquitous LMS vessel made fleeting contact with New

Caledonians at Port St Vincent on the west coast in 1840. But the Samoan teachers they wanted to land there refused to go ashore because they thought the Islanders were too fierce looking. The next year the LMS set down two teachers at Tuauru in the south, in lands owing tribute to Touru of the Isle of Pines. Touru opposed this move since at this stage he wanted a monopoly over relations with missionaries. However the two teachers found a ready reception from local chiefs, and the following year, 1843, the LMS landed another teacher, Ta'unga. This Rarotongan spent the next three years in the region and left a valuable account of local customs (which he despised) and of his trials and tribulations.[84] His host community was constantly harassed both by its mainland enemies and by Touru's warriors. In 1845 the LMS removed him and other teachers from imminent danger and transferred them to the now very promising Loyalty Islands. A visit to Tuauru the next year confirmed the wisdom of the LMS withdrawal for the area had been laid waste by Touru. The LMS, thinking that mainland New Caledonia offered much the same misfortunes as the New Hebrides, never returned.

Early Marist ventures

Farther to the north the Marists ran into similar difficulties. In 1843 Bishop Douarre arrived on a French warship to establish a mission at Balade, chosen because Cook and D'Entrecasteaux had put a name to that part of the map.[85] The presence of the warship initially gave the Marists some prestige (and power) in the eyes of the local tribe—the Puma. But as soon as the vessel left the Marists were seen as materially poor and powerless. The Puma treated them with indifference and sometimes hostility.[86] The Marists were often prisoners in their own huts, poverty stricken, and invariably short of food. After almost two years in such a plight a series of visits from French warships loaded with supplies saw their prestige soar. Some Islanders attended prayer meetings, presumably in the hope of getting some of the new provisions. In 1847 the Marists took advantage of intertribal ties and started another station further down the coast at Puébo. But the promise of expansion was illusory. A raging epidemic and subsequent famine saw the Islanders take their anger out on the priests. The Balade station was abandoned after one lay brother was killed. The rest of the Marists fled to Puébo, where they were similarly attacked, and were rescued by the timely arrival of a French warship. The commander then punished the people of Balade and Puébo with bombardments.

In spite of such setbacks, the Marists still viewed New Caledonia with some hope, unlike their forbidding fields in the Solomons and the New Hebrides. New Caledonia was, in their opinion, a major centre of population in the southwest Pacific and as yet the hated English Protestants had not gained a foothold. Furthermore, there was some indication that some chiefs were at times favourably disposed to accepting Marists, like Bwarat at Hienghène,[87] if only because of the promise of material gain or the presumed threat of French warships that occasionally sailed about the island. At least there *were* chiefs on New Caledonia, and if their support and protection could be won, missionaries would be far better off than they could ever be in the Solomons or the New Hebrides.

Bwarat and other chiefs were in a tricky situation with regard to the French warships. English sandalwood and other traders were the main European presence and influence in the region and English warships made more visits. Bwarat invited Marists to set up a mission at Hienghène in 1849. Bishop Douarre accepted his offer but was repelled by Bwarat's alleged cannibalism and, believing the Islanders were about to attack the mission, recalled his priests from Hienghène after only a month. Bwarat again asked for priests in 1853, but then changed his mind, presumably on English advice, before the Marists arrived. The official Marist view of Bwarat was that he was 'friend to the English, was hostile to the French' and a 'redoubtable defender of all savage practices, and enemy of civilisation'.[88]

The Marists felt much more confident returning to their old stations at Balade in 1851 and Puébo in 1852, where the local chiefs seemed keen to receive them. Yet again actual mission presence was treated with indifference or hostility. Mission prospects seemed bleak. Ironically, the absence of English Protestant missionaries on New Caledonia hindered Marist influence. Had such Englishmen settled amongst some tribes, Marists would have been eagerly supported by rival communities, as had happened on the Loyalty Islands. The mainland was also different from the Isle of Pines where there was just one principal chief to deal with. However, a new complexion was suddenly placed on the rather precarious Marist footholds in New Caledonia when the island was annexed by France in 1853.

The French administration

Whatever the differences in long-term goals between Marists and those responsible for France's policies in the Pacific islands, cooperation between them had usually been close. A common nationality was a unifying force in such remote areas, especially in the face of so much English presence. French naval commanders and Marist missionaries generally supported each other where they could. French annexation of New Caledonia was welcomed by the Marists who believed that they would now have a measure of security. And they rejoiced that there was no possibility of the French administration allowing English Protestant missionaries onto the island.[89]

Relations between government officials and Marists at first ran smoothly. French governors, always short of resources and personnel and eking out a rather tenuous existence with a small military garrison at Port de France, or Noumea, welcomed Marist presence in the remoter regions for they believed that it had a civilising and pacifying role. For their part, the Marists usually supported government actions including military forays against rebellious tribes since a subdued community made mission work easier. New Caledonian chiefs were well aware of the implications of this cooperation. Marists were able to open several new stations amidst welcoming tribes around the island. Other chiefs were more suspicious of the Marists and refused to accept them, though they made sure that they stayed on good terms with the government. A few chiefs actively opposed both mission and administration presence. In the late 1850s and early 1860s a number of loose tribal coalitions became involved in a series of wars. Government officials and missionaries assumed that this fighting amounted to rebellion against colonial influence. In fact the fighting was not inspired by anti-government or anti-missionary ambitions but was essentially a continuation of long-standing intertribal animosity. However, as in the Loyalty Islands, new European influences were readily integrated into existing hostilities. Some coalitions identified themselves as mission and government supporters while others rejected these labels.

The French authorities tended to have the advantage in the long run precisely because the conflicts were more between island factions than between Islanders and Frenchmen. Divide and rule with military reprisals or the threat of them became the order of the day for the governors. Some tribes became meekly submissive immediately; others were beaten into obedience. Hostile chiefs were usually deposed or exiled—Bwarat for example ended up in Tahiti—and chiefly contenders loyal to France were put in their places. The Marists reaped the benefits and by the early 1860s they were established amidst many formerly hostile communities. Even so, the missionary situation was still far from being as stable as it was on the Isle of Pines and the Loyalty Islands. From 1863 until 1870 New Caledonia was ruled by Governor Guillain who was an ardent anticleric and who harassed missionaries and tried to destroy their 'political' influence with the tribes. Chiefs loyal to the administration but anti-Christian were given every support. Tribal rivalries were again exploited by both European and Islander. Governors after Guillain usually followed a pro-missionary or neutral policy but by then relations between many New Caledonians and Frenchmen had been thoroughly soured by Guillain's and his successors' policies of compulsory acquisition of land and the resettling of defeated rebellious tribes on reservations. One consequence was major tribal uprisings against the government in 1878.[90] These were savagely put down by the French and, in the longer term, the Marists benefited. Defeated, demoralised, and government reorganised tribes were more likely to accept missionaries. By the late nineteenth century New Caledonians were forced to acknowledge that for the time being their island was undisputedly controlled by Frenchmen. Acceptance of the Catholic church was a significant aspect of this recognition.

Denouement

While missionary progress on mainland New Caledonia differed in many respects from that on the Loyalty Islands and Isle of Pines, particularly with regard to French government presence, there was still one basic common element—Christian influence infiltrated all these places through its association with chiefs or would-be chiefs who led hierarchical, tribal organisations. Whether this infiltration resulted mainly from the Islanders' initiatives as happened on the Loyalty Islands and Isle of Pines, or from manipulation by both Islander and European interests as on the mainland, the fact that communities were socially and politically organised in this way meant that Christianity of whatever brand could readily become a major influence in indigenous life in the early contact period. In addition, these Islanders' attitudes to foreigners, together with the rather more benign climate (as far as Europeans were concerned), further enabled missionaries to establish levels of comfort and security that were never achieved in the Solomons or the New Hebrides. Missionaries and their teachings were for all these reasons very much more relevant to the peoples of New Caledonia and dependencies. In contrast, Solomon Islanders and New Hebrideans, who had rather different social and political institutions, many more languages, and islands that by European standards were very unhealthy, saw little worth in what consequently was often a rather wretched mission presence.

15

Trade frontiers

At the same time as missionaries ventured into Melanesia, from the early 1840s, so too did a number of traders. And just as missionaries were forced to take account of the many new and different circumstances in these isles, so too were those in search of wealth.

SANDALWOOD

The rush and reaction

Edward Foxall spied sandalwood whilst he was a crew member on the LMS vessel visiting the Isle of Pines in 1841.[1] He told nobody until he reached Sydney where he sold his news to some merchants. They secretly despatched two ships and found that the island was indeed rich in the timber. Its chief, Touru, was initially keen to have his subjects cut and carry the wood in return for iron and axes. News of the find could not be kept secret for long on the gossipy Sydney waterfront. Within a few months more than a dozen vessels had 'secretly' sailed from New South Wales bound for the Isle of Pines. It soon became common knowledge that sandalwood was also plentiful on neighbouring New Caledonia and the Loyalty Islands, and on most of the islands in the southern New Hebrides. The rush was on, in spite of the publicity about John Williams's murder by the savages of this region. The prospects of quick profits overrode misgivings. Sydney merchants were only too keen to chance hostile Islanders and uncharted waters to take advantage of certain fortuitous circumstances: the price of sandalwood at Canton was very high in the early 1840s and the former major source of supply, Hawaii, had long been depleted. Furthermore, the East India Company's monopoly of the China trade had now disappeared, and the islands of southern Melanesia were but a few days sail from Sydney.

It was not long before the potential dangers became all too real. Early in 1842 five of the *Martha's* boat crew were murdered off Mare's eastern coast. Shortly afterward Touru of the Isle of Pines started attacking sandalwood vessels in retaliation for epidemics that had swept his island. He captured the *Star*, killing the sixteen crew and five passengers. The next year he captured the *Catherine*, which was retaken after one of the crew managed to set fire to some powder casks literally blowing off the top half of the vessel, maiming about fifty of the captors. Burnt to the waterline, the *Catherine* limped back to Sydney.[2] Traders steered clear of the Isle of Pines until after Touru's death in the mid-1840s when his successors once more encouraged peaceful trading.

Sensational publicity in New South Wales newspapers about such violent clashes between traders and Islanders was then refocused on Mare. In 1843 nine of the *Brigand's* crew were killed on the orders of Chief Yiewene of the Si Gwahma. Several weeks later the master of the *Sisters* had an argument with Yiewene and took to him with a rope's end. This was a monstrous act in Marean eyes and within seconds the *Sisters'* eleven crew were killed. The ship was stripped and set alight. Yiewene died in 1845 and his successors, like Touru's, encouraged peaceful trading, partly out of fear of retaliation by HMS *Havannah* soon after visiting the island, and partly because they appreciated the economic and political advantages that they might gain. They were also staunch supporters of the London Missionary Society teachers by this stage. Chiefs elsewhere on Mare were less peaceably inclined. They rejected both teachers and traders. Five of a party of seven convicts on the run from Norfolk Island were killed instantly when their boat came ashore. Some years later Mareans captured the *Lucy Ann* and killed the seventeen crew. Although Mare gained the reputation of 'massacre island', a large number of sandalwood traders continued to go there—to the safety of Si Gwahma lands under the protection of the Naisilines.[3] Uvea and Lifu, the other two Loyalty Islands, were not considered as dangerous as much of the Mare coastline though relations between Islanders and early traders were sometimes very tense. Andrew Cheyne who visited Lifu in 1842 left vivid accounts of his experiences.

At 3 P.M. on the 30th A large War canoe came alongside from the other side of the bay, carrying 50 men, they brought a little Sandal Wood but did not seem anxious to sell it, having come apparently for the purpose of taking the schooner; They came on like wild Bulls, and boarded the vessel in spite of us—we drew our men up across the quarter deck two deep while we were buying their wood, and after allowing them to remain on board nearly two Hours, we were at last obliged to charge on them with the bayonets, and drive them overboard. They fought hard for some time but were at last obliged to give way. These Bloodthirsty Villains still seem determined to take us, notwithstanding the lesson they got from us two days ago.

These repeated skirmishes were most harassing both to body and Mind—and kept us in a continual state of excitement as we did not know the moment we might be attacked either night or day, and required us to be constantly on the alert at night, as they would be certain to overpower us, could they catch us off our guard, or asleep.[4]

Cheyne thought that the Uveans were 'milder in their disposition' but still 'treacherous and cruel to the last degree' and most certainly not to be trusted.[5]

Cheyne also had a harrowing time at Balade on the New Caledonian mainland where he and his crew had to drive some three hundred warriors off their vessel.

We then made a rush up the half deck ladder and had to clear a footing on the deck with our bayonets: the crowd being so great at that time, that they had not room to strike with their clubs. As the men got up, they formed back to back across the deck in two divisions, one facing forward, and the other aft. At first the crowd fell back, but being pressed forward by those in the rear, and led on by the chiefs, they made a furious rush upon us, yelling like fiends, and tried to strike the bayonets off our muskets with their clubs, but without making any impression. Our men stood firm with their Muskets at the charge, and received them on the point of the bayonet. In the mean time, blood flowed fast, and the groans of those who fell, began to mingle with the yells of the combatants. At times indeed, the natives obtained a momentary superiority, which was almost immediately lost by a corresponding exertion on our part. After a desperate resistance in which they had many killed and wounded, we managed to clear the quarter deck, and leaving a few men to guard it, we joined the others, and commenced charging the natives at the gangways, amidst showers of spears and clubs thrown at us from all directions.[6]

Nevertheless, sandalwood vessels flocked to New Caledonia after detailed explorations and successful expeditions in the mid-1840s. The wood was a fine quality and many of the chiefs were keen to do business, especially Bwarat of Hienghène who became a staunch supporter of English traders. Yet there were instances of violence too. On at least seven occasions traders and Islanders ended up killing each other.[7]

The southern New Hebrides were generally approached with extreme caution; after all, the previous sandalwood expeditions of 1829–1830 to Eromanga had been a disaster, and John Williams' fate on that same island was fresh in memories. One of the earliest sandalwood expeditions to the New Hebrides in the 1840s consisted of three vessels out from Tahiti. They first called in at Tonga where they hired 67 labourers, led by Ma'afu, who were landed on Eromanga. After a few days, violence flared and one Eromangan and one Tongan were killed. The vessels next transported the Tongans to Efaté where quarrels again broke out. The Tongans shot several Efatese and drove some 60 or 70 others into some caves. They then lit fires and suffocated those inside. News of this incident 'provided missionaries with enough ammunition in their campaign against the traders to last as long as the sandalwood trade itself.'[8] Eromangan sandalwood was so good that traders were prepared to tempt fate, though they took every possible precaution. Cheyne commented that the Eromangans were 'the most barbarous race in the New Hebrides; so much so, that no Europeans have landed from any sandal-wood vessels that have touched at this island.'[9] Instead the Islanders had to swim out through the surf with their wood. But even this strategy was not foolproof. The *Elizabeth*'s boat crew of four were killed in 1845. The *Elizabeth* returned to Eromanga the next year; this time two of her boat crew were murdered. Her stubborn master, W E Jones, still persisted in trading at the island. Eventually in 1844 the *Elizabeth* was wrecked on Eromanga and the four surviving crew were killed when they reached shore. After that there are at least five recorded instances of affrays resulting in the deaths of traders and Eromangans.

The question of violence

The wide publicity given to this violence in Melanesia created the impression that the sandalwood trade was, in missionary J G Paton's oft-quoted words, 'a trade steeped in human blood and indescribable vice.'[10] The most common explanation, perpetrated mainly by the ill-fated missionaries on the New Hebrides, was that sandalwood traders were ruthless brutes, committing the most blatant atrocities in their lust for wood. The poor Islanders, the missionaries argued, naturally tried to protect themselves. Dorothy Shineberg, the revisionist historian of the sandalwood trade, calls this the 'retaliation only' theory. These views still predominate in popular literature. Yet as Shineberg has shown, the traders' notorious reputation has either been taken out of context (often deliberately) or unwittingly accepted in ignorance of other considerations about the trading frontier itself. A close examination of these violent incidents suggests that no one side had a monopoly of virtue and fair play. Just as some of the traders were at times unscrupulous and deceitful, so too were some of the Islanders doing business with them. The Islanders' hostile acts did not invariably result from white depredations—the 'retaliation only' view. Rather these actions resulted from a variety of motives ranging from spontaneous anger or consumer greed to careful plotting, often in the context of local politics. As happened elsewhere in the Pacific islands, early European visitors could become unwittingly embroiled in a web of existing jealousy and conflict.

The 'retaliation only' theory is also challenged by the more obvious fact that traders simply were not in a position to impose their will upon island communities. Their vessels were small, often in poor condition, and had few crew members, perhaps ten or fifteen at most. They were sailing for the most part in very treacherous waters, and had to do business with strange and potentially hostile people. Traders were always uncertain of the reception they might receive, at least in earlier years. Those who would buy sandalwood usually had to land in small boats along the reef-choked coastlines. The Islanders had the advantage of numbers, military strength, and local knowledge. Sandalwood traders did not have the capacity to sail around the New Caledonian and New Hebridean waters as great white predators imposing demands at will or whim. Massacres and brutality were in fact the exception rather than the rule when set against the background of the sandalwood trade in Melanesia as a whole. The thirty or forty recorded incidents of serious violence[11] that dominated publicity about the trade become far less significant in the context of the many thousands of deals between traders and Islanders that took place over several decades. The brutal elements of sandalwood trading in the southwest Pacific were far less prevalent than the anti-trade propaganda claimed. Moreover, there was often a pattern to such violence itself, namely that it was more likely to occur in early trading days at any one location when both sides were inexperienced in dealing with each other. Misunderstandings were likely to lead to conflict. Once trading became commonplace, both trader and Islander saw mutual advantages in cooperation rather than conflict. The Islanders could indeed kill European crews and capture and ransack vessels, but they soon found out that this might drive other vessels away, so depriving themselves of trade goods, or bring retaliation. They soon learnt from experience that most benefit accrued from relatively peaceful dealings, which could still include threats and sharp business practice of every kind. For the traders, few in number and in strange lands amidst potentially hostile communities, it was generally very dangerous to act in a high-handed manner. Most significantly, the traders needed the Islanders to show them where the wood was, cut it, and carry it to the shore. The traders lacked the manpower to find suitable stands of timber, chop it down, and get it out to their ships *and* fight off hostile warriors at the same time. As one trader aptly explained, 'you cannot trade with these people and fight them too.'[12] Violence did not pay.

Even the nature of the traders' presence, at least after the earliest years, indicates that the frontier was not an endless battleground. Many of the more successful sandalwood gatherers lived with the Islanders for months at a time. It became common practice for ships' masters to drop off a trader who arranged for the Islanders to collect timber which was then picked up when the vessel returned weeks or months later. Numerous permanent sandalwood depots were scattered throughout the islands where the wood was prepared and made ready for shipment to Canton. In total, at least two dozen such stations were recorded at various times, on Aneityum, Tana, Eromanga, Espiritu Santo, Isle of Pines, Uvea, and New Caledonia.[13] Several traders married island women; others employed island men and women as servants.

Contact bargaining

Contrary to the popular view that the traders held the whip hand, it was the Islanders of southern Melanesia who were dominant. Even when they had no intention of plundering a sandalwood vessel they were always using their advantage to abuse and threaten traders to push up the price of the wood. Many Europeans frequently bartered with tobacco in one hand and a pistol in the other, especially in earlier years. Even after both sides knew each other well, the Islanders were notorious for their ability to barter and haggle and deceive.

That the Islanders were far from passive and helpless is also demonstrated by their changing demands. Perhaps the Islanders' greatest single advantage was that they had the wood and if the traders wanted it they had to pay the right price. As was common throughout the Pacific islands, only for so long could Europeans get what they wanted by fobbing off trifles. Shineberg has described how the economic demands of New Caledonians and New Hebrideans followed a typical pattern, though its timing naturally varied from place to place.[14] The Islanders first showed a passion for any form of iron and steel, metal fish-hooks, glass beads, bottles, tomahawks, pots, and trinkets of various kinds. As these items glutted local economies, more sophisticated metal tools like scissors and saws were demanded, then tobacco and cloth, and finally 'superior edge-tools' and muskets. On some islands, especially in the New Hebrides, there then followed demands for more customary forms of wealth, especially pigs and certain shells. Traders were kept on their toes, and made great efforts to stock those items that would suit the changing marketplace and keep them ahead of their rivals. It was too bad for a master to arrive with a load of hoop-iron when the local people wanted tobacco, or to arrive with tobacco when the demand was for pigs. The Islanders became increasingly selective too—traders returned to Sydney with tomahawks that were not exactly the sort required, or with tobacco rejected because it was not the best negro-head. Perhaps the best examples of traders going to extreme lengths to satisfy their customers were those who went to the Solomons for tortoise shell, traded it at Tana for pigs, then took these to Espiritu Santo to exchange for sandalwood. Such patterns of supply and demand are ample evidence that commercial dealings between Europeans and Melanesians were based on mutual accommodation of each other's needs.

Economic consequences

It is difficult to examine readily and in detail the consequences of the introduction of these new goods (and in some cases an insurgence of familiar goods too) since the sociopolitical entities are so numerous, diverse, and fragmented, especially in the New Hebrides. Yet some generalisation can be offered.

Islanders in the main sought articles that were essentially substitutes for items of their own culture. Many were not always used as Europeans used them. Bottles were broken and the glass used as a cutting and scraping edge. Chisel blades were removed from handles and lashed onto existing adze handles where they replaced stone blades. Scissors were pulled apart

Pigs for muskets. Tanna. 1870.

32   '*Pigs for muskets. Tanna 1870*'.
    (*Wawn* '*Amongst the Pacific Islands*'. *Alexander Turnbull Library*)

and used as knives or heated and used to bore holes in wood. These new metal tools and artefacts were usually more effective than the wood and stones they replaced, though not necessarily so. The metal fish-hooks that replaced bone and shell ones were no better at catching fish. The real advantage of such European items was that they came ready made and so spared the Islanders months of hard work to produce, for example, their own fish-hooks. If an Islander received a hatchet, he not only did not have to make one out of stone, but perhaps he did not have to travel to or trade with regions where suitable stone was to be found. It was the same when iron pots replaced clay ones, glass beads replaced jade ornaments, European paint replaced pigment dyes, cloth replaced tapa, and dinghies replaced canoes. Not only was the effort of producing the local equivalent no longer necessary, but the Islanders were spared the effort of procuring suitable clay, jade, dyes, mulberry, and timber. In this way the various networks of trade between and amongst many islands of New Caledonia and the New Hebrides were abandoned. The excitement provided by these former journeys was now more readily available thanks to the presence of European shipping in the region.

Trading for European goods resulted in more than simple technological substitution. Even the most basic European artefact was capable of setting in motion a variety of social changes. In addition to the abandonment of local manufacture, European technology meant that more work could be done in less time, especially with the introduction of axes and steel slashers. Areas of bush could be more quickly slashed in preparation for burning off and planting. Huts could be more quickly constructed. Priorities were sometimes modified too. Seasonal cycles of planting, harvesting, and fighting, were now interrupted by year-round trading with Europeans. Sometimes food production, especially of vegetables and pigs, was increased far beyond normal subsistence requirements in order to sell surpluses to traders.[15] There were political consequences too. In New Caledonia and its dependencies, where there were entrenched élites, the more ambitious chiefs were able to aggrandize their powers by monopolising trade, often in association with a Christian mission—as did the Naisilines on Mare, Bula and Wainya on Lifu, Bazit and Whenegay on Uvea, Touru on the Isle of Pines, and Bwarat on New Caledonia.[16] In the New Hebrides, where Big-Men societies were more common, the effects could be similar, or quite the opposite as in the case of a Big-Man whose wealth based on pigs was suddenly eclipsed by underlings who bought greater numbers of pigs from traders.

The introduction of European goods into Melanesia did not cause disruption, but it did contribute to varying degrees of social, economic, and political change. In contrast to many islands in Polynesia, however, changes in lifestyles on Melanesian islands were more often than not localised. There were no leaders like the Kamehamehas and the Pomares to direct and apply such changes to the pursuit of the centralised state.

One item is commonly accused of bringing dramatic change to even the smallest Melanesian communities—the musket. The usual practical difficulties of using muskets in Pacific conditions were encountered here, along with their other technological limitations.[17] In addition, indigenous warfare throughout much of Melanesia was often of a small scale, limited, and sometimes even ritualised. It was still in deadly earnest, but the killing of large numbers of the enemy was not a feature of fighting (and nor did it become so), perhaps reflecting the lack of large political units. Large-scale warfare and mass killing can only be undertaken by leaders who can organize substantial armies. The most effective new weapons adopted throughout Melanesia at this stage were hatchets. Muskets were certainly in demand, but more for their prestige and psychological impact than for their actual killing power.[18]

Overseas travel

Nothing better illustrates the degree to which the Islanders willingly participated in the sandalwood trade than their eagerness to work for and travel with traders, so repeating what Islanders in the central and eastern

Pacific had been doing for decades. Even by the mid-1840s virtually every sandalwood vessel in the region had Islanders aboard as crews, indulging, said Erskine, their 'love of wandering'.[19] Loyalty Islanders, men from the Isle of Pines, Eromangans, Tanese, quickly developed the reputation of being excellent sailors and were sought by ships' masters. This trend intensified in the 1850s when the gold rushes in Australia caused a shortage of European labour in the islands. In addition large numbers of Islanders, hundreds in many cases, were employed on the sandalwood stations scattered throughout the region. There was even a flourishing system of migrant labour in southern Melanesian waters as entrepreneurs like Henry Burns, Andrew Henry, Hugh Mair, and James Paddon gathered labourers from their various islands and took them to sandalwood depots. Paddon was attributed with being

> *the first to work out the principle that, in order to get natives to work well, you must take them away from their own island, and leave them entirely dependent on their employer for food. He also adopted ... [the] plan of bringing them in limited numbers from different islands, so that they could not combine against their employer.*[20]

Many Islanders went far beyond Melanesian waters. Sandalwood vessels going to Canton were often crewed by them. Three-quarters of Burns's vessels *Cheetah*, *Vulture*, *Coquette*, and *Adolphus Yates* were crewed by Loyalty Islanders. Likewise, many travelled to Sydney with the traders. Robert Towns employed them on his wharves there as early as 1842. Others crossed the Pacific to California on whalers.[21]

Local produce trade

As Sydney-based sandalwood traders became more familiar with southern Melanesia, they discovered other products apart from sandalwood. Soon they were gathering bêche-de-mer and pearl shell around New Caledonia and the New Hebrides and moving on to the Barrier Reef and Torres Strait, again employing island labour. However this trade was soon overshadowed by a burgeoning commerce in island produce stimulated by the French annexation of New Caledonia in 1853 and the founding and rapid growth of Noumea.

French administrators were at once keen to find suitable products both for local consumption and, more importantly, as exports to help pay for the necessarily high level of imports for their new colony. They soon discovered considerable wealth in yams and other vegetables as well as pigs and fowls, particularly on the Loyalty Islands and the southern New Hebrides. Fleets of small vessels, licensed by the government, plied two principal routes out from Port de France—a shorter one taking in bays on the New Caledonian mainland, the Loyalty Islands, and the Isle of Pines, and a larger circuit encompassing the New Hebrides. Englishmen, who dominated New Caledonian commerce throughout the remainder of the century, owned most of the vessels, many of which had been employed earlier in the sandalwood trade. As with that enterprise, most continued to be 'principally manned' by Melanesians, particularly Loyalty Islanders, who took 'service on the understanding that they ... [were] to be returned to their own country at some future time'.[22] It was also not 'an uncommon practice for captains (white men) of small crafts plying up and down the east coast of Nouvelle Calédonie, to take unto themselves Mare or Lifu women for wives':

> *These women are, as a rule, massive, well built, and, notwithstanding a few tattooed lines on their faces, pleasant looking. They know how to splice a rope, and to take the tiller when required; they are most useful to their mates, and behave in a more creditable manner than many of the dusky females from other Pacific Islands do ... South Sea Island women, even if they are ornamental, must be useful; and white men who live with them reckon their value according as they display plenty of 'savey' as well as personal attractiveness.*[23]

Origins of labour trading

It was inevitable that with their desire to travel and participate actively in these various maritime ventures, the Islanders of southern Melanesia would sooner or later be seen as potential labourers for European farmers and planters. Benjamin Boyd, one of New South Wales's more controversial entrepreneurs and graziers, recruited some 150 Islanders from the Loyalty Islands, New Hebrides, and southern Gilberts in several expeditions in 1847. His intention was to employ them as agricultural labourers on his properties at Deniliquin in central-southern New South Wales. However more than half of his recruits refused to go beyond the New South Wales seaboard. Those who did march the 480 kilometres inland took one look at the forbidding Riverina landscape and promptly walked back to Sydney. Boyd was an unpopular figure and his enemies accused him of flooding the colony with 'unreclaimed savages' whom they claimed he had kidnapped. The allegation of kidnapping was investigated by the New South Wales government and easily proven false. Though the Islanders had no idea of what Boyd wanted them for, they had been only too willing to accompany him to the colony. All Boyd's recruits, who by now wanted to go home, were eventually repatriated on mission and other vessels.[24]

French colonists on New Caledonia in the 1850s were next to try recruiting southern Melanesians for farm work and after 1860 the French administration assisted them. Much of the recruiting was carried out by former sandalwood traders like the Englishman Andrew Henry. Most of the labourers came from the New Hebrides. Loyalty Islanders preferred working for Englishmen and certainly wanted to go further afield than New Caledonia.

Sandalwood in retrospect

By the 1850s the sandalwood market in China had slumped, and the best timber had been depleted on New Caledonia and the southern New Hebrides. Those traders still in business tended to look farther afield, to the northern New Hebrides, especially Espiritu Santo, and when supplies there eventually ran out in the early 1860s the Melanesian sandalwood trade came to an end.

While it lasted, the trade was of major importance to New Caledonians and New Hebrideans. It was the principal agency by which the European world and particularly its technology was first introduced into the region. Furthermore, sandalwood traders enabled Islanders to travel far beyond their homes, to meet other Islanders, and to go to New South Wales and beyond. Traders also introduced notions of contract labour on board vessels, on other islands, and in New South Wales. New Caledonians and New Hebrideans were thus familiar with labour recruiting two decades before the Melanesian labour trade commenced in earnest. At the same time, plantation owners in Australian colonies and Fiji whose enterprises expanded rapidly in the 1860s knew where to turn for a vast pool of labour.

LABOUR

The labour trade in history

From its beginnings in the 1860s until it ended early in the twentieth century, the Melanesian labour trade for Queensland and Fiji cotton and then sugar plantations employed well over 100 000 Islanders, mostly males aged between sixteen and twenty-five, and mostly from the New Hebrides and the Solomon Islands. More specifically, some 1100 Loyalty Islanders, 18 000 Solomon Islanders, 40 000 New Hebrideans, and 2800 New Guineans were indentured in Queensland. Figures for Fiji are less detailed, but include some 10 000 Solomon Islanders; the total number of Islanders taken to Fiji from 1877–1911 was 22 000. In addition there was some recruiting of Melanesians for plantations in other countries. Several thousand New Hebrideans and less than 1000 Solomon Islanders were recruited for New Caledonia, some 2000 Solomon Islanders went to Samoa, and 550 New Hebrideans were taken to Hawaii.[25]

If the sandalwood trade in Melanesia has had a bad press, the labour trade or 'blackbirding' as it is more commonly called, has had an atrocious one. There is a vast body of published literature dating from the 1870s to the present that condemns it as an exercise in cold-blooded kidnapping, a Pacific islands version of the earlier trans-Atlantic slave trade. Julius Brenchley wrote after a cruise on HMS *Curaçoa* in 1865:

> *What a hideous emblem of our civilisation is that bloodstained vessel throwing out, like the fangs of a grim monster, its grappling-irons to clutch and upset the canoes of the unsuspecting natives, then sending its boats to pick up such of them as had not made for land, or were not drowned; hustling and closely packing them in its hold, and, when its captives, driven mad by excitement and suffering, quarrelled among themselves, firing shot upon shot at them through the hatches during the night, killing and wounding seventy; and finally, when morning broke, throwing the dead and the wounded fastened to one another into the sea! Surely if there were felt but a hundredth part of the interest in the fate of the Polynesian that was once, and is still, taken in the fate of the African, there would have been a shout of indignant remonstrance from one end of the land to the other. But where now is the Anti-Slavery Society? Where is the really benevolent Society of Friends? Where is there the slightest flash of that frenzy of indignation not long since exhibited in the case of the Jamaica black?*[26]

More than a hundred years later many writers are no less vitriolic in their assessment of labour recruiting in Melanesia.[27] But just as modern Pacific historians have revised interpretations of the sandalwood trade, so have they done so for the labour trade, particularly Peter Corris and Deryck Scarr.[28] That there were instances of kidnapping is not denied, nor is the often considerable violence associated with recruiting brushed aside. But when put into an overall context of recruiting activities and the responses of the peoples of Melanesia over a fifty-year period, the labour trade, like the sandalwood trade, appears as more of a cooperative venture than one dominated by either side.

Recruiting in the Loyalty Islands and the New Hebrides

Recruiting vessels from Queensland and Fiji went first to those now relatively well known regions of Melanesia where traders had been operating for up to twenty years and where the Islanders had long been in the habit of working and travelling with Europeans—the southern New Hebrides and the Loyalty Islands (the mainland of New Caledonia, now a French colony, was left alone). From 1863 until 1872 some 4300 New Hebrideans and 1100 Loyalty Islanders were officially indentured on Queensland's cotton fields, and from 1864 until 1869, another 1647 labourers, mostly New Hebrideans, went to Fiji.[29] Vessels in search of labour for Fijian and Samoan plantations also ventured to the Gilbert and

Ellice Islands in the 1860s, but men from these islands proved too prone to sickness and too intractable for plantation life.[30]

The flurry of recruiting activity around the New Hebrides and the Loyalty Islands in the 1860s drew vigorous opposition from some missionary societies and other humanitarian groups. Accusations of deception, kidnapping, and cruelty on the part of the recruiters were commonplace. Two incidents in particular raised a storm of protest. When the *Young Australian* was at Api Island in the New Hebrides in 1868 some of her crew shot and threw overboard three Islanders who tried to escape from the vessel.[31] The master, Albert Hovell, and a crew member were eventually sentenced to death, though this was commuted to life imprisonment. Captain Palmer of HMS *Rosario* then came across Ross Lewin's *Daphne* at Fiji fitted out like a slave ship:

> *We found her a small schooner of forty-eight tons register, fitted up precisely like an African slaver,* minus *the irons, with 100 natives on board, who had been brought from the New Hebrides, having experienced the pleasure of a dead beat to windward for twenty-one days; they were stark naked, and had not even a mat to lie upon; the shelves were just the same as might be knocked up for a lot of pigs,—no bunks or partitions of any sort being fitted* ...[32]

This activity was invariably associated in many minds with the horrific slave raids of the Peruvians a few years earlier, in 1862–1863. Peruvian vessels had scoured the smaller and low islands from Easter Island across to the Gilberts (without reaching Melanesia) and captured some 3500 people, often in particularly brutal ways. Such was the Islanders' suffering and extremely high death rate that such 'recruiting' soon came to an end. Only 148 Islanders were successfully repatriated; the remainder died. Even more seriously, those who returned brought with them smallpox, which decimated many of their home communities.[33]

In order to placate opposition to recruiting in Melanesia, and to make sure it was not a repetition of the Peruvian experiment, the Queensland authorities in 1868 passed the Polynesian Labourers Act which was the first of a series of colonial and imperial legislation designed to regulate labour recruiting. But the protests continued and as well the Noumean administration complained to British authorities about vessels out from Australian colonies taking away Loyalty Islanders whom it considered French subjects. In 1869 the New South Wales government established a royal commission to investigate 'certain alleged cases of kidnapping' from the Loyalty Islands and the New Hebrides. A wide range of witnesses including government officials, traders, missionaries, and some of the recruits themselves were interviewed. Considerable attention was drawn to the Islanders' 'migratory disposition', and to the previous twenty years of recruiting activity about their islands. The commission stressed the point that far from being poor, ignorant wretches forced into slavery in

Queensland and Fiji by unscrupulous traffickers in black ivory, as the trade's critics claimed, many of the inhabitants of the southern Melanesian islands had been in the habit of signing contracts, travelling and working on European vessels, and labouring for Europeans since the early 1840s. Indeed, many of the Queensland and Fijian recruiting vessels themselves were manned by Melanesian crews. Since recruiting for plantation labour had flourished as a business from the mid-1860s, the commission found that there had been some isolated incidents of deception and kidnapping—concerning the *Daphne* and the *Young Australian* in particular—but that these were by no means typical of the trade as a whole.[34] Even many missionaries on the islands who deplored the system of indentured labour had to admit that most Islanders sailed away of their own free will. This was particularly true of the LMS and Marist missionaries on the Loyalty Islands who certainly made no complaints about kidnapping. On the contrary they wrote about the young men's 'great rage, almost a mania' for emigration to Queensland; 'there is always a frenzy to leave for Sidni', they said. Some Islanders lit fires at night to attract passing vessels; others swam far offshore and begged captains to let them aboard. These missionaries were also convinced that these young men left 'with their eyes open'.[35] They willingly signed the contracts binding them to three years' work on plantations in return for £6 per year. But many missionaries in the New Hebrides complained bitterly about kidnapping. This apparent contradiction of views between Loyalty Islands and New Hebrides missionaries, which initially confused people like Captain Palmer, is easily explained. Where Marist and LMS missionaries on the Loyalty Islands were glorying in their religious successes, the Presbyterian missionaries in the New Hebrides had not only failed to convert Islanders but were in great danger for their lives. These missionaries saw labour recruiting as a scapegoat for their miserable fortunes, just as they had blamed sandalwood trading earlier on. The vehemence of their opposition to the labour trade and the effective publicity they generated has left the false impression that all missionaries in the southwest Pacific were arch opponents of labour re-cruiting, which they branded as kidnapping. But missionaries elsewhere, in less dire circumstances, believed no such thing. Such was the precarious situation of the Presbyterians in the New Hebrides that they really had little knowledge of what was happening on their islands, though they had very strong views as to what they *thought* was taking place. Furthermore, some of the most outspoken critics had never visited this part of the world at all. There is every evidence that New Hebrideans responded as enthusiastically to the recruiters as did Loyalty Islanders. Eye-witness accounts paint a picture that could hardly be interpreted as kidnapping and slavery. For example, one recruiter at Tana in 1870 'found the hearts of all the men hardened against the idea of emigration to Queensland, so long had elapsed since they had seen their countrymen who had gone before.' Yet when

33   Labour recruiting in the New Hebrides.
(Photo from New Hebrides Album, *vol 1. Dixson Library, Sydney)*

these same men appeared on deck and were reunited with their kin ashore and told of their experiences,

> *a good many of the young men joined me; and as soon as their intention to leave the island was known, there was a general rush of all the women to stop them. Some . . . yielded to female influence, but most of them, indignant at being treated as children, and perhaps afraid of being laughed at by the boat's crew, insisted on getting into the boat [and signing contracts].*[36]

The royal commission of 1869 concluded

> *. . . the strongest desire is manifested by the natives, both of the Loyalty and New Hebrides Groups, to leave their homes, either to serve on board English ships, or to labour on the plantations of Queensland; and that any attempt to kidnap them would be not only unnecessary, but most impolitic, and even dangerous.*[37]

Kidnapping in the Solomons

Labour recruiting around the Loyalty Islands ended in the early 1870s mainly because most people willing and able to go to Queensland had already done so, and because the French authorities in New Caledonia now effectively claimed the Loyalty Islands as French territory. Recruiting in the southern and central New Hebrides also began to tail off from the 1870s because many Islanders were driving too hard a bargain. Recruiters out from Fiji were at a particular disadvantage since wages were half those being offered in Queensland. There was some movement of recruiting operations to the northern New Hebrides where there had been relatively little contact with the West so far. But by then recruiting ships from both Fiji and Queensland were pushing into the untapped labour source in the Solomon Islands. After the 1880s the Solomon Islands became the principal supplier of labour for Queensland and Fiji, providing about one-third of all the peoples of Melanesia who were so indentured.

The Solomons, when first visited by labour vessels in 1870, had seen very little European presence. Whalers and bêche-de-mer traders had frequented some harbours from the 1840s but overall European influence was negligible. Like the sandalwood traders who first ventured around New Caledonia and the New Hebrides in the 1840s, the labour traders entering the Solomons in the early 1870s were in unknown and dangerous regions. Again, the potential for misunderstandings and violence in the Solomons as Islander and European first met was considerable, especially since the recruiters' prime purpose was to take Islanders away from their homes.

Solomon Islanders initially had no idea of what recruiters wanted. Some were enticed aboard and willingly agreed to sail away, though they had no idea of where they were going, or why, or for how long. Invariably these people had to be locked below to prevent them from leaping overboard when they saw their islands disappearing below the horizon. In other cases, Islanders were forced aboard. The early 1870s in the Solomons were marked with numerous instances of spectacular brutality and much of the trade's evil reputation stems from some of the more publicised incidents. The crew of the *Carl*, for example, travelled through the Solomons running down canoes or holing them with lumps of iron. Ropes were lowered to the helpless swimmers who were then assisted aboard and forced below. Those who resisted were shot. Other vessels known to have operated after this fashion were the *Emma Bell* and the *Nukulau*, and there were many others. Reports of 'massacres' filtered back to the colonies. Even apparently innocent visitors were in danger at this time. Bishop Patteson was killed at Nukapu allegedly to avenge the *Emma Bell*'s kidnapping there. But, like the perpetrators of the massacres and violence associated with the earlier sandalwood trade farther south, Solomon Islanders sometimes attacked recruiting vessels for their own reasons.

Changing patterns of response

Peter Corris has argued that this period of kidnapping or 'blackbirding' in the early 1870s soon came to an end for two reasons. First, moved by public outcries over real or imagined atrocities, and under pressure from the British government, Queensland and Fiji authorities adopted various measures to regulate the trade and control its worst excesses.[38] Recruiters and their vessels had to be licensed and have government agents on board. Employers had to pay ten guineas for each recruit to cover his care, return fare, and salaries of the agents. Such regulations were wide open to abuse and the lowly paid agents were commonly addicted to the bottle and for the most part ineffective policemen. Even so, their very presence on vessels was probably of some consequence. Masters were aware that even a hint back in port about foul play might result in troublesome and expensive inquiries. Second, kidnapping soon became unnecessary for the most part.[39] The Solomon Islanders quickly learnt exactly what indenturing involved, especially when the first recruits, many of whom had been kidnapped, were returned to their islands with the goods they had bought with their wages. Many spoke favourably of plantation life and of their experiences and so inspired relatives and friends to sign on. Labour recruiting in the Solomons thenceforth followed much along the lines of the New Hebridean ventures. But while kidnapping and massacre became the exception rather than the rule, there was always a level of violence not too far below the surface. As Deryck Scarr pointed out: 'There was sometimes only a fine line between the energetic recruiting agent, sensitive to the wishes of a would-be recruit, and the outright kidnapper.'[40] On the whole however, the most successful recruiters were those who proved most reliable and trustworthy with their human cargoes. As with the sandalwood trade, violence did not pay in the long run.

By the mid-1880s recruiting vessels had touched at most places throughout the Solomons and masters had amassed considerable local knowledge. As a result they tended to stay away from some of the western islands—New Georgia, Choiseul, and Santa Ysabel—where vigorous head-hunting and slave raiding campaigns by the inhabitants thinned and intimidated populations. As recruiter William Wawn explained while sailing along Santa Ysabel:

> *The absence of any village is easily accounted for. The natives of this group are pre-eminently treacherous and blood thirsty, and they dread their nearest neighbour quite as much as they do strangers. Two or three villages could be made out in the distance, perched, like crows' nests, on peaks high up among the mountains.*[41]

Head-hunting raids also kept participants too excited and involved to want to sail away in large numbers. The gradual introduction of European firearms to these regions increased the tempo of such activities so that by the late 1890s they had reached unprecedented limits. Hundreds of heads were taken in a single raid. By this time, firearms were no longer muskets. European technology had developed breech-loading rifles with all-metal cartridges and, unlike muskets, they *were* extremely effective in Pacific conditions.[42] Wawn described how the days of the smooth-bore were over, now it was nothing 'but a repeating rifle'.[43] The leader Iqava from Roviana Lagoon on New Georgia hunted his human prey with English-built boats, 500 men, 400 rifles, and 9000 bullets.[44] Another notable leader, the Big-Man Bera, rose to unprecedented dominance in Bugota at the southern tip of Santa Ysabel through a similar reign of head-hunting terror.[45] From there he ranged far and wide with the hundreds of firearms he received from traders calling in at Thousand Ships Bay. Wawn met him in 1881 and described him as

> *much dreaded by the inhabitants of Isabel. . . . Many a ruined village attested to the devastating energy of his forays. When I met him, Captain Walsche [on another vessel] was sorting out a large quantity of 'trade', to barter with him for copra, bèche-de-mer, tortoise-shell, and other island produce.*[46]

The presence of such traders who settled or regularly visited these regions from the 1870s was also an obstacle to labour recruiting. Said Wawn,

> *Copra traders are generally opposed to the labour trade. The more men there are on the islands, to make copra and buy tobacco with it, the better for them. Besides— like the missionaries—they cannot bamboozle the 'returned' labourers so easily as they do the unsophisticated savage.*[47]

The islands which supplied most recruits were Malaita and Guadalcanal which lay outside the 'head-hunting zone' and were the most populous islands in the group, together with San Cristobal, Buka, and Bougainville. For the most part, the coastal people sailed off to Queensland and Fiji— not just because they were obviously handy to harbours and landing places, but because they deliberately prevented most interior or bush people, their arch enemies, from gaining the benefits of a period of indenture. Coastal dwellers were particularly anxious to keep a monopoly of the supply of rifles, which were the prized possessions of returning recruits. By the mid-1880s coastal communities were less willing to offer recruits. In some localities the novelty had worn off. Some Islanders became more daring and attempted to capture and loot vessels as a quicker way to riches. More commonly, however, the many individuals who wanted to sail away had already done so, and there were always self-imposed limits as to how many young men from any one settlement could be absent. Coastal communities were in danger of becoming depleted, or were depleted. Labour was not in inexhaustible supply. Combined with the increasing reluctance to continue the trade at its earlier frenzied pace was the realisation that the same benefits could be gained by staying at home. The coastal people began to play active role as intermediaries—guides, interpreters, provisioners of ships—as the recruiters tapped into a new source of labour amongst the bush dwellers. Coastal leaders were also quick to appreciate the possibilities for 'taxing' these people laden with goods on their return. They could also help to kidnap bush people and get them ready for the next recruiting ship. This was the era of the so-called passage-masters, seaside leaders who increased their authority by exploiting the trade in this fashion, like Kwaisulia of Ada Gege.[48]

The shift in recruiting patterns and in relations between bush and coastal people was aided by legislation in Queensland and Fiji in 1884 which prohibited labourers from returning to their homes with firearms, and recruiters from distributing them as presents. In the short term this legislation worked against the recruiters from Queensland and Fiji since many Islanders chose to go instead to Samoa and New Caledonia where there were no restrictions on bringing back guns. Consequently, some recruiters from Queensland and Fiji decided to press on to the still-untapped islands around New Guinea, whose inhabitants had not had much European contact and whose taste for goods did not yet run to firearms.

New Guinea interlude

In 1883–1884, 32 trips were made from Queensland to New Guinea, New Ireland, New Britain, Murua, and the D'Entrecasteaux and Louisiade archipelagos. Some 5800 Islanders were brought back to the colony.[49] Recruiters from Fiji were similarly successful. However, as in the Solomons in the early 1870s, much of this recruiting was in virgin fields and therefore marked by violence. Of the 32 voyages from Queensland, 14 were officially investigated. Numerous complaints of abuses of regulations were upheld. Some recruiters were jailed; others were banned from recruiting. In addition there was an extremely high death rate amongst these Islanders on the plantations. After a royal commission in 1885, New Guinea and surrounding islands were closed to recruiting activities, and the labour vessels returned once more to the Solomons. Here they found that the Islanders had lost their enthusiasm for going to Samoa and New Caledonia, even if they could get guns, since they found working and living conditions very much tougher and the pay less lucrative than in Fiji and especially Queensland.

In the last decades of recruitment for Queensland and Fiji, the bush people of the Solomons provided most of the labourers. Trading in these years was for the most part routine, though there were still occasional instances of bloodshed, enough to keep the anti-recruiting lobbyists in Britain and the colonies constantly outraged and agitating to put an end to the labour trade in Melanesia.

End of indenture

In Queensland the decision to stop recruiting in Melanesia was initially made in 1885 after the royal commission investigated the labour trade around New Guinea; no more licences for collecting labourers from

Melanesia were to be issued after 1890. At the same time, efforts were made to replace the large sugar-cane plantations with smaller holdings using European labour, in keeping with prevalent notions of a 'white Australia'. However, recession in the sugar industry in the early 1890s saw the Queensland government reverse its decision and recruiting was allowed to continue for a few more years. By the time the Australian colonies formed a federation in 1901 it was widely accepted throughout Queensland that labour from Melanesia had had its day. The Pacific Island Labourers Act passed by the Federal Parliament in 1901 declared that immigration would cease in 1904 and that all Pacific Islanders still in Queensland by 1906 were to be deported. About 7000 Islanders were thus returned to their homes, though several hundred chose to go to Fiji instead. Another 1600 Islanders gained exemption and were allowed to stay in Australia. The planters were cushioned against the loss of this cheap labour as the Queensland government, and the federal government after 1901, imposed a hefty duty and tax on sugar to subsidise growers for employing more expensive European labour.[50]

In Fiji the indenturing of people from Melanesia was ended because imported Indian labour proved more economical. There was now additional opposition from the British authorities in the Solomons and from European planters there who wanted to use the labour themselves. The last labour vessel arrived in Fiji in 1911. There was no enforced repatriation from Fiji and thousands of Solomon Islanders and New Hebrideans never bothered to leave.[51]

Motives and experiences

The exodus of some 100 000 people from Melanesia over a thirty-year period can no longer be explained as kidnapping. To do so, argued Corris, would be to believe that two generations of Islanders 'were so witless as to stand about on their beaches year after year and allow themselves to be kidnapped by a handful of Europeans and their henchmen. The 'black-birding' interpretation ... denies more than 100 000 Melanesians their humanity.'[52] Scarr concluded, 'As a business ... the labour trade required the substantial consent of all concerned, which was, in a considerable measure, forthcoming from the islanders who were involved with it.'[53]

Corris maintained that there were four general motives for Solomon Islanders wanting to go to the plantations, and these seem equally applicable to New Hebrideans and others: 'the great desirability of European goods, the novelty of travel, the example set by others who had returned and seemed to benefit by their experiences in a variety of ways, and pressures within their own society.'[54] The last motive would include a desire to flee from sorcerers, illness, the tyranny of leaders, or boredom. The majority of those who did sail away were not disillusioned by their experiences. While plantation life in Queensland and Fiji might appear harsh by our standards, with its long hours and hard physical labour, and while the incidence of ill health and mortality may seem high,[55] the Islanders themselves appeared relatively unconcerned about these matters. Plantation life was enjoyable at best, tolerable at worst, and usually rewarding at the end. The weekly highlight was a free half Saturday and all day Sunday. In Queensland labourers flocked to races and the 'Kanaka' shops run by Chinese and even Islanders in the towns. Saturday night was a big occasion.

From all quarters you will see swarms of Kanakas coming quietly down the middle of the street with all the graciousness that money and 'trade' drapery can make them. A tall straw hat, with a sharp silk necktie that would shame the sun at noonday, with a pipe generally a clay—sometimes a briar or a meerschaum—all this, with much gutteral chattering and laughing makes up a Bundaberg Kanaka on Saturday night and he never travels singly.[56]

In Fiji there were few such opportunities unless the labourers were near Levuka or Suva, and campfire dancing and singing were more common entertainments, as they were in remoter parts of Queensland. There was also considerable fighting amongst the Islanders as rival groups from different islands tried to establish their mark.

Some Islanders found attractions in church activity. Where they repulsed missionaries on their own islands, they found themselves a captive audience in Queensland. Those who stayed on for a second or third term of indenture—the time-expired boys—delved deeper into the pleasures of town life, especially in Queensland, where there was plenty of opportunity for drinking, gambling, and whoring at brothels operated by European, Japanese, and Aboriginal women.

Relatively few Islanders seemed to loathe their experiences in Queensland or Fiji. Indeed, one of the most compelling arguments against the labour trade being based on kidnapping and slavery is the fact that numerous Islanders made several trips to the plantations or stayed on for additional terms. Overall, about one-quarter of all recruits from the Solomon Islands in Queensland and Fiji were time-expired boys. By the 1890s this figure was approaching 50 per cent.[57] These old hands received at least double the ordinary pay, taking them to £12 per year in Queensland and half that in Fiji. They also did less work, acted as overseers and bosses of raw recruits, and generally enjoyed a higher standard of living.

The time-expired boy, as a rule, has adopted the household customs of civilization. He has a bedroom and a living room. His kitchen boasts of table and chairs and pots and plates; his wife becomes a fairly good cook. Many of the men have a slight knowledge of gardening, and all who choose are allowed on most plantations to have gardens, in which they grow vegetables for their own use.[58]

A recent economic analysis of Islanders' wage rates in Queensland has concluded that since the labour market was 'subject to forces of supply and demand' the Islanders could express considerable choice as to where they worked, who they worked for, and the type of work they wanted, such as group or individual tasks.[59]

The movement of so many people out of Melanesia in the later nineteenth century was on the whole a voluntary exodus. To work in Queensland or Fiji was seen by most as an opportunity to enrich their lives, as well as to gain status and wealth.

Consequences for island communities

Vast quantities of European goods were introduced to Melanesian islands by the labour trade. Chiefs, Big-Men, passage-masters, all received tools, firearms, cloth, tobacco in return for their services and as payment for permitting their followers to leave, or organising others to do so. Part of the recruiters' strategy was to excite the Islanders' cupidity.

> *Each boat carried a 'trade box', containing about a dozen pounds of twist tobacco, two dozen short clay pipes, half a dozen pounds of gunpowder in quarter, half, and one pound flasks, some boxes of military percussion caps, a bag of small coloured beads, a few fathoms of cheap print calico, a piece (twelve yards) of Turkey red twill, half a dozen large knives, with blades sixteen or eighteen inches long, the same number of smaller knives, half a dozen fantail tomahawks, a few Jews'-harps, mirrors, fish-hooks, and other trifles. Paint was then in frequent demand. For this we provided a tin canister of vermilion powder and some balls of Reckitt's washing blue.*[60]

When labourers were paid off after their three-year term (with their £18 in Queensland and £9 in Fiji) they rushed off to buy goods from the kanaka shops set up for the purpose. They packed clothes, tobacco, tools into 'little boxes, cedar or painted red ... about two feet long, eighteen inches broad and eighteen inches high. These must have locks and keys. These boxes they fill with anything they can collect.'[61] Ships' masters returning Islanders to their homes were sometimes driven to distraction, as one explained:

> *I had for many days ... good reason for cursing those ... chests, as the owners kept up a constant state of disturbance, never being able to decide, when their money was running short, what desirable article they would purchase next, and, when at sea, always fetching their whole property on deck every morning and bartering among themselves, both sides being always dissatisfied with the results, and insisting on bringing me into the squabble as arbitrator.*[62]

Firearms were by far the most prized possession to take home, before being prohibited in 1884. Excitement mounted as the returning recruits neared their islands:

> *Discarding the old clothes they had used as their sea 'toggery' they donned brand new tweed trousers, gorgeous shirts—red, blue, and striped; broad brimmed straw hats, with scarlet bands of Turkey twill and leather belts with pouches and sheath knives. Then came their red-painted ponderous boxes from the hold, and the lowering of them into the boats.*[63]

The goods were usually freely distributed to or taken by relatives and leaders when the recruits finally reached the beach. Someone returning with large quantities of booty and especially firearms was assured of considerable prestige even though these items might not have remained his personal property.[64] To return with nothing or little, as sometimes happened when the labourers lost their goods gambling on the ship home, was humiliating. Such men often immediately signed on for another three years abroad.

For thirty years the labour trade was responsible for a constant flow of goods into many parts of Melanesia, and there was a veritable flood when the 6000 labourers were returned en masse in 1906. Iron and steel gradually replaced wood, stone, and shell. European goods were allotted local equivalents and became new negotiables. An axe or knife or rifle became worth so many pigs or shells. European trade goods became accepted into local economies and 'ceased to have merely utilitarian or novelty value'.[65] The more this happened the more dependent communities became on having continued contact with Europeans. This provided a valuable point of entry for European planters later in the century. There was probably considerable inflation. Brides became more expensive. Some customary forms of exchange assumed lesser importance; for example, the shell-money industries on San Cristobal and Guadalcanal became obsolete.[66] Some Islanders tried their own cash cropping, as on Aoba in the New Hebrides. There the customary graded society based on pigs was undermined and the coconut tree and copra became the pivotal elements in a much more competitive society—and one that became Christian.[67]

The social consequences of the labour trade are more difficult to assess. Clearly, thousands of Islanders returned with different skills, habits, values, and expectations than those they departed with. But in many cases the veneer of civilisation was soon stripped away on return to village life. Perhaps a majority of returnees ever after kept up a public face as being slightly different in dress and domestic habits, but they nevertheless fitted fairly easily back into the routines and obligations of the community. Those who could not usually left, often to work for Europeans in the islands, or to set up small businesses of their own.[68] These people were more likely to be receptive to Christianity, especially for its promise of personal social and economic advancement and 'modern' living.

Local political consequences are easier to document. Big-Men and leaders in numerous places increased their wealth and their political authority. Some who acquired large numbers of rifles, especially before 1884, indulged in various forms of mini-imperialism, like Kwaisulia of Ada Gege, Bera of Santa Ysabel, Iqava of Roviana Lagoon, Foulanger of Malaita, and others.[69] Yet, given the socially, politically, and geographically fragmented nature of Solomon Islands and New Hebrides societies, there could be no equivalents of the monarchs of eastern Polynesia. Local strong-men emerged, but they had no means of institutionalising their authority and creating dynasties, or of extending their domain over a wider territory.

Denouement

To examine the labour trade in Melanesia in terms of culture contact, and, in rejecting the older view that it amounted to kidnapping and slavery, to stress the voluntary nature of the Islanders' mobility and its rewards for them, is not a complete picture. For in addition to its voluntary nature— 'its individual or group motivation in seeking work'—labour migration also 'entailed a consideration of the system of production in which labour is employed.'[70] In this system Melanesia was a pool or reserve of labour that was used by a vast regional market based on European capital and organisation in Queensland, Fiji, New Caledonia, Samoa, and Hawaii.[71] While an individual Islander was, from his point of view, a fairly free agent, the choices available in the longer term and from a broader perspective were fundamentally limited. The labour pool in which Islanders freely participated became itself increasingly subject to the demands and concerns of (often conflicting) interests from the other side of the globe. By 1900 much of Melanesia was still remote in European perceptions, and with the possible exception of some tribal groups in New Caledonia which had been forcibly resettled, the way of life, social organisation, and values of most Melanesian peoples were essentially unaltered. Although the effects of these overseas demands and concerns on the labour pool intensified after about 1900, after the Queensland and Fijian labour trade had ended, the basis for them was being laid from the 1870s onward.

Labour recruiting for the colonies was the main European activity in the Solomon Islands and the New Hebrides over the last three decades of the nineteenth century, but there was also a growing number of resident European traders from Sydney and New Caledonia collecting tortoiseshell, bêche-de-mer, and copra. They too employed local labour and so commenced, on a tiny scale at first, patterns of local labour migration within the Solomons and the New Hebrides. This alternative to migration to overseas plantations became predominant when recruitment for the colonies ended.

The 'free' Melanesian labourer could still choose whether to work or not, but already the choice as to *where* was being determined by European economic and political priorities. In the 1880s and 1890s European commercial activity in the Solomons and the New Hebrides became more entrenched with the arrival not only of more traders, but of planters who needed land as well as labour. These men were often backed by large Australian-based companies like Burns Philp, Levers, and the Australasian New Hebrides Company, as well as the Compagnie Calédonien des Nouvelles Hébrides from New Caledonia. Mission societies that had had such a gruelling time in these islands for much of the century now returned, often in the wake of repatriated labourers from Queensland, some of whom at least saw the church as a means of maintaining aspects of the newer life they had just experienced. There was often a relationship, usually uneasy, between renewed missionary endeavour and commercial development in the Solomons and the New Hebrides, since both missions and companies represented and provided opportunities to participate in aspects of the European world.[72]

Commercial and religious activities in Melanesia ensured the attention of nearby governments—in Queensland, Fiji, and New Caledonia—as well as Britain, France, and (bringing New Guinea into the picture) Germany. To suggest a direct collusion between particular business concerns and government policies is somewhat simplistic since the interests of business and the priorities of legislators were as much in conflict as in harmony. Furthermore, national jealousies and international rivalries in the region and beyond introduced complex elements into the commerce–government relationship. But as Colin Newbury has said, the imperial partition of Melanesia 'can be considered, not as a necessary consequence of development by particular pressure groups, but as an incidental means of regulating the disorderly process of investment, land confiscation, and labour recruiting through the clientage networks already established in the islands.'[73] In this process, the individual Melanesian played no part, but rather was subject to it as a voluntary member of a labour pool.

It is beyond the scope of this book to detail the steps by which this partition evolved. Suffice it to say that, in addition to New Caledonia being annexed in 1853, the New Hebrides came under joint British and French rule in 1906, the Solomon Islands became a British Protectorate in 1893, and New Guinea (which had still experienced extremely little European contact) was partitioned in 1884 into the German Protectorate of New Guinea and British New Guinea or Papua, which in 1906 was given to Australia.[74]

Much of the history of twentieth-century Melanesia, building on its nineteenth-century experiences, and especially the labour trade, thus became dominated by the triple concerns of plantation economies, the role of the Christian churches, and European administrations.

Epilogue

16

Considering the new historiography

The fact that by the end of the nineteenth century (and in many cases much earlier) most Pacific islands were incorporated into European empires suggests an element of inevitability. Indeed it is quite reasonable to look back on the history of the Pacific islands, at least from the days of Balboa's sighting of the ocean to the formal imposition of colonial controls, as a logical development: particular needs, ideologies, and technological developments saw the expansion of Europe overseas with people we can now label as the forerunners of empire—explorers, traders, missionaries—establishing a presence and influence in island communities that led eventually to European government involvement. From this perspective the Pacific islands, first settled by communities that subsequently became isolated from the Old World, saw a second wave of newcomers, especially from the late eighteenth century, which led to the eventual incorporation of the islands and their civilisations into global designs.

To see links between the rough positions scratched onto sixteenth-century maps and the nineteenth-century documents of annexation; or even between boardroom decisions in European capitals and the lot of labourers on Pacific plantations, is not to see the whole story. It might provide a useful superstructure for the tale of the imperial historians, but it is an *imperial* overview. Modern Pacific historians have instead examined what might be called (to continue the metaphor of architecture) a series of substructures made of different materials and for different purposes. The superstructure is not necessarily altered or distorted—after all Europe did come to the Pacific islands—so much as seen from new perspectives. The new approach, bringing the Islanders into focus and studying their activities, reveals a whole range of hitherto-ignored considerations. The imperial historians simply did not question the dominance and cultural superiority of their European subjects whose initiative, they believed, determined every course of events. Their assumptions still exist in popular views of Pacific islands history, as anyone who teaches undergraduate students can attest: for example, that explorers left behind a trail of dead Islanders whose surviving companions stared in mute amazement at the power and superiority of the strangely coloured newcomers; that missionaries imposed their will on hapless Islanders and converted them to Christianity, so instilling in island cultures the missionaries' own guilts and obsessions (or, alternatively, saving the Islanders from their own brutish lifestyles); or that traders indulged their evil ways with women and rum and were exploiters and destroyers wherever they made landfall.

Recent historical research suggests that the processes of culture contact were not always so one-sided, that Islanders were quite capable of taking their own initiative and, rather than passively accepting Europeans and their ways, either rejected or deliberately exploited the newcomers for their own reasons. Individual Islanders or whole communities made use of explorers and missionaries and traders, using, adopting, adapting, applying new ideas and customs and technologies and institutions within the context of the priorities and perceptions of their respective indigenous cultures. In some situations Europeans held the advantage; in others the Islanders did. But usually, as I have attempted to show in this book, there were many subtle and complex levels of mutual exploitation and accommodation.

If that was the response, what were the consequences for island communities? One answer to this question has been taken for granted for the last two hundred years—European entry into the Pacific meant sooner or later doom and disaster for the islands' inhabitants.[1] This long-standing tradition of a 'fatal impact' began with some of the eighteenth-century explorers who had little doubt that their coming was but a prelude to the destruction of the nobility and arcadian simplicity that they believed characterised at least some aspects of island living. As George Forster commented:

> *It were indeed sincerely to be wished, that the intercourse which has lately subsisted between Europeans and the natives of the South Sea islands may be broken off in time, before the corruption of manners which unhappily characterises civilized regions, may reach that innocent race of men, who live here fortunate in their ignorance and simplicity.... If the knowledge of a few individuals can only be acquired at such price as the happiness of nations, it were better for the discoverers, and the discovered, that the South Sea had still remained unknown to Europe and its restless inhabitants.[2]*

Cook, Bligh, and Vancouver all expressed similar sentiments.[3] These ideas were further expounded by philosophers back in Europe, like the French encyclopaedist Denis Diderot, who focused in particular on missionaries and Christianity as among the most deadly of the European influences that would head for the islands.[4] This view was confirmed by later travellers like Otto von Kotzebue who saw missionaries in action in Hawaii and Tahiti in the early decades of the nineteenth century and considered them a blight upon the happiness of mankind.[5] Perhaps the most eloquent and vitriolic publicist of the wickedness of missionaries in particular and

European civilisation in general was Herman Melville. Such civilisation was in his opinion a poison for innocent Islanders that would see them head rapidly toward extinction.[6] Those who supported the introduction of civilisation and Christianity naturally took the strongest exception to this view, and argued that if European presence was upsetting island societies it had nothing to do with their activities. They blamed instead beachcombers, whalers, traders, and various other 'scum' who had 'hung their consciences on Cape Horn' and exploited and perverted entire islands. Yet even missionaries and their apologists did not dispute the notion that the Islanders' fate was sealed: 'There seems to be a certain incompatibility between the tastes of the savage and the pursuits of civilized man, which, by a process more easily marked than explained, leads in the end to the extinction of the former; and nowhere has this shown itself more visibly than in Polynesia.'[7] Whether one believed in the nobility or ignobility of Islanders, and whoever or whatever one blamed for their situation, the result was not in question: European contact meant the demise of island peoples. Such talk of extinction long predated the evolutionary theories. What the application or rather misapplication of Darwinian and Lamarckian theories subsequently provided in the second half of the nineteenth century was a so-called scientific explanation for the ruination and depopulation of Pacific Islanders. Now the missionaries or beachcombers were not specifically destroying Pacific societies, but rather participating in the workings of certain immutable natural laws having to do with the survival of the fittest. As one exponent of the art noted, the Islanders 'have doubtless performed some allotted part in the economy of nature' and now were making fatal progress to extinction.[8] Such notions were still in vogue in the 1920s. Even those who rejected these ideas did not dispute that Islanders were culturally and biologically doomed. R L Stevenson in the later nineteenth century, and anthropologists and ethnologists like G Pitt-Rivers, WHR Rivers, and Bronislaw Malinowski in the early twentieth century, suggested that the cause of depopulation was psychological: 'Now once you make life unattractive for a man ... you cut the taproot of his vitality. The rapid dying out of the native races is ... due more to wanton interference with their pleasures and normal occupations ... than to any other cause.'[9]

By the 1930s, however, even armchair theorists had to acknowledge that Pacific Islanders were not in fact dying out—indeed some of their societies were increasing all too rapidly and outstripping resources. If depopulation itself ceased to be an issue, the notion that European contact had had nasty, bewildering, and demoralising consequences continued as strong as ever. The second world war did much to stimulate such thinking, especially amongst Americans, whose country had been so involved in the Pacific war zone. Both J C Furnas and Douglas Oliver wrote influential books about the Pacific islands which have as a central theme the idea that Europeans since the days of Cook have caused nothing but disruption and dislocation of the Islanders' lifestyles.[10] These opinions are still common enough, especially in non-academic circles, and have been given most vivid illustration in Alan Moorehead's *The Fatal Impact*: 'When Captain Cook entered the Pacific in 1769 it was a virgin ocean, pristine and savage, and its inhabitants lived a life of primeval innocence. Seventy years later firearms, disease and alcohol had hammered away at this way of life until it crumbled before them, and where Satan had sown the Protestant missionaries reaped: the Tahitians, who "had known no God but Love", came to accept the morality of an English suburb ...'[11]

All such views, from Cook to Moorehead, share certain assumptions: that Europeans were culturally and technologically superior, the Islanders implicitly or explicitly inferior, passive, and unable to cope with the white man's all-powerful way of life. This belief is usually accompanied, again either implicitly or explicitly, with feelings of guilt or shame or at least considerable unease. Furthermore, many if not all of the writers appear to have described events and situations that have derived less from observation, experience, and perceptible reality than from their own particular viewpoints and psychological urges.[12] The Noble Savage purists of the late eighteenth and early nineteenth centuries were reacting against industrialisation and social and political upheavals in Europe and saw in Pacific cultures an image of a way of life long since sadly lost to Europeans. Missionaries and traders of the early nineteenth century frequently looked for scapegoats for their own difficulties, blamed each other for their problems, and accused each other of ruining Pacific peoples. Neo-Darwinists of the later nineteenth and early twentieth centuries attempted to absolve themselves and their civilisation from responsibility for the apparently imminent extinction of Pacific races by arguing that natural laws far beyond any human capacity to stay were in inexorable motion. Anthropologists and ethnologists of the early twentieth century were still sometimes influenced by neo-Darwinian thinking, and especially by the theoretical underpinning of their developing disciplines; in particular, the concept of 'functionalism' held that an indigenous society was very fragile, and change in any one aspect would necessarily alter and then destroy all the rest. After the second world war, American writers reflected guilt at what had apparently happened to the good but unfortunate peoples of the Pacific islands, as well as their country's shouldering of the burden of economic, political, and strategic responsibility for much of the region.

Just as modern Pacific historians have rejected the view that Islanders were inferior, passive, and helpless in a contact situation, so have they also rejected the view that the end result was a fatal impact. In part this is because new research has suggested rather different conclusions should be drawn. For example the prehistorians now paint a picture of island societies before European arrival that is rather more complex than the simplistic view of their being pristine and primevally innocent. In both pre- and postcontact times there were on Pacific islands human situations with human reactions on both sides, not morality plays with the forces of evil arrayed against helpless innocents. In other words, if there was no Paradise there cannot be a Paradise Lost. Furthermore, the work of demographers, especially Norma McArthur, has now shown that for the most part the alleged depopulation of Pacific islands in the nineteenth century—the topic that so obsessed generations of commentators—is a myth, and one usually created by Europeans who looked for what they wanted to see. Most Pacific islands communities did not suffer from massive population declines because of introduced diseases or other such influences.[13] Modern Pacific historians have also drawn on the work of the more sophisticated anthropology that has developed since the 1930s. The earlier functionalists had never been interested in studying social changes in island societies after European contact, but had tried instead to create essentially static models of what those societies were like in their so-called uncontaminated stage. Changes that Europeans occasioned were seen as symptoms of decline and decay and were lamented rather than studied. Later generations of anthropologists, comprising people like Margaret Mead, Raymond Firth, Ian Hogbin, and C S Belshaw, rejected such simplistic functional analysis and adopted more dynamic models. They were especially interested in social change (or acculturation as it was commonly called). They showed that social changes in the Pacific and elsewhere were not necessarily imposed by Europeans, and that change in itself was not necessarily destructive. Changes could come as much from within island communities as from direct outside stimulus. Change could be creative. Many societies were shown to be highly adaptable. They could with relative ease shed or modify what had seemed to earlier anthropologists to be the most important and functional elements of their culture. Finally, modern Pacific historians also work from rather different premises than earlier writers. They try to do away with more blatant, European-centred value judgments, and they deny the cultural inferiority of Island peoples and their inability to think and act for themselves. They believe in the justness of these people controlling their own destinies. Modern Pacific history is certainly not value free, but its values are often very different from those of earlier generations.

As a result of these different techniques and perceptions modern Pacific historians have amassed a considerable body of evidence that leads to rather different conclusions about Pacific islands history in precolonial times than were previously advocated. There is no suggestion that Western influences were always of benefit to Pacific peoples; most modern historians make no claims that Islanders were better or worse off as a result of European contact. But their research strongly suggests that the blanket interpretation of a fatal impact cannot be sustained. To see Islanders as passive, helpless, and always persecuted and suffering at the hands of Europeans not only excludes modern research findings but, it is now argued, denies the Islanders their humanity. Change and innovation did occur, but not only when Europeans arrived. After all, the Austronesians had been on Pacific islands for thousands of years before European vessels nosed tentatively into the South Seas. Once the Europeans did come, island societies proved adaptable, resourceful, and resilient. A history of culture contact can no longer be interpreted in terms of European initiatives; the course of events was very much influenced by the nature of the Islanders' own social and political arrangements. Islanders had long been masters of their environment. When faced with Western contact they took a remarkable range of social, economic, political, and intellectual initiatives designed to exploit new opportunities and cope with new challenges. Furthermore, to focus solely on changes in island life is to lose sight of important continuities. Although at various points in the nineteenth century a political and economic control was finally assumed by European interests, this did not necessarily mean the destruction of island values, perceptions, and social organisations; to suggest that it did is to ignore the lifestyles that still flourish in many parts of the Pacific today. Injustice, intolerance, and interference can easily be documented, especially in the colonial period, but these must not be permitted to overshadow the other dimensions of the more intimate workings of island societies. It is worth quoting again J W Davidson's belief that 'the indigenous cultures . . . were like islands whose coastal regions outsiders might penetrate but whose heartlands they could never conquer.'[14] In this book I have tried to capture something of the spirit of this sentiment, at least for the period before colonial rule. The approach, as I have said, has rejected earlier assumptions and values, and has therefore come to different conclusions, but it is a product of other assumptions and values. There are no absolutes in historical interpretation. History is what we choose to see and we tend to see what we are looking for. The past has no independent existence.

Notes and References

Preface

1 J W Davidson *The Study of Pacific History* and 'Problems of Pacific history'
2 J W Davidson 'Problems of Pacific history' p 9
3 J W Davidson 'European penetration of the South Pacific' p 313
4 Howe 'Pacific islands history in the 1980s'
5 Spate 'The Pacific as an artefact' p 42
6 Dening *Islands and Beaches*; Gilson *The Cook Islands*; Macdonald *Cinderellas of the Empire*
7 This Oceanic Pacific is investigated by Spate in *The Spanish Lake*, and other volumes in preparation. See also his 'Prolegomena'.
8 J W Davidson 'Lauaki Namulau'ulu Mamoe' p 267
9 Spate *The Spanish Lake* p x

1 Whence and how

1 Useful general surveys of Southeast Asian prehistory are in Bellwood *Man's Conquest of the Pacific*, chapters 3, 7, 8; Shutler and Shutler *Oceanic Prehistory* pp 8–30. See also papers by Hutterer and Hayden in Allen, Golson, and Jones (eds) *Sunda and Sahul*.
2 Golson 'The remarkable history' p 14
3 ibid pp 14–15. See also Mulvaney *The Prehistory of Australia*; Mulvaney and Golson (eds) *Aboriginal Man and Environment*; Allen, Golson, and Jones (eds) *Sunda and Sahul*.
4 Blainey *Triumph of the Nomads* pp 234–251; Macknight *The Voyage to Marege*
5 Blainey *Triumph of the Nomads* p 237
6 ibid pp 217–29 passim
7 Some useful surveys of the 'Austronesian' advance, and of aspects of Pacific islands prehistory in general are Bellwood *Man's Conquest of the Pacific*; Howells *The Pacific Islanders*; Pawley and Green 'Dating the dispersal of the Oceanic languages'; Shutler and Marck 'On the dispersal of the Austronesian horticulturalists'; Shutler and Shutler *Oceanic Prehistory*; Shutler 'Radio carbon dating and Oceanic prehistory'; Jennings (ed) *The Prehistory of Polynesia*.
8 Green 'New sites with Lapita pottery' pp 1–2
9 Chowning *An Introduction* pp 9–13; Bulmer 'Settlement and economy in prehistoric Papua

New Guinea'; Watson and Cole, *Prehistory of the Eastern Highlands*

10 Pawley and Green 'Dating the dispersal of the Oceanic languages'

11 Chowning, *An Introduction* pp 4–5

12 Shutler and Shutler *Oceanic Prehistory* pp 55–77

13 Garanger 'Incised and applied-relief pottery'; Golson 'Lapita ware and its transformations'; Green 'Lapita pottery and the origins of Polynesian culture'; Green 'New sites with Lapita pottery'; Green 'Lapita'

14 Green 'New sites with Lapita pottery' p 2

15 For example, Bellwood has suggested that the Lapita makers may have come up to 1000 years after an earlier aceramic 'Austronesian' settlement of island Melanesia (*Man's Conquest of the Pacific* pp 255, 275).

16 Alkire *An Introduction* pp 5–10; Bellwood *Man's Conquest of the Pacific* chapter 10; Shutler and Shutler *Oceanic Prehistory* pp 90–4

17 Shutler and Shutler *Oceanic Prehistory* p 69

18 Howells 'Computerised clues' pp 3–4. This argument is further developed in Howells *The Pacific Islanders* pp 213–63. (However, Howells has since modified his views in the light of recent discoveries about early Lapita communities in island Melanesia; see Howells 'Physical anthropology' p 284.) Other supporters of a Micronesian route include Peter Buck, who argued that plants and animals entered Polynesia via Melanesia but Polynesian man came via Micronesia (*Vikings of the Sunrise* chapter 5), and Roger Duff, who believed that tanged Polynesian adzes derived from the

Philippine region through Micronesia (*Stone Adzes of Southeast Asia* p 16).

19 Green and Davidson 'Melanesian origin of Polynesian culture'; Bellwood *Man's Conquest of the Pacific* pp 281–2

20 Green and Davidson 'Melanesian origin of Polynesian culture' p 73

21 Shutler and Shutler *Oceanic Prehistory* pp 79–81; Shutler 'Radio carbon dating' p 225

22 Groube 'Tonga, Lapita pottery, and Polynesian origins'. Since Groube published this article more recent findings of earlier settlement dates for Samoa give it equal claim with Tonga to be the 'Polynesian homeland'. However, the overall argument remains valid.

23 Pawley and Green 'Dating the dispersal of the Oceanic languages' pp 18–19, 43–5

24 Shutler and Shutler *Oceanic Prehistory* pp 82–3. Earlier, but as yet out-of-context dates have been found for the Marquesas. These would put first settlement back about 300 years (to the first century AD) and this is thought to be not unreasonable; see ibid p 83, and also Pawley and Green 'Dating the dispersal of the Oceanic languages' p 22.

25 Shutler and Shutler *Oceanic Prehistory* pp 84–7. See also Bellwood 'Dispersal centres in east Polynesia'; Sinoto 'An archaeologically based assessment of the Marquesas'.

26 Pawley and Green 'Dating the dispersal of the Oceanic languages' p 21

27 For a study of the historiography of Polynesian origins see Bellwood *Man's Conquest of the Pacific* pp 303–11; Howard 'Polynesian

origins and migrations'.

28 Groube 'Tonga, Lapita pottery, and Polynesian origins' p 313

29 For example, Shutler and Marck 'On the dispersal of the Austronesian horticulturalists'; Pawley and Green 'Dating the dispersal of the Oceanic languages'; Bellwood *Man's Conquest of the Pacific* chapter 5

30 For example, Howells *The Pacific Islanders* pp 30–79

31 For example, Emory 'East Polynesian relationships as revealed through adzes'

32 For example, Yen 'The development of agriculture in Oceania'; Bellwood *Man's Conquest of the Pacific* chapter 6

33 Heyerdahl actually proposes two waves of migration into eastern Polynesia. The first settlers were 'islanders of Andean origin' who, among other things, built the stone statues on Easter Island. Sometime later an 'East Asiatic element' entered Polynesia at Hawaii having first travelled to the northwest American coast from Southeast Asia via the Japan current. See his *American Indians in the Pacific*, *Aku-Aku*, and *Sea Routes to Polynesia*.

34 See for example Golson 'Thor Heyerdahl and the prehistory of Easter Island'. See also Lanning 'South America as a source'; Bellwood *Man's Conquest of the Pacific* pp 361–77.

35 Yen *The Sweet Potato and Oceania*; O'Brien 'The sweet potato'

36 Ward 'The dispersal of the coconut' p 28 (quoted with the author's permission). See also his 'The viability of floating coconuts'.

37 Sharp *Ancient voyagers in Polynesia* pp 16–17, 33–4, 71, passim

38 ibid chapter 2

39 ibid chapter 3

40 For example see Golson (ed) *Polynesian Navigation*

41 Lewis *We the Navigators* chapters 2, 3, 4

42 ibid p 104

43 ibid chapter 5

44 ibid p 142

45 ibid chapter 6

46 Lewis ' "Expanding" the target in indigenous navigation' p 95

47 Lewis *We the Navigators* chapter 10. See also Lewis 'The Pacific navigators' debt to the ancient seafarers of Asia'. For a definitive survey of canoe types see Haddon and Hornell *Canoes of Oceania*.

48 See for example, Gladwin *East is a Big Bird*; Finney (ed) *Pacific Navigation and Voyaging*.

49 Levison, Ward, and Webb *The Settlement of Polynesia* p 11

50 ibid chapter 4

2   *Civilisations in the making*

1 The literature on New Guinea prehistory is now immense. A succinct survey is Bulmer 'Settlement and economy in prehistoric New Guinea: A review of the archaeological evidence'.

2 For example, Golson's excavations of the Kuk site in the highlands near Mt Hagen have revealed a most remarkable 9000 year sequence of drainage ditch constructions. See his 'No room at the top'.

3 Bulmer 'Settlement and economy in prehistoric New Guinea' pp 67, 68

4 Green *A First Culture History of the Solomon Islands* p 13

5 ibid p 17

6 ibid p 22

7 ibid
8 Garanger *Archéologie des Nouvelles-Hébrides*
9 Garanger 'Incised and applied-relief pottery' p 62
10 ibid p 65
11 Shutler and Shutler *Oceanic Prehistory* p 66. R Shutler has advanced the hypothesis that 'by 10 000 years ago, a non-Austronesian, aceramic, pre-Neolithic, tumuli-building people were in Island Melanesia, on New Guinea and Ile des Pins, and that eventually evidence for similar early occupation of islands between New Caledonia and New Guinea will be found', 'Radiocarbon dating and Oceanic prehistory' p 222.
12 Shutler and Shutler *Oceanic Prehistory* p 66
13 ibid pp 64–6. See also Shutler 'Pacific island radiocarbon dates, an overview' pp 15–18; Garanger 'Incised and applied-relief pottery' p 63; Golson 'Both sides of the Wallace Line' pp 554–76.
14 Barrau *Subsistence Agriculture in Melanesia* p 21 passim
15 Green 'A suggested revision of the Fijian sequence'
16 Palmer 'Fijian pottery technologies'
17 Garanger 'Incised and applied-relief pottery' p 62
18 Pawley and Green 'Dating the dispersal of the Oceanic languages' pp 17, 46–7
19 France *The Charter of the Land* p 6
20 Palmer 'Ring-ditch fortifications on windward Viti Levu'
21 Green and Davidson *Archaeology in Western Samoa* 2: 281
22 A brief survey of Tongan prehistory is given by Poulsen 'Archaeology and prehistory'
23 ibid p 14

24 See Latukefu *Church and State in Tonga* chapter 1; Rutherford *Friendly Islands* pp 27–39; Cummins 'Tongan society at the time of European contact'
25 Green and Davidson *Archaeology in Western Samoa* 2: 224. See also Janet Davidson 'Samoa and Tonga'.
26 Green and Davidson *Archaeology in Western Samoa* 2: 224
27 ibid 2: 253
28 ibid 2: 244
29 ibid 2: 241–2
30 ibid 2: 242–3
31 ibid 2: 282
32 Pawley and Green 'Dating the dispersal of the Oceanic languages' p 18
33 ibid p 19
34 Green 'West Polynesian prehistory' p 105
35 ibid p 106
36 ibid p 107
37 Sinoto 'Position of the Marquesas' and 'An archaeologically based assessment'
38 Shutler and Shutler *Oceanic Prehistory* p 83
39 ibid p 84
40 Emory 'A re-examination of east Polynesian marae' p 75
41 Goldman *Ancient Polynesian Society* p 177
42 Oliver *Ancient Tahitian Society* 2: 1122
43 ibid
44 Cordy 'Cultural adaptation and evolution in Hawaii'
45 Kirch 'The chronology of early Hawaiian settlement' p 118
46 Cordy 'Cultural adaptation and evolution in Hawaii' p 186
47 ibid p 181n5
48 Finney *Hokule'a*
49 There are some excellent surveys of New Zealand prehistory, in particular Simmons 'Economic

change in New Zealand prehistory'; Green *Adaptation and Change in Maori Culture*; Bellwood *Man's Conquest of the Pacific* chapter 13; Janet Davidson 'The Polynesian foundation'; Brailsford *The Tattooed Land.*

50 Janet Davidson 'The Polynesian foundation' p 3

51 Classic expression of the Great Migration theory was given by S P Smith in *Hawaiki: The Whence of the Maori* and *Lore of the Whare Wananga.*

52 Simmons *The Great New Zealand Myth*

3   *Ethnographic moments*

1 McArthur 'The demography of primitive populations' pp 1097–101

2 For example, McArthur *Island Populations of the Pacific* and *Introducing Population Statistics*; McArthur and Yaxley *Condominium of the New Hebrides: A Report on the First Census of the Population*

3 For example, Roberts *Population Problems of the Pacific*; Brown *Peoples and Problems of the Pacific*

4 McArthur, Saunders, and Tweedie 'Small population isolates: A micro-simulation study' pp 322, 325

5 Golson 'The Pacific islands and their prehistoric inhabitants' p 29

6 Pirie 'Polynesian populations: Review' p 180

7 Amherst and Thomson (eds) *The Discovery of the Solomon Islands* 1: 89, 146

8 Markham (ed) *The Voyages of Pedro Fernandez de Quiros* 1: 150

9 ibid 1: 27

10 Bougainville *A Voyage Round the World* p 249

11 Beaglehole (ed) *The Journals of Captain James Cook* 2: 850

12 ibid 1: 278

13 ibid 3: 1, 629

14 Whether yaws was widespread throughout the islands is a matter of debate. Some researchers claim it has been positively identified only in Australia and New Guinea; see Watt 'Medical aspects and consequences of Cook's voyages' p 151. For another view see Pirie 'The effects of treponematosis and gonorrhoea on the populations of the Pacific islands'.

15 Beaglehole (ed) *The Journals of Captain James Cook* 2: 540

16 ibid 2: 450; 3: 2, 1365–66

17 Oliver *Ancient Tahitian Society* 1: 484–5

18 Quoted in ibid 1: 485

19 Beaglehole (ed) *The Journals of Captain James Cook* 3: 1, 612

20 For example, Houghton *The First New Zealanders*; Pietrusewsky *Prehistoric Human Skeletal Remains from Papua New Guinea and the Marquesas*; Snow, *Early Hawaiians*

21 Beaglehole (ed) *The Journals of Captain James Cook* 3: 1, 611

22 Houghton *The First New Zealanders* chapter 7

23 Pietrusewsky *Prehistoric Human Skeletal Remains* pp 33, 127

24 Snow *Early Hawaiians* pp 11–12

25 ibid p 10

26 Houghton 'Prehistoric New Zealanders' p 214

27 For a brief survey of the argument see Bellwood *Man's Conquest of the Pacific* p 95.

28 Brookfield with Hart *Melanesia* pp 68–77

29 For opposing viewpoints see G S Parsonson 'The problem of Melanesia' and Chowning 'The real Melanesia'.

30 Hogbin and Wedgwood 'Local

grouping in Melanesia'

31 Alkire *An Introduction to the Peoples and Cultures of Micronesia*; Bellwood *Man's Conquest of the Pacific* pp 105–6

32 Oliver *Ancient Tahitian Society* 1: 44

33 Beaglehole (ed) *The Journals of Captain James Cook* 1: 120

34 ibid 2: 261–2

35 Golson 'The Pacific islands and their prehistoric inhabitants' p 23; Bellwood *Man's Conquest of the Pacific* pp 320–1

36 Golson 'The Pacific islands and their prehistoric inhabitants' pp 20–21

37 Barrau 'Histoire et préhistoire horticoles de l'Océanie tropicale'; Bellwood *Man's Conquest of the Pacific* pp 136–41

38 The following survey of plant cultivation comes mainly from Barrau *Subsistence Agriculture in Melanesia* and *Subsistence Agriculture in Polynesia and Micronesia*. See also Bellwood *Man's Conquest of the Pacific* pp 142–8.

39 Beaglehole (ed) *The Journals of Captain James Cook* 2: 538

40 ibid 1: 247

41 ibid 1: 583–4

42 ibid 1: 282

43 ibid 1: 121–2

44 ibid 2: 252, 272

45 Brookfield with Hart *Melanesia* pp 324 ff

46 ibid pp 328–9

47 Bedford *New Hebridean Mobility* pp 15–21; Davenport 'Red-feather money'; Howe *The Loyalty Islands* p 8

48 Janet Davidson 'Western Polynesia and Fiji'; Kaeppler 'Exchange patterns in goods and spouses: Fiji, Tonga and Samoa'

49 For example, Leach 'Four centuries of community interaction and trade in Cook Strait, New Zealand'

50 For example, Sahlins 'Poor man, rich man, Big-Man, chief: Political types in Melanesia and Polynesia'

51 A most useful recent discussion is Douglas 'Rank, power, and authority'.

52 Amherst and Thomson (eds) *The Discovery of the Solomon Islands* 1: 154

53 For example, Hogbin and Wedgwood 'Local grouping in Melanesia'; Burns et al 'Melanesian Big Men and the accumulation of power'

54 Oliver *A Solomon Island Society*; Hogbin *A Guadalcanal Society*

55 Allen 'Rank and leadership in Nduindui'

56 Guiart 'Native society in the New Hebrides'

57 Douglas 'Rank, power, and authority'; Chowning 'Leadership in Melanesia'

58 Hogbin '"Polynesian" colonies in Melanesia'

59 Guiart *Structure de la Chefferie en Mélanésie du Sud*

60 Goldman *Ancient Polynesian Society* pp 20–1 passim

61 Alkire *An Introduction to the Peoples and Cultures of Micronesia* passim; Bellwood *Man's Conquest of the Pacific* pp 104–6

62 Sahlins *Social Stratification in Polynesia* pp 248–9 passim

63 Goldman *Ancient Polynesian Society* pp 20–1, 567–70

64 Dening *Islands and Beaches* p 264

4 *Suspected continents*

1 Oliver, W H 'Yesterday's loss' (*Out of Season* [poems] Wellington, 1980) p 31

2 Much material in this chapter

comes from Spate *The Spanish Lake*; Beaglehole *The Exploration of the Pacific*; Sharp *The Discovery of the Pacific Islands*; Friis (ed) *The Pacific Basin*.

3 Stanley of Alderley (ed) *The First Voyage Round the World by Magellan* pp 64–5

4 ibid p 68

5 Spate *The Spanish Lake* p 85

6 Brand 'Geographical exploration by the Spaniards' p 130

7 Maude *Islands and Men* pp 35–83

8 Jack-Hinton *The Search for the Islands of Solomon*

9 Beaglehole *The Exploration of the Pacific* p 105

10 Celsus Kelly *La Austrialia del Espiritu Santo* pp 82–3

11 Gallego in Amherst and Thomson (eds) *The Discovery of the Solomon Islands* 1: 51

12 ibid p 52

13 Pearson 'The reception of European voyagers'

14 Markham (ed) *The Voyages of Pedro Fernandez de Quiros* 1: 18

15 ibid

16 ibid pp 24–5

17 ibid p 26

18 Shineberg 'Guns and men'

19 A quite contrary opinion is held by Langdon in his controversial *The Lost Caravel*. See also his 'The European ships of Tupaia's chart'. He argues that a Spanish vessel, *San Lesmes*, was wrecked in the Tuamotu Islands in 1526 and that the survivors had a major cultural and genetic effect throughout eastern Polynesia and New Zealand. He believes that survivors from other early Spanish vessels lost elsewhere in the Pacific probably had a similar impact. These hypotheses have been received rather coolly on the whole by Pacific historians and prehis-

torians. Many accept that Langdon may have a case for early European presence in the Tuamotus, though whether this was from the *San Lesmes* or later (though still pre-Cook) vessels is very much open to question, but they are dubious about his claims for its impact and extent. However in spite of all the opinions both for and against Langdon, there has been little detailed examination of his evidence; but see Driessen 'Outriggerless canoes and glorious beings'.

20 See Beardsley *Guam Past and Present*; Carano and Sanchez *A Complete History of Guam*.

21 Spate *The Spanish Lake* p 289

22 Brand 'Geographical exploration by the Spaniards' p 143

23 Beaglehole *The Exploration of the Pacific* p 111

24 Sharp *The Discovery of Australia*

25 Quoted in Broek 'Geographical exploration by the Dutch' p 159

26 Sharp (ed) *The Voyages of Abel Janszoon Tasman* p 45

27 British and French entry to the Pacific is discussed in Beaglehole *The Exploration of the Pacific* chapters 8, 9; Dunmore *French explorers in the Pacific* vol 1.

28 See Beaglehole (ed) *The Journals of Captain James Cook* and *The Life of Captain James Cook*.

29 For example, Fry 'Alexander Dalrymple and Captain Cook'; Hoare *The Tactless Philosopher*

30 Watt 'Medical aspects and consequences of Cook's voyages' pp 154–6

31 ibid p 135, passim

32 Fisher and Johnston (eds) *Captain James Cook and his Times*

33 Ruggles 'Geographical exploration by the English' p 245

34 Bougainville *A Voyage Round the*

World pp 218–19

35 ibid p 228
36 ibid p 257
37 Bernard Smith *European Vision and the South Pacific* chapter 5
38 Pearson 'European intimidation and the myth of Tahiti'
39 G Robertson *The Discovery of Tahiti* p 137
40 ibid
41 ibid p 143
42 ibid p 148
43 ibid p 154
44 ibid p 160
45 ibid p 166
46 ibid p 180
47 Pearson 'European intimidation and the myth of Tahiti' p 217
48 Cook *A Voyage to the Pacific Ocean* 2: 136
49 Vancouver *A Voyage of Discovery* 1: 145
50 McArthur 'Essays in multiplication'
51 On this question see Pirie 'The effects of treponematosis'; Van der Sluis *The Treponematosis of Tahiti*; Howard Smith 'The introduction of venereal disease into Tahiti'; Watt 'Medical aspects and consequences of Cook's voyages'.
52 McArthur *Island Populations of the Pacific* chapter 5

5   *The wealth of islands*

1 Frost *Convicts and Empire*
2 Young 'Australia's Pacific frontier'; Hainsworth *The Sydney Traders*
3 ibid. See also J W Davidson *Peter Dillon of Vanikoro*.
4 Maude *Islands and Men* pp 178–232
5 Im Thurn and Wharton (eds) *The Journal of William Lockerby*
6 Shineberg *They Came for Sandalwood*
7 Begg and Begg *The World of John Boultbee*; McNab *Murihiku and the Southern Islands* and *The Old Whaling Days*; Morton *The Whale's Wake*; Tapp *Early New Zealand*; Wright *New Zealand 1769–1840*
8 Quimby 'Hawaiians in the fur trade'
9 Morton *The Whale's Wake*
10 Wilkes *Narrative of the United States Exploring Expedition* 5: 484
11 Davidson *Peter Dillon*
12 Oliver *The Pacific Islands* pp xxii, 103, 107. See also Moorehead *The Fatal Impact*; Furnas *Anatomy of Paradise*; Doumenge *L'Homme dans le Pacifique Sud*; Price *The Western Invasion of the Pacific*.
13 F D Bennett *Narrative of a Whaling Voyage* 1: 72
14 Quoted in Kuykendall *The Hawaiian Kingdom vol 1 1778–1854* p 90; see also pp 89–90; Bradley *The American Frontier in Hawaii* pp 60–71.
15 F D Bennett *Narrative of a Whaling Voyage* 1: 209–10
16 Morton *The Whale's Wake*
17 Turnbull *A Voyage Round the World* p 497. See also Morton *The Whale's Wake*.
18 A J Morrell *Narrative of a Voyage* p 36
19 Hargreaves 'The Maori agriculture of the Auckland province'
20 Fanning *Voyages to the South Seas* pp 61–3
21 Ward 'The Pacific *bêche-de-mer* trade'
22 Diapea *Cannibal Jack* p 56
23 F D Bennett *Narrative of a Whaling Voyage* 1: 339
24 McCormick *Omai*
25 Bradley *The American Frontier in Hawaii* p 33
26 Quoted in Quimby 'Hawaiians in the fur trade' p 101
27 Turnbull *A Voyage Round the*

World p 231. See also Archibald Campbell *A Voyage Round the World* p 154.

28 Quoted in Stackpole *The Sea-Hunters* p 387

29 Bradley *The American Frontier in Hawaii* pp 227–8; Dodge *New England and the South Seas* p 47

30 Turnbull *A Voyage Round the World* p 506

31 Quoted in Ward 'The Pacific *bêche-de-mer* trade' p 113n1. See also Morton *The Whale's Wake.*

32 B Morrell *A Narrative of Four Voyages to the South Sea* p 372, and see also p 374.

33 J W Davidson *Peter Dillon* p 95

34 Turnbull *A Voyage Round the World* p 209

35 ibid p 400

36 ibid p 506

37 Beechey *Narrative of a Voyage to the Pacific* 1: 303–4

38 The following material on beach-combers owes much to Maude *Islands and Men* pp 134–77; Ralston *Grass Huts and Warehouses* and 'The beach communities'.

39 B Morrell *A Narrative of Four Voyages to the South Sea* pp 441ff

40 Turnbull *A Voyage Round the World* p 156

41 'Jackson's Narrative' in Erskine *Journal of a Cruise* p 465

42 Diapea *Cannibal Jack* p 57

43 Patterson *Narrative of the Adventures and Sufferings* p 84

44 Turnbull *A Voyage Round the World* p 272

45 O'Connell *A Residence of Eleven Years* p 105

46 ibid pp 113–5

47 'Jackson's Narrative' in Erskine *Journal of a Cruise* pp 412–3

48 A Campbell *A Voyage Round the World* p 97

49 ibid pp 118–19

50 ibid p 103

51 Quoted in Ralston *Grass Huts and Warehouses* p 24

52 Bargatzky 'Beachcombers and castaways as innovators'

53 Dening *Islands and Beaches* p 133

54 Robarts *The Marquesan Journal of Edward Robarts* pp 46–7

55 ibid p 47n4

56 Erskine *Journal of a Cruise* pp 461–2

6   *To recover the remnant*

1   Corney *The Quest and Occupation of Tahiti*

2   ibid 2: 332

3   Much of this chapter relies heavily on Gunson *Messengers of Grace.*

4   ibid p 2

5   ibid pp 12–15

6   ibid p 43

7   ibid p 34

8   Cairns *Prelude to Imperialism* p 74

9   Coates, Beecham, and Ellis *Christianity the Means of Civilization* pp 171, 174 quoted in Gunson, *Messengers of Grace,* p 269

10   Havard-Williams (ed) *Marsden and the New Zealand Mission* p 14

11   Binney *Legacy of Guilt* p 7

12   Quoted in Bernard Smith *European Vision* pp 106–7

13   Buddle *The Aborigines of New Zealand* p 51

14   Quoted in Gunson *Messengers of Grace* p 197

15   Gunson *Messengers of Grace* p 270

16   Coates, Beecham, and Ellis *Christianity the Means of Civilization*

17   Gunson *Messengers of Grace* p 269

18   ibid pp 268–9

19   Quoted in ibid p 272

20   Gunson *Messengers of Grace* p 34

21   Sorrenson 'How to civilize savages'

22   Gunson *Messengers of Grace* chapters 2–4

23 ibid p 48
24 Lovett *The History of the London Missionary Society* p 120
25 Wilson *A Missionary Voyage* p 140
26 ibid
27 Lovett *The History of the London Missionary Society* p 172

7   *Pomares of Tahiti*

1   Oliver *Ancient Tahitian Society* 2: chapter 18
2   ibid 3: chapter 25; Newbury's introduction to Davies *The History of the Tahitian Mission* pp xxxv–xxxviii
3   Handy *History and Culture in the Society Islands* pp 77ff
4   Newbury 'Te Hau Pahu Rahi'
5   Newbury's introduction to Davies *The History of the Tahitian Mission* p xxxvi
6   Oliver *Ancient Tahitian Society* 2: chapter 22
7   ibid 3: 1179ff
8   G Robertson *The Discovery of Tahiti* pp 203–4
9   Beaglehole (ed) *The 'Endeavour' Journal of Joseph Banks* 1: 266
10 Beaglehole (ed) *The Journals of Captain James Cook* 1: 85
11 Beaglehole (ed) *The 'Endeavour' Journal of Joseph Banks* 1: 305
12 ibid 1: 274; Beaglehole (ed) *The Journals of Captain James Cook* 1: 85
13 Beaglehole (ed) *The 'Endeavour' Journal of Joseph Banks* 1: 385
14 Oliver *Ancient Tahitian Society* 3: 1234
15 Beaglehole (ed) *The Journals of Captain James Cook* 2: 206
16 ibid 2: 410
17 ibid 2: 385–6
18 ibid 2: 387
19 ibid 3: 1, 197
20 ibid 3: 1, 211n
21 ibid 3: 1, 214

22 Bligh *A Voyage to the South Sea* 1: 375
23 ibid 1: 378
24 ibid 2: 28
25 ibid
26 Rutter (ed) *The Journal of James Morrison* pp 100–101
27 Oliver *Ancient Tahitian Society* 3: 1259; Newbury's introduction to Davies *The History of the Tahitian Mission* p xxxviii
28 Vancouver *A Voyage of Discovery* 1: 144
29 ibid 1: 143
30 ibid 1: 100
31 ibid 1: 105
32 Turnbull *A Voyage Round the World* p 139
33 See chapter 6.
34 Quoted in Oliver *Ancient Tahitian Society* 3: 1305
35 ibid 3: 1306
36 Turnbull *A Voyage Round the World* p 154; Davies *The History of the Tahitian Mission* pp 53ff
37 Turnbull *A Voyage Round the World* pp 153–4
38 Davies *The History of the Tahitian Mission* p 86
39 Turnbull *A Voyage Round the World* pp 132, 134, 149
40 ibid p 382
41 J W Davidson 'European penetration of the South Pacific' p 10
42 Quoted in Oliver *Ancient Tahitian Society* 3: 1313
43 Davies *The History of the Tahitian Mission* pp 75–6, 78
44 ibid p 32
45 ibid
46 Quoted in Oliver *Ancient Tahitian Society* 3: 1311
47 Newbury's introduction to Davies *The History of the Tahitian Mission* p xlii
48 Maude *Islands and Men* p 212
49 Davies *The History of the Tahitian Mission* p 195

50 Ellis *Polynesian Researches* 3: 132
51 Davies *The History of the Tahitian Mission* p 203
52 A French version of this code is in the *Journal de la Société des Océanistes* 8, 1952, pp 5–26
53 J W Davidson 'European penetration of the South Pacific' p 17
54 ibid p 18
55 Davies *The History of the Tahitian Mission* p 209
56 G S Parsonson 'The literate revolution'
57 Gunson 'Pomare II of Tahiti and Polynesian imperialism'
58 Quoted in ibid p 68
59 J W Davidson 'European penetration of the South Pacific' p 350
60 Quoted in Gunson 'Pomare II of Tahiti and Polynesian imperialism' p 70
61 Ellis *Polynesian Researches* 3: 250, 251, 258
62 Davies *The History of the Tahitian Mission* p 233
63 ibid p 233n
64 ibid pp 233–234n
65 ibid pp 349–50
66 ibid p 234
67 Beechey *Narrative of a Voyage*, 1: 290–2
68 ibid 1: 304–5
69 Kotzebue *A New Voyage Round the World* 1: 172
70 F D Bennett *Narrative of a Whaling Voyage* 1: 81
71 Gunson 'An account of the Mamaia'
72 For accounts of political developments in Tahiti from the 1830s see, for example, Langdon *Island of Love*; Newbury *Tahiti Nui*.

8   *Kamehamehas of Hawaii*

1 The best general accounts are Bradley *The American Frontier in Hawaii*; Daws *Shoal of Time*; Kuykendall *The Hawaiian Kingdom 1778–1854*.
2 Fornander *An Account of the Polynesian Race* vol 2; Kamakau *Ka Po'e Kahiko*; Malo *Hawaiian Antiquities*
3 Malo *Hawaiian Antiquities* pp 60–1
4 Beaglehole (ed) *The Journals of Captain James Cook* 3: 1, 597–8
5 ibid 3: 1, 512–3
6 ibid 3: 2, 1215
7 Kamakau *Ruling Chiefs of Hawaii* pp 117–21
8 Beaglehole (ed) *The Journals of Captain James Cook* 3: 2, 1151
9 Vancouver *A Voyage of Discovery* 2: 135–43
10 Kamakau *Ruling Chiefs of Hawaii* p 147
11 Odgers 'Western contact with Hawaii'
12 Kamakau *Ruling Chiefs of Hawaii* pp 142–58
13 Vancouver *A Voyage of Discovery* 2: 122
14 ibid 2: 155ff; 3: 31ff
15 ibid 2: 155, 163–4; 3: 18
16 ibid 2: 123, 131
17 ibid 3: 29–30
18 Kamakau *Ruling Chiefs of Hawaii* pp 168–74
19 A Campbell *A Voyage Round the World* p 97
20 Odgers 'Western contact with Hawaii'
21 The most lively account is Daws *Shoal of Time* chapter 2.
22 Turnbull *A Voyage Round the World* pp 204–5. See also Campbell *A Voyage Round the World* p 122
23 Campbell *A Voyage Round the World* p 97
24 Golovnin *Around the World* p 200
25 Turnbull *A Voyage Round the World* p 227
26 Kamakau *Ruling Chiefs of Hawaii*

p 231

27 Kuykendall *The Hawaiian Kingdom 1776—1854* pp 61—89
28 Golovnin *Around the World* p 196
29 ibid p 191; Campbell *A Voyage Round the World* pp 91, 112, 119; Lisiansky *A Voyage Round the World* pp 116, 133
30 Campbell *A Voyage Round the World* pp 152—3
31 Lisiansky *A Voyage Round the World* p 115
32 Turnbull *A Voyage Round the World* p 224
33 Golovnin *Around the World* p 203
34 ibid p 204
35 Campbell *A Voyage Round the World* p 153
36 Golovnin *Around the World* p 280
37 Kotzebue *Voyage of Discovery* pp 308, 316, 349
38 Kamakau *Ruling Chiefs of Hawaii* p 220
39 Arago *Narrative of a Voyage* p 92
40 This topic is investigated in detail by Davenport 'The "Hawaiian cultural revolution"'; Harfst 'Cause or condition'; Levin 'The overthrow of the kapu system'; Webb 'The abolition of the taboo system'.
41 Ellis *Polynesian Researches* 4: 204
42 Levin 'The overthrow of the kapu system' p 402
43 Arago *Narrative of a Voyage* p 139
44 Golovnin *Around the World* p 209
45 Levin 'The overthrow of the kapu system'
46 Davenport 'The "Hawaiian cultural revolution"' p 19
47 Kotzebue *Voyage of Discovery* p 98
48 Ellis *Polynesian Researches* 4: 287
49 Bingham *A Residence of Twenty-one Years* p 79
50 Quoted in Kuykendall *The Hawaiian Kingdom 1778—1854* p 89
51 Ellis *Polynesian Researches* 4: 397. See also Kuykendall *The Hawaiian Kingdom 1778—1854* pp 89—90; and Bradley *The American Frontier* pp 60—71
52 Ellis *Polynesian Researches* 4: 410
53 Daws 'Honolulu in the nineteenth century'; Ralston *Grass Huts and Warehouses*
54 F D Bennett *Narrative of a Whaling Voyage* 1: 208
55 Bingham *A Residence of Twenty-one Years* p 81
56 ibid p 70
57 ibid p 87
58 ibid p 103
59 ibid p 145
60 ibid
61 Ellis *Polynesian Researches* 4: 41
62 Quoted in Kuykendall *The Hawaiian Kingdom 1778—1854* p 106. See also Bradley *The American Frontier* pp 141—4; Bingham *A Residence of Twenty-one Years* pp 205, 212.
63 Bingham *A Residence of Twenty-one Years* p 281
64 Kotzebue *A New Voyage Round the World* 2: 206
65 Quoted in Kuykendall *The Hawaiian Kingdom 1778—1884* p 106
66 Quoted in G S Parsonson 'The literate revolution' p 53
67 Kotzebue *A New Voyage Round the World* 2: 256—9
68 ibid 2: 255
69 Kuykendall *The Hawaiian Kingdom 1778—1854* pp 121—6
70 F D Bennett *Narrative of a Whaling Voyage* 1: 220
71 ibid 1: 233
72 ibid 1: 231
73 On Hawaiian political history for the remainder of the century see Bradley *The American Frontier*; Daws *Shoal of Time* chapters 4—7; Kuykendall *The Hawaiian Kingdom 1778—1854*, *The Hawaiian Kingdom 1854—1874*, and *The Hawaiian Kingdom 1874—1893*.

9 *Taufa'ahau of Tonga*

1 Cummins 'Tongan society'; Latukefu *Church and State* chapter 1; Rutherford *Friendly Islands* pp 27–39; Gunson 'The *hau* concept of leadership'
2 Beaglehole (ed) *The Journals of Captain James Cook* 3: 1, 174
3 ibid 3: 1, 177
4 Cummins 'Tongan society'; Latukefu *Church and State* chapter 1
5 Beaglehole (ed) *The Journals of Captain James Cook* 3: 2, 1013; see also p 1021
6 ibid 3: 2, 1310
7 Cummins 'Tongan society' pp 66–7
8 Martin *An Account of the Natives* 1: 80
9 Gunson 'The coming of foreigners' p 96
10 Orange (ed) *Life of the Late George Vason*
11 ibid p 169
12 Martin *An Account of the Natives* 1: 74–5
13 Orange (ed) *Life of the Late George Vason* p 175
14 ibid p 186
15 Martin *An Account of the Natives* 1: 85–6
16 Gunson 'The coming of foreigners' p 102
17 Martin *An Account of the Natives* 1: 57–68
18 ibid 1: 88–9
19 ibid 1: 94–5
20 ibid 1: 98
21 ibid 1: 86
22 ibid 1: 139, 157
23 ibid 1: 163
24 ibid 1: 236–7
25 ibid 1: 167
26 Gunson 'The coming of foreigners' pp 103–5; Latukefu *Church and State* p 21
27 Gunson 'The coming of foreigners' pp 109–10
28 Latukefu 'The Wesleyan mission'
29 Latukefu *Church and State* p 61
30 On Taufa'ahau see Latukefu *Church and State* and 'King George Tupou'.
31 Farmer *Tonga and the Friendly Islands* p 216
32 Lawry *Friendly and Feejee Islands* p 6
33 Cummins 'Holy war'
34 Quoted in Latukefu *Church and State* p 111
35 Farmer *Tonga and the Friendly Islands* p 324
36 West *Ten Years in South-Central Polynesia* p 287; see also Farmer *Tonga and the Friendly Islands* pp 323–6
37 Laracy 'The Catholic mission'
38 Latukefu *Church and State* Appendix A
39 ibid Appendix B
40 Nothling 'Charles St Julian'
41 Rutherford *Shirley Baker and the King of Tonga* and *Friendly Islands* pp 154–72
42 Latukefu *Church and State* Appendix C
43 ibid p 247
44 Latukefu *Church and State* Appendix D
45 Scarr *Fragments of Empire* chapter 5; Fusitu'a and Rutherford, 'George Tupou II and the British Protectorate'

10 New Zealand

This chapter owes much to the publications of, and discussions with, John Owens.

1 Beaglehole (ed) *The Journals of Captain James Cook* 2: 117
2 ibid 1: 284

3 ibid 3: 1, 60–1
4 Houghton *The First New Zealanders*
5 Brailsford *The Tattooed Land* p 8
6 Beaglehole (ed) *The Journals of Captain James Cook* 1: 281
7 See chapter 3
8 For surveys of Maori social and political organisation see Best *The Maori*; R Firth *Economics of the New Zealand Maori*; Metge *The Maoris of New Zealand*.
9 Elder (ed) *The Letters and Journals of Samuel Marsden* p 118
10 A Parsonson 'The expansion of a competitive society' p 49
11 Bowden '*Tapu* and *mana*' p 60
12 ibid
13 A Parsonson 'The expansion of a competitive society' and 'The pursuit of mana'
14 Beaglehole (ed) *The Journals of Captain James Cook* 3: 1, 71
15 Dunmore *French Explorers in the Pacific* 1: 148–53
16 ibid 1: 181–90
17 Crozet *Crozet's Voyage* pp 49, 63
18 B Smith *European Vision* pp 86–7
19 McNab *Murihiku*; Morton *The Whale's Wake*; Tapp *Early New Zealand*
20 McNab (ed) *Historical Records* 2: 535–51
21 ibid 1: 254–5
22 ibid 1: 255
23 Savage *Some Account of New Zealand*
24 Quoted in McNab *From Tasman to Marsden* p 118
25 Nicholas *Narrative of a Voyage* 2: Appendix 3
26 Yarwood *Samuel Marsden*
27 Havard-Williams (ed) *Marsden and the New Zealand Mission* pp 14, 36, 41
28 Binney *Legacy of Guilt* p 132
29 McNab (ed) *Historical Records* 1: 304, 419, 423–4

30 Binney *Legacy of Guilt* pp 16–17; McNab (ed) *Historical Records* 1: 293–309; McNab *From Tasman to Marsden* pp 125–37; Nicholas *Narrative of a Voyage* 2: 71–6; Owens *Prophets in the Wilderness* 35–6
31 Nicholas *Narrative of a Voyage* 1: 25
32 ibid 1: 26–7, 48
33 ibid 1: 40
34 ibid 1: 43
35 Binney *Legacy of Guilt* p 32
36 Cruise *Journal of a Ten Months' Residence* p 54
37 Wright *New Zealand* p 139; see also p 150
38 Binney *Legacy of Guilt* chapter 3; Cruise *Journal of a Ten Months' Residence* p 55; Wright *New Zealand* pp 86–90
39 Quoted in Wright *New Zealand* p 87
40 ibid
41 Quoted in Urlich 'The introduction and diffusion of firearms' p 400
42 Elder (ed) *The Letters and Journals of Samuel Marsden* p 333
43 Binney *Legacy of Guilt* p 34
44 S P Smith *Maori Wars* pp 9–88; Urlich 'The introduction and diffusion of firearms' pp 399–403
45 S P Smith *Maori Wars* pp 89–95
46 Vayda *Maori Warfare* p 24
47 S P Smith *Maori Wars* pp 96–128; Burns *Te Rauparaha* chapter 13
48 Binney *Legacy of Guilt* pp 56–62
49 S P Smith *Maori Wars* pp 183–4
50 ibid pp 181ff; G S Parsonson 'The life and times of Hongi Hika'
51 G S Parsonson 'The life and times of Hongi Hika' p 6
52 Burns *Te Rauparaha*
53 ibid p 133; Urlich 'The introduction and diffusion of firearms' p 404
54 Urlich 'The introduction and

diffusion of firearms' p 407

55 Wright *New Zealand* chapter 5;
Vayda 'Maoris and muskets'

56 Urlich 'The introduction and
diffusion of firearms' and
'Migrations of the North Island
Maoris'

57 Ballara 'The role of warfare' p 503,
passim; see also 'Settlement
patterns'

58 G S Parsonson 'The life and times
of Hongi Hika'

59 Elder (ed) *The Letters and Journals
of Samuel Marsden* p 387

60 Owens 'New Zealand before annexation' pp 45–6

61 Ballara 'The role of warfare' p 504

62 ibid

63 Earle *Narrative of a Residence* pp
167–8

64 G S Parsonson 'The life and times
of Hongi Hika' p 8

65 A Parsonson 'The expansion of a
competitive society' p 55

66 S P Smith *Maori Wars* p 130

67 Nicholas *Narrative of a Voyage* 1:
49–50

68 McNab (ed) *Historical Records* 1:
628. See also Elder (ed) *The Letters
and Journals of Samuel Marsden* pp
113, 382

69 Binney *Legacy of Guilt*

70 On Henry Williams see Rogers *Te
Wiremu*; and Fisher, 'Henry
Williams' leadership of the CMS
mission'.

71 Owens *Prophets in the Wilderness*

72 Wright *New Zealand*

73 Binney 'Christianity and the
Maoris'

74 Owens *Prophets in the Wilderness*
p 147; see also his 'Christianity and
the Maoris' and 'Religious disputation'; and Howe 'The Maori
response to Christianity' pp 34–7

75 Howe 'The Maori response to
Christianity'. See also Owens,
'New Zealand before annexation'

pp 37–8

76 Parr 'Maori literacy'

77 Owens 'Missionary medicine and
Maori health'

78 For example, Howe 'The Maori
response to Christianity' p 41

79 Binney *Legacy of Guilt* p 17

80 For example, Dieffenbach *Travels
in New Zealand* 2: 72, 108

81 See examples in Howe 'The Maori
response to Christianity' pp 34–7

82 Wright *New Zealand* chapter 9;
Binney 'Papahurihia'

83 See for example Peter Adams
Fatal Necessity; McLintock *Crown
Colony Government* part 1; Tapp
Early New Zealand.

84 Wright *New Zealand* chapters 4, 5

85 For example, Oliver and Thomson
Challenge and Response chapters 9,
10

86 Dieffenbach *Travels in New Zealand*
2: 83. See also Pool *The Maori
Population.*

87 Morton *The Whale's Wake*

88 Owens 'New Zealand before annexation' p 42

89 Dieffenbach *Travels in New Zealand*
1: 191. See also Earle *Narrative of
a Residence* p 136.

90 Owens 'New Zealand before annexation' p 53

91 A Parsonson 'The expansion of a
competitive society' and 'The
pursuit of mana'

92 Sorrenson 'How to civilize
savages'

11 Samoa

1 The best general surveys of
Samoan social and political or-
ganisation are J W Davidson
Samoa mo Samoa chapter 2; Gilson
Samoa chapters 1, 2.

2 George Turner *Nineteen Years*
p 287. See also John Williams

A Narrative of Missionary Enterprises p 454

3 See chapter 3

4 John Williams *A Narrative of Missionary Enterprises* p 454

5 Wilkes *Narrative* 2: 103

6 Erskine *Journal of a Cruise* p 156

7 Wilkes *Narrative* 2: 153

8 George Turner *Nineteen Years* p 280

9 Wilkes *Narrative* 2: 148

10 George Turner *Nineteen Years* p 287

11 Gilson *Samoa* p 52

12 Wilkes *Narrative* 2: 153

13 Bougainville *A Voyage Round the World* p 281

14 La Pérouse *A Voyage Round the World* 3: 71, 75, 82, 109

15 Kotzebue *A New Voyage* 1: 258

16 Maude *Islands and Men* pp 143–4

17 W P Morrell *Britain in the Pacific Islands* p 53; John Williams *A Narrative of Missionary Enterprises* pp 352–3

18 Wilkes *Narrative* 2: 99–100; George Turner *Nineteen Years* pp 106–9. See also Freeman 'The Joe Gimlet or Siovili cult'.

19 Daws *A Dream of Islands* pp 23–69

20 Williams *A Narrative of Missionary Enterprises* pp 262–3

21 ibid p 490

22 George Turner *Nineteen Years* p 103; Gilson *Samoa*, p 73

23 John Williams *A Narrative of Missionary Enterprises* p 288

24 ibid p 363

25 ibid p 454

26 Garrett 'The conflict between the London Missionary Society and the Wesleyan Methodists'

27 Wilkes *Narrative* 2: 130

28 Quoted in Gilson *Samoa* p 74

29 John Williams *A Narrative of Missionary Enterprises* pp 378–9

30 ibid p 464. See also Erskine *Journal*

of a Cruise p 99

31 George Turner *Nineteen Years* p 31

32 John Williams *A Narrative of Missionary Enterprises* pp 489–90

33 Gilson *Samoa* chapters 4, 5

34 Gunson *Messengers of Grace* p 281

35 Erskine *Journal of a Cruise* p 131

36 Murray *Forty Years' Mission Work* p 103

37 Wilkes *Narrative* 2: 130

38 ibid 2: 129

39 Gilson *Samoa* pp 128–9

40 ibid p 133

41 Erskine *Journal of a Cruise* p 63

42 ibid p 65

43 ibid pp 76, 101

44 ibid p 44

45 ibid pp 86, 87

46 George Turner *Nineteen Years* p 305

47 Ralston *Grass Huts and Warehouses* pp 79–80. See also Ralston 'The pattern of race relations'.

48 Gilson *Samoa* pp 147–9

49 ibid pp 242ff

50 ibid chapter 11; J W Davidson *Samoa mo Samoa* pp 45–7

51 On these events see Gilson *Samoa* chapters 11, 12.

52 On Steinberger and his regime see Gilson *Samoa* chapter 13; J W Davidson *Samoa mo Samoa* pp 48–58.

53 Rigby 'Private interests and the origins of American involvement'

54 On later nineteenth century Samoan politics see J W Davidson *Samoa mo Samoa* pp 58–75; Gilson *Samoa* chapters 14–16; Kennedy *The Samoan Tangle*; Masterman *The Origins of International Rivalry*; Scarr *Fragments of Empire* chapter 4.

55 Stevenson *A Footnote to History* p 5

56 George Turner *Nineteen Years* pp 291–2

12   *Fiji*

1   France *Charter of the Land* pp 3–5
2   ibid p 4. See also his 'The Kauni-
    toni migration'.
3   For example, Derrick *A History of
    Fiji* pp 5–7
4   Reid 'The fruit of Rewa' p 2
5   For general surveys of Fijian
    social and political organisation
    see Derrick *A History of Fiji* chap-
    ter 1; France *Charter of the Land*
    chapter 1. For older views see for
    example Thomson *The Fijians*;
    Thomas Williams *Fiji and the
    Fijians* vol 1.
6   Lawry *Friendly and Feejee Islands* p
    48
7   Derrick *A History of Fiji* p 9
8   France *Charter of the Land* pp
    11–13
9   Derrick *A History of Fiji* pp 23–4
10 Im Thurn and Wharton (eds) *The
    Journal of William Lockerby*
11 Shineberg 'Guns and Men' pp
    78–9
12 Im Thurn and Wharton (eds) *The
    Journal of William Lockerby* pp 56,
    109
13 France *Charter of the Land* pp
    21–2; Scarr, 'Cakobau and
    Ma'afu' p 96
14 Ward 'The Pacific *bêche-de-mer*
    trade' p 110
15 France *Charter of the Land* p 22
16 Derrick *A History of Fiji* p 53;
    Wilkes *Narrative* 3: 61
17 Derrick *A History of Fiji* p 56;
    Wilkes *Narrative* 3: 77
18 Scarr 'Cakobau and Ma'afu' pp
    96–8; Waterhouse *The King and
    People of Fiji* p 53; Wilkes *Narrative*
    3: 61
19 Wilkes *Narrative* 3: 54, 56
20 ibid 3: 66. See also A Lady
    [Wallis] *Life in Feejee* pp 24–5.
21 Quoted in Scarr 'Cakobau and
    Ma'afu' p 99. See also Waterhouse

The King and People of Fiji p 97
22 Belcher *Narrative of a Voyage* 2: 55;
    Wilkes *Narrative* 3: 97–102
23 Wilkes *Narrative* 3: 67
24 Waterhouse *The King and People of
    Fiji* p 63
25 'Jackson's Narrative' in Erskine
    Journal of a Cruise pp 454–5,
    464–5, 472; Im Thurn and
    Wharton (eds) *Journal of William
    Lockerby* pp 256–62
26 Schütz (ed) *The diaries and cor-
    respondence of David Cargill* p 159
27 Derrick *A History of Fiji* pp 76–8
28 Quoted in ibid p 83. See also
    Rowe *The Life of John Hunt* p 164;
    A Lady [Wallis] *Life in Feejee* p
    165.
29 Erskine *Journal of a Cruise* pp 167,
    171, 180, 214
30 ibid p 185
31 ibid p 186
32 A Lady [Wallis] *Life in Feejee* p
    224
33 Erskine *Journal of a Cruise* p 171
34 ibid p 173; Wilkes *Narrative* 3: 47
35 Scarr 'Cakobau and Ma'afu' pp
    102–3
36 Derrick *A History of Fiji* p 95
37 ibid p 103
38 Waterhouse *The King and People of
    Fiji* pp 279–80
39 ibid pp 280–1
40 On early culture contact in Lau
    see Reid 'The view from Vatu-
    waqa'; and Young 'The response
    of Lau to foreign contact'.
41 Schütz (ed) *The Diaries and
    Correspondence of David Cargill* p 65
42 ibid p 83
43 Calvert *Fiji and the Fijians* 2: 35;
    Schütz (ed) *The Diaries and
    Correspondence of David Cargill* pp
    92, 111; Reid 'The view from
    Vatuwaqa' p 161
44 Schütz (ed) *The Diaries and
    Correspondence of David Cargill* p
    162

45 Calvert *Fiji and the Fijians* 2: 32
46 ibid 2: 26
47 ibid 2: 29
48 Wilkes *Narrative* 3: 155–6
49 Belcher *Narrative of a Voyage* 2: 54
50 Calvert *Fiji and the Fijians* 2: 40
51 ibid 2: 46
52 Erskine *Journal of a Cruise* p 170
53 Derrick *A History of Fiji* p 125
54 ibid p 128
55 Scarr 'Cakobau and Ma'afu' p 107
56 Derrick *A History of Fiji* p 130.
   See also Reid 'Crusaders'.
57 Waterhouse *The King and People of
   Fiji* p 189
58 ibid
59 ibid pp 223–5
60 ibid p 229
61 Quoted in ibid pp 245–6
62 ibid pp 243–4
63 ibid p 257
64 ibid p 293
65 Legge *Britain in Fiji* p 11
66 ibid p 68
67 ibid pp 27–35; Derrick *A History
   of Fiji* pp 138–48
68 France *Charter of the Land* chapter
   3; Ralston *Grass Huts and Warehouses* pp 168–9; Stokes 'The Fiji
   cotton boom'; Young 'Evanescent
   ascendancy'
69 Derrick *A History of Fiji* pp 158–
   9; France *Charter of the Land* pp 73–
   4; Legge *Britain in Fiji* pp 64–5
70 Derrick *A History of Fiji* pp
   163–6; France *Charter of the Land*
   pp 78–83; Legge *Britain in Fiji* pp
   66–9
71 France *Charter of the Land* pp 83–7
72 Scarr 'Creditors and the house of
   Hennings'
73 France *Charter of the Land* pp
   87–90
74 Quoted in Derrick *A History of
   Fiji* p 196
75 On the Cakobau government and
   British annexation see Derrick *A
   History of Fiji* pp 202–250; France

Charter of the Land pp 92–101;
Legge *Britain in Fiji* pp 78–137;
Scarr *Majesty of Colour*, vol 1 and
'John Bates Thurston, Commo-
dore J G Goodenough'.

13   The making of Melanesia

1 Quoted in J W Davidson *Peter
   Dillon* p 88
2 Erskine *Journal of a Cruise* p 1
3 Wallis (ed) *Carteret's Voyage* 1:
   163–4
4 ibid 1: 172, 175, 194, 196
5 Bougainville *A Voyage Round the
   World* p 290. The 'leprosy' was
   probably yaws. True leprosy was
   not introduced to the Pacific islands until the later nineteenth
   century.
6 ibid p 318–19
7 Quoted in Dunmore *French
   Explorers* 1: 103
8 Dunmore 'A French account of
   Port Praslin'
9 Dunmore *French Explorers* 1:
   136–43
10 Beaglehole (ed) *The Journals of
   Captain James Cook* 2: 460–526
11 ibid 2: 466
12 ibid 2: 462, 464
13 ibid 2: 539
14 ibid 2: 546
15 J W Davidson *Peter Dillon* chapters 8–11; Jack-Hinton *The Search
   for the Islands of Solomon* pp 296,
   338–40
16 Quoted in J W Davidson *Peter
   Dillon* p 90
17 Shineberg *They Came for
   Sandalwood* pp 17–22
18 John Williams *A Narrative of
   Missionary Enterprises* pp 430–1
19 ibid p 6
20 For one recent account see Daws
   A Dream of Islands pp 65–6.
21 Erskine *Journal of a Cruise* p 2

14   Mission frontiers

1 Laracy *Marists and Melanesians* p 15
2 On Catholic missionary entry into the Pacific see Gunson *Messengers of Grace* pp 26–7; Laracy *Marists and Melanesians* pp 12–3; Wiltgen *The Founding of the Roman Catholic Church in Oceania.*
3 Laracy 'Xavier Montrouzier' p 129
4 Laracy *Marists and Melanesians* p 15
5 ibid p 17
6 ibid pp 18–22
7 ibid pp 22–30
8 Laracy 'The first mission to Tikopia'
9 Jones to LMS, 30 September 1865, South Seas Letters, LMS Archives
10 Murray *Missions* p 139
11 Belcher *Narrative of a Voyage* 2: 58–9
12 Murray *Missions* p 140
13 George Turner *Nineteen Years* p 6
14 ibid p 13
15 ibid p 84
16 ibid pp 15, 82
17 ibid pp 24, 34, 89–92
18 Murray *Missions* pp 146–50
19 ibid p 213
20 ibid p 186
21 ibid p 184
22 ibid pp 184–6
23 ibid p 32
24 ibid p 12
25 ibid pp 152–6
26 ibid p 151
27 Erskine *Journal of a Cruise* p 302; Inglis *In the New Hebrides* p 41
28 Inglis *In the New Hebrides* p 41
29 Erskine *Journal of a Cruise* p 302; Shineberg *They Came for Sandalwood* pp 100–103
30 Miller (ed) *Misi Gete* pp 59, 86
31 Shineberg *They Came for Sandalwood* pp 104–5
32 Murray *Missions* p 131

33 For example, Miller (ed) *Misi Gete* pp 341–3
34 ibid p 141
35 Inglis *In the New Hebrides* p 77
36 ibid
37 Miller (ed) *Misi Gete* p 180
38 George Turner *Nineteen Years* p 494
39 Paton (ed) *John G Paton* pp 62–148; Murray *Missions* p 166
40 Shineberg *They Came for Sandalwood* pp 124–5
41 Quoted in McArthur 'And, behold, the plague' p 277
42 ibid passim
43 Murray *Missions* p 401
44 McArthur, unpublished paper on the New Hebrides, p 19
45 ibid p 19
46 McArthur 'And, behold, the plague' p 282
47 Paton (ed) *John G Paton* p 152
48 McArthur, unpublished paper on the New Hebrides, pp 24, 33
49 ibid p 22
50 ibid pp 22–24
51 Murray *Missions* pp 415–22; H A Robertson *Erromanga* pp 73–6
52 Paton (ed) *John G Paton* p 162
53 ibid pp 148–219
54 Brenchley *Jottings* p 194
55 ibid p 202
56 ibid p 203
57 ibid pp 300–305
58 Paton (ed) *John G Paton* p 298
59 Steel *The New Hebrides* p 179. On the controversy see also ibid pp 171–9; Brenchley *Jottings* pp 305–318; Paton (ed) *John G Paton* pp 297–304.
60 See Steel *The New Hebrides*; H A Robertson *Erromanga*
61 Most of the material for this section comes from Hilliard 'Bishop G.A. Selwyn and the Melanesian Mission' and 'John Coleridge Patteson: Missionary Bishop of Melanesia'.

62 Quoted in Hilliard 'John Coleridge Patteson' p 179
63 George Turner *Nineteen Years* p 84
64 ibid p 83
65 Murray *Missions* p 441
66 This section is based on Howe *The Loyalty Islands*.
67 Quoted in ibid p 26
68 See Guiart *Structure de la Chefferie*
69 Murray *Missions* p 277
70 Quoted in Howe *The Loyalty Islands* p 7
71 Murray *Missions* p 300
72 Quoted in Howe *The Loyalty Islands* p 26
73 Murray *Missions* p 311
74 Quoted in Howe *The Loyalty Islands* p 27
75 F A Campbell *A Year in the New Hebrides* p 139
76 Quoted in Howe *The Loyalty Islands* p 32
77 MacFarlane *Story of the Lifu Mission* p 22
78 Quoted in Howe *The Loyalty Islands* p 20
79 Shineberg *They Came for Sandalwood* pp 33–4
80 Murray *Missions* p 295
81 George Turner *Nineteen Years* pp 412–16
82 Shineberg *They Came for Sandalwood* pp 102, 111–12
83 Pisier *Kounié* p 143
84 Crocombe and Crocombe (eds) *The Works of Ta'unga*
85 See Douglas 'A contact history of the Balad people'
86 Douglas 'A history of culture contact' pp 48–9. Much of the following material comes from this thesis.
87 On Bwarat see Douglas 'Bouarate of Hienghène'
88 Quoted in ibid p 46
89 This section is based on Douglas 'A history of culture contact', 'Bouarate of Hienghène', and 'Conflict and alliance'.
90 See Latham 'Revolt re-examined'; Dousset *Colonialisme et Contradictions*

15   Trade frontiers

1 Material on the sandalwood trade comes mainly from Shineberg *They Came for Sandalwood*.
2 ibid chapter 3
3 ibid pp 47–51, 65. See also Howe *The Loyalty Islands* pp 22–4
4 Shineberg (ed) *The Trading Voyages* pp 96–7
5 ibid p 127
6 ibid pp 139–40
7 Shineberg *They Came for Sandalwood* pp 75–9
8 ibid p 61
9 Quoted in ibid p 70
10 Paton (ed) *John G. Paton* p 130
11 See Shineberg *They Came for Sandalwood* appendix 2
12 Quoted in ibid p 168
13 ibid appendix 3
14 ibid chapter 12
15 Douglas 'The export trade in tropical products'; Howe *The Loyalty Islands* chapter 10
16 Douglas 'Bouarate of Hienghène'; Howe *The Loyalty Islands* passim
17 Shineberg 'Guns and men'
18 Howe 'Firearms and indigenous warfare'
19 Erskine *Journal of a Cruise* p 342
20 Inglis *In the New Hebrides* p 201
21 Howe 'Tourists, sailors and labourers'
22 Quoted in ibid p 26
23 Anderson *Notes of Travel* p 159
24 Howe 'Tourists, sailors and labourers' pp 28–31
25 J A Bennett 'Immigration, "blackbirding", labour recruiting?'; Corris *Passage, Port and Plantation* appendix 1; Price with Baker

'Origins of Pacific island labourers'

26 Brenchley *Jottings* p x

27 For example, Docker *The Black-birders*; Holthouse *Cannibal Cargoes*; Oliver *The Pacific Islands* p 127

28 Corris *Passage, Port and Plantation*; Scarr 'Recruits and recruiters'; Giles *A Cruize in a Queensland Labour Vessel*

29 Corris *Passage, Port and Plantation* p 24; Price with Baker 'Origins of Pacific island labourers'

30 Scarr 'Recruits and recruiters' p 226

31 George Palmer *Kidnapping in the South Seas* pp 51–3

32 ibid p 108

33 Maude *Slavers in Paradise*

34 Howe 'Tourists, sailors and labourers' pp 34–5

35 Quoted in Howe *The Loyalty Islands* p 93

36 Hope *In Quest of Coolies* p 43

37 Quoted in Howe 'Tourists, sailors and labourers' p 35

38 Corris *Passage, Port and Plantation* pp 27–9. On these various regulations see Parnaby *Britain and the Labour Trade*.

39 Corris *Passage, Port and Plantation* pp 29ff

40 Scarr 'Recruits and recruiters' p 245

41 Wawn *The South Sea Islanders* p 224

42 Shineberg 'Guns and men' p 82

43 Wawn *The South Sea Islanders* p 9

44 Corris *Passage, Port and Plantation* pp 29–30

45 Jackson 'Headhunting'

46 Wawn *The South Sea Islanders* p 219

47 ibid p 223

48 Corris *Passage, Port and Plantation* pp 33ff and chapter 4

49 Corris '"Blackbirding" in New Guinea waters'

50 Parnaby *Britain and the Labour Trade* pp 186–99

51 ibid pp 180–6

52 Corris, letter in *The Australian* 17 November 1973

53 Scarr *Fragments of Empire* p 139

54 Corris *Passage, Port and Plantation* p 59

55 See ibid chapter 5; Saunders 'The black scourge' and 'The Pacific Islander hospitals'.

56 Quoted in Corris *Passage, Port and Plantation* p 85

57 ibid pp 49–51

58 Quoted in ibid p 87

59 Shlomowitz 'Markets for indentured and time-expired labour' p 91, passim. See also Saunders 'Troublesome servants'.

60 Wawn *The South Sea Islanders* pp 8–9

61 Quoted in Howe *The Loyalty Islands* p 106

62 Hope *In Quest of Coolies* p 16

63 Melvin *The Cruise of the Helena* p 15

64 ibid pp 17–18

65 Corris *Passage, Port and Plantation* p 105

66 ibid p 114

67 Allen 'The establishment of Christianity and cash cropping' pp 32–3

68 Corris *Passage, Port and Plantation* pp 118, 145–6

69 ibid chapter 4. See also Corris 'Kwaisulia of Ada Gege'.

70 Newbury 'The Melanesian labour reserve' p 3

71 ibid p 4

72 On these themes see for example Allen 'The establishment of Christianity and cash cropping'; J A Bennett 'Oscar Svensen'; Corris *Passage, Port and Plantation* chapter 6; Hilliard 'Colonialism and Christianity'; Thompson 'Commerce, Christianity and colonialism'.

73 Newbury 'The Melanesian labour reserve' p 23

74 See for example Brookfield

Colonialism, Development and Independence; S Firth 'German firms in the western Pacific' and 'The transformation of the labour trade'; Griffin et al *Papua New Guinea*; Hempenstall *Pacific Islanders under German Rule*; Scarr *Fragments of Empire*.

16   *Considering the new historiography*

1 This tradition is examined more fully in Howe 'The fate of the "savage" in Pacific historiography'.
2 Forster *A Voyage Round the World* 1: 303, 368
3 Cook *A Voyage to the Pacific Ocean* 2: 136; Bligh *Captain Bligh's Second Voyage* p 74; Vancouver *A Voyage of Discovery* 1: 145
4 Diderot *Supplément au Voyage de Bougainville*
5 Kotzebue *A New Voyage Round the World*
6 Melville *Omoo* and *Typee*
7 Russell *Polynesia* p 469
8 Forbes 'On the extinction of certain races of men' p 321
9 Malinowski *Argonauts of the Western Pacific* p 465
10 Furnas *Anatomy of Paradise*; Oliver *The Pacific Islands*
11 Moorehead *The Fatal Impact* cover description
12 Baudet *Paradise on Earth* p 6
13 McArthur *Island Populations*; McArthur and Yaxley *Condominium of the New Hebrides*. The one major island where later nineteenth century depopulation seemed unquestionable—New Caledonia—has recently been examined by Dorothy Shineberg (in an unpublished paper). She has concluded that this was not the case since calculations of the supposed pre- and post-decline populations have been erroneously interpreted (personal communication).
14 J W Davidson 'Lauaki Namulau'ulu Mamoe' p 267

Bibliography

Only those sources which have been cited in notes and references or which gave relevant background information appear in this bibliography. For a more comprehensive list of published sources see, for example, C R H Taylor *A Pacific Bibliography: Printed Matter Relating to the Native Peoples of Polynesia, Melanesia and Micronesia* 2nd edn, Oxford, 1965. For later publications see the annual bibliography in the *Journal of Pacific History*.

Abbie, A A *The Original Australians* London, 1969

Adams, Henry *Memoirs of Arii Taimai E, Marama of Eimeo, Terirere of Tooarai, Teriinui of Tahiti, Tauraatua I Amo* Paris, 1901

Adams, Peter *Fatal Necessity: British Intervention in New Zealand 1830–1847* Auckland, 1977

Alkire, William H *An Introduction to the Peoples and Cultures of Micronesia* Reading, Mass, 1972

Allen, J, J Golson, and R Jones (eds) *Sunda and Sahul: Prehistoric Studies in Southeast Asia, Melanesia and Australia* London, 1977

Allen, M R 'The establishment of Christianity and cash cropping in a New Hebridean community' *The Journal of Pacific History* 3, 1968, 25–46

—— 'Rank and leadership in Nduindui, northern New Hebrides' *Mankind* 8, 1972, 270–82

Amherst, Lord, and Basil Thomson (eds) *The Discovery of the Solomon Islands by Alvaro de Mendaña in 1568* 2 vols, London, 1901

Anderson, J W *Notes of Travel in Fiji and New Caledonia with some Remarks on South Sea Islanders and their Languages* London, 1880

Arago, Jacques Etienne Victor *Narrative of a Voyage Round the World . . . during the Years 1817, 1818, 1819, and 1820* London, 1823

Ballara, Angela 'The role of warfare in Maori society in the early contact period' *Journal of the Polynesian Society* 85, 1976, 487–506

—— 'Settlement patterns in the early European Maori phase of Maori society' *Journal of the Polynesian Society* 88, 1979, 199–213

Bargatzky, Thomas 'Beachcombers and castaways as innovators' *Journal of Pacific History* 15, 1980, 93–102

Barrau, Jacques *Subsistence Agriculture in Melanesia* Honolulu, 1958

—— *Subsistence Agriculture in Polynesia and Micronesia* Honolulu, 1961

—— 'Histoire et préhistoire horticoles de l'Océanie tropicale' *Journal de la Société des Océanistes* 21, 1965, 55–78

Baudet, Henri *Paradise on Earth: Some Thoughts on European Images of Non-European Man* New Haven, Conn, 1965

Beaglehole, J C *The Exploration of the Pacific* London, 1966

—— *The Life of Captain James Cook* London, 1974

Beaglehole, J C (ed) *The 'Endeavour' Journal of Joseph Banks 1768–1771* 2 vols, Sydney, 1962

—— (ed) *The Journals of Captain James Cook on his Voyages of Discovery* 3 vols, Cambridge, 1955, 1961, 1967

Beardsley, Charles *Guam Past and Present* Rutland, Vt, 1964

Bedford, R D *New Hebridean Mobility: A study of circular migration* Canberra, 1973

Beechey, F W *Narrative of a Voyage to the Pacific and Beering's Strait . . . in the ship 'Blossom'* vol 1, London, 1831

Begg, Alison 'The conversion to Christianity of the South Island Maori in the 1840s and 1850s' *Historical and Political Studies* 3, 1972, 11–17

Begg, A Charles, and Neil C Begg *The World of John Boultbee Including an Account of Sealing in Australia and New Zealand* Christchurch, 1979

Belcher, Edward *Narrative of a Voyage Round the World Performed in Her Majesty's Ship 'Sulphur' during the Years 1836–1842* vol 2, London, 1843

Bellwood, Peter 'Dispersal centres in east Polynesia with special reference to the Society and Marquesas islands' in *Studies in Oceanic Culture History* vol 1, edited by R C Green and M Kelly, Honolulu, 1970, pp 93–104

—— 'The prehistory of Oceania' *Current Anthropology*, 16, 1975, 9–28

—— *Man's Conquest of the Pacific* Auckland, 1978

—— *The Polynesians: Prehistory of an Island People* London, 1978

—— 'Indonesia, the Philippines and Oceanic prehistory' *Journal de la Société des Océanistes* 36, 1980, 148–55

Bennett, F D *Narrative of a Whaling Voyage Round the Globe, from the Year 1833 to 1836* 2 vols, London, 1840

Bennett, J A 'Immigration, "blackbirding", labour recruiting? The Hawaiian experience 1877–1887' *Journal of Pacific History* 11, 1976, 3–27

—— 'Oscar Svensen: a Solomons trader among "the few"' *Journal of Pacific History* 16, 1981, 170–89

Berndt, R M, and C H Berndt *The World of the First Australians* London, 1964

Best, Elsdon *The Maori* 2 vols, Wellington, 1924

Bingham, Hiram *A Residence of Twenty-One Years in the Sandwich Islands* New York, 1969

Binney, Judith 'Papahurihia: Some thoughts on interpretation' *Journal of the Polynesian Society* 75, 1966, 321–31

—— *The Legacy of Guilt: A Life of Thomas Kendall* Auckland, 1968

—— 'Christianity and the Maoris to 1840: A comment' *New Zealand Journal of History* 3, 1969, 143–65

Blainey, Geoffrey *Triumph of the Nomads: A History of Ancient Australia* Melbourne, 1975

Bligh, William *A Voyage to the South Sea . . . in His Majesty's Ship the 'Bounty' . . .* 2 vols, London, 1792

—— *Captain Bligh's Second Voyage to the South Sea* edited by Ida Lee, London, 1920

Bougainville, Louis-Antoine de *A Voyage Round the World . . . in the frigate 'La*

Boudeuse' and the store ship 'L'Etoile' ... translated by J R Forster, London, 1772

Bowden, Ross '*Tapu* and *mana*: Ritual authority and political power in traditional Maori society' *Journal of Pacific History* 14, 1979, 50–61

Bradley, H W *The American Frontier in Hawaii: The Pioneers 1789–1843* Stanford, Calif, 1942

Brailsford, Barry *The Tattooed Land: The Southern Frontiers of the Pa Maori* Wellington, 1981

Brand, Donald D 'Geographical exploration by the Spaniards' in *The Pacific Basin: A History of its Geographical Exploration* edited by Herman R Friis, New York, 1967, pp 109–44

Brenchley, Julius L *Jottings During the Cruise of the H.M.S. 'Curaçoa' Among the South Sea Islands in 1865* London, 1873

Broek, Jan O M 'Geographical exploration by the Dutch' in *The Pacific Basin: A History of its Geographical Exploration* edited by Herman R Friis, New York, 1967, pp 151–69

Brookfield, H C *Colonialism, Development and Independence: The Case of the Melanesian Islands in the South Pacific* Cambridge, 1972

Brookfield, H C, with Doreen Hart *Melanesia: A Geographical Interpretation of an Island World* London, 1974

Brou, B *Histoire de la Nouvelle-Calédonie: Les Temps Modernes, 1774–1925* Noumea, 1973

Brown, John Macmillan *Peoples and Problems of the Pacific* 2 vols, London, 1927

Buck, Peter *Vikings of the Sunrise* Christchurch, 1954

Buddle, Thomas *The Aborigines of New Zealand* Auckland, 1851

Bulmer, Susan 'Settlement and economy in prehistoric Papua New Guinea: A review of the archaeological evidence' *Journal de la Société des Océanistes* 31, 1975, 7–75

Burns, Patricia *Te Rauparaha: A New Perspective* Wellington, 1980

Burns, Tom, Matthew Cooper, and Bradford Wilde 'Melanesian big men and the accumulation of power' *Oceania* 43, 1972, 104–12

Cairns, H A C *Prelude to Imperialism: British Reactions to Central African Society 1840–1890* London, 1965

Calvert, James *Fiji and the Fijians* vol 2, *Mission History*, London, 1858

Campbell, Archibald *A Voyage Round the World, from 1806 to 1812* Honolulu, 1967

Campbell, F A *A Year in the New Hebrides, Loyalty Islands and New Caledonia* Melbourne, 1873

Carano, P, and P C Sanchez *A Complete History of Guam* Rutland, Vt, 1964

Choris, Louis *Voyage Pittoresque Autour du Monde* Paris, 1822

Chowning, Ann 'The real Melanesia: An appraisal of Parsonson's theories' *Mankind* 6, 1968, 641–52

—— *An Introduction to the Peoples and Cultures of Melanesia* 2nd edn, Menlo Park, Calif, 1977

—— 'Leadership in Melanesia' *Journal of Pacific History* 14, 1979, 66–84

Coates D, John Beecham, and William Ellis *Christianity the Means of Civilization: Shown in the Evidence Given Before a Committee of the House of Commons on Aborigines* ... London, 1837

Cook, James *A Voyage towards the South Pole and round the World* 2 vols, London, 1777

Cook, James *A Voyage to the Pacific Ocean* vol 2, London, 1784

Cordy, Ross H 'Cultural adaptation and evolution in Hawaii: A suggested new sequence' *Journal of the Polynesian Society* 83, 1974, 180–91

Corney, B G *The Quest and Occupation of Tahiti by Emissaries of Spain During the Years 1772–1776* 3 vols, London, 1913, 1914, 1919

Corris, Peter ' "Blackbirding" in New Guinea waters, 1883–4: An episode in the Queensland labour trade' *Journal of Pacific History* 3, 1968, 85–105

—— 'Kwaisulia of Ada Gege: A strongman in the Solomon Islands' in *Pacific Islands Portraits* edited by J W Davidson and Deryck Scarr, Canberra, 1970, pp 253–65

—— *Passage, Port and Plantation: A History of Solomon Islands Labour Migration 1870–1914* Melbourne, 1973

Crocombe, R G, and Marjorie Crocombe *The Works of Ta'unga: Records of a Polynesian Traveller in the South Seas 1833–1896* Canberra, 1968

Crozet, Julien M *Crozet's Voyage to Tasmania, New Zealand, the Ladrone Islands, and the Philippines in the years 1771–1772* translated by H Ling Roth, London, 1891

Cruise, Richard A *Journal of a Ten Month's Residence in New Zealand* London, 1824

Cummins, H G 'Holy War: Peter Dillon and the 1837 massacres in Tonga' *Journal of Pacific History* 12, 1977, 25–39

—— 'Tongan society at the time of European contact' in *Friendly Islands: A History of Tonga* edited by Noel Rutherford, Melbourne, 1977, pp 63–89

Davenport, William 'Red-feather money' *Scientific American* 206, 1962, 94–104

—— 'The "Hawaiian cultural revolution": Some political and economic considerations' *American Anthropologist* 71, 1969, 1–20

Davidson, J W European penetration of the South Pacific 1779–1842, PhD thesis, Cambridge University, 1942

—— *The Study of Pacific History: An Inaugural Lecture Delivered at Canberra on 25 November 1954* Canberra, 1955

—— 'Problems of Pacific history' *Journal of Pacific History* 1, 1966, 5–21

—— *Samoa mo Samoa: The Emergence of the Independent State of Western Samoa* Melbourne, 1967

—— 'Lauaki Namulau'ulu Mamoe: A traditionalist in Samoan politics' in *Pacific Islands Portraits* edited by J W Davidson and Deryck Scarr, Canberra, 1970, pp 267–99

—— *Peter Dillon of Vanikoro: Chevalier of the South Seas* Melbourne, 1975

Davidson, J W, and Deryck Scarr (eds) *Pacific Islands Portraits* Canberra, 1970

Davidson, Janet 'Western Polynesia and Fiji: the archaeological evidence' *Mankind* 11, 3, 1978, 383–90

—— 'Samoa and Tonga' in *The Prehistory of Polynesia* edited by Jesse D Jennings, Canberra, 1979, pp 82–109

—— 'The Polynesian foundation' in *The Oxford History of New Zealand* edited by W H Oliver with B R Williams, Wellington, 1981, pp 3–27

Davies, John *The History of the Tahitian Mission, 1799–1830* edited by Colin Newbury, London, 1961

Daws, Gavan 'Honolulu in the nineteenth century: Notes on the emergence of urban society in Hawaii' *Journal of Pacific History* 2, 1967, 77–96

—— *Shoal of Time: A History of the Hawaiian Islands* Toronto, 1968

—— *A Dream of Islands: Voyages of Self-discovery in the South Seas* New York, 1980

Dening, Greg *Islands and Beaches: Discourse on a Silent Land, Marquesas 1774–1880* Melbourne, 1980

Derrick, R A *A History of Fiji* vol 1, Suva, 1950

Diapea, William *Cannibal Jack: The True Autobiography of a White Man in the South Seas* London, 1928

Diderot, Denis *Supplément au Voyage de Bougainville* edited by H Dieckmann, Paris, 1955

Dieffenbach, Ernest *Travels in New Zealand* 2 vols, London, 1843

Docker, Edward *The Blackbirders: The Recruiting of South Sea Labour for Queensland, 1863–1907* Sydney, 1970

Dodd, Edward *Polynesian Seafaring* New York, 1972

Dodge, Ernest S *New England and the South Seas* Cambridge, Mass, 1965

Douglas, Bronwen 'A contact history of the Balad people of New Caledonia 1774–1845' *Journal of the Polynesian Society* 70, 1970, 180–200

—— 'The export trade in tropical products in New Caledonia 1841–1872' *Journal de la Société des Océanistes* 27, 1971, 157–69

—— A history of culture contact in north-eastern New Caledonia 1774–1870, PhD thesis, Australian National University, 1972

—— 'Bouarate of Hienghène: Great chief in New Caledonia' in *More Pacific Islands Portraits* edited by Deryck Scarr, Canberra, 1978, pp 35–57

—— 'Rank, power, authority: A reassessment of traditional leadership in South Pacific societies' *Journal of Pacific History* 14, 1979, 2–27

—— 'Conflict and alliance in a colonial context: Case studies in New Caledonia 1853–1870' *Journal of Pacific History* 15, 1980, 21–51

Doumenge, François *L'Homme dans le Pacifique Sud* Paris, 1966

Dousset, Roselène *Colonialisme et Contradictions: Etude sur les Causes Socio-historiques de l'Insurrection de 1878 en Nouvelle-Calédonie* Paris, 1970

Driessen, H A H 'Outriggerless canoes and glorious beings: Pre-contact prophecies in the Society Islands' *Journal of Pacific History* 17, 1982, 3–28

Duff, R *Stone Adzes of Southeast Asia* Christchurch, 1970

Dumont d'Urville *Voyage Pittoresque Autour du Monde* Paris, 1839

Dunmore, John *French Explorers in the Pacific* 2 vols, Oxford, 1965, 1969

—— 'A French account of Port Praslin, Solomon Islands, in 1769' *Journal of Pacific History* 9, 1974, 172–82

Earle, Augustus *A Narrative of a Nine Months' Residence in New Zealand in 1827* Christchurch, 1909

Elder, J R (ed) *The Letters and Journals of Samuel Marsden, 1765–1838* Dunedin, 1932

—— *Marsden's Lieutenants* Dunedin, 1934

Elkin, A P *The Australian Aborigines* Sydney, 1938

Ellis, William *Polynesian Researches During a Residence of Nearly Eight Years in the Society and Sandwich Islands* 4 vols, London, 1831

Emory, Kenneth P *Stone Remains in the Society Islands* Honolulu, 1933

—— 'East Polynesian relationships as revealed through adzes' in *Prehistoric Culture in Oceania* edited by I Yawata and Y H Sinoto, Honolulu, 1968, pp 151–69

—— 'A re-examination of east Polynesian marae: Many marae later' in *Studies in Oceanic Culture History* vol 1, edited by R C Green and M Kelly, Honolulu, 1970, pp 73–92

—— 'The Societies' in *The Prehistory of Polynesia* edited by Jesse D Jennings,

Canberra, 1979, pp 200–221

Erskine, J E *Journal of a Cruise Among the Islands of the Western Pacific* London, 1853

Fanning, Edmund *Voyages to the South Seas ... Between the Years 1830–1837* New York, 1838

Farmer, Sarah S *Tonga and the Friendly Islands* London, 1855

Finney, Ben R *Hokule'a: The Way to Tahiti* New York, 1979

Finney, Ben R (ed) *Pacific Navigation and Voyaging* Wellington, 1976

Firth, Raymond *Economics of the New Zealand Maori* Wellington, 1972

Firth, Stewart 'German firms in the western Pacific islands, 1857–1914' *Journal of Pacific History* 8, 1973, 10–28

—— 'The transformation of the labour trade in German New Guinea 1899–1914' *Journal of Pacific History* 11, 1976, 51–65

Fisher, Robin 'Henry Williams' leadership of the CMS mission to New Zealand' *New Zealand Journal of History* 9, 1975, 142–53

Fisher, Robin, and Hugh Johnston (eds) *Captain James Cook and his Times* Vancouver, 1979

Forbes, A L A 'On the extinction of certain races of men' *New South Wales Medical Gazette* 3, 1873, 216–321

Fornander, A *An Account of the Polynesian Race* vol 2, London, 1880

Forster, George *A Voyage Round the World, in His Britannic Majesty's Sloop 'Resolution' ... During the Years 1772, 3, 4, and 5,* 2 vols, London, 1777

France, Peter 'The Kaunitoni migration: Notes on the genesis of a Fijian tradition' *Journal of Pacific History* 1, 1966, 107–13

—— *The Charter of the Land: Custom and Colonisation in Fiji* Melbourne, 1969

Freeman, J D 'The Joe Gimlet or Siovili Cult: An episode in the religious history of early Samoa' in *Anthropology in the South Seas* edited by J D Freeman and W R Geddes, New Plymouth, 1959, pp 185–200

Friis, Herman R (ed) *The Pacific Basin: A History of its Geographical Exploration* New York, 1967

Frost, Alan *Convicts and Empire: A Naval Question 1776–1811* Melbourne, 1980

Fry, Howard T 'Alexander Dalrymple and Captain Cook: The creative interplay of two careers' in *Captain James Cook and His Times* edited by Robin Fisher and Hugh Johnston, Vancouver, 1979, pp 41–57

Furnas, J C *Anatomy of Paradise* London, 1950

Fusitu'a, 'Eseta, and Noel Rutherford 'George Tupou II and the British Protectorate' in *Friendly Islands: A History of Tonga*, edited by Noel Rutherford, Melbourne, 1977, pp 173–89

Garanger, José 'Incised and applied-relief pottery, its chronology and development in southeastern Melanesia, and extra areal comparisons' in *Studies in Oceanic Culture History* vol 2, edited by R C Green and M Kelly, Honolulu, 1971, pp 53–65

—— *Archéologie des Nouvelles-Hébrides* Paris, 1972

Garrett, John 'The conflict between the London Missionary Society and the Wesleyan Methodists in mid-19th century Samoa' *Journal of Pacific History* 9, 1974, 65–80

Giles, W E *A Cruize in a Queensland Labour Vessel to the South Seas* edited by Deryck Scarr, Canberra, 1968

Gill, W W *Life in the Southern Isles* London, 1876

Gilson, R P *Samoa 1830 to 1900: The Politics of a Multi-cultural Community* Melbourne, 1970

—— *The Cook Islands 1820–1950* Wellington, 1980

Gladwin, Thomas *East is a Big Bird: Navigation and Logic on Puluwat Atoll* Cambridge, Mass, 1974

Goldman, Irving *Ancient Polynesian Society* Chicago, 1970

Golovnin, V M *Around the World on the 'Kamchatka' 1817–1819* translated by Ella Lury Wiswell, Honolulu, 1979

Golson, Jack 'Thor Heyerdahl and the prehistory of Easter Island' *Oceania* 36, 1965, 38–83

—— 'Lapita ware and its transformations' in *Studies in Oceanic Culture History* vol 2, edited by R C Green and M Kelly, Honolulu, 1971, pp 67–76

—— 'Both sides of the Wallace Line: New Guinea, Australia, Island Melanesia and Asian prehistory' in *Early Chinese Art and its Possible Influence in the Pacific Basin* vol 3, edited by N Barnard, New York, 1972, pp 533–95

—— 'The Pacific islands and their prehistoric inhabitants' in *Man in the Pacific Islands*, edited by R Gerard Ward, Oxford, 1972, pp 5–33

—— 'The remarkable history of Indo-Pacific man' *Journal of Pacific History* 7, 1972, 5–25

—— 'No room at the top: Agricultural intensification in the New Guinea highlands' in *Sunda and Sahul: Prehistoric Studies in Southeast Asia, Melanesia and Australia* edited by J Allen, J Golson, and R Jones, London, 1977, pp 601–638

Golson, Jack (ed) *Polynesian Navigation: A Symposium on Andrew Sharp's Theory of Accidental Voyages* Wellington, 1962

Green, R C 'A suggested revision of the Fijian sequence' *Journal of the Polynesian Society* 72, 1963, 235–53

—— 'West Polynesian prehistory' in *Prehistoric Culture in Oceania* edited by I Yawata and Y H Sinoto, Honolulu, 1968, pp 99–109

—— 'Lapita pottery and the origins of Polynesian culture' *Australian Natural History* 17, 1973, 332–37

—— *Adaptation and Change in Maori Culture* Albany [Auckland], 1977

—— *A First Culture History of the Solomon Islands* Auckland, 1977

—— 'New sites with Lapita pottery and their implications for an understanding of the settlement of the western Pacific' *Working Papers in Anthropology, Archaeology, Linguistics* 51, University of Auckland, 1978

—— 'Lapita' in *The Prehistory of Polynesia*, edited by Jesse D Jennings, Canberra, 1979, pp 27–60

Green, R C, and Janet Davidson 'Melanesian origin of Polynesian culture' *Pacific Islands Monthly*, September 1972, p 73

Green, R C, and Janet Davidson (eds) *Archaeology in Western Samoa* 2 vols, Auckland, 1969, 1974

Green, R C, and M Kelly (eds) *Studies in Oceanic Culture History* 3 vols, Honolulu, 1970, 1971, 1972

Griffin, James, Hank Nelson, and Stewart Firth *Papua New Guinea: A Political History* Richmond, Vic, 1979

Groube, L M 'Tonga, Lapita pottery, and Polynesian origins' *Journal of the Polynesian Society* 80, 1971, 278–316

Guiart, Jean 'Native society in the New Hebrides' *Mankind*, 4, 1953, 439–46

—— *Structure de la Chefferie en Mélanésie du Sud* Paris, 1963

Gunson, Niel 'An account of the Mamaia or visionary heresy of Tahiti 1826–1841' *Journal of the Polynesian Society* 71, 1962, 209–243

—— 'Pomare II of Tahiti and Polynesian imperialism' *Journal of Pacific History* 4, 1969, 65–82

—— 'The coming of foreigners' in *Friendly Islands: A History of Tonga* edited by Noel Rutherford, Melbourne, 1977, pp 90–113

—— *Messengers of Grace: Evangelical Missionaries in the South Seas 1797–1860* Melbourne, 1978

—— 'The *hau* concept of leadership in Western Polynesia' *Journal of Pacific History* 14, 1979, 28–49

Haddon, A C, and James Hornell *Canoes of Oceania* Honolulu, 1975

Hainsworth, D R 'Exploiting the Pacific frontier: The New South Wales sealing industry 1800–1821' *Journal of Pacific History* 2, 1967, 59–75

—— *The Sydney Traders: Simeon Lord and His Contemporaries 1788–1821* Melbourne, 1971

Handy, E S C *History and Culture in the Society Islands* Honolulu, 1930

Harfst, Richard 'Cause or condition: Explanations of the Hawaiian cultural revolution' *Journal of the Polynesian Society* 81, 1972, 437–47

Hargreaves, R P 'The Maori agriculture of the Auckland province in the mid-nineteenth century' *Journal of the Polynesian Society* 68, 1959, 61–79

—— 'Changing Maori agriculture in pre-Waitangi New Zealand' *Journal of the Polynesian Society* 72, 1963, 101–17

Havard-Williams, P (ed) *Marsden and the New Zealand Mission: Sixteen Letters* Dunedin, 1961

Hawkesworth, John *An Account of the Voyages for Making Discoveries* 3 vols, London, 1773

Hempenstall, Peter J *Pacific Islanders Under German Rule: A Study in the Meaning of Colonial Resistance* Canberra, 1978

Henderson, G C *Fiji and the Fijians 1835–1856* Sydney, 1931

Henderson, G C (ed) *The Journal of Thomas Williams, Missionary in Fiji, 1840–1853* 2 vols, Sydney, 1931

Henry, Teuira *Ancient Tahiti* Honolulu, 1928

Heyerdahl, Thor *The Kon-Tiki Expedition* London, 1950

—— *American Indians in the Pacific: The Theory Behind the Kon-Tiki Expedition* London, 1952

—— *Aku-Aku: The Secret of Easter Island* London, 1958

—— *Sea Routes to Polynesia* London, 1968

Highland, G A et al (eds) *Polynesian Culture History* Honolulu, 1967

Hilliard, David 'Bishop G A Selwyn and the Melanesian Mission' *New Zealand Journal of History* 4, 1970, 120–37

—— 'John Coleridge Patteson: Missionary bishop of Melanesia' in *Pacific Islands Portraits* edited by J W Davidson and Deryck Scarr, Canberra, 1970, pp 177–200

—— 'Colonialism and Christianity: The Melanesian Mission in the Solomon Islands' *Journal of Pacific History* 9, 1974, 93–116

—— *God's Gentlemen: A History of the Melanesian Mission 1849–1942* St Lucia, Qld, 1978

Hoare, Michael E *The Tactless Philosopher: Johann Reinhold Forster* Melbourne, 1976

Hogbin, H Ian ' "Polynesian" colonies in Melanesia' *Journal of the Polynesian Society* 49, 1940, 199–220
—— *A Guadalcanal Society: the Kaoka Speakers* New York, 1964
Hogbin, H Ian, and C H Wedgwood 'Local grouping in Melanesia' *Oceania*, 23, 1953, 241–276; 24, 1953, 58–76
Holthouse, Hector *Cannibal Cargoes* Adelaide, 1969
Hope, James L A *In Quest of Coolies* London, 1872
Houghton, Philip 'Prehistoric New Zealanders' *New Zealand Medical Journal* 87, 1978, 213–16
—— *The First New Zealanders* Auckland, 1980
—— 'Pre-historic Maoris in New Zealand' typescript
Howard, A 'Polynesian origins and migrations: A review of two centuries of speculation and theory' in *Polynesian Culture History* edited by G A Highland et al, Honolulu, 1967, pp 45–101
Howe, K R 'The Maori response to Christianity in the Thames-Waikato area, 1833–1840' *New Zealand Journal of History* 7, 1973, 28–46
—— 'Firearms and indigenous warfare: A case study' *Journal of Pacific History* 9, 1974, 21–38
—— 'The fate of the "savage" in Pacific historiography' *New Zealand Journal of History* 11, 1977, 137–54
—— *The Loyalty Islands: A History of Culture Contacts 1840–1900* Canberra, 1977
—— 'Tourists, sailors and labourers: A survey of early labour recruiting in southern Melanesia' *Journal of Pacific History* 13, 1978, 22–35
—— 'Pacific islands history in the 1980s: New directions or monograph myopia?' *Pacific Studies* 3, 1979, 81–90
Howells, William 'Computerised clues unlock a door to Polynesia's past' *Pacific Islands Monthly* May 1972, pp 67–9
—— *The Pacific Islanders* Wellington, 1973
—— 'Physical anthropology' in *The Prehistory of Polynesia* edited by Jesse D Jennings, Canberra, 1979, pp 271–85
Im Thurn, Everard, and Leonard C Wharton (eds) *The Journal of William Lockerby, Sandalwood Trader in the Fijian Islands During the Years 1808–1809* London, 1925
Inglis, John *In the New Hebrides: Reminiscences of Missionary Life and Work* London, 1887
Jack-Hinton, Colin *The Search for the Islands of Solomon 1567–1838* Oxford, 1969
Jackson, K B 'Head-hunting in the Christianization of Bugotu' *Journal of Pacific History* 10, 1975, 65–78
Jennings, Jesse D (ed) *The Prehistory of Polynesia* Canberra, 1979
Kaeppler, Adrienne C 'Exchange patterns in goods and spouses: Fiji, Tonga and Samoa' *Mankind* 11, 3, 1978, 246–52
Kamakau, S M *Ruling Chiefs of Hawaii* Honolulu, 1961
—— *Ka Poʻe Kahiko: The People of Old* Honolulu, 1964
Kirch, P V 'Halawa dune site (Hawaiian Islands): A preliminary report' *Journal of the Polynesian Society* 80, 1971, 228–36
—— 'The chronology of early Hawaiian settlement' *Archaeology and Physical Anthropology in Oceania* 9, 1974, 110–19
Kirk, R L, and A G Thorne (eds) *The Origin of the Australians* Canberra, 1976
Kelly, Celsus *La Austrialia del Espíritu Santo* 2 vols, Cambridge, 1966

Kelly, Marion 'Some problems with early descriptions of Hawaiian culture' in *Polynesian Culture History* edited by G A Highland et al, Honolulu, 1967, pp 399–410

Kennedy, Paul M *The Samoan Tangle: A Study of Anglo-German-American Relations 1878–1900* Dublin, 1974

Kotzebue, Otto von *Voyage of Discovery in the South Sea ... Undertaken in the Years 1815, 16, 17 and 18* London, 1821

—— *A New Voyage Round the World in the Years 1823, 24, 25 and 26* 2 vols, London, 1830

Kuykendall, Ralph S *The Hawaiian Kingdom 1778–1854, Foundation and Trans-formation* Honolulu, 1938

—— *The Hawaiian Kingdom 1854–1874, Twenty Critical Years* Honolulu, 1953

—— *The Hawaiian Kingdom 1874–1893, The Kalakaua Dynasty* Honolulu, 1967

Langdon, Robert *Tahiti: Island of Love* Sydney, 1968

—— *The Lost Caravel* Sydney, 1975

—— 'The maritime explorers' in *Friendly Islands: A History of Tonga* edited by Noel Rutherford, Melbourne, 1977, pp 40–62

—— 'The European ships of Tupaia's chart: An essay in identification' *Journal of Pacific History* 15, 1980, 225–32

Lanning, Edward P 'South America as a source for aspects of Oceanic cultures' in *Studies in Oceanic Culture History* vol 1, edited by R C Green and M Kelly, Honolulu, 1970, pp 175–82

La Pérouse, J F G de *A Voyage Round the World in the Years 1785, 1786, 1787 and 1788* 3 vols, London, 1798

Laracy, Hugh 'The first mission to Tikopia' *Journal of Pacific History* 4, 1969, 105–9

—— 'Xavier Montrouzier: A missionary in Melanesia' in *Pacific Islands Portraits* edited by J W Davidson and Deryck Scarr, Canberra, 1970, pp 127–45

—— *Marists and Melanesians: A History of Catholic Missions in the Solomon Islands* Canberra, 1976

—— 'The Catholic mission' in *Friendly Islands: A History of Tonga* edited by Noel Rutherford, Melbourne, 1977, pp 136–53

Latham, Linda 'Revolt re-examined: The 1878 insurrection in New Caledonia' *Journal of Pacific History* 10, 1975, 48–63

Latukefu, Sione 'King George Tupou I of Tonga' in *Pacific Islands Portraits* edited by J W Davidson and Deryck Scarr, Canberra, 1970, pp 55–75

—— *Church and State in Tonga: The Wesleyan Methodist Missionaries and Political Development, 1822–1875* Canberra, 1974

—— *The Tongan Constitution: A Brief History to Celebrate Its Centenary* Nuku'alofa, 1975

—— 'The Wesleyan mission' in *Friendly Islands: A History of Tonga* edited by Noel Rutherford, Melbourne, 1977, pp 114–35

Lawrence, P, and M J Meggitt (eds) *Gods, Ghosts and Men in Melanesia* Melbourne, 1965

Lawry, Walter *Friendly and Feejee Islands: A Missionary Visit ... in 1847* London, 1850

Leach, B F 'Four centuries of community interaction and trade in Cook Strait, New Zealand' *Mankind* 11, 3, 1978, 391–405

Legge, J D *Britain in Fiji, 1858–1880* London, 1958

Levin, Stephenie Seto 'The overthrow of the *kapu* system in Hawaii' *Journal of the Polynesian Society* 77, 1968, 402–30

Levison, M, R G Ward, and J W Webb *The Settlement of Polynesia: A Computer Simulation* Canberra, 1973

Lewis, David ' "Expanding" the target in indigenous navigation' *Journal of Pacific History* 6, 1971, 83–95

—— 'The gospel according to St Andrew' *Journal of Pacific History* 7, 1972, 223–5

—— *We, the Navigators: The Ancient Art of Landfinding in the Pacific* Canberra, 1973

—— 'The Pacific navigators' debt to the ancient seafarers of Asia' in *The Changing Pacific: Essays in Honour of H.E. Maude* edited by Niel Gunson, Melbourne, 1978, pp 46–66

—— 'The great canoes of the Pacific' *Hemisphere* 25, 1980, 66–76

Lisiansky, Urey *A Voyage Round the World in the Years 1803, 4, 5, and 6 . . .* London, 1814

Liverpool, C G S *Three Years on the Australia Station* London, 1868

Lovett, R *The History of the London Missionary Society, 1795–1895* vol 1, London, 1899

McArthur, Norma *Introducing Population Statistics* Melbourne, 1961

—— 'Essays in multiplication: European seafarers in Polynesia' *Journal of Pacific History* 1, 1966, 91–105

—— *Island Populations of the Pacific* Canberra, 1967

—— 'The demography of primitive populations' *Science* 167, 1970, 1097–101

—— 'And, behold, the plague was begun among the people' in *The Changing Pacific: Essays in Honour of H.E. Maude* edited by Niel Gunson, Melbourne, 1978, pp 273–84

—— unpublished paper on the New Hebrides, typescript

McArthur, Norma, I W Saunders, and R L Tweedie 'Small population isolates: A micro-simulation study' *Journal of the Polynesian Society* 85, 1976, 307–26

McArthur, Norma, and J F Yaxley *Condominium of the New Hebrides: A Report on the First Census of the Population 1967* Sydney, 1968

McCormick, E H *Omai: Pacific Envoy* Auckland, 1977

Macdonald, Barrie *Cinderellas of the Empire: Towards a History of Kiribati and Tuvalu* Canberra, 1982

MacFarlane, Samuel *The Story of the Lifu Mission* London, 1873

Macknight, C C *The Voyage to Marege': Macassan Trepangers in Northern Australia* Melbourne, 1976

McLintock, A H *Crown Colony Government in New Zealand* Wellington, 1958

McNab, Robert *Murihiku and the Southern Islands* Invercargill, 1907

—— *The Old Whaling Days: A History of Southern New Zealand from 1830 to 1840* Christchurch, 1913

—— *From Tasman to Marsden: A History of Northern New Zealand from 1642 to 1818* Dunedin, 1914

McNab, Robert (ed) *Historical Records of New Zealand* 2 vols, Wellington, 1908, 1914

Malinowsky, Bronislaw *Argonauts of the Western Pacific* London, 1922

Malo, David *Hawaiian Antiquities* Honolulu, 1951

Markham, A H *The Cruise of the 'Rosario' Amongst the New Hebrides and Santa Cruz Islands, Exposing the Recent Atrocities Connected with the Kidnapping of Natives in the*

South Seas London, 1873

Markham, Clements (ed) *The Voyages of Pedro Fernandez de Quiros, 1595 to 1606* 2 vols, London, 1904

Martin, John *An Account of the Natives of the Tonga Islands in the South Pacific Ocean . . . Compiled and Arranged from Extensive Communications of Mr William Mariner, Several Years Resident in those Islands* 2 vols, London, 1827

Masterman, Sylvia *The Origins of International Rivalry in Samoa 1845–1884* London, 1934

Maude, H E *Of Islands and Men: Studies in Pacific History* Melbourne, 1968

—— *Slavers in Paradise: The Peruvian Labour Trade in Polynesia* Canberra, 1981

Melville, Herman *Typee: A Peep at Polynesian Life During a Four Months' Residence in a Valley of the Marquesas . . .* New York, 1963

—— *Omoo: A Narrative of Adventures in the South Seas* New York, 1963

Melvin, J D *The Cruise of the Helena: A Labour Recruiting Voyage to the Solomon Islands* edited by Peter Corris, Melbourne, 1977

Mercer, P M, and C R Moore 'Melanesians in North Queensland: The retention of indigenous religious and magical practices' *Journal of Pacific History* 11, 1976, 66–88

Metge, Joan *The Maoris of New Zealand: Rautahi* London, 1976

Millar, David 'Whalers, flax traders and Maoris of the Cook Strait area' *Dominion Museum Records in Ethnology* 2, 6, 1971, 57–74

Miller, R S (ed) *Misi Gete: John Geddie, Pioneer Missionary to the New Hebrides* Launceston, 1975

Moorehead, Alan *The Fatal Impact: An Account of the Invasion of the South Pacific 1767–1840* Harmondsworth, 1968

Morrell, Abby Jane *Narrative of a Voyage* New York, 1833

Morrell, Benjamin *A Narrative of Four Voyages to the South Sea . . . From the Year 1822 to 1831* New York, 1832

Morrell W P *Britain in the Pacific Islands* Oxford, 1960

Morton, Harry *The Whale's Wake* Dunedin, 1982

Mulvaney, D J *The Prehistory of Australia* London, 1969

Mulvaney, D J, and Jack Golson (eds) *Aboriginal Man and Environment in Australia* Canberra, 1971

Murray, A W *Missions in Western Polynesia: Being Historical Sketches of these Missions from their Commencement in 1839 to the Present Time* London, 1863

—— *Forty Years' Mission Work in Polynesia and New Guinea, from 1835 to 1875* London, 1876

—— *Wonders in the Western Isles,* London [n d]

Newbury, Colin 'Te Hau Pahu Rahi: Pomare II and the concept of inter-island government in eastern Polynesia' *Journal of the Polynesian Society* 76, 1967, 477–514

—— 'The Melanesian labour reserve: Some reflections on Pacific labour markets in the nineteenth century' *Pacific Studies* 4, 1980, 1–25

—— *Tahiti Nui: Change and Survival in French Polynesia, 1767–1945* Honolulu, 1980

Nicholas, J L *Narrative of a Voyage to New Zealand* 2 vols, London, 1817

Nothling, Marion 'Charles St Julian: Alternative diplomacy in Polynesia' in *More Pacific Islands Portraits* edited by Deryck Scarr, Canberra, 1979, pp 19–33

O'Brien, P J 'The sweet potato: Its origin and dispersal' *American Anthropologist*

74, 1972, 342–65

O'Connell, J F *A Residence of Eleven Years in New Holland and the Caroline Islands* edited by S H Riesenberg, Canberra, 1972

Odgers, Stephen 'Western contact with Hawaii and the rise of Kamehameha I' paper, Department of History, Australian National University [n d]

Oliver, Douglas *A Solomon Island Society: Kinship and Leadership Among the Siuai of Bougainville* Cambridge, Mass, 1955

—— *The Pacific Islands* rev ed, Harvard, 1961

—— *Ancient Tahitian Society* 3 vols, Canberra, 1974

Oliver, W H, and Jane M Thomson *Challenge and Response: A Study of the Development of the Gisborne East Coast Region* Gisborne, 1971

Oliver, W H, with B R Williams (eds) *The Oxford History of New Zealand* Wellington, 1981

Orange, James (ed) *Life of the Late George Vason of Nottingham . . .* London, 1840

Owens, J M R 'Christianity and the Maoris to 1840' *New Zealand Journal of History* 2, 1968, 18–40

—— 'Religious disputation at Whangaroa 1823–7' *Journal of the Polynesian Society* 79, 1970, 288–304

—— 'Missionary medicine and Maori health: The record of the Wesleyan mission to New Zealand before 1840' *Journal of the Polynesian Society* 81, 1972, 418–36

—— 'The unexpected impact: Wesleyan missionaries and Maoris in the early nineteenth century' *Proceedings of the Wesley Historical Society (New Zealand)* 27, 6, 1973, 1–37

—— *Prophets in the Wilderness: The Wesleyan Mission to the New Zealand* Auckland, 1974

—— 'New Zealand before annexation' in *The Oxford History of New Zealand* edited by W H Oliver with B R Williams, Wellington, 1981, pp 28–53

Palmer, Bruce 'Ring-ditch fortifications on windward Viti Levu, Fiji' *Archaeology and Physical Anthropology in Oceania* 4, 1969, 181–97

—— 'Fijian pottery technologies: Their relevance to certain problems of southwest Pacific prehistory' in *Studies in Oceanic Culture History* vol 2, edited by R C Green and M Kelly, Honolulu, 1971, pp 77–103

Palmer, George *Kidnapping in the South Seas, Being a Narrative of a Three Months' Cruise of H.M. Ship Rosario* Edinburgh, 1871

Parnaby, O W *Britain and the Labour Trade in the Southwest Pacific* Durham, 1964

Parr, C J 'Maori literacy, 1843–67' *Journal of the Polynesian Society* 62, 1963, 211–34

Parsonson, Ann 'The expansion of a competitive s⹎ ⹎ety: A study in nineteenth-century Maori social history' *New Zealand Journal of History* 14, 1980, 45–60

—— 'The pursuit of mana' in *The Oxford History of New Zealand* edited by W H Oliver with B R Williams, Wellington, 1981, pp 140–67

Parsonson, G S 'The literate revolution in Polynesia' *Journal of Pacific History* 2, 1967, 39–57

—— 'The problem of Melanesia' *Mankind*, 6, 1968, 571–84

—— 'The life and times of Hongi Hika' *Historical News* (University of Canterbury), 44, 1982, 1–8

Paton, James (ed) *John G Paton, D.D. Missionary to the New Hebrides: An Autobiography* London, 1902

Patterson, Samuel *Narrative of the Adventures and Suffering of Samuel Patterson*

Providence, R I, 1825

Pawley, Andrew 'On the internal relationships of eastern Oceanic languages' in *Studies in Oceanic Culture History* vol 3, edited by R C Green and M Kelly, Honolulu, 1972, pp 1–141

Pawley, Andrew, and R C Green 'Dating the dispersal of the Oceanic languages' *Oceanic Linguistics* 12, 1973, 1–67

Pearson, W H 'European intimidation and the myth of Tahiti' *Journal of Pacific History* 4, 1969, 199–217

—— 'The reception of European voyagers on Polynesian islands' *Journal de la Société des Océanistes* 26, 1970, 121–53

Pietrusewsky, Michael *Prehistoric Human Skeletal Remains from Papua New Guinea and the Marquesas* Honolulu, 1976

Pirie, Peter 'Polynesian populations: Review' *Australian Geographical Studies* 6, 1968, 175–81

—— 'The effects of treponematosis and gonorrhoea on the populations of the Pacific islands' *Human Biology in Oceania* 1, 1971–72, 187–206

Pisier, Georges *Kounié ou L'Ile des Pins* Noumea, 1971

Polack, J S *New Zealand: Being a Narrative of Travels and Adventures During a Residence in that Country Between the Years 1831 and 1837* 2 vols, London, 1838

—— *Manners and Customs of the New Zealanders* 2 vols, London, 1840

Pool, D Ian *The Maori Population of New Zealand 1769–1971* Auckland, 1977

Poulsen, Jens 'Archaeology and prehistory' in *Friendly Islands: A History of Tonga* edited by Noel Rutherford, Melbourne, 1977, pp 4–26

Price, A Grenfell *The Western Invasions of the Pacific and its Continents* Oxford, 1963

Price, C A, with Elizabeth Baker 'Origins of Pacific island labourers in Queensland, 1863–1904: A research note' *Journal of Pacific History* 11, 1976, 106–21

Quimby, George I 'Hawaiians in the fur trade of north-west America 1785–1820' *Journal of Pacific History* 7, 1972, 92–103

Ralston, Caroline 'The beach communities' in *Pacific Islands Portraits* edited by J W Davidson and Deryck Scarr, Canberra, 1970, pp 77–93

—— 'The pattern of race relations in 19th century Pacific port towns' *Journal of Pacific History* 6, 1971, 39–59

—— *Grass Huts and Warehouses: Pacific Beach Communities of the Nineteenth Century* Canberra, 1977

Rathje, William L 'Melanesian and Australian exchange systems: A view from Mesoamerica' *Mankind* 11, 3, 1978, 165–74

Reid, A C 'The fruit of Rewa: Oral traditions and the growth of the pre-Christian Lakeba state' *Journal of Pacific History* 12, 1977, 2–24

—— 'The view from Vatuwaqa: The role of Lakeba's leading lineage in the introduction and establishment of Christianity, *Journal of Pacific History* 14, 1979, 154–67

—— 'Crusaders: The religious and relationship background to Lakeban expansion in the 1850s' *Journal of Pacific History* 16, 1981, 58–69

Rigby, B 'Private interests and the origins of American involvement in Samoa, 1872–1877' *Journal of Pacific History* 8, 1973, 75–87

Robarts, Edward *The Marquesan Journal of Edward Robarts* edited by G M Dening, Canberra, 1974

Roberts, S H *Population Problems of the Pacific* London, 1927

Robertson, George *The Discovery of Tahiti: A Journal . . . 1766–1768* edited by Hugh Carrington, London, 1948

Robertson, H A *Erromanga: The Martyr Isle* London, 1902

Rogers, Lawrence M *Te Wiremu: A Biography of Henry Williams* Christchurch, 1973

Rogers, Lawrence M (ed) *The early Journals of Henry Williams, Senior Missionary in New Zealand of the Church Missionary Society, 1826–1840* Christchurch, 1962

Rowe, G S *The Life of John Hunt, Missionary to the Cannibals* London, 1860

Ruggles, Richard I 'Geographical exploration by the English' in *The Pacific Basin: A History of its Geographical Exploration* edited by Herman R Friis, New York, 1967, pp 221–55

Russell, M *Polynesia: A History of the South Sea Islands, Including New Zealand . . .* London, 1853

Rutherford, Noel *Shirley Baker and the King of Tonga* Melbourne, 1971

Rutherford, Noel (ed) *Friendly Islands: A History of Tonga* Melbourne, 1977

Rutter, Owen (ed) *The Journal of James Morrison, Boatswain's Mate of the Bounty . . .* London, 1935

Sahlins, Marshall D *Social Stratification in Polynesia* Seattle, 1958

—— 'Poor man, rich man, Big-man, chief: Political types in Melanesia and Polynesia' in *Peoples and Cultures of the Pacific* edited by Andrew P Vayda, New York, 1968, pp 157–76

Saunders, Kay 'The black scourge' *Exclusion, Exploitation and Extermination: Race Relations in Colonial Queensland* edited by Raymond Evans, Kay Saunders, and Kathryn Cronin, Sydney, 1975, pp 147–234

—— 'The Pacific Islander hospitals in colonial Queensland: The failure of liberal principles' *Journal of Pacific History* 11, 1976, 28–50

—— '"Troublesome servants": The strategies of resistance employed by Melanesian indentured labourers on plantations in colonial Queensland' *Journal of Pacific History* 14, 1979, 168–83

Savage, John *Some Account of New Zealand . . .* London, 1807

Scarr, Deryck 'John Bates Thurston, Commodore J G Goodenough, and rampant Anglo-Saxons in Fiji' *Historical Studies: Australia and New Zealand* 11, 43, 1964, 361–82

—— *Fragments of Empire: A History of the Western Pacific High Commission 1877–1914* Canberra, 1967

—— 'Cakobau and Ma'afu: Contenders for pre-eminence in Fiji' in *Pacific Islands Portraits* edited by J W Davidson and Deryck Scarr, Canberra, 1970, pp 95–126

—— 'Recruits and recruiters: A portrait of the labour trade' in *Pacific Islands Portraits* edited by J W Davidson and Deryck Scarr, Canberra, 1970, pp 225–51

—— 'Creditors and the house of Hennings: An elegy from the social and economic history of Fiji' *Journal of Pacific History* 7, 1972, 104–23

—— *The Majesty of Colour: A Life of Sir John Bates Thurston* vol 1, *I, the Very Bayonet* Canberra, 1973

Scarr, Deryck (ed) *More Pacific Islands Portraits* Canberra 1979

Schmitt, R C 'New estimates of the pre-censal population of Hawaii' *Journal of the Polynesian Society* 80, 1971, 237–43

Schütz, Albert J (ed) *The Diaries and Correspondence of David Cargill, 1832–1843* Canberra, 1977

Sharp, Andrew *Ancient Voyagers in the Pacific* Wellington, 1956

—— *The Discovery of the Pacific Islands* Oxford, 1960

—— *The Discovery of Australia* Oxford, 1963

—— *Ancient Voyagers in Polynesia* Auckland, 1963

—— 'David Lewis on indigenous Pacific navigation' *Journal of Pacific History* 7, 1972, 222–3

Sharp, Andrew (ed) *The Voyages of Abel Janszoon Tasman* Oxford, 1968

Shineberg, Dorothy *They Came For Sandalwood: A Study of the Sandalwood Trade in the South West Pacific 1830–1865* Melbourne, 1967

—— 'Guns and men in Melanesia' *Journal of Pacific History* 6, 1971, 61–82

Shineberg, Dorothy (ed) *The Trading Voyages of Andrew Cheyne 1841–1844* Canberra, 1971

Shlomowitz, Ralph 'Markets for indentured and time-expired Melanesian labour in Queensland, 1863–1906: An economic analysis' *Journal of Pacific History* 16, 1981, 70–91

—— 'Indentured Melanesians in Queensland: A statistical investigation of recruiting voyages, 1871–1903' *Journal of Pacific History* 16, 1981, 203–8

Shutler, R 'Pacific island radiocarbon dates: An overview' in *Studies in Oceanic Culture History* vol 2, edited by R C Green and M Kelly, Honolulu, 1971, pp 13–27

—— 'Radiocarbon dating and Oceanic prehistory' *Archaeology and Physical Anthropology in Oceania* 13, 1978, 215–28

Shutler, R, and J C Marck 'On the dispersal of the Austronesian horticulturalists' *Archaeology and Physical Anthropology in Oceania* 10, 1975, 81–113

Shutler, R, and M E Shutler *Oceanic Prehistory* Menlo Park, Calif, 1975

Simmons, D R 'Economic change in New Zealand prehistory' *Journal of the Polynesian Society* 78, 1969, 3–34

—— *The Great New Zealand Myth* Wellington, 1976

Sinoto, Y H 'Position of the Marquesas Islands in east Polynesian prehistory' in *Prehistoric Cultures in Oceania* edited by I Yawata and Y H Sinoto, Honolulu, 1968, pp 111–18

—— 'An archaeologically based assessment of the Marquesas as a dispersal center in east Polynesia' in *Studies in Oceanic Culture History* vol 1, edited by R C Green and M Kelly, Honolulu, 1970, pp 105–32

Smith, Bernard *European Vision and the South Pacific 1768–1850: A Study in the History of Art and Ideas* Oxford, 1969

Smith, Howard M 'The introduction of venereal disease into Tahiti: A re-examination' *Journal of Pacific History* 10, 1975, 38–45

Smith, S Percy *Hawaiki: The Whence of the Maori* Wellington, 1910

—— *Maori Wars of the Nineteenth Century: The Struggle of the Northern Against the Southern Maori Tribes Prior to the Colonisation of New Zealand in 1840* Christchurch, 1910

—— *The Lore of the Whare Wananga: Or Teachings of the Maori College on Religion, Cosmogony, and History* 2 parts, New Plymouth, 1913, 1915

Snow, Charles Ernest *Early Hawaiians: An Initial Study of Skeletal Remains from Mokapu* Lexington, Ky, 1974

Sorrenson, M P K 'How to civilize savages: Some "answers" from nineteenth century New Zealand' *New Zealand Journal of History* 9, 1975, 97–110

—— *Maori Origins and Migrations: The Genesis of Some Pakeha Myths and Legends* Auckland, 1979

Spate, O H K 'Prolegomena to a history of the Pacific' *Geographica Polonica* 36,

1977, 217–23

—— ' "South Sea" to "Pacific Ocean": A note on nomenclature' *Journal of Pacific History* 12, 1977, 205–11

—— 'The Pacific as an artefact' in *The Changing Pacific: Essays in Honour of H.E. Maude* edited by Niel Gunson, Melbourne, 1978, pp 32–45

—— *The Spanish Lake* Canberra, 1979

Specht, Jim, and J Peter White (eds) *Trade and Exchange in Oceania and Australia* issue of *Mankind* 11, 3, 1978

Spencer, J E, and G A Hale 'The origin, nature and distribution of agricultural terracing' *Pacific Viewpoint* 2, 1961, 1–40

Stackpole, Edouard A *The Sea Hunters: The New England Whalemen During Two Centuries 1635–1835* Philadelphia, 1953

Stanley of Alderley, Lord (ed) *The First Voyage Round the World by Magellan: Translated From the Accounts of Pigafetta and Other Contemporary Writers* London, 1874

Steel, Robert *The New Hebrides and Christian Missions* London, 1880

Stevenson, R L *A Footnote to History: Eight Years of Trouble in Samoa* London, 1967

Stokes, Evelyn 'The Fiji cotton boom in the eighteen-sixties' *New Zealand Journal of History* 2, 1968, 165–77

Suggs, Robert C 'The *Kon-Tiki* myth' in *Cultures of the Pacific: Selected Readings* edited by Thomas G Harding and Ben J Wallace, New York, 1970, pp 29–38

Tapp, E J *Early New Zealand: A Dependency of New South Wales 1788–1841* Melbourne, 1958

Thompson, Roger C 'Commerce, Christianity and colonialism: The Australasian New Hebrides Company, 1883–1897' *Journal of Pacific History* 6, 1971, 25–38

Thomson, Basil *The Fijians: A Study of the Decay of Custom* London, 1908

Turnbull, John *A Voyage Round the World in the Years 1800, 1801, 1802, 1803 and 1804* London, 1813

Turner, George *Nineteen Years in Polynesia: Missionary Life, Travels, and Researches in the Islands of the Pacific* London, 1861

—— *Samoa: A Hundred Years Ago and Long Before* London, 1884

Turner, J G *The Pioneer Missionary: Life of the Rev. Nathaniel Turner* Melbourne, 1872

Urlich, Dorothy 'The introduction and diffusion of firearms in New Zealand 1800–1840' *Journal of the Polynesian Society* 79, 1970, 399–410

—— 'Migrations of the North Island Maoris 1800–1840: A systems view of migration' *New Zealand Geographer* 28, 1972, 23–35

Vancouver, George *A Voyage of Discovery to the North Pacific Ocean and Round the World . . .* 3 vols, New York, 1967

Van der Sluis, Isaac *The Treponematosis of Tahiti: Its Origin and Evolution, A Study of the Sources* Amsterdam, 1969

Vayda, A P *Maori Warfare* Wellington, 1960

—— 'Maoris and muskets in New Zealand: Disruption of a war system' *Political Science Quarterly* 85, 1970, 560–84

Wade, W R *A Journey in the Northern Island of New Zealand* Hobart, 1842

Wallis, Helen (ed) *Carteret's Voyage Round the World 1766–1769* 2 vols, Cambridge, 1965

[Wallis, Mary Davis] 'A Lady' *Life in Feejee, or, Five Years Among the Cannibals* London, 1851

Ward, R Gerard 'The Pacific *bêche-de-mer* trade with special reference to Fiji' in *Man in the Pacific Islands: Essays on Geographical Change in the Pacific Islands* edited by R Gerard Ward, Oxford, 1972, pp 91–123

—— 'The dispersal of the coconut: Did it float or was it carried?' seminar paper, Department of Human Geography, Australian National University, 1977

—— 'The viability of floating coconuts' *Science in New Guinea* 7, 2, 1980, 69–72

Waterhouse, Joseph *The King and People of Fiji: Containing a Life of Thakombau; With Notices of the Fijians, Their Manners, Customs and Superstitions Previous to the Great Religious Reformation of 1854* London, 1866

Watson, V D, and J D Cole *Prehistory of the Eastern Highlands of New Guinea* Canberra, 1978

Watt, James 'Medical aspects and consequences of Cook's voyages' in *Captain James Cook and His Times* edited by Robin Fisher and Hugh Johnston, Vancouver, 1979, pp 129–57

Wawn, William T *The South Sea Islanders and the Queensland Labour Trade* edited by Peter Corris, Canberra, 1973

—— 'Amongst the Pacific Islands 1870–1874' MS, Alexander Turnbull Library, Wellington

Webb, M C 'The abolition of the taboo system in Hawaii' *Journal of the Polynesian Society* 74, 1965, 21–39

West, Thomas *Ten Years in South-Central Polynesia ... the Friendly Islands and Dependencies* London, 1865

Wilkes, Charles *Narrative of the United States States Exploring Expedition During the Years 1838, 1839, 1840, 1841, 1842* 5 vols, Philadelphia, 1845

Williams, John *A Narrative of Missionary Enterprises in the South-Sea Islands ...* London, 1838

Williams, Thomas *Fiji and the Fijians* vol 1, *The Islands and Their Inhabitants* London, 1858

Wilson, James *A Missionary Voyage to the Southern Pacific Ocean ...* London, 1799

Wiltgen, Ralph M *The Founding of the Roman Catholic Church in Oceania 1825 to 1850* Canberra, 1979

Winslow, J H (ed) *The Melanesian Environment* Canberra, 1977

Wright, Harrison M *New Zealand, 1769–1840: Early Years of Western Contact* Cambridge, Mass, 1959

Yarwood, A T *Samuel Marsden* Melbourne, 1968

Yawata, I, and Y H Sinoto (eds) *Prehistoric Culture in Oceania* Honolulu, 1968

Yen, Douglas E 'The development of agriculture in Oceania' in *Studies in Oceanic Culture History* vol 2, edited by R C Green and M Kelly, Honolulu, 1971, pp 1–12

—— *The Sweet Potato and Oceania: An Essay in Ethnobotany* Honolulu, 1974

Young, John M R 'Australia's Pacific frontier' *Historical Studies* 12, 47, 1966, 373–88

—— 'Evanescent ascendancy: The planter community in Fiji' in *Pacific Islands Portraits* edited by J W Davidson and Deryck Scarr, Canberra, 1970, pp 147–75

—— 'The response of Lau to foreign contact: An interdisciplinary reconstruction' *Journal of Pacific History* 17, 1982, 29–50

Young, John M R (ed) *Australia's Pacific Frontier: Economic and Cultural Expansion into the Pacific, 1795–1885* Melbourne, 1967

Index